"Opportunity is missed by most people because it is dressed up in overalls and looks like work."

These words of truth were spoken by Thomas Edison. The material contained in this book represents an opportunity. An opportunity to radically transform the bottom line of your company. An opportunity to turn your people into profit minded employees. An opportunity to make both your managers and employees understand that the game of business is about producing profits, not products or services.

Please do not miss out on the opportunities afforded you within this book by being intimidated by its size.

We assure you that the few hours spent reading, digesting, and applying the material contained in this book will produce returns you cannot even begin to imagine.

Compared to the hundreds of business books we read each year, we can honestly say we have seen few others that provide as much actionable advice as this book does. We have seen no others that will impact your bottom line in the dramatic manner that "In Pursuit of Profits" will.

You have an opportunity in your hands. An opportunity that you can't afford to miss simply because it looks like work.

LeeMar Publishing
Suite 178
319 Centre Ave
Route 123
Rockland, MA 02370

More of what others have to say about
"In Pursuit of Profits"

"<u>Everyone in your company should have a copy of this book. I bought one for each of my employees. So should you. It is that good.</u> At the very least get a copy of this book for every one of your officers, division heads, departments heads, managers, and supervisors."

"A winner."

"If you want to make a great deal more money tomorrow, read this book today."

"Learn how to double your profits for far less than the cost of a decent dinner."

"If you were one of my students I would give you an A+."

"As far as business books go, this one is a page turner."

"Learn how to dramatically lower your cost of doing business."

"If you only read one business book this year make it In Pursuit of Profits."

"If you want to start increasing your profits instead of just talking about it, read this book."

"Mr. Welch has shown us there is another way besides increasing sales to significantly improve profits. Perhaps a far better way."

"Just one idea from this book added $100,000 to my bottom line."

"In Pursuit of Profits should be required reading for every one of your employees."

"For many companies the strategies in this book could mean the difference between thriving and just surviving or, in some cases, surviving at all."

"It has been said that one good idea can make you rich. Derrick Welch has given you over 1,000. <u>This book is a complete guide on not only how to dramatically increase your profits but also on how to dramatically improve your company.</u> If you can't double your profits after reading this book you simply are not trying very hard."

"Should be given to every employee right along with the employee handbook."

"If you think your people have already cut costs to the bone you should read this book. Better yet, give a copy to each of them."

"This book is at least 6 times the size of your average business book. There is nothing average about this book. If you are serious about doubling your profits read it."

"The bigger your business the more you probably need to read this book. It will show you how to take back the control you lose with size."

"A million dollars worth of ideas."

"If increased profits are important to your business, you must read this book."

"At last, a title that tells the truth."

"Put a copy of this book in the hands of each one of your employees. You will never get a better return on your investment."

"This book reminded me and <u>my employees</u> why we are in business. Not to make products, not to deliver services, not to solve problems. Too many of us had lost sight of the fact we are in business to make money."

"Learn how to slash costs in every area of your business without any sacrifice in quality or service."

"Another name for this book could be The Art of Total Cost Control."

In Pursuit of Profits

How To At Least Double Your Profits Without Increasing Your Sales

Including 1,000 Cost Control, Expense Reduction, And Income Producing Strategies You Can Start Using <u>Today</u> To Dramatically Increase Your Bottom Line.

By

Derrick W. Welch

LeeMar Publishing

Other books by the author:

A Businessman's Book of Wisdom (Available spring of 1995)

In Pursuit of Excellence (Available spring of 1995)

ISBN 1-886262-00-4

Today we live in a suit happy society in which no one takes responsibility for anything. Between lawyers and the government, business has less and less control each year and more and more liability. Like it or not, and I don't, this is the world we live in. Therefore, I must add the following disclaimer:

This publication contains the opinions and ideas of its author and is designed to provide useful advice in regard to the subject matter covered. It is sold with the understanding that the author and publisher are not engaged in rendering legal, accounting or other professional services.

The author and publisher specifically disclaim any responsibility for any liability, loss or risk, personal or otherwise, which is incurred as a consequence, directly or indirectly, of the use and the application of any of the contents of this book. If these terms are not agreeable to you please return this book to the publisher for a full refund within 30 days of purchase.

With that said, I will also point out that I will claim no credit for any fiscal success you enjoy as a result of reading and implementing my ideas. After all, fair is fair.

Cover Design by Katherine Conley

Dedication

"The credit belongs to the man who is actually in the arena, whose face is marred by dust and sweat and blood; who strives valiantly; who errs and comes short again and again; who knows the great enthusiasms; the great devotions, and spends himself in a worthy cause; who at the best knows the triumph of high achievement; and who, at the worst, if he fails, at least fails while daring greatly, so that his place shall never be with those cold and timid souls who know neither victory nor defeat."

Theodore Roosevelt

This book is dedicated to the businessmen and women who have made this great country what it is today. You will never get the credit you deserve.

Acknowledgments.

Despite what anyone might tell you, no one writes a book alone. Many of my thoughts and ideas are a result of trial and error rooted in actual experience. I have found out what works and what does not the hard way, from failing. Others have come from many fine businessmen and women, who I have had the pleasure of learning from over the years. Others are just plain common sense.

Yet, still others have come from watching and learning from the mistakes of others. Therefore, much of my knowledge has been developed over the years from sources that, regrettably, I cannot properly credit here.

It is my hope that you will use these ideas and strategies to make your business more profitable or to climb higher up the corporate ladder. If I can play some small part in helping you achieve your goals, my efforts will be well rewarded.

I also wish to publicly thank my wonderful wife Dianne and my two daughters, who are my pride and joy, Jessica and Joanna. Without their constant support this book would never have been written. They have endured countless hours without my company as I worked day and night for many months putting the ideas you read here on paper.

I suspected this was a tremendous hardship, but I can't help but wonder why they keep asking me when I am going to start my next book. It seems that I might have overestimated the enjoyment of my company.

Finally, I wish to thank my parents who have always been a never ending source of support and encouragement to me. You could never be more proud of me than I am of you.

Table of Contents

A message from the author

My goal is a simple one. It is to help your company, large or small, become more profitable. Dramatically more profitable, in fact. In this book I will show you not only what to do to accomplish this, but how to do it as well.

If you are a business owner I will show you how to make stunning improvements to your bottom line. If you are a division or department head, manager, supervisor, or an employee, you can use these ideas and strategies to bolt up the corporate ladder as you will find few things in your career that will boost your stock more than efforts and ideas that improve your employer's bottom line.

This book will show you ways to slash costs in every area of your business without sacrificing quality or service. The strategies I will show you are not theoretical or complex. They do not consist of any academic or idealistic bull. You will find no such nonsense in my books or publications. Quite the opposite. They are simple common sense strategies that can be used by any business, large or small, private or public, for profit and non profit.

If you were walking down the street and saw a $100 bill lying on the ground would you stop and pick it up? Many of these strategies take no more effort than this and will enable you to make a great deal more money. These are proven workable strategies that can dramatically transform your business. Depending on the size of your company the ideas and strategies in this book could easily add tens of thousands, hundreds of thousands, or even millions of dollars or more to your bottom line each year.

Yes, you can double your profits without increasing your sales and, in fact, you can do this while sales are actually declining. I know, I have helped many companies do it.

But this book goes beyond that. It will also show you a new way to conduct the daily operations of your business. It is about making your company a better company in all areas of your operation. It will show you how to change the thinking of your management team and your employees. It will help you create a common goal for your management and staff to work toward in unity.

It will show you how to get your people thinking long term and not just short term. It will show you how to develop a proactive management style instead of merely being reactive and it will show you why this is so important. This book will remind your people why you are in business. It will make them think like few other books have. I hope it will help you improve every area of your business.

This book is about a program of Total Cost Control.

So, while the focal point revolves around controlling and reducing expenses, please read my ideas, concepts, and strategies with an open mind for I will show you many ways to dramatically improve your company and, by doing so, your bottom line.

Yes, you can easily double your profits without increasing your sales and yes, this book will show you how to do that and more. But it cannot be accomplished without the involvement of your management personnel and your employees. They are the key. Therefore, if you are serious about doubling the profits of your company it is vital that a copy of this book be placed in the hands of each of your officers, division heads, department heads, managers, supervisors, and, if possible, employees.

The strategies I will be giving you extend to every area of your business. Only by placing a copy of this book in the hands of the people responsible for managing within each area of your business will you be able to realize the maximum gains in profitability possible.

The small investment that it will take to put a copy of this book in the hands of your employees, or at least your key people, will pay you dramatic dividends for years to come. It is an investment in your people, your bottom line, and the future of your company.

To help you accomplish this in the most economical way possible I have made arrangements with the publisher to enable you to order additional copies of this book based on the discount schedule outlined on the order form at the end of this book.

If I can help you accomplish your goals in a more direct manner I stand ready to help. I can be reached through my publisher at 1-617-499-1970.

My best,

Derrick W. Welch

P.S.   My apologies if I offend you, your business, or how you conduct business. That is not my goal. My goal is to help your company become the best company it can be. A company driven to be cost efficient is a company driven to improve every area of its operation.

To those of you who might lose business or sales from customers who follow my strategies, rest assured, by following a program of Total Cost Control you can become a better, more competitive company and win those customers back.

Preface

A young boy sat high up on a hill mesmerized by the scene below. The flashing lights, the screams of terror, the cries of merriment. Alone he sat and watched and listened. There was an air of excitement and anticipation coupled with a feeling of deep sadness.

He was watching the highlight of every young child's summer go on without him. He was watching the carnival that came to town but once a year. He listened to the high pitched shrieks of horror coming from the spooky house and from high atop the Ferris wheel. He heard the squeals of laughter coming from inside the fun house. His mouth watered at the aroma of cotton candy and roasted hot dogs. He wondered if the bearded lady really had a beard and if the two headed man was indeed real. His imagination ran wild.

He spotted his friends darting from game of chance to game of chance. However, to a young boy few things were more frustrating than not having any money to go to the carnival. How was he to impress the young ladies with his skill at winning the games and daring the rides if he had no money?

The carnival was in town for only one week each year and each night they had a fireworks display. The fireworks display was free. So, the first night he walked through the carnival and watched his friends ride rides that today would turn his stomach and try games of chance that he now knows offered odds only slightly better than winning the lottery.

He sat on that hill later that first night overlooking the carnival, alone, but surrounded by hundreds of other people, watching the fireworks display. In those days they had displays that lasted for up to an hour. What a night.

The next day the young boy returned and, once again, sat on that hill and waited for the carnival to open. As he sat there he noticed a number of shiny objects in the grass around him. What do you think they were? Coins. Dozens and dozens of coins. Coins that had fallen out of the pockets of those hundreds and hundreds of people who had been sitting on the hill watching the fireworks from the night before.

Within a few minutes he had picked up over $5.00 in change. He picked up pennies, nickels, dimes, quarters, and even an occasional silver dollar. Within an hour he had over $10.00. The young boy sat there in amazement.

The night before hundreds of people had just walked over that money. Why did they not see it? It was a well lit area. They just weren't looking. The young boy was.

The young boy, flushed with his sudden fiscal good fortune, sat and thought about how this had occurred and where else he might find money lying around. The carnival would not be open for another hour so he got up and walked down to the midway. He looked and looked. He found money under the rides that had fallen out of the rider's pockets. He found money in front of the concession stands. He found money in front of the games of chance.

Yes, mostly what the young man found were nickels and dimes but they added up to dollars. A lesson the young boy never forgot.

The point of this story is that the answer to that young boy's problem was right in front of him. All he had to do was look around. You can do the same. That little boy found money everywhere he looked. I will show you how to find the money that is lying all around your company. You see, I was that young man.

Derrick W. Welch

BOOK ONE

IN PURSUIT OF PROFITS

TOTAL COST CONTROL

Chapter 1. The simplicity of business.

"There is only one rule of business and that is: Make the best quality you can at the lowest cost possible. "

Henry Ford

Being in business today can be a very complex process, but making more money in business is not that complex. The basic business formula is that <u>your profit equals your revenue minus your cost</u>. **Therefore, any way you look at it there are really only three basic ways to increase your profits.**

You can either increase sales, decrease expenses, or do both. Most businesses seek to find ways to increase sales. They plan, set goals, develop new products, hire new salespeople, run sales, and actively pursue an increased base of sales and customers in thousands of other ways. Yes, increasing sales is the top priority of most businesses and the only priority of many.

But increasing sales costs money. In most cases a great deal of money. Marketing costs money. Advertising costs money. Each of these efforts can severely hinder your cash flow. Furthermore, finding the proper formula to increase sales is often an elusive quest. Trial and error coupled with educated guesswork is normally the method employed by most companies in their never-ending quest to increase sales. At best, expensive and most often, ineffective, strategies.

Most companies look outside to solve their profit problems and by doing so realize limited success and often create even more problems. But, like it is with each of us, the fastest path to improvement is normally to look within. Unfortunately, most companies, like most people, will only look within when all other options are exhausted.

Reducing costs costs nothing, actually saves money, can dramatically improve your cash flow and profits, often increases productivity, and has countless secondary benefits for any company. Think about this, if you increase sales by $1,000 you spent money to get that sale and you might realize a net bottom line pretax profit (after selling expenses, operating costs, cost of goods sold, etc.) of $20 to $50 if you are like most companies who show a net pretax profit of 2% -5% per year or less.

But now think about this, if you reduce costs by that same $1,000 you have just increased your bottom line by $1,000. The cost was zero. In fact, you have improved your cash flow by eliminating the cost associated with increasing sales and by the $1,000 you saved.

Think about these examples. A $4,000 reduction in costs for a company that has a pretax profit ratio of 4% is equal to a gain in sales of $100,000. A 1% reduction in costs for a company that has $10,000,000 in sales and a 5% pretax profit ratio puts $95,000 pretax dollars on the bottom line.

This means this company's profit went from $500,000 to $595,000 simply by cutting costs 1%. They have just increased their pretax profits by 19% simply by decreasing their costs 1%. Think about this, a 19% increase in pretax profits without increasing sales a penny. To realize this same increase in profits through increased sales this company (at a 5% profit level) would need to increase sales $1,900,000.

Look at a company with $1,000,000,000 in sales and a 2.5% pretax profit ratio. In this case the company has costs of $975,000,000 and a pretax profit of $25,000,000. A 1% reduction in total costs would result in a dollar savings of $9,750,000. This mere 1% reduction in costs has added $9,750,000 directly to the bottom line of this company. A 1% decrease in costs has produced a 39% increase in profits.

I assure you few things in business can be accomplished with less effort that will have such a dramatic effect on your bottom line.

Thinking in these terms will reinforce the dramatic effect cost control and cost reduction can have on your bottom line. Clearly, dollars saved by reducing expenses and controlling costs can have a very direct and very dramatic effect on the profit picture of your company, with a fraction of the effort and cost of the increase in sales that would be required to produce the same increase in profits.

But few companies make any serious ongoing effort to try and reduce or control costs. Those that do might spend only a fraction of the time and effort they spend on increasing sales, on decreasing and controlling costs. Oh, sure they may talk about cutting and controlling costs and they may even take a few obvious steps to do something about it, but normally that is the extent of their short term efforts in this area.

Imagine not paying much, if any, attention to 50% of your success formula. But this is exactly what happens in all too many companies. I would be willing to bet that this is exactly what happens in your company. A company with strong financial management can survive many other types of mismanagement, but no matter how strong management is in other areas, without strong financial management a company will never reach the levels of profitability they could, and should reach. In fact, they might not even survive very long.

Reducing and controlling costs can keep you in business or at the very least dramatically increase your profitability. Increasing and uncontrolled costs are hurting your company in hundreds of ways. Increased costs drain profits and devastate your cash flow. They force you to raise prices, which in turn makes you less competitive and, as a result, lose sales. Uncontrolled costs can put you out of business.

You must keep costs down during tough times to survive. During good times it is just as important to control and reduce costs. This will help you build a solid fiscal and operational foundation so you can survive the difficult times that are sure to come and it will allow you to increase profits, expand your marketing efforts, and improve your company during the good times.

Ineffective financial management can affect every area of your business not just the bottom line. It reduces profits which affects the pay and benefits you give your people. This negatively affects your ability to hire the best people you can. It affects your ability to provide a higher rate of return to your stockholders. It affects your borrowing ability as you can be perceived as a higher credit risk. This could result in lower lines of credit, higher rates, poor terms, and even affect your ability to get credit at all.

It affects your ability to develop new products and market them. It affects your ability to upgrade your facility and equipment which can severely hamper your efforts to improve production, which in turn makes you less competitive. Yes, ineffective financial management severely hurts your company in hundreds of ways.

However, like a tea kettle on the stove, the areas of cost control and expense reduction are usually ignored until the warning whistle blows. But why? The benefits of controlling and reducing costs are so obvious and can produce such a dramatic effect in most companies, why are they so often neglected?

In Pursuit of Profits. How To At Least Double Your Profits Without Increasing Your Sales.

Well, one reason is that many managers have strong training and background in sales, management, marketing, administration, personnel, customer service, and many other conventional areas. But very few, if any, have training in cost control and expense reduction.

How could they? Schools don't teach it. Most managers, executives, and owners don't practice it. Where would they learn it?

Cost control and expense reduction are perhaps the two most neglected areas of management in any company. Yet, they are possibly the areas of management that can have the most dramatic effect on your bottom line and, in fact, your entire operation, with the least amount of effort.

So why don't more companies and more employees give this vital area the attention it deserves? Some other reasons that come to mind are:

* **Convenience**. It is always easier to take the easy way. Often just another word for being lazy.

* **Ignorance**. They just don't know how to control costs.

* **Laziness.** They just don't try, or make the effort to learn how or to think of better ways.

* **Loyalty.** Blind loyalty to certain suppliers, companies, or sales representatives.

* **Who cares attitude.** Many management personnel and employees simply don't care about profits. They see no direct connection to their jobs, advancement, or income with reducing or controlling costs. In other cases managers or even company officers have many other things on their agenda. They are more concerned with building a power base, increasing staff and budgets, and taking care of their own individual goals regardless of the bottom line impact to the company. These are the people more concerned with bureaucracy and politics than with productivity and profitability. These people thrive in large organizations and must be rooted out at all costs.

* **Indifference.** They don't care. It is not their money.

* **Low priority.** Many other more visible and pressing matters must be addressed.

* **No incentive**. You have given them no reason to.

* **Example.** They follow the example, or lack of the example, of management and ownership. This will be discussed in depth later on.

Each of these problems can be overcome and I will show you how throughout this book. But let me give you a tip now. **The key to everything in business and in fact in life, is thinking and asking questions.** Thinking about what the problem is and thinking of ways to overcome that problem.

If you found money on the street you would stop to pick it up wouldn't you? You have money lying all over your company, all you need to do is look for it. **I will show you how to find it. It will be up to you and your people to pick it up!**

Controlling costs and reducing expenses is not being cheap. It is not being a bean counter. Getting the best buy for your money is being an intelligent businessman or woman. Eliminating waste is the only smart thing to do. Anyone who thinks cost control is being cheap has no right calling themselves a business person.

The alternative to total cost control is overpayment, waste, and inefficiency. Which do you think characterizes the better business person? Watching the bottom line and getting the best value for your money in order to ensure maximum profitability should be the goal of anyone in business. **I would call this doing your job. I would call this financial management.**

Proper financial control is critical to not only the growth of a business but for its very survival. Without proper financial control all cost related management will be of a reactive nature. Reactive management is one small step above no management. A very small step in many instances.

Reactive management takes place after the damage has already been done. The problem has been allowed to come into existence. It attempts to correct a problem. In the areas of cost control and expense reduction reactive management takes place after the cost has been incurred. The drain on profits has taken place. Reactive management then tries to find ways to lower the cost.

Proactive management attempts to make sure that the problem never exists. We will cover this more in a later chapter.

Chapter 2. The 5% solution.

"Cost reduction is the best way to increase profitability."

> *Victor Tabbush, Ph.D.*
> *Associate Dean*
> *John E. Anderson Graduate School of Management*
> *UCLA*

Recent studies have shown that the majority of companies in this country make a pretax profit, as a percentage of sales, of 5% or less. **If you think I am just referring to small companies think again. The median profit, as a percentage of sales, of the Fortune 500 in 1991 was only 3.1%. In 1992 this dropped to 2.4%. In 1993 it was 2.9%. Let me repeat this. In 1993 the median profit of 500 of the largest companies in this country, as a percentage of sales, was only 2.9%.**

<u>If you are one of these companies you can at least double, and most likely much more than double, your pretax profits simply by reducing costs 5%.</u>

If you currently enjoy a profit ratio, as a percentage of sales, that exceeds 5%, congratulations! You are in the minority. You are exceeding the average and excelling where others are not. But please do not skip this chapter. You can do better. Much better. In fact, unless your profit ratio is extremely high, the concepts I will show you here should prove to be nearly as effective for your company as they are for those companies making a profit ratio of 5% or less. Plug your ratio into the formulas I show you and see how dramatic the bottom line results can be for your company.

Furthermore, while the profit ratios in the specific examples may not be directly applicable to your overall operations they may be directly applicable to many of your profit centers, divisions, or departments. In any case, setting goals in the manner I will show you in this chapter will produce significant improvements to your bottom line.

Your pretax profit ratio is simply your bottom line profits before taxes, divided by your total gross sales. For example, if your pretax profit for your last fiscal year was $250,000 you would simply divide this by your total sales to get your pretax profit ratio. If your total sales were $10,000,000 you would divide $250,000 (pretax profit) by $10,000,000 (gross sales) to arrive at your pretax profit ratio of .025 or 2.5%.

If your profit ratio, as a percentage of sales, is less than 5% , you can use it to replace the 5% example I am using with your % and read as though I am talking to you directly. **The point I am trying to make, is that the way to double your profits is to reduce your costs by an amount equal to your pretax profits as a % of sales.**

Of course, this will also work with 1%, 2%, 3%, or 4%. I have chosen to use 5% in my example solely because 5% or less is the pretax profit percentage of the majority of companies in this country.

So, while I have called this chapter the 5% solution it could just as easily have been called the 1% solution or the 4% solution or whatever percentage that is equal to your pretax profit as a percentage of sales from your last fiscal year. The concept is the same. Take your pretax profit ratio and decrease costs by this percentage, while holding sales level, and you will come very close to doubling your profits.

Let me demonstrate this using a larger company as an example. If you have $10,000,000,000 in sales and a 5% pretax profit your costs are $9,500,000,000. This means 95% of the income from your sales goes to cover your costs. Your pretax profit is $500,000,000. If you can lower your costs by only 5% you will increase your profit to $975,000,000. Your original $9,500,000,000 of costs times .05 = $475,000,000. This is how much you will have added to your bottom line. Your profits have risen from $500,000,000 to $975,000,000.

You have nearly doubled your profits. Let me put these numbers in perspective for you. **With an average of 249 business days a year excluding holidays, this company just added $1,907,630 per day to the bottom line. That's right, nearly $2 million dollars per day!** In an 8 hour day this is $238,453 per hour or $3,974 per minute. Accomplished simply by lowering costs by 5%! How much per day would you add to your bottom line by doubling your profits?

To realize the same increase in profits at the existing 95% cost ratio, this company would have to increase sales to nearly $20,000,000,000. Which would you think would be the way to go? Could you increase sales from $10,000,000,000 to $20,000,000,000? If so, how? At what cost?

Remember, we are talking about doubling your sales to achieve the same bottom line result that can be accomplished by merely holding sales level and reducing costs 5%. Doubling this company's sales would be an almost impossible task to accomplish in any reasonable length of time. However, cutting their costs by an amount that will allow them to double, or even triple, their pretax profits can be done in a very short time and quite easily.

The concept is the same no matter what your sales are. For example, if your sales are $50,000,000 and you have the same 5% pretax profit ratio your pretax profits are $2,500,000, leaving your costs at $47,500,000. If you can lower your costs by 5% they will drop by $2,375,000. This was arrived at by taking 5% or .05 of your remaining costs which were $47,500,000. Your new pretax profit level is $4,875,000. You have nearly doubled your profits without increasing your sales a penny.

To realize this same profit increase by increasing sales, you would have had to increase sales by $47,500,000 or, in other words, you would have nearly had to double sales. The way to determine how much of a sales increase you would need to match the added profits realized by cutting your costs is to simply take the added profit realized by your cost cutting efforts and divide it by your pretax profit ratio.

In this case, by cutting costs only 5% you would have realized an added pretax profit of $2,375,000 as I have shown you above. To find the increased level of sales you would need to create an added pretax profit of $2,375,000, you would simply divide this figure by your pretax profit ratio of 5%. Remember, at a 5% pretax profit ratio, 95% of all sales income is going to cover costs associated with that sale and your operation. Therefore, only 5% of the amount of that sale ends up on your bottom line.

In this example, $2,375,000 divided by .05 = $47,500,000. This is the added amount of sales you would need to realize the same pretax profit increase of $2,375,000 if you average a 5% pretax profit ratio. You can cross check this by multiplying this increased sales figure by .05. $47,500,000 x .05 = $2,375,000.

There you have it. You would need to nearly double your sales from $50,000,000 to $97,500,000 to realize the same profit increase that you can obtain by merely cutting your costs by 5%. Imagine that. You can nearly double your profits by simply cutting costs an amount equal to your pretax profit ratio. Compare the effort required to cut costs by a mere 5% to the cost and effort required to double your sales. One can be done very easily and the other can't. It is just that simple!

It doesn't matter if your sales are $100,000 or $100,000,000,000, it works the same way.

In Pursuit of Profits. How To At Least Double Your Profits Without Increasing Your Sales.

Double your sales or reduce costs by 5%?

Trying to double your sales could put you out of business and, at the very least, would result in serious growing pains and a severe cash flow problem. Even if you could double your sales how many years would it take? Just think about our example of the $50 million dollar company. Think about this. Which do you think is more easily achieved, turning this company into a $100 million dollar company or cutting costs by 5%?

Reducing your costs by 5% is not very difficult, can be done in a very short time, involves no growth, and improves your cash flow. **In fact, you should be easily able to decrease costs much more than this.** Trying to increase sales by 100% will take a bit more doing. The choice would appear to be a very simple one.

Triple your profits without increasing your sales.

If you can cut costs by a percentage equal to double that of your last year's pretax profit ratio without increasing sales you will nearly triple your profits.

For example, if you are among the millions of companies producing **less than** a 5% pretax profit cutting your costs 5% will have even more dramatic results. For example, if your pretax profit is 2.5% look what happens. Sales of $1,000,000 with costs of $975,000 would produce a pretax profit of $25,000. By lowering your costs by 5% you would save $48,750 and increase your pretax profit to $73,750. This is determined by taking 5% of your $975,000 costs which is $975,000 x .05 = $48,750. This added pretax profit of $48,750 combined with your previous pretax profit of $25,000, gives you a new bottom line pretax profit of $73,750.

You have nearly tripled your profit without increasing sales one penny. All you have done is lower your costs by an amount equal to double your last year's pretax profit ratio. To realize this same added pretax profit by increasing sales, using the same 2.5% pretax profit ratio, you would have to increase your sales to $2,950,000. In short, you would need to triple sales to triple profits.

Of course, if your pretax profits are 2.5% you can nearly double your profits simply by reducing costs a matching 2.5% as I have shown in previous examples.

If you think that reducing costs is simply too difficult, let me say two things. First, you are wrong. Think can do, not can't do. Remember these words:

"If you think you can do a thing
or think you can't do a thing, you're right."

Henry Ford

"The difference between the impossible
and the possible
lies in a person's determination."

Tommy Lasorda

Secondly, I will point out that even if you fail to accomplish your goal of reducing costs by an amount equal to your pretax profit ratio, and there is no reason you should fail, you will still realize dramatic bottom line success. Think about this. If you are a $50,000,000 company with a pretax profit ratio of 5%, your pretax profits are $2,500,000 and your costs are $47,500,000. If you are successful in only decreasing your costs by 1%, you will have added $475,000, or over $1,907 per day, to your bottom line, thereby increasing profits from $2,500,000 to $2,975,000 or 19%.

If you attempted to realize this same gain in profits by increasing sales with the same 5% pretax profit ratio, you would need to increase your sales by $9,500,000 or 19%. Check the numbers yourself. $9,500,000 x .05 = $475,000. $9,500,000 divided by $50,000,000 = .19. $50,000,000 x 1.19 = $59,500,000. There is no magic here. A 1% reduction in costs has produced a 19% increase in profits which is equal to a 19% increase in sales at a pretax profit ratio of 5%.

You see, in this game even failure can produce astounding success. How much would a 1% reduction in costs mean to the bottom line of your business?

Reducing costs without decreasing costs.

No, that sentence is not a typo. In the examples I have given you so far we have actually reduced costs by lowering the dollar volume of those costs. For example, when we lowered costs in our example of the company with $50,000,000 in sales and a pretax profit ratio of 5%, we actually lowered the dollar volume of the costs from $47,500,000 to $45,125,000. We lowered costs 5% or $2,375,000. This increased our profits from $2,500,000 to $4,875,000 without increasing sales.

But you can also effectively reduce costs by holding the dollar amount level while you increase sales. To demonstrate this we will use the same numbers of $50,000,000 in sales, $47,500,000 in costs and $2,500,000 or 5% in pretax profits. If you increase sales to anything over $50,000,000 while holding your costs at $47,500,000 you have effectively reduced costs.

For example, if sales increase to $52,500,000 and costs stay at $47,500,000 you have reduced your costs as a percentage of sales from 95% to 90.5%. Costs of $47,500,000 against sales of $50,000,000 equals a 95% cost ratio. However, costs of $47,500,000 against sales of $52,500,000 equals a 90.5% ratio. Simply put, you have held costs while increasing sales thereby lowering your overall cost ratios.

Had your cost to sales ratio remained at 95%, when your sales increased from $50,000,000 to $52,500,000, your costs would have risen from $47,500,000 to $49,875,000 ($52,500,000 x .95 = $49,875,000) . This would have left you a profit of $2,625,000 on your sales of $52,500,000.

However, since you have held your costs stable at $47,500,000, while increasing sales to $52,500,000 your profit increased to $5,000,000. Imagine that. **Your sales went up only 5%, but since you held costs stable, your pretax profits went up 100%.**

What you have done is achieve nearly the same results whether it was by decreasing costs by 5% while sales stayed level or by holding costs stable and increasing sales by 5%. Here you have held your costs stable while increasing your sales by an amount equal to your last year's pretax profit ratio which, in this example, was a mere 5% and, by doing so, produced a 100% gain in pretax profits from $2,500,000 to $5,000,000. If you recall, when we lowered costs by 5% without any increase in sales, pretax profits went from $2,500,000 to $4,875,000. In both cases a 5% change produced an increase in pretax profits of nearly equal amounts. **There is no magic here. It works!**

In this example, we did not cut actual costs by one cent. Instead, we simply held costs while effecting a very minor increase in sales. We are simply getting more for our money with a resulting increase in productivity. In the previous examples we cut costs to accomplish the same result without increasing sales one penny.

Now, if your sales were $50,000,000 and your pretax profit ratio had only been 2.5%, your profits would have been $1,250,000 and your costs would have been $48,750,000. In this case, if you were able to increase your sales the same 5% while holding costs stable as we reviewed above, your total sales would still have risen to

In Pursuit of Profits. How To At Least Double Your Profits Without Increasing Your Sales.

$52,500,000 but your profits have now increased to $3,750,000. You have tripled profits merely by holding costs stable and increasing sales 5%.

What you have done is increase sales at a ratio equal to double that of what your pretax profit ratio had been while holding costs stable. Now, of course, in order to hold costs stable while increasing sales, you need to decrease actual costs in some areas to offset those product related costs that are a fixed part of the product or service you are selling. But remember, we are talking total overall costs and not individual costs.

If you tell me that you can't hold costs while increasing sales I will tell you once again you are wrong.

"If we did all the things we were capable of doing
we would literally astound ourselves."

Thomas Edison

Think of how you can, not why you can't. If you tell me that you can't hold costs level while increasing sales or that you can't decrease costs despite level sales, I will suggest to you that perhaps you should think about another way to make a living or that you have the wrong people working for you. If this is the case, please call me right away, I think you need my help.

Now, think about this. If you are able to decrease costs while increasing sales a percentage that is greater than your previous year's pretax profits percentage your results will be even more impressive. Much more impressive.

Again, I will tell you that holding costs while increasing sales or decreasing costs while sales are level is not very difficult. I know, I have done this many times with many companies. It can be done. It will take time and it will take effort, but most importantly it takes a commitment to getting it done.

Think about what your profits would be if you can lower your costs by an amount equal to double your last year's pretax ratio while increasing your sales by the same ratio.

Look what would happen. If your sales are $1,000,000 and your pretax profit ratio is 2.5% ($25,000) by decreasing costs 5% while sales stay level, your profits would go from $25,000 to $73,750 as your costs have dropped from $975,000 to $926,250. Now if you are also able to increase sales 5%, your sales would go from $1,000,000 to $1,050,000. Sales of $1,050,000 with costs of $926,250 leaves you with a pretax profit of $123,750.

Think about this. All you have done is lower your total dollar costs 5% while increasing sales a mere 5% and your profits have gone from $25,000 to $123,750. **A 5% decrease in actual costs and a 5% increase in sales has produced a 495% increase in bottom line pretax profits.**

How much would you have to increase sales at a 2.5% pretax profit ratio to increase that original $25,000 in profits by 495%? Well, in our example a 495% increase in profits equates to $123,750. This means you would need to increase profits by $98,750 from your original profit figure of $25,000. As I have shown you earlier, to find out how much we need to increase sales to reach this added profit goal we simply take the added profit goal and divide it by your pretax profit ratio. Here we would divide $98,750 by .025 to find out that we would need to increase sales by $3,950,000 to increase our profits by $98,750.

This means our sales would have to increase from $1,000,000 to $4,950,000 to realize the same profit of $123,750 if our expense ratio stayed at 97.5%. $4,950,000 x .025 = $123,750.

Take a minute and think about what I am showing you here. Increasing your sales from $1,000,000 to $4,950,00 will be a formidable task to say the least. Depending on your type of business and growth stage, it may even appear to be an impossible task. But think about lowering your costs a mere 5% while increasing your sales only 5%. One effort seems impossible and one seems easily obtainable. Yet, both have the same bottom line results.

Can you do this in your company? Of course you can! It does not matter whether you have $100,000 a year in sales or if you are a Fortune 500 company. The principles and benefits are the same.

The overwhelming majority of business managers and owners in this country think that the way to increased profits is to increase sales. Countless books have been written on this subject and seminars teaching companies how to increase sales are held every day, in every city, in the country.

But I have shown you that there is another way to increase profits. A much easier and, perhaps, more effective way, to generate significantly increased profits. I will cover this more in another section but I am also showing you a way to do much more than just increase profits. **I am also showing you a way that can change the very way your company operates in every area. A way that can dramatically increase productivity, morale, service, quality, and yes, profitability.** A program of total cost control can indeed accomplish each of these things and we will discuss this much more in an upcoming chapter.

For now, you will notice that in all the examples I have given you I have used a % goal not a dollar amount goal. There is a reason for this. **It is because perception and credibility are critical to your efforts in these areas.**

Simply put, a % solution is a good motivating objective to employ. Staying with the 5% solution, you will find this is a very attainable goal and one in which your employees will believe they can accomplish.

Think about a $1,000,000,000 company with a pretax profit of 5% trying to reduce costs by 5%. This would mean this company is trying to reduce costs from $950,000,000 to $902,500,000. They are trying to cut costs by $47,500,000. Do you think your employees would perceive a goal of reducing costs by $47,500,000 to be more attainable than a goal of reducing costs by a mere 5%?

People must think the objective they are working towards is worthwhile and can be reached. A cost reduction of $47,500,000 is such a large number it will either have little meaning to them or it will scare the hell out of them. **If they do not think the goal can be accomplished I can assure you it will not be accomplished. If it has no meaning their efforts will reflect this. If it scares them they will feel it cannot be accomplished and therefore it will not be.**

But a 5% reduction in costs neither intimidates nor seems meaningless. Remember, perception is reality for the holder of that perception. If you tell me our objective is to reduce costs by 5% I will see this as both a worthwhile goal and a very attainable goal. If you tell me we must reduce costs by $47,500,000 I will ask how and doubt whether such lofty goals are even possible. I will wonder where we could possibly save this kind of money. I would wonder where you drank your lunch. I would wonder if my job was safe and if you were sane.

Yet, both have the same dramatic effect on your bottom line.

When I tell you our goal is to reduce total costs by 5% you begin to think of ways to do this. I can, and will, give you hundreds of ways you can reach this very attainable goal. I will show you ways to reduce many costs by 20%, 30%, or even 100%.

In Pursuit of Profits. How To At Least Double Your Profits Without Increasing Your Sales.

Of course, you can save 5% and a great deal more. This is the type of mentality you must have and you must foster in those who work for you. There are hundreds of ways large and small in which you can save 5% and much more. Yes, I know that in some cases you will be unable to reduce a cost by 5% and, in fact, you will do well just by being able to control them.

But there are many places in which you can easily reduce actual dollar costs by 10%, 20%, even 50% or more. I also know that you should very easily be able to increase sales while holding your dollar costs stable. By doing this you effectively accomplish the same thing as an actual dollar cost reduction.

For example, if your people produce more you have lowered a cost. If you have a person making $20,000 a year who produces 10,000 widgets a year, your labor cost per widget is $2. If they increase their productivity and now can produce 12,000 widgets a year, you have lowered your per widget cost to $1.67 each. You have lowered your per widget labor cost by 16.5% without lowering the actual dollar cost one penny.

If you have a store that costs you $50,000 per year to lease and you sell 50,000 items a year, or a factory that costs the same to lease and produces 50,000 widgets a year, your per sale or per widget facility, related cost is $1. Now if you can increase your sales or order output to 60,000 items a year you have dropped your facility related overhead cost for each sale or item to .83 each. Again, here you have not decreased actual dollars spent but, instead, increased your output thereby effectively accomplishing a decrease in costs as a percentage of the sale. In this example a 17% effective decrease in costs. Improving your quality thereby lowering rejects and returned goods also accomplishes the same thing.

Please do not be side tracked by these simplistic examples. I am well aware that other factors exist beyond the ones I am showing you here, focus in on the concepts.

However you do it, increase sales or output while holding costs or cutting actual dollars spent, the overall goal is the same. **Think overall and not just individual costs.** Think of the areas in which you can reduce costs 1% or 2%, think of the areas in which you can easily reduce costs 25% or 50% or more.

This can also be done by decreasing costs more aggressively while sales are going down. I have also done this. If you are able to decrease more than a $1 in costs for every $1 lost in sales your profits will increase despite the loss in sales. Remember, when you lose a dollar in sales you do not lose a dollar in profits because only a small portion of the dollar in sales is actually profit.

This is how you maintain or increase profits during difficult times. In some cases intentionally losing sales can be a very effective strategy to increase profits if you can couple it with a greater drop in expenses. If you have low profit or no profit sales, intentionally shedding yourself of these sales may enable you to reduce overhead at an even greater rate, thereby creating a desirable situation.

Think about this. Plug your pretax profit percentages into these formulas and see the impact cost control and expense reduction can have on your company.

Chapter 3. Questions are the key.

"Why and how are words so important that they cannot be too often used."

Napoleon

It was Kipling who gave us what was perhaps the greatest advice for business success and, in fact, success in life, that has ever been given. He told us the key to success in all areas when he said **"I had six honest serving men. They taught me all I knew. Their names were: where and what and when and why and how and who."**.

The late great Earl Nightingale suggested we add two more friends to this group. They are, which and if. I suggest you add as many more as you can to this group.

Whether you are seeking to find ways to increase sales or control and reduce costs, questions are the key. Whether you are striving to improve your customer service or the quality of your product, questions are the key. Asking the questions and developing the answers are the keys to any and all success you will have in business. Questions like:

Which is better?	If we make that purchase what is the payback period?
If we do this what happens?	Why do we do it that way?
Why do we need this?	Why do we buy that many?
Why do we buy that few?	What are we planning to do with them?
Why do we buy from them?	Why do we only get one bid?
Why do we do it this way?	Why don't we do it this way?
Who else can we use?	Who else can do this?
Who else can we sell to?	Who uses this?
Where else can this be done?	Where else can we get this?
Where is that used?	What is it used for?
What can we do to reduce costs?	What can we do to improve productivity?
What can we do to improve quality?	What can we do to improve our service?
What steps can we take to streamline?	When do we do that? Why?
When do we buy that? Why?	When do we need to re-inventory? Why?
How else can we do this function?	How else can that be done?

In Pursuit of Profits. How To At Least Double Your Profits Without Increasing Your Sales.

How can we do it better, faster, cheaper?

How can we improve quality, service, profits?

How can we reduce waste?

How can we sell more to that customer?

How can we cut costs? Why not?

Is there a better way? There always is!

If we do not do that what happens?

If we do this will we improve quality?

If we do this will it improve service?

If we do this will it increase profits?

Which is better? Why?

Which provides us with better quality?

Which is cheaper?

Which is best for our customer?

What is bought ?

Why is it bought?

What do we use it for?

Why do we need it?

Why can't we do without it?

What do we get in return for this cost?

Why is it worth it?

Why are we not buying in this quantity?

Why do we buy in the quantity?

Why do we not buy more to save on the unit cost?

Who else can provide what we need?

Why don't we buy less and free up cash for other uses?

Why are we paying that much?

Why do we not deal with another company?

Why are we not paying less?

What do they provide us that someone else can't?

Why are we dealing with them?

How many other bids have we gotten?

Who are they from?

Why so few?

Why so many?

Why do we do this at all?

What does this add?

Is this effort cost justified?

What if?

Why?

Is it costing us more to do this than we are saving?

What do we buy that can be combined with other purchases to get a better overall deal?

How can we replace that with equal quality for less?

What are other companies charging for that product or service?

What are other companies paying for that product or service?

Will this process or step add value to our product or service or does it produce added profit?

You see my point I am sure. You must ask questions and seek out the answers. You must also justify the answers. **You must never stop asking. If you are not continuously asking the questions and reacting to the answers you are either assuming or stagnating. Either one can be deadly to your business.**

As we continue on I will begin to focus more and more of my comments on the areas of cost control and expense reduction, but please do not limit your thinking to these areas only. Questions are certainly, but not exclusively, the key to reducing and controlling costs.

"I do not believe you can do today's job with yesterday's methods and still be in business tomorrow."

Nelson Jackson

Questions are also the key to improvements in every area of your company and by improving other areas of your organization you will not only be reducing and controlling costs, but also be providing a better product and service. I will be focusing more on the areas of cost control and expense reduction simply because that is what the major thrust of this publication is. Not because these are the only areas for which questions are important. They are equally important in every other area of your business.

For example, do you know your competitions products, services, and prices? Do you know what else your customers could buy that you can provide? Do you even know who your customers are? Do you know what your market potential is? Do you know what your market share is? What other markets exist for your product or service? How do you know what opportunities are out there if you do not know the answers to these questions? How can you formulate a marketing plan if you do not have complete knowledge of your market?

You must review every phase of your business from the front office to customer service, from manufacturing and distribution to quality control and shipping. You might get depressed when you see how much money your company spends on these areas and you surely will be upset when you see how much is squandered each year. But even so you will be shocked when you see how little effort it will take to find huge savings and to make major improvements in how you conduct business.

Do you know how your products are produced and distributed? Do you know what goes into your product or service? I don't mean a general idea, I mean specifics. How much material at what cost? How much time at what cost?

Is your product flow or order processing set up to maximize time, quality and productivity and reduce costs? If you don't know how can you expect to control costs, improve or control quality, and improve productivity? Why do you do these things this way? How can you find a better way if you don't know how it is being done now and why?

Examine every single area that you spend money on. Every single area. There are very few areas in which you cannot save money. From sales to order entry. From production to distribution. From the showroom to the storefront. From accounts receivable to accounts payable. You can always improve how you do things. You must find ways to conduct business more efficiently, eliminate needless steps, improve productivity, reduce errors, increase sales, reduce expenses, and control costs.

In Pursuit of Profits. How To At Least Double Your Profits Without Increasing Your Sales.

"There is a better way for everything. Find it."

Thomas Edison

Always strive for improvement in every area of your business. Always look for ways to do it better, faster, less expensive. Look for ways to sell your product or service to more markets and for higher prices. Never overlook the small savings or improvements. Just as finding 1,000 was to save $1 will add up to a savings of $1000, numerous small improvements will equate to major improvements. The Japanese call this type of management thinking "Kaizen". A more radical version of this type of thinking is popularly known in this country as "reengineering". Call it what you will, it does not matter, just adopt this type of thinking.

Tom Peters once said "Do 1,000 things just 1% better and soon you'll be 1,000 % better.". He is right. You must always be asking yourself if that is the best you can do. Your people must keep asking the same thing. **The quest for improvement must be never-ending. But you will never be able to do this unless you ask the questions.** Why do you do what you do the way you do it? Why do you not do it another way? What are you spending your money on, with who, and why? Why not in another manner with another company? **Ask the questions. They are the key to the door of improvement.**

"If you are satisfied with the best you have done you will never do the best you can."

Martin VanBee

Never assume you or your people can't do better. <u>Always assume you can do better.</u> Let me give you one small example of how an assumption proved to be very costly at one company. One of the many products this company offered was a Christmas label strip. This was simply a strip of peel off labels. Banks around the country would buy them and give them out one strip at a time to their customers around the holidays.

For years this company shrink wrapped these in packages of 250 and sold them in a minimum quantity of 1,000. The shrink wrapping was time consuming and costly. We asked them why. Why did they need to be shrink wrapped? How did they know if this was important to the customer? What, if any, difference did packaging make to their customers?

They asked the questions and found the answers. The answer in this case was that the customer either couldn't have cared less about the packaging or did not like the shrink wrap as it simply meant more work for them to unwrap. After years of doing it the way they always did and assuming that was what the end user wanted they found out differently. They now bulk package. They save between $20,000 and $30,000 per year and their customers are either happier or neutral about this change.

You must think and analyze every area of your business. Not just the bigger, more likely to yield larger savings, areas, but every area. From packaging to promotion, from procedures to personnel, you must keep striving to improve your organization. **But never should you compromise on the quality of your product or service. This is not what total cost control is all about.**

Look at the example I gave you above. Did this company sacrifice quality in any way to save money? No, they improved productivity, improved customer satisfaction, and by doing so, improved profitability. **This is what total cost control is all about.**

You should constantly be reviewing every area of your operation to seek ways in which you can improve. Use common sense. From office expenses to customer service, from distribution and production to quality control and shipping, you will be shocked at how little effort it will take to improve your operations, reduce waste and redundancy, and realize huge savings.

You should look at every process in your company, from sales to order entry to order fulfillment, your objective should be to streamline all areas of how you process your work. The question is "is this the most expedient and efficient way to do the job?".

Does the work flow properly? Can I move equipment or functions to speed things up? Can I alter sequences of processing to make things quicker or less wasteful or less redundant? Are all steps needed? Should each step be done by the person or departments now doing them?

From the way you sell things to the way you buy things, it is up to you to improve things. Improvement is always possible in everything we do.

The overriding question is if you were starting from scratch what would be the way you would organize and layout each and every one of these functions? If you are not in line today with what that ideal setup would be, you had better start making changes. An effective "flow" of work will reduce costs, improve quality and productivity.

I must warn you that you will get depressed when you see how much money you or your people have squandered over the years in the form of poor purchasing practices, redundant labor efforts, needless purchases, poor quality, wasted steps, inefficient processes, and hundreds of other areas. But the good news is that you will find you can make major improvements to your operation and significantly improve your bottom line with very little effort.

Forget the way it has always been done. Forget the fancy names like "reengineering" and "Kaizen". Use your God given common sense. You possess the greatest thinking machine ever created and it sits right between your two ears. You own it, free and clear. All you need to do is put it to work.

Resource

Reengineering The Corporation by Michael Hammer & James Champy. Published by Harper Business.

Chapter 4. The domino effect.

"Business is like a game of chess. It takes strategy and a series of small victories to win."

Derrick W. Welch

Did you ever play dominos as a child? If you did, you know that one of the most enjoyable things to do with those spotted wooden blocks was not to play the game of dominos, but to stand them up on their ends, one after another, and then to knock the first one over. When you knocked the first one over it in turn fell on the second one, which in turn fell on the third one, which in turn fell on the fourth one, and this sequence continued until the last domino in line fell over. The primary action you took was to knock over the first block. The secondary result was that you knocked all the others over as well. Your action of knocking over one caused a series of secondary actions. **I call this the domino effect.**

It is the same way in life. Every action you take in life produces a number of secondary results beyond the primary result you see. In every area of life this is true. If your actions are positive you will realize many positive secondary benefits as a direct or indirect result of your primary action. The same thing is true in business and the same thing is true for inaction.

For example, if you have an employee who comes in late every day you may be forced to terminate him if his actions cannot be modified. His actions cause a reaction on your part. If your primary action is to take no action, the primary result will be that the problem will continue. The secondary results are that you may have a morale problem among other employees who resent the fact that this employee is allowed to come in late all the time. You will have a problem with your productivity since this person cannot be counted on. You may face a discrimination suit if you discipline another employee for the same attendance problems when you did nothing about the problem employee. You see your inactions also produce many results beyond the primary one.

Now if you had taken action against this employee and your primary action was to terminate him, you have also caused a number of secondary results. You now may need to hire a new employee or, at the very least, reassign his job duties. You may suffer a temporary reduction in productivity. You may face higher unemployment rates as this employee may file for unemployment and get it despite your objections. You may see improved attendance as you have now sent a message to other employees. You see the results of your primary actions ripple out well beyond the primary and most visible result. **A domino effect is created.** The same thing will happen in your cost control and expense reduction efforts.

Your primary cost control and cost reduction efforts will often produce significant secondary savings beyond the obvious ones you see and have planned on. As you read my strategies I will most often focus on the primary savings involved so as not to be redundant by listing every secondary savings every time, but you should be aware of them. **The secondary savings produce significant results and they are critical to your program of total cost control.**

For example, if I install a high speed plain paper fax to replace my old slow thermo paper fax the obvious savings will be reduced phone bills due to the more rapid transmission times realized by the utilization of a high speed fax when compared to the old slower fax. But the domino effect, or secondary savings, also includes reduced labor as less time is spent at the fax, reduced usage of your photo copier and labor as plain paper faxes do not need to be photocopied as the thermo paper ones most often do. This also reduces repairs on the copier and lowers your consumable costs. This trickles down to improved cash flow which gives you other opportunities to use the saved money. You will also see improved productivity due to the labor savings, reduced accounts payable activity as you are buying fewer copier supplies and a longer life for your copier. This also results in reduced trash disposal costs. The domino effect has produced savings and benefits that extend far beyond the obvious and primary benefit of reduced phone bills.

Look at payroll for example. If you are able to reduce a $500,000 payroll by 5% you will cut your payroll costs by $25,000. The primary effect in this case is the actual dollar reduction of $25,000 in payroll. But the domino effect also provides you with a number of significant secondary savings.

In this case you would also reduce unemployment insurance costs, workers' compensation costs, health insurance costs, perhaps disability and group life insurance costs as well as a host of other taxes, insurance, and benefit costs that are all indexed to your payroll costs. Since the United States Chamber of Commerce has estimated that these payroll indexed "hidden costs" amount to a dollar value of 30% or more of the employee's base earnings, you have also saved at least an added $7,500. The domino effect has produced a number of very significant savings.

Yes, many times the secondary results of your primary action will be small and the savings apparently not very significant. **But this is what total cost control is all about.** You are realizing a primary gain and by doing so you are enjoying many secondary benefits that increase your overall savings and will improve your company in many other ways.

The quest for total cost control itself is a program that affords you tremendous secondary benefits. A program of total cost control has the primary goal of dramatically increasing your profitability but is has other benefits that reach far beyond your bottom line. Nowhere will the domino effect be seen more than in a company that has decided to institute a program of total cost control.

"In a balanced organization, working toward a common objective, there is success."

T.L. Scrutton

When you embrace a program of total cost control you are embracing a way of doing business that extends well beyond simply saving money and increasing profits. You are creating a focus for your company. You are creating an objective for every single person in your company. You are creating a culture for your organization. You are creating an internal mission statement that will guide the actions of all who are in your organization. You are instituting an evolutionary program designed to embark on a never-ending journey of improvement.

You are seeking to improve every area of your operation. From how you produce and deliver products and services, to how you purchase and inventory products. From how you sell to how you service, you are constantly seeking ways to do it better, faster, and at a lower cost.

Your people have a common goal with your company. You are bringing individual objectives in line with corporate objectives. If you follow the advice I will be giving you in this book you will see stunning improvements in the morale of your employees. This will lead to improved productivity, improved attendance, better service, increased quality, and a greater commitment from your people in every area of your company. All of which leads to greater profitability. It is a self-perpetuating cycle. The domino effect works in large and small ways. **In the game of business which I call "the pursuit of profits", the domino effect will be one of your best weapons.**

Chapter 5. Do you know where your money goes and what you get in return? Financial Reports - - Your report card.

"Your bottom line is like your waistline, if you don't watch it constantly you might not like what it turns into."

Derrick W. Welch

In school, report cards are used to measure progress and overall academic results, in business your financial reports are used to measure progress and financial results. Without them you have no way of knowing how well you are doing or how poorly you are doing. I have a friend who runs a small business and I asked him once how things were going for him. He responded by telling me that he was having a lot of fun and was very busy but he had no idea if he was making money.

Now I can't speak for you, but if I wanted to have fun and stay busy I would go to Disney World and not into business. The objective in business is to make profits. Not to provide jobs. Not to have fun. Not to keep busy. The objective is to make a profit. Without profit you have no business. Without profit you do not need to worry about anything else because you won't be in business. A successful business will indeed provide jobs, pay taxes, and keep you busy. But a successful business is a profitable business.

You cannot afford to wait and review financial reports once a year or even every quarter. If you do this, by the time you find out if you have a problem it will have already cost you money. You need to be able to monitor the results of your expense reduction and cost control efforts each and every month. This will enable you to act and react based on your cumulative results.

Having these reports is not enough. You and your management people must have a basic understanding as to how to read them. You must know what goes into each cost category. You can't find ways to control costs and save money unless you know how your money is being spent now. I do not just mean a general idea. I mean specifically what your expenses are. Line by line, cost area by cost area. You must know what you spend and why. You must make sure every expense is justified.

You must know what is going up and why. You should be setting goals for each expense category (we will discuss this later) and only by reviewing your financial reports will you be able to effectively see if you are meeting those goals.

Are your selling expenses too high? Are your operating expenses too high? Do you know what goes into these costs? Look line by line. Know what makes up each cost category.   Have a detailed chart of accounts. The more detail you have the more effective your cost control and expense reduction efforts. If you don't know the answers to these questions how can you possibly expect to control your costs?

Only by reviewing your financial reports and the details that make them up, will you know if you are meeting your goals. This is very clear cut. You have no subjective view here. Either you are or are not meeting your cost reduction and cost control goals.

You should look beyond the line item number and see what went into making up that cost. Many expense categories are made up of numerous costs, you must look at these individual costs to see how the total cost was arrived at and what you are effectively controlling or better yet reducing, and what you have to work on. It is up to you to know what makes up each line item expense on your financial reports.

It has been my experience that many business owners and managers have no real idea as to what makes up each line item expense. If they review the individual expense categories they do so by analyzing the total dollar value of that number. I suggest you take this a step further and find out what makes up the line item total. Only then will you be able to engage in true total cost control.

It is not enough to know that your office supply expenses have gone down by 10%. This is great, but can you do better? What steps have you taken that have worked and what steps have not produced the results you are seeking? Unless you know what goes into the overall line item total for office supplies you have no way to know the answers to these questions. **Without the answers you have no direction for your next action.**

Beyond the line item expense categories you need to be on top of other key concerns. What is your net profit? What is your pretax profit? You must have profit to survive. You are in business to make money. You need to grow, to improve your operations, upgrade your facility, upgrade equipment, hire better employees, engage in R & D, pay your stockholders a return on their investment, etc.. To accomplish these things you need profits.

Are your sales falling? Why? If so, are you cutting costs to neutralize this loss of sales so that you can maintain profitability? Do you know your financial ratios? Are they good for your type of business? What do others in your industry have for ratios? How do yours match up? You had better know this. Your investors and your banker will sure be looking at these ratios.

What is your cost of sales ratio? Is this good? Why? What are you doing right? What are you doing wrong? You must have these financial reports completed in a timely manner and they must provide you with enough detail to allow you to see what is going on. You must also know what makes up every line item in your financial reports.

No, you do not need to be an accountant, but you must know how to read your financial reports in order to monitor what is going up and what is coming down. This is the only way you will know where you are doing well and where you need to improve your efforts. **Think of your financial reports as your road map to financial control because that is exactly what they are.**

The financial reports will point the way for you. They will tell you if you are meeting your objectives. There is no subjective view here. If your goal is a 25% reduction in outside office supply costs, the financial reports will clearly show you how effective your efforts have been in accomplishing this goal. If you have set a goal to reduce printing by 10%, by comparing year to date and monthly comparative income statements for the current and previous year, you will be able to see if you are meeting that goal.

Look beyond the numbers. It is very important that you look beyond the actual dollar numbers and review your ratios as well. The ratios I am speaking of here are your costs to sales expense ratios. Knowing the dollar amount and monitoring it for actual dollar increases or decreases is very important as we have discussed but it does not tell the whole tale. Not by any means.

For example, let's say you have a payroll of $1,000,000 and it is your goal to reduce this by 5% over the next year. Concentrating on the dollar amount this means that your goal over the next year is to reduce your payroll costs by $50,000. By looking at your actual dollar costs each month it will be very easy to determine how well or how poorly you are doing in your efforts to reach this goal.

But remember, I have shown you that the other way to reduce costs is to increase sales while holding costs stable. In this case what if your dollar cost did not go down at all? Instead it stayed the same or perhaps even increased a bit. If you are merely looking at the dollar costs and not the ratio of the cost to your overall sales, it will appear that your efforts to reduce these costs have failed. But if sales have gone up this is not the case at all.

Let's say your sales were $10,000,000 when your payroll was $1,000,000. A year later you look at your year end figures and you see that your payroll costs increased to $1,050,000. You have not only failed to lower your costs but worse than that they have increased right? Perhaps not.

Unless you know your ratios you cannot be sure if your efforts paid off or not. If you knew your ratios, you knew that when your payroll was $1,000,000 and your sales were $10,000,000, your payroll was 10% of your sales. Using our example, if sales the next year stayed at $10,000,000 and your payroll did increase to $1,050,000, yes, you have failed in your cost control efforts as they applied to this cost center. Not only did your dollar costs increase by 5% or $50,000, but instead of decreasing your ratio as a percentage of sales it increased from 10% to 10.5%. All and all a dismal performance on your part.

But what if your sales increased from $10,000,000 to $12,000,000? If you are looking just at the dollar figure of your costs you still think you have failed in your efforts, but when you look at your ratios you see that quite the opposite is true. You have not failed, instead you have done a tremendous job.

What is that you say? How long have I been out in the sun? Hold on a minute, don't have me committed just yet. What you have done by only allowing your payroll costs to increase a dollar amount equal to 5% while you increased your sales by 20%, is to effectively cut your costs much more than 5%.

You see now your payroll costs are only .875% of your total sales. If you recall, they had been 10% of your total sales. Had your payroll remained at 10% of your total sales, when your sales increased to $12,000,000, your payroll would have increased from $1,000,000 to $1,200,000. But your payroll is only $1,050,000. So instead of failing, when your costs rose to $1,050,000 instead of falling to your dollar goal of $950,000, you have actually done much better. No, you did not cut this cost by $50,000 as you had wanted to, instead you have effectively cut this cost by $150,000.

Only by knowing and examining your ratio of cost to sales would you have known this. Let me demonstrate this further by showing you some actual costs from one small business I worked with.

1990		
Sales	$2,194,925	
Actual Payroll	$ 445,203	
As a % of sales	20.3%	

In 1990 this company had sales of $2,194,925 with an actual payroll of $445,203. The ratio of payroll to sales as you can see was 20.3%. By 1992 sales had increased to $2,750,386. But as you can see payroll also increased to $502,515. If you had been looking only at the dollar costs and not the ratios, you would see that payroll had increased by over $55,000. When sales are increasing or decreasing, only by looking at your ratios can you tell how well or poorly you really have done in controlling your costs.

1992		
Sales	$2,750,386	
Actual Payroll	$ 502,515	

In this case, this company increased sales 25% during this time frame and if you figure the ratios, you will see that they had only increased payroll during this same time by 12.8%. Remember, in 1990 this company had a payroll of $455,203 which was a cost ratio to sales of 20.3%. But in 1992, their payroll of $502,515 represented a cost ratio of only 18%.

The bottom line here was that for this company payroll as a % of sales actually decreased 2.3%. By reducing payroll as a % of sales by 2.3% they had effectively reduced payroll costs by $56,000 while increasing sales $556,000. Had their payroll as a % of sales remained at 20.3%, 1992 payroll levels would have been $558,328 instead of $502,515. They now had fewer people, producing more.

I hope these examples show you how important it is to look at both your actual dollar costs and your ratios of each cost to sales. Only by knowing both will you know how well you really are doing.

If your software does not determine these for you or if you are a very small company and generate manual financial reports, you must take the time to figure them out yourself each month. It won't take long and it is simple to do. All you need to do is divide the dollar amount of each line item by your total sales. For example, if your utility costs are $55,000 per year and your total sales are $5,000,000, you simply divide $55,000 by $5,000,000 to determine that your utility costs as a percentage of sales are 1.1%.

You must always watch your ratios of costs to sales. The goal must be to hold or decrease your cost ratios as a percentage of sales during periods of increased sales and lower them during periods of decreasing sales. This may sound obvious to some of you and it may sound confusing to others.

What I am saying is that you must know what percentage of sales your cost ratios are and as your sales increase or decrease these ratios must be adjusted accordingly if you are to maintain or increase profits.

For example, if your sales are $100,000,000 and your payroll costs represent 15% of the gross sales, payroll is costing you $15,000,000. If sales fall to $90,000,000 and your payroll remains at $15,000,000, as a percentage of sales your payroll has now increased to 16.7%.

This is unacceptable. While you may look at the actual dollar amount of payroll and think that you don't have a problem because payroll has not gone up, you are wrong. Yes, indeed payroll stayed at $15,000,000. But as a percentage of sales payroll went up while sales went down.

Had you maintained the payroll to sales ratio of 15%, your payroll would have fallen as sales fell. Had this occurred your payroll would have fallen to $13,500,000. This is .15 x $90,000,000. The end result is that your payroll has effectively gone up $1,500,000. You did not react to your falling sales by lowering your payroll costs as a percentage of the gross sales.

Looking at a situation when sales are rising we can see how effective holding payroll can be. Let's say that sales rose from $100,000,000 to $110,000,000. Again, if your payroll had been 15% of gross sales at the $100,000,000 sales level your actual dollar cost was $15,000,000. If you hold this ratio as sales increased to $110,000,000, your payroll would increase to $16,500,000.

Yes, you have held payroll costs as a percentage of sales at 15%. But if you had held the actual dollar cost of $15,000,000 while your sales increased to $110,000,000 you would have reduced your percentage of sales payroll ratio to 13.6%. In this latter case you did not decrease your actual payroll costs $1 but you effectively reduced your costs by $1,500,000 since you held the dollar cost at the previous level while sales increased, thereby driving down your ratio of payroll as a percentage of gross sales.

You must look both at the dollar figure and the ratio of your costs as a percentage of gross sales. To look at only one will give you a distorted picture. You must always at least maintain your current profit margins, while striving to increase them, regardless of whether sales are decreasing or increasing. The way to do this is to hold or lower these ratios while you are also holding or lowering the actual dollar cost. There is no magic here. Just simple logic.

Chapter 6. What is your management style and the style of your management people? It can make a huge difference!

"One of the great failings of today's executive is his inability to do what he's supposed to do."

Malcolm Kent

There are two basic types of management. One is a proactive management style and the other is a reactive management style. There is, of course, a third type of management style that I have seen all too frequently and that is the manager who does nothing and hopes that the problem takes care of itself and goes away or that someone else will resolve the problem. These so called managers are most often procrastinators or are incapable of making a decision. You might call this type of manager the hemorrhoidal manager. They just sit on the problem and hope it goes away.

We will waste not a minute talking about this type of manager or owner. They will ruin the strongest of companies. I know that this is not the type of manager or owner that you are, otherwise you would not be reading this book. Therefore, let's move back to our discussion about proactive and reactive managers.

In my opinion the majority of managers at all levels are reactive. The reactive manager manages, as the word indicates, by reacting to a situation or set of circumstances that has developed. Costs are high so they react by trying to determine how to lower those costs. Returned products are increasing in number so they look for ways to improve quality. Bills are late in going out so they seek ways to speed up the billing process.

Past due accounts are paying even slower so the reactive manager seeks out ways to speed up collections and get those past due bills in. Absenteeism is high so the reactive manager takes actions to stem this problem. Complaints are coming in more frequently so the reactive manager takes steps to improve customer service.

*"**It is never very clever to solve problems. It is far cleverer not to have them.**"*

E.F. Shumacher

In each and every case they have reacted to a problem. **This is the problem.** They have let the problem come into existence. They must now deal with the problem. Occasionally the reactive manager will act in a proactive manner but this is much more infrequent.

The proactive manager is a manager who is often taken for granted. You see, the goal of the proactive manager is to think short and long term. He thinks today about tomorrow. His goal is to prevent problems from ever coming into existence. Of course, he must also manage as needed in a reactive style usually addressing problems created by reactive employees, but unlike the reactive manager, the proactive manager does this much less frequently since he has prevented so many problems from ever coming into existence.

The proactive manager is a rare and invaluable talent. Unfortunately, the very strengths of the proactive manager are what often leads him to be so unappreciated. By thinking short and long term, by planning ahead with foresight and decisiveness, the proactive manager never has to deal with many of the problems that the reactive manager must contend with.

The illusion of course is that the reactive manager is busier and therefore a more valuable manager. After all, look at all the problems he deals with every day. Look at all the fires he must put out. His desk is always a mess, covered with problems and projects. On the other hand how important can the proactive manager be? He does not look that busy. His desk is normally clear and well organized. He does not put out fires and handle problems all day long. He is often taken for granted and under appreciated. His department or division runs so much smoother than all the others it almost seems to run itself. Too good for his own good? Perhaps.

But which way would you rather have your company, division or department run?

By thinking both short and long term the proactive manager improves every area he is responsible for. He thinks of yesterday, today, and tomorrow. He learns from yesterday's mistakes and missed opportunities to take steps to insure that they will not occur again in the future. When he must manage in a reactive manner he does so as quickly as possible considering the circumstances and does so in a decisive manner. He does not let the embers smolder. He puts the fire out.

He capitalizes on strengths while working to improve weaknesses in every area. He works to make sure it is done right the first time and by doing so does not have to worry about how to fix it or redo it when a problem comes up. By being proactive he helps his company in numerous ways that are never seen. After all, you can see a correction to a problem but it is very difficult to see the problems that were prevented from ever occurring as a result of steps taken by the proactive manager weeks, months, or even years before.

An in depth discussion of these management styles will be the subject of another book but, in short, the proactive manager saves you money, time, and frustration. In fact, he will save you a great deal of each of these.

The exact same managerial philosophy used by the proactive manager will serve you best in the area of cost control. The best time to control costs will be at the beginning of any project or purchase. As we go along I will show you many examples of how you can accomplish this and what type of benefits it will provide you.

But it will be up to you to think in a preventive or proactive manner in conjunction with every area of operations that you are responsible for. It will be up to you to foster this style and attitude in others. Control your quality at the beginning and you will have fewer rejects, reduced service demands, and an improved reputation for quality. This means lowers costs and higher selling prices. This means increased profits.

Hire right to begin with and you will have more loyal and productive employees. This means you will turn out better quality, lower cost work. This means less time hiring and training new employees. This means increased profits and better morale.

No matter what area of your business or department we are talking about, do it right the first time and you won't find yourself having to manage in a reactive style as often in the future. Think and act with an eye to both today and tomorrow.

If you take steps at the beginning to prevent problems or costs in the future, you will have no need to worry about the problem later on. In the area of cost control this is as applicable as it is in any other area. Let me give you a few examples of what I am talking about.

Taking the time to hire right will save you personnel problems and costs. If you hire without taking the time to see enough people to enable you to hire the best person you can afford and if you hire without thoroughly checking out the person you are considering, it could be a very costly mistake.

Morale problems could result. Reduced productivity and / or quality could occur as a result of a poor hiring decision that could have been avoided. Increased sick time and workers' compensation costs could result if you hired a person with a poor or questionable history in these areas.

Higher unemployment costs could also result if you are forced to, and are able to, correct the hiring mistake. This does not even consider the tremendous waste of time spent training an employee who did not work out and should have not been hired and the cost of hiring and training a new employee to replace this one. Nor does it consider the potential wrongful termination suit that could come in this suit happy society we live in.

Look at machinery. You purchase the lowest cost piece of equipment you can to resolve your immediate need. You think only of the short term. In the long term however, your consumable costs are much higher than they would have been with the higher priced alternative product. The lower cost machine may break down more often and since it has a poor warranty you will be paying higher service costs. Don't forget the lost time which lowers productivity and hinders your ability to service your customers.

By doing your homework you might have found out that the higher cost machine had a much better maintenance record and lower operating costs and as a result in the long run would have saved you money, time, and frustration. You may have prevented numerous related problems by thinking about and analyzing both the short term and long term results of your actions and decisions.

What about lease rates for your facility? By properly negotiating a lease with an eye on both today and tomorrow you can save yourself significant amounts of money. A proactive manager would consider the rate today and build in controls to contain the rate each and every year of the lease. They would also include options for extensions as well as escape clauses. The proactive manager would dictate that all potential problem clauses are removed or negated. They do not want to deal with the cost or expense 5 years down the road.

Take a proactive attitude in everything you do. It will be much easier and less costly to prevent the problem from ever coming into existence. Think of this as a form of preventive maintenance for every thing you do. Think. Plan ahead. Be proactive and not just reactive.

I have a very high spirited Dalmatian named Niki. When I got Niki I took a proactive action by having my yard fenced in. Had I been reactive I might have found myself chasing her all over the neighborhood and might have even lost her. I know, I know, a bad example, but I hope you see my point. It is much easier to never let her out than it is to try and get her back home. I simply took steps to make sure I never have to deal with the problem.

Let me give you another example of a proactive strategy. Whenever possible you should put policies in place designed to utilize the lowest cost, best value method possible unless otherwise specified and justified. For example, your overnight shipment policy should state that all overnight shipments must be justified and must go for afternoon, not morning, delivery. This will not only cut down on the number of overnight shipments, but it will also insure that the vast majority of shipments that must go overnight go scheduled for afternoon delivery. This will reduce your costs in this area by at least 30% to 40% when compared to not having such a policy.

If you do not have a control policy and procedure in place your people will send many more overnight shipments than they should and you can be sure that 99% of these will be scheduled for a much more costly AM delivery thereby costing you an added 30% or more.

This is being proactive. You are controlling costs by preventing them from becoming a problem by planning ahead. Instead of looking for ways to cut 30% to 40% out of your costs in these areas you are preventing the costs from ever reaching the 30% to 40% higher level. Even if you can figure out how to cut costs in this area you are doing so only after you have already absorbed this added cost for a number of years. Do you see the benefits of planning ahead?

In this case you could develop a checklist that must be completed for every overnight shipment. The person requesting the overnight shipment in your company would be required to turn in this completed sheet in along with the request for the overnight shipment.

This checklist would require responses to questions like:

• Does it have to go overnight?

• Why must it go overnight?

• Can the reason that caused this be corrected to avoid future occurrences of this type of problem?

• Can it be faxed instead with original sent by regular mail? Why not?

• Can it be sent by electronic mail instead with a hard copy sent by regular mail? Why not?

• Who is authorizing this?

• What is the material?

• Who is the customer?

• Can they be billed?

I would also add a line on the form that clearly indicated that unless otherwise specified the shipment in question will be sent for an afternoon delivery.

This type of checklist does a number of things. It makes the person requesting the shipment think about the real need for overnight delivery, this will cut down overnight shipments. It makes them take responsibility which will always make people think twice. It provides them with reminders of alternative methods for sending the information. It provides a written record of who sent the material, why, what it was, and if the customer can be billed.

This will allow your bookkeeping people to cross check bills from the overnight carrier and to add applicable charges to the customers invoice thereby recovering costs that might have otherwise slipped through. It will allow you to monitor activities for any abuses. If you have an employee, manager, or department who is using overnight services a great deal you can identify them and find out why. Is it legitimate or is it due to procrastination or poor organization?

Once any problem is identified you can develop the needed steps to resolve it. This is a good example of a proactive and reactive combined series of actions. It will also insure that any overnight package or letter that must go out, will go out for the much lower cost afternoon delivery and not the very costly morning delivery unless an exception is requested and cost justified.

Compare a proactive policy like the one I described to one that lets anyone who wants to, send anything they want to, anywhere, overnight with little or no record keeping. **Depending on your annual volume of overnight shipments this proactive strategy could easily save you thousands, tens of thousands, or even hundreds of thousands of dollars or more a year.**

For example, if you send 100 overnight letters a week, each scheduled for a.m. delivery, depending on the carrier you use, your costs will range from $47,000 per year to over $80,600 per year. By reducing the number of overnight shipments and implementing the other proactive steps I have outlined you should be able to reduce this cost by 30% or more with little effort.

This will save you between $14,000 and $24,000 per year using only a 30% savings ratio. Now take this a step further and think about how many added sales you would need to make to add an equal amount of net pretax profit to your bottom line?

Well, if your profit ratio is 2.5% you would need to increase your sales by $560,000 to $960,00 simply to add the same amount of profit to your bottom line!

How can you apply proactive strategies in your company? Think! How else? What are you waiting for? Get going with the needed steps to put those strategies in place.

Chapter 7. Your employees. You can't do it without them.

"I not only use all the brains I have, but all that I can borrow."

Thomas Woodrow Wilson

Owners and managers can do a great deal to reduce and control expenses. I will give you hundreds of strategies that can be implemented at the ownership and management level. I would expect that you will be able to develop hundreds of additional ways in which your company can reduce expenses and control costs. But at some point your program of total cost control must be taken to the next level, you must integrate your employees. **For it is your employees who will make or break your program of total cost control by their actions and inactions.**

However, before you involve your employees in any of the ways I will be outlining, you should implement as many of the strategies, policies, and procedures that I will give you as possible and as many more as you can think of.

You see, when you involve your employees you may find the most effective way to do this will be through some type of program that will require your company to spend money to make money. By this I mean, some type of program that rewards your employees for their efforts or lets them share directly in the rewards of their efforts.

Therefore, it is very important that you take as many steps as possible to realize as many savings as you can before you implement any type of shared savings program with your employees. The first phase should be undertaken and implemented by management and you can also involve employees to a point by using the recognition incentives I will outline. Eventually you can go to the shared savings incentives type of strategy.

There is no point giving money away. For example, if you are a $10,000,000 company with a pretax profit ratio of 5%, your costs are $9,500,000. If you can implement polices and procedures that result in a 10% reduction in costs you have added $950,000 to your bottom line. If after doing this you feel that you have done all you can from a management level you will then want to take the next step and directly involve your employees in your program of total cost control. Of course, to some point they already have been involved and hopefully you have begun laying a solid foundation for your program of total cost control.

Now, if you had immediately involved your employees in a monetary way in a program of total cost control without doing all you could at the executive level first, depending on the type of employee involvement program you use, you might be sharing much of the $950,000 with them. This, of course, means reduced profits for the company.

For example, if you institute a program whereby you share a percentage of the savings with your employees you will be giving them money that you did not need to share. If you have a program that directly shares the savings with your employees you have just given away part of that $950,000 that you did not need to. All I am trying to say here is that you should undertake as many ways to save money that you can before you begin sharing the savings. Get the easy savings first and then look for help at the next level.

Of course, if you are planning on rewarding your employees in some manner that does not involve directly sharing the savings, such as a flat reward system or a recognition system of some sort, by all means involve them right away.

In Pursuit of Profits. How To At Least Double Your Profits Without Increasing Your Sales.

Why reward them or recognize them at all?

Why not just tell them what to do? After all you know their jobs don't you? How could they suggest changes that you couldn't? As an owner or manager you might think you know your employees jobs as well as they do and therefore you can institute cost control polices as well as they can.

Don't kid yourself, this simply is not true. How many jobs are in your company that you could just walk out into the office or production floor and just do? I mean completely be able to do that job as efficiently and effectively as the person who normally does that job. Not many I am sure. Give your people credit.

Unless you are doing their job day in and day out, you can not possibly be intimate with the details of the job they do. If you aren't and you can't be, then you will never be able to uncover all the ways they can to do that job better and to cut costs in conjunction with that job. Even if you could, it is still up to them to implement the changes.

Furthermore, if you recall our earlier discussions you will remember that one of the ways to effectively reduce costs was to improve productivity. Another was to improve quality. Unless your employees have an incentive to do better or do more, why would they? You might think they need to do this because you say so or because this is their job. But don't be naive.

"No man will work for your interests unless they are his."

David Seabury

People generally improve performance because it benefits them to do so. Not because you say so. Sure in the short term your negative incentive of threatening and demanding might work, but in the long term I can assure you it will not.

You must have, and you must get your employees to have, a cost savings and improvement mind set. How we look at things and how we think of things determines our mind set. Many employees never think of saving money for the company. They worry about only their own job. They see no or little direct connection to the bottom line profits of the company and their job or advancement.

It is my contention that you will be able to take a program of total cost control only so far without directly involving your employees and allowing them to share in the results in a monetary manner or with an ongoing recognition program. Yes, you will be able to begin a program of total cost control on your own at the beginning. In fact, for the fiscal reasons I have already outlined, this may be the way you should start such a program. You want to cut and control as many costs as you can on your own before you start sharing profits.

Yes, you can involve your employees to a large degree by setting expectations and monitoring how well they live up to them and we will discuss this more later. But at some point, if you wish to transform your company in the manner I have outlined in previous chapters, you are going to need to reward and recognize your employees. Unless you do this your results will never be as good as they can be.

Your employees must know that they are important to your company and they must know their efforts are needed and appreciated. Telling them is fine and important. Showing them is far more effective and meaningful. You can tell me how much you appreciate me all day long, but how long do you think I will keep putting in extra effort and generating ideas that line the pockets of the company and return me nothing but verbal appreciation? Not very long I assure you. I have never yet found a bank that accepts deposits of appreciation.

If you want your people doing the best they can day in and day out while constantly looking for ways to do it better and save you money, you had better start thinking of showing them and not just telling them! Whether you involve them through a program of recognition, shared savings, or flat rewards, at some point if you want their involvement and commitment, you better start showing yours.

How can you get your employees committed to total cost control?

Here are a few ideas to foster employee involvement and enthusiasm.

* **Create an idea of the month program.** The winners could receive a gift, money, time off, recognition, or any one of a hundred other rewards.

* **Get support at home**. The reward can also be for someone else in the family. A weekend away. Depending on the value of the idea the reward could vary.

* **Give the employee that had the idea a percentage of the first year savings that result from his or her idea**. If you have your people working in teams foster the team attitude and reward the team.

* **Give the employee or team 100% of one month's worth of the net savings.** If they find a way to save $12,000 a year they get $1,000. Remember, if you share savings in a monetary manner do so based on the **net** savings not the gross savings.

* **Feature the employee or team in a company newsletter or sales bulletin.** Recognition can go a long way.

* **Send a note of thanks and recognition to the employee's home.** Give them a sense of pride among their family members.

* **Use savings bonds to reward people.** You can get them for 1/2 the face value and they have full value recognition. Give them to the employee or in the name of the employee's children. This latter idea lets the employee's family know what a good job they are doing and how much you appreciate it. This will go a long way toward fostering loyalty and maximum effort from your employee. The support of the family is a very strong motivational factor.

You must be willing to try ideas. All ideas must be given consideration. No idea is too big or too small. Pennies add up to dollars. Acknowledge all ideas, both large and small. Not only because it is the right thing to do, not only because savings or improvements resulting from small ideas can add up to major savings or improvements, but also because it reinforces involvement.

You want your people understanding you recognize and appreciate their efforts and ideas no matter how small they may be. You want them to think "wow, I like the fact the company listened to me and acknowledged my idea. I am going to think even more and try even harder". You want others to see the recognition given and this will compel them to become more involved as well. You want your blue collar workers knowing that they can impact the company with their minds and not just their physical efforts. You want them involved.

You want your employees to understand their main responsibility is to produce profits not products and services. Products and services are merely the vehicles used to generate the profits.

Also remember, the more ideas you have, the more ideas you will get. By this I mean, ideas submitted by your employees will cause you to develop even more ideas. It may be a modification of the idea they submitted. It may be an idea that came from your thinking in a new direction that you had not thought of before you read your employee's idea.

Never simply dismiss an idea out of hand. Even if you know it is unworkable you want your people to feel as though you are considering it. **If you dismiss the idea you dismiss the individual.** You should never do this. If you do, don't expect that employee to ever give you another idea.

Besides, what makes you think your opinion is right? There are thousands of success stories that could be told that happened because individuals refused to accept the opinion of someone who told them that they or their idea was no good. In fact, this is exactly why many employees leave to start their own business. To avoid passing judgment on your own, consider reviewing ideas by committee to get a more balanced view of the value of the idea.

To foster teamwork, consider having your people work in teams to submit ideas. This fosters teamwork within the group or department and competition within the organization. It will also serve to stop ideas from reaching you that clearly are not workable. The team atmosphere and input will serve to suppress many of the really unacceptable ideas.

Teams efforts will also help foster an attitude of all employees on one team working toward the same goal. After all, one way to save money is to increase productivity and even those who may not develop ideas to save money, may be very helpful in a number of less tangible ways such as improved attendance, improved quality, better service, increased productivity, and improved internal customer service.

Never forget how fast ideas that result in small savings can quickly add up to serious savings. Fifty ideas that save $1,000 each will save you $50,000. How many sales do you have to make to net out $50,000 in added profit?

Listen to your employees. They will be your best source of creative ideas. They will tell and show you how to cut and control costs, improve your product and process, improve your service and quality. They will make your company what you want it to be.

Assign people to have specific areas of responsibility in reducing or controlling costs. For example, charge one person with responsibilities for office supplies and another for cutting and controlling inventory costs. You cannot and should not, try to do it all by yourself. No one can. Not you, not me.

You must practice and demonstrate total cost control everyday. Why do you think NFL teams practice everyday all week long? They do it to be ready on game day. They do it because their efforts during the week are what lay the foundation to win on Sunday.

You must practice total cost control everyday. Your game day comes at the end of the year and the score is your bottom line. Your employees are your best source of how to accomplish your goals. Not only from an implementation standpoint, but as importantly from an idea standpoint.

If you think I am overestimating the importance of involving your employees think about this. According to the November 16th, 1992 issue of Industry Week, in 1991 over 48,000 ideas were submitted by employees at American Airlines. The savings resulting from these ideas exceeded $58,000,000 in just the year 1991. In 6 years of the savings suggestion program American Airlines has saved over $250 million.

From ideas that saved large amounts, all the way down to the employee who noticed that most passengers did not eat the olives in their salad, American Airlines listened. By the way, by eliminating the olives in the salads they serve AA saved over $40,000 per year. Think about this. Over 10 years this adds up to over $400,000.

They share a portion of all first year savings in the form of points that can be redeemed for gifts. But they also reward every employee who submits an idea, even those whose ideas are rejected, with a base level of points. They are encouraging and rewarding all who participate regardless of the merit of the idea. **You should too!**

Furthermore, if a team was involved, they reward the entire team in addition to the employee whose idea was used and they reward supervisors with a percentage of the points given to each of their employees. They want involvement and encouragement at every level and they have taken steps to get it. **So should you!**

That same year, employees at Nippondenso-Manufacturing U.S.A, in Battle Creek, Michigan provided suggestions that produced savings of nearly $1,700,000.

According to Industry Week, it cost Nippondenso about $45,000 to run the suggestion program that resulted in the employee generated ideas that saved this money. A 38-1 return on their investment. Think about that. Furthermore, this savings of $1.7 million came from only 5% of the ideas. The remaining 95% of the ideas resulted in savings that could not be so specifically measured. Does the domino effect come to mind?

Nippondenso does not reward employees with a percentage of the savings or even in a direct monetary manner. Instead, they reward employees for ideas with points that can be redeemed for gifts. The average reward was said to be only 8 points each worth about $1. Nearly 73% of all employees participated in the suggestion programs. Think of that. **Nearly 73% of all employees working together toward a common goal of corporate improvement. This is exactly what I want to happen in your company. This is my vision for your company. This is my vision of total cost control.**

These are simply a few examples that demonstrate the dramatic effect employee involvement can have on a company's bottom line. But beyond the bottom line there are many secondary benefits. From improved morale to improved productivity, your employees can be the key to the fiscal success of your organization. **But only if you let them.**

" Fail to honor people they fail to honor you."

Lao Tzu

They must know their ideas are wanted, needed, will be considered, and whenever possible, be used. If they feel otherwise you will lose out on one of the most important resources you have. Communication must be frequent and open. Appreciation must be shown and recognition must be given, on a timely basis. You must make it known how important their input is to you and the overall success of the company. They must also know that you welcome all ideas both large and small.

Textron Aerostructures received ideas that represented over $6 million in savings from their employees. They improved communications between management and employees. They encouraged ideas that would result both in small savings or improvements, as well as those that could result in significant savings or improvements.

Textron sends every employee who submits an idea a thank you note. If the idea is implemented, they provide the employee a $50 gift certificate and each year the most innovative ideas are rewarded with a $500 award.

An interesting fact about Textron's suggestion program was that they had at first instituted a fairly complex suggestion system that shared part of the savings with the employees. They moved away from this system to their current system because they felt the process was too intimidating due to the complexity of the suggestion process and they felt employees were only submitting ideas with significant savings or improvement potential.

They now use a simplified suggestion form that asks what the current method is, what the suggested method is and what the advantages are of the new method. They also realize how important the ideas that result in small savings and slight improvements are and therefore aggressively solicit these as well.

The top people at Textron clearly understand that little things can result in big improvements and that dimes add up quickly to dollars. From purchasing to procedures, Textron adopted ideas that saved money and improved the company. From technology to a commitment to total quality management, Textron adopted ideas that have changed their company for the better.

Think about how such a program can work in your company.

Never overlook the little ideas. According to a report in Industry Week, the Employee Involvement Association (EIA), formally the National Association of Suggestion Systems, compared savings from United States suggestion systems and Japanese suggestion systems. The results serve to reinforce the need to solicit and implement as many suggestions, large or small, as possible.

The EIA found that in 1990, in the United States, the net savings per suggestion was $7,102. That same year in Japan it was only $129. However, the Japanese suggestion programs were by far and away more successful and profitable than those in the United States.

How could that be? After all I just pointed out individual suggestions in this country produced savings over 55 times greater than those of Japanese companies. The reason the Japanese suggestion systems were so much more effective overall was that they successfully encouraged a much higher level of employee involvement.

The Japanese built their programs with the goal of not only involving as many employees as possible, but also of involving all employees in an ongoing basis to insure continued improvement. According to the EIA data, each employee in Japan submits an average of 32 ideas per year. Each American employee submits an average of only 17 ideas per year. Furthermore, in Japan, of the 32 ideas submitted on average per employee, 28 of them are adopted. While in the United States the implementation ratio of ideas submitted is less than 1 out of 20.

Japanese companies do a far better job of securing employee involvement on an ongoing basis. It is no coincidence that they utilize a much higher percentage of ideas submitted. After all, how many times would you submit an idea if it never got used? The bottom line is that in Japan the average savings per suggestion, per employee, was $3,612 compared to $386 in the United States. Does it pay off to actively solicit and implement both large and small ideas? Nearly 10 to 1 it does.

Many companies will offer the employee a cash reward for any implemented idea that results in a cost savings. This cash reward is often based on a percentage of the first year savings. This can also be done for new product ideas that increase sales.

If you do choose to develop a bonus pool with the intent of sharing savings with employees, consider distributing the pool from the previous year during the current year on a monthly basis. This provides a monthly reminder to your employees of the benefits they share in and it allows the money to earn additional interest.

As you can see by these random ideas and thoughts, employee involvement is a critical part of a successful program of total cost control. There are many methods you can use to foster and reinforce this involvement but no matter what type of employee involvement and / or suggestion program you undertake it should contain the following elements:

◆ It should be consistent with your company's overall operational and quality strategy.

◆ It should encourage participation among all employees and management.

◆ It should provide for immediate recognition.

◆ It should provide for feedback to those making suggestions whether or not the suggestion is used.

◆ It should be simple to participate in, administer, and monitor.

If you are using a cost saving pool in which a percentage of all savings resulting from your cost control and expense reduction efforts is to be used to benefit or reward your employees either individually or collectively, make sure the contributions to the pool are based on **net savings or net income only** and make sure you are letting your employees know how much has been put in that pool and how much has been dispersed.

This will help keep your employees interested in your efforts and it will provide visual evidence and tangible incentive of how their efforts are benefiting them and the company. It will also show them how well they are doing in a dollars and cents manner.

Remember, no matter what type of employee involvement system you put in place you should not discourage any idea. Ideas for new products or services. Ideas for ways to reduce costs. Ideas to improve quality. Ideas, good or bad, lead to other ideas. You do not wish to stifle any creativity. Even if you only get one workable idea per month that will give you 12 per year. This could translate into thousands and thousands of dollars saved each year. Year after year.

Let me give you one small example. For years employees at one company I worked with used a disposable cotton pad to clean their machinery. They spent about $1,500 per year on these pads. The employees in this department suggested to the owners that they switch to rags from a rag company that dropped off clean and picked up dirty rags each week. The rags cost .06 each and they would need about 50 per week. This would cost $156 per year. They saved nearly $1,344 per year and they liked the rags better. But, remember, there is a domino effect.

First of all, over a ten year period the company will save over $13,440. They also have happier employees who are using a product they prefer. Furthermore, the company has also saved another 5% in sales tax, cut down on their trash bill, and taken a step to be environmentally sensitive as they now recycle.

The owners never thought of this. They were too busy thinking of bigger issues. This was a small matter to the owners but a larger matter to the employees who suggested it. I will take every small idea like this I can get. Would you? Remember, 1,000 ideas of this size would save you $1,344,000 per year and $13,440,000 over ten years. Savings that go directly to your bottom line!

Resource

EIA, 1735 North Lynn Street, Suite 950, Arlington, VA 22209-2022. 1-703-524-3424.

"1001 Ways to Reward Employees". By Bob Nelson. Publisher - Workman. This is a very useful book.

Chapter 8. Goals.

"Goals are dreams we convert to plans and take action to fulfill."

Zig Ziglar

You must have goals. You probably have goals to improve customer service and sales, goals to increase market share and profits, and goals to improve quality, but do you have goals to control and decrease expenses? Do you ever even think about these areas? Do you talk about cutting and controlling expenses in a general manner and then do little or take some steps that quickly fall by the wayside?

You must set goals, establish timetables for fulfilling those goals, and you must make your expectations known. Keeping them a secret will insure that they are not accomplished. How can your objectives and expectations be fulfilled if those responsible for accomplishing them know nothing about them?

You must be specific in your cost control and cost cutting goals. Generalities will not work. You must have specific goals for specific expense areas to be accomplished within specific time periods. You must communicate these goals to your people. If your people do not know your goals how can they ever achieve them?

Set expectations for all areas of your company. From cost control to quality, from productivity to sales. Properly set and met expectations will not only serve to make every area of your company better, but it will also lower your costs.

For example, if you currently produce 50 items per hour with a reject rate of 2 per 50 produced and the hour of labor for all parties involved cost $100, your labor cost per unit in this phase of production is $2.08. This is the $100 cost divided by the 48 acceptable units. If you're able to raise production by 20% and decrease rejects to 1 per hour you would be producing 59 acceptable units for the same $100 cost. You have not lowered your costs by 1 cent but you have produced more acceptable units for the same cost. Your cost per unit is now $1.69. You have, in effect, lowered your production costs per unit by nearly 19% without lowering your dollar costs at all.

Lower costs per unit will produce a higher profit without raising the selling price or, if your prefer, you could lower the selling price to reflect some of the reduced costs while still realizing a higher profit than you had at 50 units per hour and a 4% reject ratio. This should allow you to generate more sales and therefore more economies of scale in your production and purchasing efforts, which would ultimately lead to even higher profits.

Communicate with your employees. Issue weekly or at least monthly updates informing your employees how well their efforts at controlling and reducing costs are going. I feel very strongly about the importance of communicating with your employees. Not just in the area of cost control and expense reduction, but in all areas of your company.

I feel you should always tell them how they are doing, how the company is doing, what your plans for the future are, what needs to be done better and on and on. Get your employees involved in your company by keeping them informed. You must share information with your people. You can't ask them to meet expectations you set and then never share with them how well their efforts are paying off. How else will they know? Show them. Share information with them on a very consistent basis. They must have feedback to reinforce their positive efforts and redirect their ineffective efforts. If you are not communicating you can't expect commitment. Have you ever turned on the TV during a football game and watched for 5 or 10 minutes without once ever seeing the score? It will drive you crazy and cause you to get very frustrated. You must see the scoreboard to know the score. Your people must see the scoreboard as well.

How else will they know how they are doing? How else will they know where they are doing well and where they must work harder? What are the results of their efforts? What more can they do? What else should they be working on? How do their efforts impact your bottom line?

Your people must know the answers to these questions. They must feel as though you trust them. If you trust them why are you not sharing information with them? Are their efforts important to you? How do they know this unless you are sharing information with them? If you do not trust them then get people on your staff you do trust.

It does not get much simpler than this -- no communication, no commitment. How can you expect the people in your company to be excited or enthusiastic about controlling and reducing costs if they do not know what they are now? How can you expect quality to be improved if they do not know how many rejects you now have?

I am not saying you need to share complete financial reports with your employees. I am not saying you need to share salaries with your employees. But, you must share financial information with them if you expect them to control costs. You can do this with a condensed version of your financial reports. You can do this by showing costs as a percentage of sales. You can simplify what you show them.

How you show them and in what form is up to you, but you must be providing a guideline by which your people can judge their efforts. Let your people in your different departments know what their costs are and what makes up those costs. If you have an order entry department, make sure your order entry people know what those costs are for their department and what goes into them. How else can you expect them to try and control and reduce those costs?

Of course you want them to help control costs in all areas of your company. Of course you want to encourage suggestions about how you can improve any area of the company regardless of the area the employee making the suggestion works in. But you must start by informing them of their own area.

Start involving your people by meeting with your key people each week or at least once a month and make sure they are doing the same with their people within their departments. The sole purpose of these meetings should be to discuss ways to reduce and control costs, eliminate unneeded steps and processes, improve production (which cuts your cost of sales), improve quality (which reduces rejects and therefore saves money), improve market penetration (including ideas for new products and services), improve internal and external customer service, and to give them feedback on how well their efforts are going.

It is critical that these meetings are productive. Wasted meetings are all too common. Make sure yours are productive. You should be setting these meetings in advance and it should be known to everyone that you expect not only a progress report pertaining to ongoing efforts and accomplishment of goals, but that you also expect them to come to the meeting with one or two new ideas as to how you can reduce costs, control costs and improve profits by improving operations, improve quality, service ETC..

Your efforts must be ongoing and you must be ever vigilant. Controlling costs and reducing expenses is not a one time occurrence. Goals will keep your efforts and the efforts of your people on track. You must constantly monitor your efforts to see how successful you are at reaching them. By monitoring your efforts you will know what is working and what is not and this will point the way of any needed adjustments in your individual strategies.

Break your overall goals into small individual goals. A goal of cutting a large dollar figure from your costs may scare your people or appear to be unattainable. Break the goal down into costs savings per area or department. Use a percentage instead. For example, do not set a goal of cutting costs by $300,000 if your current costs are $2,000,000, instead set a goal of cutting cost by 15%. Break the 15% goal into % goals in 15 different areas that will equate to the same dollar total. Simplify and make the goals appear more digestible and attainable.

The accomplishment of the individual goal for each cost area will lead to the fulfillment of your overall goals. Keep your people informed of how well things are going. **By keeping them informed you keep them involved.**

Think you can, not you can't. **Set expense reduction goals just like you set sales goals. Reaching your expense reduction goals will be far easier, and much more profitable, than reaching your sales goals.**

Set your goals, communicate them to your employees, establish a timetable for meeting the goals and hold them accountable for meeting them. Do not set goals too far out. A goal to be met or realized in 5 or 10 years just isn't going to work. It is too far out and it conveys no sense of urgency. It you have long term goals, and you should, break them into short term goals and communicate these to your people. These will appear much more attainable and will be more readily embraced by those responsible for accomplishing them.

"Never tell people how to do things, tell them what to do and they will surprise you with their ingenuity."

General George S. Patton

Give your people the tools needed to meet the goals and give them the authority to take the steps needed to meet the goals. Do not set your goals too low or too high. Make them aggressive but realistic. If you set them too low your people will be underachieving. Too high and they will be viewed as unattainable. But I would set them on the high side. By setting them high even if you fall short of your goals you will have accomplished more than if you had set them low and accomplished those lesser goals.

My mother has often told my daughters that they should grow up and become hair dressers or secretaries or even court stenographers. These are the expectations she has set in her mind for my daughters. These are the expectations she would like them to establish in their minds.

She suggests they aspire to this level and no higher. My point is not to diminish those who work in these capacities. My point is instead, to point out the problem with setting low expectations. My daughters both have unlimited capabilities. I do not know what they can accomplish or even what they wish to accomplish. But I do know that aspiring to a lower level occupation will never allow them to reach their full potential. It will never push them to develop and use their capabilities.

They are much more capable than this. You are much more capable than you may think. Your people are much more capable than you probably give them credit for. **Set the expectations high. Aim high. Did you ever go to a carnival and play the games of chance? Have you ever gone to a bar and ordered a drink? The best rewards are always on the top shelf.**

Mediocrity is always well within reach. Excellence is too.

Chapter 9. You must "Walk the Talk".

"Example is not the main thing in influencing others. It is the only thing."

Albert Schweitzer

As an owner or manager you must demonstrate your commitment to a program of total cost control. You must walk the talk. You cannot say one thing and do another. Doing so will be the end of any efforts by anyone else.

Let me give you an example. The division head pulled up in his brand new company van having just returned from an out of state convention of highly questionable value that took place in a warm weather state in the middle of a cold northeastern winter. Later that day his brand new executive conference table and chairs were delivered. The employees watched as the delivery folks rolled the brass and leather chairs down the hall to his office.

Things must be going awfully well they thought. Profits sure must be high. Thoughts of big raises immediately came to mind.

How do you think they felt later on that day when they were told raises would only be 2% that year and that due to low profits that was all the division could afford? Do you think that manager had any credibility? How anxious would you be to do all you could to control costs?

How do you think the employees felt when they heard about the $200 dinner at a French restaurant the manager enjoyed while at the convention? Or how about the $100 rounds of golf each day at a private country club? What about the $250 a night room rate?

Do you think these employees would be giving this company all they had? Do you think they had any incentive to control costs and reduce expenses? If you do, you had better think again.

I know first hand, if the owners or managers do not have and demonstrate the commitment, the employees never will. It must start at the top. Think about how destructive it is to ask your employees to dedicate themselves to a program of cost control and cost reduction while the owners go around wasting money in a thousand and one ways.

It will not work. It will create resentment. I have seen it happen first hand. **All efforts to improve your company and increase profits will be doomed if a strong and committed ownership and management does not exist.** Employees follow the lead of management. They follow your example. If you think they will work hard to control and reduce costs while you do not, you had better think again. You might like to think that they will since they are the employee and you are the employer, but don't kid yourself.

Let me give you just a few examples of the type of things I have seen first hand from owners, managers, supervisors, division heads, and many others in some management capacity who have no right to expect employees to embrace a program of total cost control.

• Working short weeks.

- Leaving early and coming in late.

- Paying themselves excessive and unjustified salaries.

- Having employees handle personal work.

- Buying expensive cars that are not needed or justified.

- Having the company buy products for their personal use.

- Paying no attention to the company.

- Taking long lunches.

- Having the company pay for unneeded conventions so they can get free trips.

- Having the company pay for nights out.

- Not doing the job.

- Wasting money on highly questionable memberships.

- Wasting money on conventions and trade shows that amount to little more than a free vacation.

- Having excessively large offices furnished very expensively.

- Putting personal agendas and activities ahead of corporate objectives.

We are talking about show and tell. You cannot tell your employee to do one thing and show them something else. You might like to think you can, but you are wrong. You might think they will do what you say because after all you are the boss, but you are wrong. Do not be naive. They will do as you do, not as you say.

"It is commitment, not authority that produces results."

William L. Gore

If the owners and managers are not committed to a program of total cost control you are wasting your time. I know from first hand experience that you can put out all the memos and edicts you want but without accompanying action, support, and commitment from the owners and management your results will be poor or non existent.

Employees will not bust their butts to reduce or control costs, improve quality or improve service if they see the owners and management throwing money away through stupid and careless mistakes, abuses of position, procrastination, extravagance, bad decisions or anything like this. Would you?

Instead of developing a common goal and improving morale, you will have poor morale, resentment, and an attitude of "the hell with them". You will create dissension and foster an "us against them" mentality. This will be true even if you have an incentive or savings sharing program. If fact, it will be especially true in this case as employees will feel management is robbing them of income or recognition through their greed, inactions, incompetence and lack of commitment to the program. **They would be right!** Simply put, they will feel they are doing the job and management or ownership is either reaping the benefits or sabotaging their efforts and costing them and the company money. This simply will not work. How can you expect commitment from employees if it is not demonstrated by management and ownership?

The only result you will see is an attitude of "why should we support this program when they don't or when they spend or waste all we save?", or "we fight to keep costs down, improve the product and process and they spend the money thereby depleting our incentive pool". They will not fight for nickels and dimes while others throw away dollars. How long would you shovel sand in the ocean?

"You must demonstrate commitment before you can demand it."

Derrick W. Welch

People will follow your actions not your words. If you demand they do one thing while you do another, which do you think your people will mirror? If you preach cost control, increased productivity, honesty, and integrity and then take time off from work on false pretenses or use company labor and materials for personal projects what do you think your people will do? You will be laying a foundation of abuse, dishonesty, lack of integrity, poor morale. Abuse by managers and owners set the pattern and example for abuse by employees. If you do not care or do not live by the rules you expect them to, neither will they. **Your actions cause a reaction.**

Excellence has a price. The price is eternal vigilance. Without commitment you will never achieve excellence. Make no mistake about it. You can't state what you want and do nothing about it. You can't claim to be committed to your company and leave early whenever you want to watch your children play a school sport or to play golf.

You cannot have it both ways. **You are either committed to excellence or you are not.** There is no in-between. This is true for all areas of your organization, not just cost control. A story told by Bob Hope that points out the need for commitment.

A couple went to the doctor's. The husband had not been feeling well for some time and was both concerned and depressed. After a complete examination the doctor asked the man to wait in the waiting room while he spoke to the man's wife. The doctor advised the wife "your husband is a very sick man and he is going to need a great deal of care.". The wife replied "I will do whatever it takes to get my husband better, we have a lot of money so that is not a problem.". She continued "I am a very successful businesswoman and there is nothing more important to me than my husband.".

The doctor stated "well to be sure there will be some expenses but what your husband really requires is a great deal of personal attention. You are going to have to quit your job and stay home with him everyday. He will need home cooked meals everyday, tender loving care and much reassurance.". The wife indicated her acknowledgment and went out to the waiting room where her husband quickly asked her what the doctor had said. The wife replied sadly "he said you are going to die.".

How committed are you? Are you willing to put in the effort required to insure the health of your business? Complete commitment to total cost control must be demonstrated at the top. Like a pebble dropped in a pool of water, the effects ripple out. There must be a commitment demonstrated, not just talked about, at the top.

Chapter 10. Small one time savings do not matter. Bull!!

"Beware of little expenses. A small leak will sink a great ship."

Benjamin Franklin

I recently read a paragraph in a book supposedly on the subject of cost control. This paragraph stated that you should not worry about being overcharged small amounts on one time purchases as this type of activity has no real impact on your bottom line. It went on to state that you should only worry about ongoing or repetitive purchases.

Think about this. Think about it some more.

The author of that book has stated that small one time savings have no real impact on the bottom line. He has, in effect, stated that it is acceptable to overpay on one time and less frequent purchases.

These statements make my blood boil. How could any businessperson feel it is acceptable to ever overpay for anything? How can anyone with a half a brain say that small savings have no impact on the bottom line?

Now I may not be a math whiz, but it would seem to me if I save $100 I add $100 to my bottom line. If I do this 100 times I have saved $10,000. If I have added $10,000 to my bottom line and my profits were only $100,000 last year I have increased my profits by 10%.

This type of idiotic thinking has no place in a program of total cost control. This type of thinking has no place in any business. If you have someone who agrees with this type of thinking you had better get rid of them as soon as possible. They are costing you money.

While I agree that you must be concerned with ongoing costs (what a news flash he has given us) I could not disagree more strongly with this author's comments regarding the unimportance of small one time savings. Beyond the obvious savings involved in making sure you do not overpay for anything, you must also consider the attitude that is fostered by disregarding overpayments.

The mentality behind this type of thinking will doom your cost control and cost reduction efforts. Who decides what is an acceptable overpayment? What a stupid premise. Who decides which purchases are frequent enough to worry about and which are not? Another moronic premise. All costs are significant enough to worry about. This is what total cost control is all about.

If you are running a business with sales and expenses that run in the millions or billions each year you will have a tendency to think little of small amounts of money. Saving $100 as discussed earlier won't seem like much and in fact, may not even seem to justify your attention.

This is wrong. This is stupid. This is ignorant. What else can I say to insult you enough to make you change your thinking in this area? This is poor business. This type of thinking will doom your cost control efforts to failure or at the very least prevent you from ever truly mastering total cost control. If you think like this you must change your thinking.

If you find 20 areas in which you can reduce costs by $350 you have just saved $7,000. I am sure that a $7,000 savings would get your attention. If not, why are you bothering to read this book? If last year you made a $30,000 profit and you add $7,000 to it you have increased your profit by 23%.

Do you see how apparently small savings can have very large impacts on your bottom line? If your average net pretax profit on a sale is 5% (I said net profit not gross) you would have had to increase your sales by $140,000 to realize this same bottom line net gain. $140,000 x .05 = $7,000. Think how hard and how costly increasing sales $140,000 would be.

I hope you see my point. Unless you realize the effect small savings can have on your bottom line you will never realize the savings you could and should achieve. Just as details matter, so do small expenses, one time or ongoing.

Let me be very clear here, I am not advocating only small savings, in fact I have and will give you many strategies that will show you how to save large amounts of money, but you cannot and should not overlook small savings. This is what total cost control is all about. The word "total" does not mean some. It does not mean just the big ones. It does not mean most. Words have meaning. The word "total" means exactly that!

Finding 1000 ways to save $100 is just as effective on the bottom line as finding one way to save $100,000. **I want you to do both.** If you found a $10 bill on the ground you would get excited wouldn't you? You would stop and pick it up wouldn't you? What is the difference between finding that $10 bill on the ground and saving $10 for your business?

If your answer is one goes in your pocket and the other goes in your company's pocket, you are not committed to a program of total cost control. If your answer is that there is no difference, then you see my point that small savings, like small ideas and small details, matter and matter a great deal.

Your objective is to think, and get your people to think, that the company's money is the same as their money. Would you be happy if you lost $20 or overpaid for something by $50. Of course not. But how unhappy or even concerned are you or your people if they waste $20 or $50 of the company's money? Not concerned enough I assure you.

This is exactly what you must change. This is what you must overcome.

A number of years ago I took my family to the local fair. At the exhibit for "Billy the ape boy" I gave the barker a $20 bill for two $1 tickets. My daughter just had to see Billy. The line was long and we were being hurried into the tent. Billy's show was starting and I could hear the young girls screaming in fright. In all the excitement and confusion I never even looked at my change. Once inside I noticed I had only gotten back $3. I had been taken for $15. This ruined my day. All day I was mad at myself because I had been foolish enough to get taken this way.

How long do you think most people would think about wasting $15 of the company's money? I doubt most would think about it at all. You can help change this attitude among your people by keeping open communication with them and demonstrating this correct attitude yourself whenever possible in a visible manner. You must be sincere and you must manage with a style that reflects an attitude of total cost control. To do anything else will undermine any and all other activities you undertake.

Your people must understand that the fiscal stability and profitability of the company directly affects them. No profits or low profits means no raise or low raises. The same holds true with bonuses, company sponsored employee activities, and benefits. It also holds true with jobs.

In Pursuit of Profits. How To At Least Double Your Profits Without Increasing Your Sales.

You will be amazed at how much your employees can save you. You will be shocked at how much they can cost you if they think nothing of the company's money or if they see no relationship between corporate profitability and their job or income. Many employees feel exactly this way. Hard to believe but true.

"Only those who are ignorant ignore problems."

Derrick W. Welch

You cannot have, nor should you tolerate, an attitude or mentality that disregards savings of a few cents an item or a few dollars on an order. Rest assured the mundane can make a big difference on your bottom line. Saving money on the small items that are often overlooked or ignored can produce large savings which translate into significantly increased profits.

If you save $50,000 one time or save $1,000 fifty times, is the result not the same? In fact, finding many ways to save small amounts should be easier as there are so many more opportunities to save small amounts. In fact, by saving money on small things you may realize significantly larger overall savings.

How? Think about it. If you save $50,000 in one area and it is a one time savings that is the total of your savings. However, if you save $1000 in fifty different ways or areas many of these will be savings on recurring costs. This means the savings are ongoing indefinitely. For example, if you have fifty areas in which you have saved $1000, you have a first year savings of $50,000. But if 50% of these savings are not one time but ongoing, you will save much more than this over a long time.

Let's assume for this example that twenty five of the fifty areas in which you have reduced costs by $1000 are areas in which these savings will be repeated each year. Over the next 10 years this $25,000 first year savings becomes a total savings of $275,000. This is the first year savings of $25,000 combined with the savings over the next ten years of $25,000 per year. Add to this the $25,000 of one time savings from that first year and your fifty $1000 savings from the first year have become $300,000 by the end of the 11th year. And this is only using the savings based on costs in that first year and not the added savings you have picked up from price increases that would have occurred on the costs you no longer have.

Nor does this include any savings from the many secondary areas affected by the domino effect. Think of total cost control as a game of chess. To win the battle it requires a series of small victories.

Yes, the large savings are important, very important, and yes, savings on repetitive purchases are important, but never overlook the small savings.

Chapter 11. Money has a cost.

"Discovery (of a solution) consists of looking at the same thing as everyone else and thinking something different."

Albert Szent-Gyorgyi

When I speak about the "cost of money" I am talking about just that. Let me explain it here so I will not need to bore you by repeating the same definition whenever I talk about it. All money has a cost. Money is either used to make you money or you have lost the opportunity for your money to make you money. Or at least to make you as much as it could.

If you are borrowing money to operate your business this money has a price. The price, of course, is the interest you are paying on the money while you are borrowing it. If you have money that you are holding in the form of cash in a low interest bearing account or short term investment, this money may also be costing you money.

How? Simple. Let's say you are in a good cash flow situation and you have a cash balance of $50,000. You know this money will be needed for operational expenses in the near future so you let it sit in your business checking account or a short term liquid investment account. Let's say you are earning 5% interest during this time.

It might seem that this money is working for you making you money, and indeed it is. But the question is whether or not this is the most effective use of that money. If your money is in one place it cannot be in another at the same time. Obvious right? Well, if your money is tied up in the bank you must ask yourself if this is the best place for it? Is there another use you could put this money to in order to earn more money?

For example, can you pay some bills off early and take a trade discount of 2%. I will cover this more later but for now think and understand money has a cost. If your $50,000 sits in the bank earning 5% interest you will earn $2,500 per year. Now I know I have not factored in compound interest but I want to give a simple example of how you should think.

If you have the cash sitting for 30 days you will have earned 1/12th of this $2,500 or $208. But what if you had used that $50,000 to pay off bills early and get a 2% discount? A 2% discount on $50,000 is $1,000. A simplistic example to be sure, but even using this you have increased the return on your money by **500%.**

Leaving your money in the bank had a cost to you. A lost opportunity cost. An opportunity to use this money to make you more money. But you must consider your cash flow, no matter how effectively you might otherwise use your money, you only have so much of it to use and therefore the availability of cash must be considered.

Money does have a cost. If I have used $10,000 to pay an invoice early that offered me a 1% discount I have saved $100. If I used that same money to pay a bill early that offered me a 2% discount I have doubled my return on the use of that money as I have saved $200.

Do you see my point? Now put aside any cash flow question for a minute while I make another point.

Now what if I did not pay any bill off early, but instead put that $10,000 in an investment for 12 months paying me 10%? Have I not done even better by earning $1000 on my money? It would seem so, but this is not the case.

By paying an invoice off early to take advantage of an early payment discount you will save much more than the discount. When you earn a 2% discount by paying an invoice early you are earning a return far greater than 2%. Unless you understand this there will be no way you can properly determine whether the best use of your money is to pay the invoice off and take the discount or not.

The formula is simple so don't despair. I promised you no complex formulas and no complex formulas is exactly what you will see.

Here's the formula.

$$\text{Effective annual interest} = \frac{365 \times \text{discount rate}}{\text{Number of days payment must be made ahead of the due date to earn this discount.}}$$

So if a supplier offers you terms of "2/10 net 30" what is the effective rate of interest? Well, first of all he is offering you a 2% discount if you pay in 10 days. The normal terms are 30 days. This means that to get the 2% discount you must pay 20 days early. For this example we are assuming that you would normally comply with the 30 days terms.

For the sake of this example let us say the amount of the bill in question is the same $10,000 we have been talking about. This is what your formula looks like.

$$\text{Effective annual interest} \quad \frac{365 \times .02}{20} = .365.$$

Your effective annual interest rate is 36.5%. Obviously even if you had to borrow the money to pay off this invoice your rate of return will be well worth it.

Looking at the dollar value, at 10% interest your $10,000 earned you $1000 per year or $2.74 per day. By using this money to pay that invoice you saved $200 or 2% of the $10,000 invoice amount. One use provided you with $200 while the other provided you with $54.80. (20 days x .274). One use gave you a return 360% larger than the other.

Do not think I am suggesting paying off discounted invoices as the only option you want to look at. I have simply chosen this often overlooked strategy as an example. You must always consider all your options for using your money. The goal is to seek out the most profitable option available to you at any given time.

Never forget that money has a cost. How you use it can make a great deal of difference to your bottom line.

Chapter 12. Let's get started.

"The way to do things is to begin."

Horace Greley

I have always found that if I read a book or attend a seminar and get even one good idea the time and money I have spent in getting that one idea was well spent. **On the following pages I will give you hundreds of strategies you can use to start dramatically improving your bottom line today.**

Without knowing your business I cannot hope to give you the best possible strategies for your organization. Instead, I have attempted to give you many strategies, some of which my be right for you and others of which may be of limited or no use to you. All should make you think. Take what works as is and use it. Take other strategies and modify them for your use. Use others to spur your own thoughts on policies and procedures that are specific to your business. Don't simply read the strategy and say "well that might work for someone else but not for my company".

Think.

If my strategy does not work for you or you disagree with it, think of others. You are as smart and creative as I am. Probably even more. Look at the overall picture. I am sure I could find many more ways to reduce and control your costs and improve your efficiency by improving your operations if I was working only with your company. I am not smarter than you. You can do it.

Do not limit your efforts to looking at a line item cost and think only of how you can cut that cost. Always strive to be proactive and make every cost you are considering justify itself. **Look for ways to justify not incurring the cost, not ways to justify incurring it. There is a big difference between these two types of attitudes. One seeks to find a way not to incur a cost while the other seeks to justify incurring the cost.**

If you feel you cannot or do not want to, then hire me to do it for you. Either way, do it.

I will give you the tools but only you and your people can apply them. I can give you ideas but only you can take them and use them. Only you can modify them to fit your business. Only you can improve on them. It is up to you to expand on my ideas and to think of many more on your own.

I also want to point out that many of the strategies I will be giving you are applicable in many other areas beyond the ones I have chosen to demonstrate their applications in conjunction with. It would be impossible for me to show every possible application within the context of each area of the many different kinds of businesses and operational structures that exist.

In a few cases I have applied some strategies to other applications to demonstrate this. However, please think about each strategy I give you and how you might be able to apply them to other areas of your business. Also think of how you can modify them and apply them.

Since these strategies apply to all types and sizes of companies, in some cases I will demonstrate the potential fiscal impact using larger numbers than in other cases. This has been done simply to give you an idea of how much might be saved in different size companies. Please simply project the savings based on your own costs in the area I am reviewing. Do not forget about the domino effect. In some cases I will point out some of the added benefits produced by the domino effect but in many cases, in the interest of brevity, I will not.

If an idea I have given you is one you simply can't use or strongly disagree with, just move on to the next one. Do not get hung up on differences we might have in one area. Our goal is the same -- to dramatically increase the profitability of your business! Expand beyond what I show you. Ask the questions. Be creative.

"Creativity can solve almost any problem. The creative act, the defeat of habit by originality, overcomes everything."

George Lois

The late Earl Nightingale, much like Abraham Lincoln, would often use a short story to make his point. One of his stories comes to mind as an effective way to demonstrate the importance of asking questions and thinking creatively.

According to the story, many years ago when a person who owed money could be thrown into jail, a merchant in London had the misfortune to owe a huge sum of money to a mean money lender. The money lender, who was old and ugly, fancied the merchant's beautiful young daughter and he proposed a bargain.

He said he would cancel the merchant's debt if he could have the girl instead. Well, both the merchant and the daughter were horrified at this suggestion so the cunning money lender proposed that they let providence decide the matter. He told them that he would put a black pebble and a white pebble into an empty bag and that the girl would have to pick out one of the pebbles.

If she chose the black pebble, she would become his wife and her father's debt would be canceled. If she chose the white pebble she would stay with her father and the debt would still be canceled. But, if she refused to pick a pebble, her father would be thrown in jail and she would starve.

Well, reluctantly the merchant agreed. They were on a pebble strewn path in the merchants garden at the time as they talked. The money lender stooped down to pick up the two pebbles. As he did, the girl, sharp eyed with fright, noticed that he picked up two black pebbles and put them into the money bag. He wasn't taking any chances. He then asked the girl to decide her fate and that of her father.

Now I will interrupt this story to ask you, what would you have advised the girl to do?

The choices seem bleak. If you advise her to take a pebble to save her father she must sacrifice herself. If you advise her to refuse to take a pebble or to expose the money lender as a cheat, her father goes to jail. What would you advise her to do? Is there any way she can save both herself and her father?

If there was ever a time that showed the importance of creative thinking and innovation, this was certainly it. I will tell you what she did on the next page.

Well, the girl reached into the money bag to pick a pebble. Without looking at it she fumbled it and let it fall to the path where it became lost among all the others. "How clumsy of me" she said. "But, don't worry, you'll be able to tell the color of the one I took by the color of the one remaining.".

Since the remaining pebble was of course black, it must be assumed that she had taken the white pebble. Since the money lender could not dare to admit his dishonesty, the father's debt was forgiven and the girl remained with her father.

Creative thinking, innovative approaches to problem solving, and the ability to adapt to ever changing circumstances can be the sole reason a business survives. All too many think that these terms and functions apply only to areas like marketing, advertising, packaging, and new product development. **They are wrong.**

Creativity and innovation must be demonstrated throughout all levels of a company. These qualities should be fostered by management in employees. These functions must be undertaken by someone within an organization, if that organization is to survive and grow. You must constantly be asking the questions and seeking the answers.

You cannot just talk about cost control and expense reduction once or twice a year and then sit back and wait for all the rewards of the efforts you hope for. You must work every day, all year long, to get the maximum results. You must be ever vigilant. This is not a one shot project. You must communicate and motivate. You must demonstrate your commitment by your actions. If you do not you are wasting your time. This is what total cost control is all about.

Be passionate about cost control. Be passionate about expense reduction. Be passionate about quality. Be passionate about improvement in every areas of your company. Celebrate success in each of these areas.

Depending on your size, the ideas and strategies I will am giving you can be worth thousands, hundreds of thousands or even millions of dollars or more to your company. Sound a bit far fetched? I assure you it is not. Think short and long term. For example, if I show you 500 ways to save $1,000, I have shown you how to save $500,000. Over ten years alone this will save you $5,000,000. I will show you how to save far more than this.

If your company is large enough, consider having a cost control officer. A position such as this can pay for itself many times over in a larger company. I am not talking about a controller or CFO. Those positions are not the same thing. I am talking about a bottom line watch dog. Someone whose sole responsibility is to eliminate waste, improve productivity, and watch the impact of every activity on the bottom line. I am talking about a guardian of the gate. As you read through my strategies you will realize the type of responsibilities I am suggesting for this type of position. As you will see, they are quite a bit different than the responsibilities of the more traditional financial management positions.

Do not be limited by my strategies or the strategies and ideas of anyone else. Think. You can come up with dozens, even hundreds of ways that I have not thought about or can't give you since I do not know the workings of your business. If you do please send them to me so that I can share them with others.

"Give me a man with common sense, for he has the rarest of all commodities."

Derrick W. Welch

In Pursuit of Profits. How To At Least Double Your Profits Without Increasing Your Sales.

Many of the strategies I will be giving you are little more than common sense. But most business people simply never think of them and never turn their attention to the area of cost control and cost reduction.

You do not need to be a master negotiator to save big money. Sure it helps to have some basic negotiating skills, but I will show you how to save a great deal of money without any skills in this area. I am sure that you have heard the statement about there always being someone who is faster, stronger, or smarter. I am sure you agree with these statements as they are indeed true. Well, then you should agree that there is always a source selling what you need at a lower price, with better quality, with faster delivery, offering better terms or rates.

It is up to you to find the source offering the best value to you. **I doubt there is anything that you now purchase for which you could not save money on without sacrificing any quality or service. In most cases I doubt realizing this objective will even require much effort.**

Why is it that some sources will be able to offer you a better value than others? Why can one source sell you the exact same product or service or a comparable one at a much lower price than another source can?

There are many reasons for this and I have listed a few for you below.

• They may be offering a loss leader.

• They may purchase or produce in large quantities thereby enabling them to offer them to you at a lower cost.

• They may have lower overhead costs. This could include lower pay scales, higher producing equipment, lower facility costs, one may be union and one may not be.

• They may have better management which is reflected in a more efficient operation.

• They may pay lower commissions.

• They may not pay any commissions and instead may only sell direct.

• They may have read this book and as a result find themselves much more profitable and competitive.

This may surprise you but the lowest price is not always the best value. I rarely purchase the most expensive and often I will not purchase the cheapest. It depends of course on what I am buying, but you must look beyond just the price of a product or service. Yes, price is always a factor. A big factor. But never the only factor. Other factors to consider when evaluating vendors for the best value are terms, volume discounts, rebates, free shipping, credit limits, service, and quality.

The combination of all of these elements are what makes up your best value. Whenever I talk about best or lowest price I am talking about best value. The lowest price will not always be the best value. The lowest price is the goal but never at the expense of quality or service. So let me be clear. Lowest prices are the goal but only among qualified vendors. Vendors who provide both the quality, service, and terms you must have.

I do not want you to sacrifice quality or service for cost. You cannot afford late deliveries, inferior products, poor service, billing and shipping errors or any other type of problem. If you are dealing with suppliers that do not live up to your expectations in these areas drop them. Drop them regardless of the cost savings they offer. You are looking for the best value and the best value goes beyond just having the lowest prices.

With the tools I will be giving you, you should be able to get the best price or very close to it in most cases while realizing a high level of service and quality. You will often continue to use the same product or service and purchase it from the same source you now use, but you will be able to purchase it cheaper.

My objective is to show you how much money can be saved with a little effort. Darn little effort in most cases. I also want to get you to think, to think how to do far better than what I have shown you. To accomplish this at times I will resort to being very blunt. My apologies if this offends you as that is not my goal.

It has been estimated that the majority of businesses overpay on day to day purchases by up to 30%. This does not surprise me at all. We are going to put a stop to this idiocy.

We are going to change the way you purchase products and services so that you can purchase the exact same things you now do, assuming you can't find a way to do without them or replace them with a more economical item or method, for a great deal less money. Why pay 20%, 30% or more for the exact same product or service? **If you can't get your current vendors to, or find a new source to conduct business with that will, give you a 10% to 30% savings compared to what you are now paying, you are either doing one heck of a job now in controlling costs or you are not trying at all.**

If you cannot reduce the total costs in your company by at least 5% or more, again you are either already doing an excellent job in controlling costs or you are not trying at all. <u>Which is it?</u>

"Nothing pains some people more than having to think."

Martin Luther King, Jr.

Use the greatest thinking machine ever invented. You already own it. It resides between your ears.

I could find dozens or even hundreds of additional ways to save your company money and increase profits if I was writing for, or working specifically with, your company. However, many, if not most, of these ideas and strategies will work for any company including yours.

Remember, do not be limited by the application I might have chosen to use to demonstrate a concept or strategy. In fact, do not be limited by anything I have written. Adapt, modify, and apply to your company. Expand on my ideas. They are not an end, they are merely a beginning. The concept may be as effective, or even more effective, in another area of your company beyond the area I have chosen to demonstrate the strategy.

The late Sam Walton, founder of Walmart, had ten cardinal rules for running his business. One of those ten rules was "Control your expenses better than your competition". If it worked for Mr. Walton I suspect it can work for you too.

"Always bear in mind that your own resolution to success is more important than any other one thing."

Abraham Lincoln

Let's get started!

BOOK TWO

1,000 COST CONTROL, EXPENSE REDUCTION, AND INCOME PRODUCING STRATEGIES YOU CAN START USING <u>TODAY</u> TO DRAMATICALLY INCREASE YOUR BOTTOM LINE.

Some comments to guide you.

It has been a difficult task to assign every strategy to an area of business that fits universally within every type of company or organization. Quite frankly this is an impossible task. The internal and external operational structures simply vary too much from company to company to make this feasible.

However, in the interest of some type of systematic presentation, I have listed each strategy under what might be construed as "generic" sections that are germane to many businesses. Please do not be limited by my feeble attempts to properly place each strategy in a particular section. Adapt and apply as many strategies as you can within your business. If something I have listed under facility here falls under operations in your company use it in your operations or modify it so you can use it.

Think where else can you use this concept? In what other areas of your operations will that strategy work? Ask the questions. No matter where I have placed a strategy, if it works for you, or can be modified by you to work for your company, use it and use it in as many places as possible.

Please also understand that I attempted to demonstrate the potential savings in my strategies using figures for both large and small companies. The concepts are the same for any size company. The only difference is that the larger your company is the larger your savings are likely to be.

Please just project your savings based on your actual costs.

Always remember just one good idea can save you a small fortune.

Chapter 13. Banking / Loans / Lines of credit.

"If you cannot make money on one dollar -- if you do not coax one dollar to work hard for you, you won't know how to make money out of one hundred thousand dollars."

E. S. Rinnear

Interest costs. You must be aggressive in your efforts to control all costs. Interest costs are no different than any other cost. One way to reduce these costs, assuming you have a line of credit you can access as needed, is to send payments out even though you do not have the cash to cover them and then do not borrow until the next day or if the payments were made to out of state firms, until two days or even three days later.

If you send payments out today and borrow money today to cover them, you are needlessly running up interest charges. Even borrowing tomorrow to cover these payments is very conservative. The only way these checks could even clear your account the next day is if they were in state, delivered the next day (By the post office? Fat chance!) deposited in the recipient's account the same day and cleared through that bank to your bank, all in one day. This sequence of events is unlikely.

I would prefer to be even more aggressive and unless there was some chance the party I mailed the check to was going to bring it into my bank to cash it, I would borrow two or three days later and to ensure that I ran no risk, I would make sure my bank would cover any overdrafts that may happen from time to time.

All you are doing is projecting when the payments sent out will hit your account and planning your borrowing needs accordingly. Every day you refrain from borrowing you save money. I used these strategies with one company to reduce interest costs by 40% with very little effort. Be as aggressive as you can be without jeopardizing your good credit.

Always pay your line of credit whenever possible. If you borrow throughout the year on a revolving line of credit you should always pay back on the note whenever possible, even if it means you will still have to turn around and borrow on the note again in a few days. Many companies that borrow on operating notes or lines of credit, borrow during part of the year and later in the year they pay back. During the season of the year they borrow they never think of paying anything back. This is a mistake. You should always strive to pay back something on the note whenever possible, even if for only a very short time and even if only a small amount. You must be aggressive in this area to cut your borrowing costs.

Think. How can you do this if money is so tight you must always be borrowing? One way to do this is, if you have a deposit to make on Friday that will cover checks that you plan on sending that day, pay back the loan for the amount of the deposit instead of making the deposit. Then on Monday or Tuesday, or even Wednesday, if the checks went out of state, borrow the amount needed back again to cover the outstanding checks.

If you were able to do this each weekend you would be saving 2 days of interest charges out of 7 (or 28.5%) on the amount of the money you paid back. You are using the float to your advantage. This is what banks do every day with your money. Always use the float to your advantage. Don't just use this strategy on weekends use it any day and everyday you can. To make it as easy as possible, make sure that your bank gives you the option of calling in payments and amounts you need to borrow. This way a simple phone call will be all that is needed to instruct them to transfer borrowed funds into your account and to deduct funds being paid back out of your account.

You can pay back uneven amounts. Do not fall into the even amount or large amount line of credit repayment mentality. Too many people feel they must pay back loan amounts in even amounts such as $1,000 or $5,000 or $10,000. So instead of paying back $4,300, they will hold this money in deposit until they can pay back an even increment of $5,000. This is foolish. Pay back whatever you can whenever you can. Every dollar you pay back will reduce your interest costs. Your goal is to reduce interest costs not worry about round amounts or the bank's convenience. Pennies add up to dollars.

You know, you can borrow in odd amounts. Don't borrow on your credit line in even increments only. Like paying back, many companies are inclined to borrow in even amounts. Borrowing in even amounts makes as much sense as paying down in even amounts. This is to say, none at all. Why would you borrow $20,000 when you only need $17,000? The only reason I can think of that would make sense is if you could invest the extra money in a higher yielding, no risk, fully insured, and liquid investment vehicle. If you find one of these please let me know I could use it.

Remember who the customer is. If you conduct all your banking business with one bank, I.E. loans, checking, money market, investments, payroll, etc., make sure that you are getting discounts on some of these services and better rates on others. You are a high volume customer who should not pay list rates or earn standard rates. All published bank charges are list prices nothing more. Preferred customers always will pay less and earn more than others. You are a preferred customer.

Always look for a safety net. Try to develop a borrowing relationship with more than one bank. They won't like this but you are not in business to please the bank. The same logic that dictates you should have more than one supplier for any product or service applies here. I would suggest a primary lender and a secondary lender. If the primary lender changes lending polices or runs into fiscal problems, (not uncommon today) you already have an alternative source of credit established and will be much more likely to be able to expand on it.

How does this reduce costs? Simple, if your primary bank gets taken over, shuts down, or stops issuing you credit, you will lose sales, disrupt your production schedule, and it could possibly even cost you your business. If your business needs credit to produce, sell, and pay bills, without credit you may not survive.

Saving while owing makes no sense. If you have an outstanding line of credit that you can access as needed and you have an outstanding balance, don't keep cash in the bank or in any investment vehicle that yields less than the interest you are paying on the line of credit.

Keeping money in the bank at 3% interest makes no sense when you are borrowing at 9%. Instead this money should be used to pay down the note or take advantage of early payment discounts or for some other more profitable use. Reducing the cost of money and maximizing the return on your money is a very important part of any cost control program. It is vital to your total cost control efforts.

I know of one company who had $100,000 in cash in the bank at the end of their fiscal year. They also had a $70,000 operating note outstanding. They did not want to pay on the note because they knew that they would have to borrow again in the next 2 to 4 weeks so they felt there was little point in paying back the note. The note was incurring a 10% interest charge while their $100,000 was earning 4% while on deposit.

Had they paid off the note and borrowed it again in 30 days, they would have saved the 6% spread for 30 days on the $70,000. This would have added $350 to their bottom line. This may not sound like much but if you saw $350 lying on the ground would you not stop to pick it up? That little boy at the carnival so many years ago sure would have. If you won't pick it up call me I 'd be happy to. This is what total cost control is all about.

Put your business out to bid. As you look into establishing sources of credit, to save time and obtain the best terms, bid your requirements out. Write to the various banks in your area and advise them of your borrowing needs, provide a brief explanation of your company, and request information on the terms and rates they would offer you assuming approval of your credit needs. This will save you time, which always saves you money, and you are much more likely to secure the best rates and terms since you will only apply to the banks offering the best rates and terms.

Always ask for more than you expect to need. Always seek a credit line higher than the amount you anticipate needing. This will accomplish a number of things. First, it will look good if you are always well under your credit line and secondly, you will have added credit available to you in the event you need it or find a strong opportunity to use it.

Since you won't need to seek approval for added credit you will not need to justify your use of it and will not need the bank's approval. You will also eliminate any fees they may charge you for reevaluating your new or increased loan request. I don't know about you, but the fewer people that have input and control into my business the better.

One final note on this. Do not let your bank charge you a fee for unused credit availability. This is a self-serving policy some banks use to generate added income with no risk at all.

The loan officers work for you. An excellent source of low cost borrowing walks in and out of your doors every day. Your employees. By borrowing money from your employees you accomplish many things:

- You increase your available credit since you are not accessing your bank credit line for this money.

- You reduce your cost of borrowing since you will pay your employees a much lower rate of interest.

- Your employees will earn a higher rate of interest than they will with most other uses of their money.

These latter two benefits are accomplished since there will normally be a 5% to 7% spread between what banks are paying on deposit accounts and what they are charging on commercial loans. You will simply pay your employees an amount in the middle.

If you are borrowing at 10% and the average saving account (where most blue collar workers keep their money) is paying 3%, you will pay them a rate of 5% or 6%. This will increase their return on their money by 66% to 100% and will decrease your cost of borrowing by 40% to 50%.

Everybody wins except the bank, which is exactly the way it should be. If you use this strategy I would make the arrangement payable at your option or on demand by the employee (if they need it just access your credit line to pay them) and I would review the rate paid each year to ensure you are not over or under paying.

This strategy enables the company to save money while helping it's employees to earn more. Your employees now also have a vested interest in the company which should result in higher levels of productivity, service, and stronger cost control. Finally, by lending the company money they have helped reduce a cost which should help them in the long run. Not only is the company fiscally stronger, but if you follow my advice and share these savings with the employees they will see direct returns.

When to get out of the passenger's seat and start driving. You must have a good source of credit to operate your business. Even during the good times you want to maintain a relationship with an ongoing source of credit. But remember that dealing with a bank is a two way street. The bank would prefer you think it is a one way street with them calling the shots but don't fall for this.

Don't fall into the position that many banks try to put you in. They want you to think that they are in charge, that they are doing you a favor and that they call the shots. This is rubbish. You are the customer. They are the supplier. You can find another bank much sooner than they can find a new customer.

Like lawyers and doctors, bankers often put themselves up on a pedestal. You seek and they decide what to grant, when, and under what terms and conditions. They think they are in charge and you meekly follow. This of course is bull. Don't fall in line like so many others do. They forget, and want you to forget, who the customer is. It is up to you to remind them.

Banks spend a great deal of money to promote their services and products and they need customers. Don't ever forget that loans are products and various other accounts are products. This is what they sell and this is how they make their money and stay in business.

You are the customer. You should have a great deal of input into the entire process including the rates, amounts, and terms of any loan or line of credit. Of course, some customers are in a stronger position than others and I strongly recommend you look into alternative sources of funding before you start giving ultimatums, but don't fall into the subservient role bankers try to put you in.

The best way of all to keep the cost of borrowing down is to control the costs at the time you make the loan. Like other proactive strategies this results in an invisible savings since you are making sure you do not incur high costs and therefore will have less need to cut them later.

Once you have selected the bank you wish to do business with, let them go through the loan approval process. You want them to have time and money invested in the process before you start to take control and dictate some of the terms. If you try to dictate terms, rates, or other conditions at the beginning of the process you are not likely to get very far.

Once approval is given you should be presented with a letter of commitment (if not ask for one). This letter will spell out all the terms and conditions under which the bank has agreed to make the loan. Notice at this point the bank is in the driver's seat and you are along only for the ride. At least that is what the banker thinks.

This is about to change. At this point they have thoroughly checked your company and decided they want your business. The positions have turned. They want your business and they think they have it. Here is where you start turning the tables in your favor. You want to review each and every area of the letter of commitment. You are doing this for two reasons, first you want to make sure that all terms are agreeable to you (which at this stage should never be the case) and secondly, you want to be able to add any conditions that you want.

Don't misunderstand me here, I do not want you to play hardball and risk losing the commitment. But, I do want you to understand that you do have many options at this point. Some of the things I look to alter in my favor are:

♦ **Fees.** I do not pay for the privilege of being their customer and letting them make money off of me.

♦ **Rates.** I always request a rate at least 1 full percentage point below what they are asking. For example, if you run an average balance of $3,000,000 and you can get a rate 1% lower than they want you could save up to $30,000 per year.

♦ **Rate Cap.** I want to make sure that no matter what happens over the term of the loan the rate I am charged will not exceed a specific amount.

♦ **Reduced collateral.** I want options and allowing the bank to indirectly own my assets eliminates options. This includes funds on deposit requirements.

♦ **Zero balance for 30 day clause.** Many banks will want your line of credit to have a zero balance for at least one 30 day period during each 12 months of the loan. I have no way of knowing if circumstances will make this difficult or even impossible. Even if I have the ability to comply with this clause, I want the option of not having to. There are too many other options I may want to use the money for. Therefore, I always seek to modify this to an amount equal to no more than 10% of the total line.

Remember these are "list prices". You should never pay list prices.

The last line of credit I closed with a bank had 30 terms and conditions listed in the commitment letter including all of those described above. I was successful in turning 20 of those into conditions that were much more favorable to my company. Included in those 20 were all of those described above. How hard was this? It took two phone conversations each lasting about 15 minutes.

These negotiations should be done in a very amicable and non-threatening manner. Depending on how bad you need the loan you should be willing to back off on areas they are obviously very firm on and instead go for those you sense some flexibility on.

You should also start this process well before you need the credit or well before your current line expires. This will give you the option of finding other sources of credit (which you should have already looked into) in case there are points you will not agree to and the bank will not concede. Let me also point out that by negotiating strongly you are demonstrating to the bank the cost effective manner in which you conduct your business.

Buy your checks from anyone but your bank. Don't buy your company checks from your bank. Buy them from the check manufacturer or from a business forms distributor. You will receive faster service and cut your costs by up to 50%.

Here are some alternative sources for you.

Resources

Deluxe	1-800-328-0304
NEBS	1-800-225-9550
Checks in the Mail	1-800-733-4443
Current	1-800-533-3973
Designer Checks	1-800-239-9222
Custom Direct	1-800-272-5432

In Pursuit of Profits. How To At Least Double Your Profits Without Increasing Your Sales.

Collect today, deliver tomorrow. Consider offering advance payment discounts for orders with long lead times. When you produce an order that won't be shipped for months you are tying up cash in the production of that order. This hurts your cash flow and costs you an opportunity to use those funds for more profitable purposes.

It is even more expensive if you are borrowing to produce that order. In many cases a very effective strategy to improve your cash flow and gain added money you can use to make or save more money, is to offer an advance payment discount of 2% to 4% to your customers if they prepay for the order when they place it.

For example, if you take an order in February that sells for $20,000 that won't be delivered until 9 months later and you offer a 3% discount for prepayment you are offering a discount of $600. If you had to borrow the money needed to produce this order at 10% and your gross profit on the order is $4,000, you need to borrow $16,000 for 9 months.

At the 10% interest we are using in this example, it will cost you $1,200 in interest for these 9 months. But your discount to your customer was only $600. You have reduced your borrowing cost in this case by 50% and increased your cash flow. Of course, if you use this strategy make it clear in writing that any added charges that have been incurred, including shipping, will be billed at the time the order is shipped.

This strategy should also result in increased sales since you are now offering a more attractive price to your customers. You are also creating a larger credit line for your company since you are not tapping into your credit line as frequently. For example if your credit line is $1,000,000 and you are able to have your customers prepay $100,000 you have effectively created a $1,100,000 credit line. You have also eliminated your credit risk and collection costs.

Have your accountant or MIS people set up a simple system to make sure that sales and AR reflect the proper amounts. Some computer systems have difficulty handling advance payments that go beyond the current billing period. You want to make sure full credit for the total sale is applied to your income statement and that your accounts receivable accurately reflects what has been paid and what is due from your customer as a result of added charges.

Shop to save. Shop around for the best bank to place your company checking account. They are not all equal. Quite the opposite in fact. You will find a big difference in the deposit requirements, service fees, and rates paid. Contrary to what most borrowers think, you do not need to keep all your business with your lending bank.

Banking fees will vary significantly. Let me give you an example. I made three calls to check on commercial checking account costs, fees, and balance requirements. I called a large commercial bank, a small commercial bank, and a savings bank in my area. The monthly fees ranged from a low of $5 to a high of $12. **One bank cost 240% more than another for the exact same service**.

Turning to fees for each check paid, they ranged from .15 per check to .18 per check. Deposit fees ranged from a cost of .25 per deposit and .05 per item to .75 per deposit and .08 per check deposited. These are tremendous differences. By properly shopping for these services you can save at least 30% to 50% or more when compared to a higher priced service. Depending on your monthly checking account activity the dollar savings can be significant.

This one strategy alone will save you many times the cost of this book!

Keep your eye on the stability of your bank. Once it was unheard of for a bank to go out of business. Not so anymore. You cannot afford a disruption to your source of credit. I suggest you have a primary source and a secondary source of credit to eliminate any chance of your credit becoming unavailable. Also make sure that any bank you are conducting business with is insured by the Federal Government. In today's banking climate you cannot afford to assume they are insured federally and you should never risk losing even one dollar.

Have your daily deposits deposited into a money market fund. You are making deposits every day aren't you? If not, you are losing money. Deposit every day into a money market fund and only transfer what you need, when you need it, into your checking account. The money market fund will pay higher rates of interest without any loss of liquidity.

Are you overlooking even more sources of credit? Let your suppliers be your bank, especially during periods of poor cash flow. Use the float to your advantage. By this I mean, do not pay within 30 days unless you have a compelling reason to do so such as an early payment discount.

Corporate credit is not like consumer credit. Stretch 30 days to 45 or 60 days. Do not go past due 120 days. This is too long and is unfair to those who you owe money. It could also affect your relationship with those suppliers. Unless of course they don't ask you for payment which happens much more often than you would think. In that case don't pay until they press you to.

Stretching a past due 45 to 60 days will be acceptable to many companies. In fact, many large companies and many companies in certain types of industries, never pay any sooner than 60 days. That is how they operate and if you want to do business with them these are the payment terms you can expect. The float is a significant part of how banks make their money. You can do the same thing.

Suppose you have $1,000,000 in payables and you do not pay them until they are 60 days past due instead of the normal 30 days past due. Let us also say that you have to borrow to cover these bills. If you borrowed at 10% to pay these bills at 30 days instead of 60 days, you will have paid an added 30 days interest. At 10%, your interest on $1,000,000 would be $8,330 per month. By delaying your borrowing for 30 days you have saved $8,330. This does not even consider the added savings you will realize by putting your money towards an income producing application during those 30 days instead of using it to pay bills.

Pay your bills but during times of poor cash flow, just pay them slower. By doing this each month, depending on your size, you can easily save tens of thousands of dollars or more per year in the form of reduced interest costs and gain the opportunity to use your money in the short term for profit producing activities. Money that goes right to your bottom line.

If you accept charge cards make sure you are electronically processing them. If you are still using the old manual imprinting machines you are losing money. Not only are you taking longer to get credit for your charge receipts, but you are also working harder to get your payment processed. By using an electronic charge device your credits can get posted to your account overnight and since you have less paperwork you will be greatly reducing your labor and record keeping costs. Finally, by using an electronic charge device you will be able to reduce your bank related processing charge by up to 50%.

This can add up to thousands or even hundreds of thousands of dollars or more each year depending on your charge card sales volume. Dollars that go right to your bottom line. For example, if you are able to reduce your bank rate by 2% and you process $2,000,000 per year in charge receipts you will be adding $40,000 directly to your bottom line and thousands more in indirect savings resulting from reduced labor and the reduction of the float.

At a 5% pretax profit ratio you would need to increase your sales by $800,000 to realize the same increase in profits.

Shop around for the best charge card processing rates. All banks and all credit card companies do not charge the same rates. Even a rate reduction of 1% can add up to thousands, hundreds of thousands, or even millions of dollars a year in bottom line profits depending on your volume each year.

Chapter 14. Company Cars.

"I would rather have people laugh at my economies than weep at my extravagance."

King Oscar II of Sweden.

Please note - IRS regulations are ever-changing so check to make sure that any of these strategies you choose to use are in compliance with the current IRS rules. By understanding the current rules you can also create new strategies or modify these strategies to accomplish your total cost control objectives in this area.

If you don't offer company cars my advice is don't. Consider providing a company car very carefully. You are buying a rapidly depreciating asset with costs that will increase every year. A company car can easily cost you $600 per month or more. Look at your costs. It is not just the loan or the purchase price of the car. You must also consider insurance, sales tax, excise tax, maintenance, and gas.

You must also consider the lost opportunity of this money. Remember, we are striving for total cost control. We must think long and short term. We must think of lost and gained opportunities for the money involved. Company cars are very costly, difficult to take back once given, and represent one more hassle you could have with the IRS. Other than that they are great.

Instead of providing company cars to your people have them use their own cars as needed for company business and reimburse them according to the current IRS rules. This way you are only paying them for direct company use and you will not be saddled with insurance, maintenance, and other auto related costs. Depending on the amount of use involved, this can save you thousands of dollars each year. Base the reimbursement rate according to the current IRS mileage rate.

For example, if the reimbursement rate is .29 per mile, your employee would have to use his car over 2,000 miles per month on company business to cost you $600. This is of course very unlikely.

As always, check with your accountant on the current regulations and in this case the current allowable mileage rate. You should also check with your lawyer and insurance agent to make sure you have no liability under this type of arrangement. Of course, you want to check with your insurance agent first. Why? Simple. If he can provide you with the answer it will cost you nothing. Your lawyer will most likely know less and charge you up to $125 per hour to go find out. He may even be calling your agent for the answer.

To be fair to your employees, you should also consider paying them for any added insurance costs they may incur as a result of using a personal car for company business.

If you choose to provide them company cars, charge your people back for the percentage that they use for personal use. By having your employee reimburse you for any and all personal use you are being both fair and cost conscious. I am talking about a reimbursement based on all auto costs including insurance, maintenance, gas, etc..

Determine the amount of these costs and have your employee reimburse you for the percentage of these that represent the percentage of the time he uses the car personally. For example, if your costs are $5,000 per year and the employee uses the car 40% of the time for personal use, they would pay you back $2,000. This can be paid to you weekly, monthly, or yearly. What you have done is provide your employee a vehicle while cutting the cost of doing so by 40%.

If you have 100 company cars you have just added $200,000 to your bottom line per year.

If you pay gas for your employee's company car pay only for the portion used on company business.

Avoid all non-productive, ego satisfying, options when you purchase any company car. They will not only add to the cost of the car, but remember the domino effect works both ways. A higher priced car will result in higher sales tax, higher insurance costs, higher excise tax, and higher maintenance costs. Cut the options and cut your costs.

Consider insurance costs when you consider the purchase of a company car. The cost of insuring the car must be a key element in the cost analysis and decision making process on what car to buy. Purchasing the right car can save you hundreds of dollars a year in insurance costs and thousands of dollars over the life of the car.

Don't take the dealer's word about costs. They are apt to low ball you with a rounded off figure in an attempt to remove that issue from your decision process on buying the car. Contact the insurance companies before you even make an offer on any car you are considering.

If you still purchase a high insurance cost car and ignore my advice, at least use the high insurance cost issue as a tool to reduce the purchase price of the car. Let the salesman know that the high cost of the insurance is the reason you can't buy the car and watch how fast the price comes down on the car. In fact, I would suggest using this technique in conjunction with any auto purchase even if the insurance cost is not a key issue to you.

Are you getting all the discounts you should be getting? Make sure that all available discounts are being given to you including low mileage, safe driver, air bags, auto seat belts, multiple cars insured with same company, multiple policies with same company, anti theft devices, etc..

You will not always get them automatically. This is one reason to bid out this coverage every year. Those interested in getting your business will be reviewing this coverage for you in hopes of finding ways to provide you better coverage at the same or lower costs.

Shop for the best value in insurance. Rates can vary tremendously in most states. Do not assume that all rates will be the same with each company. Unless the insurance rates in your state are dictated by the government you will find huge differences in costs and coverage from one company to another. Even if your rates are state mandated you should still shop around as you can still find some deals that are better than others.

If you insure more than one company car make sure you are shopping around for the company that will give you the best multiple car discount for the coverage you are seeking. You should be able to at least get a 10% to 15% discount or more depending on the insurance company and the number of cars you will be insuring.

Always find out what discount programs or rates you may be entitled to on your insurance. Don't ever assume that your agent or company will make you aware of, or see that you get all discounts available to you. Assuming anything will almost always be a mistake. Assumption must never replace effort.

Always look into the cost of an anti theft device and / or alarm system. Weigh this cost against any savings you will get on your insurance and the deductible on your policy that you would have to pay if the car was stolen. Both of these factors must be considered before you can determine the fiscal feasibility of the alarm system. A secondary consideration is the disruption to your company as a result of the car being stolen.

If you purchase company cars make sure that you are checking the dependability and repair record in a publication like Consumer Reports. I know of no better source to consult when you are considering making a purchase like this. Remember, the history of this type of car paints a picture of what you can expect in the future. What I am telling you is to read not only the review of the new model of the car you are considering buying, but also the past history of this model and the manufacturer of this model.

You want to examine as much information as possible to make an intelligent purchase. A purchase that no matter how you look at it will cost you money for years to come. The only question is how much?

Your goal is to take every proactive step you can to minimize that cost. If you buy a car with a poor rating you have bought a bad value. If you buy a car from a manufacturer with a poor performance history you have made a poor purchasing decision. You must do all you can to ensure that you are buying the best value.

If you reimburse gas costs make sure you are checking the mileage projections of any car you are considering buying. Gas cost is a consumable cost just like a consumable cost of any other piece of equipment you own. It should be evaluated just like any other piece of equipment you would consider buying. Let me give you an example. If you buy a company car that will be driven 25,000 miles per year with the average miles per gallon (MPG) being 20 and an average per gallon of gas cost of $1, this car will cost $1,250 per year to run just on fuel costs.

However, if you purchase a car that averages 30 MPG you will reduce this cost to $833 per year. What have you done? You have reduced your costs in this area by 33%. You have saved $417 per year. Over 4 years you have saved $1,668 based only on today's gas costs. You must think short and long term. How many sales would you have to make just to cover $1,668 in costs? Now multiply this by the number of company cars you have.

Make sure you review your options with your insurance company over the identified garage location of any company vehicle. A word to the wise. Make sure you get written confirmation from your agent or carrier on this issue. You want to find out if you can indicate that the car is garaged out of the company location or the employee's home. One will most likely be a lower rated area than the other. The difference in garage location could significantly lower your rates. Let me give you an example.

I know one company who provided a company car to an employee who lived in a high risk rated city. The insurance cost was over $1,800 per year. The next year the insurance agent suggested the company switch insurance carriers and that they indicate to the new carrier that the car in question would be garaged at the location of the company and not the employee.

The company happened to be located in a very low risk rated city. The company figured the insurance agent knew what was best, requested this advice in writing and saved over $700 per year by following this advice.

They cut their costs by well over 33% and saved $700 per year. Over the next 4 years they saved over $2,800. I am sure you understand why they wanted the agent's recommendations in writing.

Make sure that every employee who drives a company car keeps the tires properly inflated. Remember, this is company equipment and you darn well better make sure that it is taken care of properly. Making sure that the tires are properly inflated not only will reduce wear and tear on your tires, thereby reducing your replacement costs, but it will also improve your gas mileage and makes the car safer to drive.

A safer car will reduce the likelihood of an accident, which will help protect your employee, keep your insurance costs as low as possible, and protect your asset. It also helps reduce your potential for liability. Remember, everything you do, both positively and negatively, has a domino effect. Your actions or inactions will always produce costs or benefits that extend far beyond the obvious immediate effect seen.

Look into the potential savings you might realize by increasing your deductible. Depending on the state you live in and the coverage you carry, you may find that you can save 5% to 15% on your insurance costs by increasing the deductible. You want to ask what the rate reduction would be if you increase your deductible to $300, $500, and $1,000. Then weigh the savings versus the added risk and determine if taking a higher deductible is cost justified.

Keep your car tuned up. A properly tuned car will burn up to 10% less gas than a car that needs a tune up.

Be careful where you finance you company car. A man I know is a finance manager for a major automobile dealership in my area. This is a fancy title that means he sells loans and warranty packages to customers. Now most people do not know that loans are a very important source of income for the dealership. They are also a large part of the personal income the finance manager earns.

How? Why? Are not all loans the same whether you get one at a bank or dealership? No, they are not. The dealership works with wholesale loan rates. The finance sources they work with provide them with a base rate each day. This is the rate that the dealership will be charged for all automobiles they sell. Any rate they charge above this represents income to the dealership and commission to the finance people. Let me give you an example of what I am trying to say.

Let us say that Honest Abe's Autos uses the Screw You Finance Company as one of their financing sources. Screw You tells Honest Abe that for all loans they approve that day they will charge a base rate of 7%. Honest Abe can charge any rate they want at or above this base rate. If they charge 9% they have just earned an amount equal to this 2% difference. The finance manager or employee will earn a commission on this "sale". This means that the higher the rate they can charge the more money they and the dealership makes. They will generally charge a rate 1% to 6% higher than the base rate. The more they think they can screw you without losing the loan or the sale, the more they will.

They are not doing you a favor by financing your car. Let me repeat that. They are not doing you a favor by financing your car. They want you to think they are but they are not. They are making a sale and you are the customer. Their goal is to charge you the most they can without risking losing the loan.

Your job as a student of total cost control, is to secure the best deal you can on every phase of the purchase, including the loan. It does you no good to save $1,000 on the purchase price only to give it back in the form of an interest rate higher than you should be charged.

Think of the loan rate they quote you as a list price. We never pay list price. They will try many tricks to get you to pay the higher rate including drawing all the paperwork up with the rate they want you to pay. They want you to think that the rate they plugged in is the rate and you have no options. They want you to think they are doing you a favor. They want you to think that all your negotiating was over when you made the deal on the car.

Don't you make the mistake of falling for this. You want to shop rates well before you ever set foot in that dealership. You must know what a good rate is. You must then indicate to the finance people that you would just as soon go to the source offering the lowest rate that you have found unless they can do better. Notice I did not say unless they matched the rate. You want a lower rate. After all you did just buy a car here did you not?

You are a customer are you not? You are making a second purchase with this dealership are you not? Well then, you darn well better be able to get a better rate. Just accepting the dealer rate for the sake of convenience or expediency can end up costing you thousands of dollars. To do so is inexcusable!

Don't purchase disability or life insurance on the auto loan. They will most often include it in the paperwork as though it is required or routine. It is neither. It is another product designed to make money off of you. The rates are a complete rip off. For the amount of money they charge you for these coverages you could buy 10 times the coverage from a life insurance company.

You are paying to protect their loan. I can buy $100,000 of term life for less than the cost of the life insurance premiums they would charge me on a loan for an $18,000 car. Doing this, if I died the loan would be paid off with $82,000 left over. Do not buy it. If it is in the contract do not sign it. Make them do the paperwork over.

Please note that this goes for any loan you get, from any source, for any business purchase. If you feel you must have life insurance or disability coverage to protect you, then find another source for it. You will pay much less and have much greater coverage.

Don't buy the "pork package". Don't purchase extended warranties for your company car. My friend the finance manager calls these "pork packages". These can cost $1,800 or more and are full of restrictions, exclusions, and conditional loopholes. You also pay for them up front, or worse, you add them to the amount financed.

Very often you must also follow a dealer determined maintenance schedule to remain eligible for the extended warranty. Required maintenance, that of course, will cost you more than it should. My suggestion is do not buy one. Instead shop right and check out the car as I have indicated in other strategies.

Whenever possible try to find a source other than a dealership to have both routine maintenance and needed repairs done. It has been my experience that repairs at dealerships cost 25% to 100% more and take much longer than those done by a dependable garage.

Remember who is paying for the car. I know many companies that allow employees to select any car they wish within a certain price or payment range. This is wrong. You must employ a cost control attitude. You are purchasing the car. You are paying for the car and all related costs. You must control the process.

Furthermore, you lose any chance to secure discounted purchases. If you are buying more than one car from a dealership at one time or within a reasonable period of time, you darn well better be seeking and receiving a better deal. If you let employees select the car and dealership you lose all leverage.

If you are paying for gas or reimbursing gas costs, make sure that your employees are buying the lowest priced brand name gas even if it means pumping it themselves. I never buy anything but economy or regular no lead gas. I have never found any compelling reasons to purchase the super duper, high octane, clean my engine while I drive, take out the trash, do it all, gasoline. My car has always run just fine on regular or economy no lead.

If your people are buying the highest or, a higher priced, gas than they could be purchasing they may be paying overpaying by 30% to 40%. What do they care it is your money?

In my area many stations match the prices of the pump it yourself stations. They have no choice if they want to compete. It is very easy to find a low priced gas station in almost any city in the country. Even if your people have to pump it themselves.

They could even pay the person next to them at the other pump it yourself station to pump the gas for them and still come out with a savings. If they pump 15 gallons and save .30 cents per gallon you could pay the person next to you $2 to pump your gas and still save $2.50.

If you are overpaying by .30 cents per gallon and you use 15 gallons per week you are overpaying by $4.50 per week or $234 per year. This is $2,340 over ten years. Multiply this times the number of cars you are paying gas costs for.

You must establish proactive controls in every area of your business. In the example above your control would be that you will only reimburse up to a preset rate per gallon. They would have to provide you receipts that indicated not only the total gas bill, but also the per gallon rate. If the per gallon rate they paid exceeded the per gallon rate you have established they have a problem as you will only reimburse at the established rate.

Make sure that all repairs on your company cars are being conducted at reputable and reasonably priced repair shops. This will normally mean non union shops. Without making a comment about unions, I will say I see no point in paying a wage 2 to 3 times higher to a union shop when I can get the same job done for a great deal less at a non union shop. Total cost control is the objective, not union support.

A dealership or union shop might charge you $60 to $80 per hour when a local garage or non union shop might charge you $25 to $35 per hour for the same job. Lower overhead and lower wages equate to lower costs for you. Following this strategy could easily save you 40% to 50% on your repair and maintenance costs.

Make sure that a written estimate of repairs is always provided. If the repair is a large one, solicit more than one estimate. When you authorize a job make sure, in writing, that you advise the shop that they are not authorized to exceed the cost of the estimate without your authorization.

You must remain in control and you must make sure they know you mean business and expect to be treated in an honest and fair manner. You are the customer. Never forget this. Your goal is to make sure that all repairs conducted are legitimate and are done in an economical manner.

Make sure that all repair bills are compared to your written estimate. You want to avoid getting ripped off by unneeded or overpriced repair or maintenance work. You must control the process and having proper controls in place will allow this to happen. Proper controls in this area can save you hundreds or even thousands of dollars per year per company car.

Make sure that all repairs and maintenance estimates include a timetable. You want the work done as rapidly as possible without increasing the cost. You must make sure that your written authorization includes a statement about your expectations on the time required to make the needed repairs or conduct the needed maintenance.

I strongly suggest that this written authorization, which by the way is a purchase order, includes a penalty for any delays. This is only fair. After all you will probably be forced to rent a car for your employee during the time the company car is in the garage or at the very least your employee will be inconvenienced. Why should you suffer the costs of needless delays? Isn't it about time this industry started operating as most other business do?

Make sure your employees are keeping a log of all miles driven. Not only is this required by the IRS, but it will also be a valuable tool in aiding you to determine what percentage of driving is for business and what is being used personally.

Always try to get a loaner car for the period required while your company car is in the shop. A loaner car will rarely be offered, but you would be surprised at how often one will be given if requested as a condition of allowing the shop to service your car. A loaner car will eliminate inconvenience and the cost of a rental car.

Make sure that all company cars have the oil changed according to the owners manual suggested schedule. This should be done not at the dealership, but instead at a quick drive through oil change shop. The service will be excellent, the costs much lower, and your employee will have virtually no inconvenience. These type of places will also check a number of other things on your car at no cost.

Consider the changing of your oil and filter at regular intervals as an insurance policy. This will go a long way toward reducing larger expenses over a period of time. A secondary benefit is that your car will get better overall mileage.

If you feel you absolutely must have an executive company car for the image your company is trying to project, buy one executive car and make any other company cars small affordable subcompacts. This way you will have the desired car for image, while keeping your costs down in conjunction with your other company cars. There is no need to have more than one executive car. The one executive car can simply be used by whoever needs it for the desired image you are trying to project.

Never buy the new model cars. Instead, wait until the end of the year when the new models are coming out and buy the old model. You still get a brand new car but you will pay far less. You will also save on sales tax, excise tax, and insurance. You will also save on interest as your base loan amount will be much lower.

In Pursuit of Profits. How To At Least Double Your Profits Without Increasing Your Sales.

<u>**Look into buying a good used car**</u>. On average a two year old car will sell for 60% less than the cost of a new car. Furthermore, you will save on insurance, sales tax, and excise tax. If you finance it you will also save on your loan interest costs.

<u>**Do not purchase a new company car every 3 or 4 years.**</u> Tell me whatever reason you want to justify this and I will tell you bull. If you are buying a new company car every three or 4 years you are doing it for ego and status. <u>These reasons have no place in a total cost control program.</u> No place whatsoever. You should be keeping your company car at least 5 to 7 years.

At one time the late Sam Walton, founder of Walmart, was listed as the richest man in America. He drove a vehicle that was ten years old. If it was good enough for Mr. Walton shouldn't it be good enough for you and me? I think Mr. Walton was also sending a message that started at the top to his employees about controlling costs.

<u>**A very effective method to purchase the car you want at the best price is to first determine what car is best suited to your needs and then solicit bids on this car from the dealerships in the area.**</u> One of the most frustrating and, to many, intimidating parts of buying a car, is having to deal with the sales force of a dealership and all the games they play. Furthermore, you almost always walk away wondering if you could have made a better deal somewhere else.

Yes, you could go to a number of dealers and work out the best deal you can with each and then purchase the overall best deal, but you still must put up with the games of the sales force and this is time consuming.

Instead of doing this, simply identify what the car you want is, including the options you are seeking, and then send a letter to each appropriate dealership asking them to submit a written price quote to your company for the exact car you have specified. Establish a time frame for the quote and request that all costs be included and that the delivery time be indicated. Tell them you will only accept written quotes and that you are securing more than one.

In essence what you are doing is treating the purchase of a company car like you would or should treat any other major purchase. What a novel idea. Imagine applying proper purchasing procedures to buying an automobile. I suspect that not one in a hundred companies who buy company cars follow anything remotely like proper purchasing procedures. Save yourself headaches and money and be that one in a hundred!

Of course, if you are buying multiple cars over any length of time you should be getting significant discounts from any dealer you use. This should be pointed out to all dealers you solicit bids from.

<u>**Make sure that any new car you buy has an inspection sticker.**</u> This is a real pet peeve of mine. Why should you spend $15,000 to $20,000 to buy a new car and then have to spend the time and money to go get a sticker? If the dealership that sold you the car does not offer stickers let them take it somewhere and get one.

Chapter 15. Credit and Collections.

"Buy low, sell high, collect early, and pay late."
Dick Levin

Past due accounts cost you money and a good deal of it. Every day an account is not paid you are losing money in a number of ways. You are losing money because you are borrowing to run your business and interest charges could be reduced if you can speed up your collections and pay the loan back sooner. You are losing money because you are spending time, effort, and materials trying to collect your money.

You are losing money because the money you are owed is not being used to make you money in the form of deposits or any number of lost opportunities to make your money earn money or save you money. **You must control this process and you must control it aggressively and systematically.**

You also must find ways to reduce your collection costs both internally and externally. You must take steps to decrease the average period for your receivables. Every day you improve the time it takes for you to get paid will save you money. Money that goes right to your bottom line profit. Write offs will cost you even more and they must be prevented.

To avoid these problems you must have a systematic collection process. It must be planned and proactive. These strategies will help you do this. Your accounts payable is also an area in which you can reduce costs and improve your cash flow and I have included a number of strategies to help you accomplish this.

How much money is in your wallet? You must have a handle on your cash flow. For small companies even if this is a weekly or at least a monthly handwritten ledger tracking receivable and payables. You need to know what your obligations are, what is going out and when it must be paid and what is due in the form of receivables and when it is due. Cash is the lifeblood of any company. Unless you can effectively project your cash position you will never be able to completely engage in total cost control. You will spend far too much time and money reacting to cash drains and cash demands.

If you have a cash flow problem you must know why and how you can correct it. Think of this like having a cut, unless you know where the cut is and how bad it is you will never be able to stop the bleeding in time. You can be a profitable and growing company but without a strong cash flow you can go out of business.

Do you have a receivable problem? The only way you will ever be able to improve the turnaround time of your receivables is to know what your receivable status is at any given time. If you asked 100 business owners what the average turnaround time of their receivables is or what the current status of their outstanding receivables was, I would be shocked if 10% could give you a specific answer.

How can you control what you do not even know the status of? Do you know how much you have outstanding now? Do you know how much is 30 days past due? 60 days? 90 days? Do you even know how much you wrote off last year and what, if anything, is being done to collect that money? You must run and analyze aging reports or review manual lists at least once each month. I would prefer that you do it every week. You must stay on top of these accounts. How can you systematically collect these accounts if you don't even know the various stages of delinquency they are in?

In Pursuit of Profits. How To At Least Double Your Profits Without Increasing Your Sales.

If you are not computerized then you must be small enough that you should have no problem in manually reviewing the status of these accounts every week. You must not only know the status of your past due accounts, but you must keep a record of your collection efforts including letters and calls.

You must be able to quickly verify that each step that should be taken to collect your money is being taken. You are trying to reduce the cost of collections by getting on your past due accounts early. You will also reduce write offs by not letting these accounts slip into an uncollectible stage.

Your reports should also include when the order in question was completed and shipped so that you can simultaneously monitor how quickly your invoices are getting out. If you have an account that is 30 days past due based on the date of your invoice, but the invoice did not get out until 30 days after the order was shipped, you have two problems. You are getting your invoices out 30 days too late and your 30 day past due account is really 60 days past due.

Have you given up on your write offs? I hope not. Yes, just because you wrote it off doesn't mean all collection activity should cease. Circumstances change and so can your debtor's ability to pay. Even after you have written an account off you should still be making periodic collection efforts. This will be especially true when a personal guarantee from the debtor is involved. Every dollar you collect is a dollar of profit at this stage.

Errors result in delayed payments. Make sure each and every invoice you send out is clear, easy to read, and, most of all, accurate. Many customers would like nothing better than to delay paying your invoice because of errors in billing. When you indicate the wrong shipping location, the wrong quantity, left off the P.O. #, etc., they may wait for 30 days or more, or until you try to collect it, to tell you why they have not paid and then they request a new invoice and start the 30 day count all over again after they receive the revised invoice.

What are your chances of collecting? You must monitor your accounts receivables very carefully. It is very important to be as proactive as possible in this area. You need to be polite but firm early on and become more aggressive as your past due accounts reach and exceed 30 days past due. Do not feel uncomfortable doing this. After all you have performed in accordance with the customer's wishes and delivered the order or performed the service. You have every right to expect prompt payment and they have an obligation to promptly pay in accordance with your terms.

According to Dun & Bradstreet statistics, you have a 93.8% chance of collecting an account that is 30 days past due. The longer the delinquency, the less likely you are to collect it at all. At 60 days you will only collect 85.2% of your past due accounts. At 90 days this drops to 73.6%. At 180 days past due you will only collect 57.8% of your past due accounts and it goes downhill from there. Get on them early and stay on them until you collect the money you are owed.

Put the odds in your favor. Make your terms 10 days net. If they pay within 10 days you have reduced your normal collection time by at least 20 days and greatly improved your cash flow by doing so. If they do not, you will be able to send them a past due statement after the 10 days are up. This will give you at least two shots at collecting them in the first 30 days instead of one.

You should send a statement on all past due accounts every 15 days. Since your terms are net 10, (aren't they?) in the first month you have billed and sent a statement.

Derrick W. Welch

My experience has shown that well over 90% of all accounts will pay either from the original invoice or the first statement. You will have sent both in the first 25 days and not have had to make one phone call or send one past due letter. This should result in significantly moving up the length of time it takes to collect the vast majority of accounts. This reduces your collection efforts and costs while improving your cash flow.

You invoice them when? Do not bill your customers on a monthly basis. If you are selling a product or service you should bill the customer as soon as the product is delivered or the service is rendered. Better yet, if applicable to your business, you should request payment at the time the service is rendered or product shipped.

If you do bill monthly as part of an ongoing service relationship, I suggest you alter these terms to bill no later than every two weeks and preferably every week. This will reduce your float time on these receivables by 50% to 75%. By getting your receivables in sooner you will greatly improve cash flow. An improved cash flow will save you money as it reduces your borrowing needs and it provides you with an opportunity to use the funds sooner to make or save you money in other areas of you business.

A sale is only a sale if you get paid. Make sure that you have a firm credit policy both for new accounts and credit limits on existing accounts. This should include a written statement about your policy and a credit application that includes the various clauses I will give you and the terms you have established.

You should have someone on staff that checks out each application or, at the very least, the credit application of a new customer seeking an amount over a specific preset dollar value. Your sales people may not like this but unless you are making sales to customers who are going to pay you, you are better off not making the sale. I would rather lose the sale which costs me nothing, than make the sale, produce and provide the product or service, and not get paid which costs me a great deal.

A no risk or at least limited, risk sale. The best way to control your past due problems are to eliminate them by getting paid up front. This is possible for many businesses as they are paid before they ship any orders. If you are not one of these lucky companies that can get away with this, you should at least get 50% of the money up front on all new customers. This should be enough to at least offset your costs if they do not pick the item up or do not pay your invoices. It also gives them a vested interest in accepting the order since they have already paid 50%.

Delayed billing is costing you dearly. You must get your billing out the same day or within a day of the date you ship the customer's order or provide the service. Surveys of accounts payable managers around the country have indicated that the vast majority of invoices they receive **arrive 30 to 45 days after the product** was delivered or the service was rendered. **This is a disgrace.**

If you are taking this long to generate invoices this is costing you a great deal of money and represents very poor customer service and financial management. Every day you delay getting the billing out you are losing profits. If added staff is needed to get the billing out during busy times then bring them in.

Think about what this is costing you. Let me give you an example. Just this week I received a $20,000 invoice for a shipment I received over a month ago. If this company borrows money at 10%, it has just cost them $166 by not getting my invoice to me for 30 days. It will cost them another $166 if I do not pay for another 30 days. They have let me float this money already for 30 days by not getting my invoice to me on time.

In Pursuit of Profits. How To At Least Double Your Profits Without Increasing Your Sales.

If the net pretax profit on this order was 5% this company had a projected bottom line profit of $1,000. By not billing me for 30 days, and by me not paying for at least 30 more days, they have lost $332. They have given up 33% of their net pretax profit on this order simply because they did not bill me in a timely manner. If I do not pay for 60 days after I get the invoice they have lost nearly 50% of the profit on this order. You must think like this and, get your people to think like this, if you are to maximize your profits. **This is total cost control!**

To avoid having to hire extra help from an outside temporary agency you should cross train employees from another department in how to bill or at least in how to handle the mundane tasks that your AR people must do such as filing, sorting, inserting, and mailing. I am talking about both billing and past due statements. Both are very important. I have had companies wait weeks, and in some cases months, before they billed me for items. When this happens I am in no hurry to pay that bill since I figure they were in no hurry to send it so they must be in no hurry to get paid.

"Men Who Say it cannot be done, should not interrupt those doing it."

Chinese proverb.

There is no acceptable excuse for not getting those bills out on time. If for some reason you do not have all costs to bill out, get them. If this is not possible then send a partial billing. Find ways to do it, not reasons why you cannot do it. If you have to, send out a manual bill if that is what it takes to get the bill out. You can always put it in the computer later. Delays can happen due to computer problems, months not being closed out, and a hundred other reasons. Work around them and get those invoices out.

The bigger the invoice the better the cash flow. If for some reason you cannot get your bills out on time then you should at least make sure that all your larger invoices are sent out. Don't just let your AR people go along billing based on ship dates, order numbers, or in any other sequence, unless you can get your billing out on time.

It makes no sense to spend days billing out small orders while you have very large orders sitting there waiting to be billed. If you can't get them all out on a timely basis at least bill the ones that will have the largest fiscal impact and result in the biggest improvement to your cash flow.

Use your fax to speed up your receivable collections. A good low cost way to improve the response to your past due notices is to fax them. You will be very surprised at the increase in response that you get when you fax a past due notice. I think there are a number of reasons for this. Faxes are hard copies that are harder to ignore than a phone call.

Faxes are seen by others in the company since someone picks it up and brings it to the party it is being sent to. This means others in the company know your customer is behind on his bills and this is not something your customer will want their employees to know. They can't say they didn't get a fax. The fax conveys a greater sense of urgency than a letter or phone call. Try it. It will cost you less than a call or a letter and should provide a better response.

Credit costs! If you accept credit cards as a method of payment you should establish a minimum amount the customer must charge in order to use a credit card. The cost of accepting credit cards is much higher than the cost of accepting cash. A higher cost to you means lower profits. By at least setting a minimum amount on all charge card purchases you will reduce this cost / lost profit to some degree by realizing a higher sale per transaction.

Progress billing improves cash flow and reduces risk. If your business sells large orders that are custom produced you should not only get some money up front, but you should also progress bill the job at various stages during the production process. This will reduce the amount of money you are tying up which reduces your costs, lowers your borrowing needs, and reduces the risk of non payment or delayed payment.

An almost risk free sale. Consider shipping COD if you do not have money up front and you have any concern whatsoever about your ability to collect payment on a timely basis. Make sure you are including your COD costs in the amount to be collected.

Who is in charge? Do not let your salespeople call the shots on your collection activity. This is a common problem with small companies. The salespeople often want to handle collections with kid gloves and will do all they can to influence your collection activities.

Do not allow this. Your interest is in collecting the money you are owed. Yes, you want to do all you can to avoid hurting your chances of conducting business with this company in the future but not at the expense of not collecting your money.

I have seen many instances when the salesperson convinced the company not to aggressively pursue collections, even up to the point where an account was running more than 6 months past due before a strong letter was even sent. I have also seen sales representatives talk companies into taking high risk orders with no up front money and I have seen those companies suffer the losses on these types of orders. Who works for who? Sometimes this isn't as clear as it ought to be.

Are you including all your costs? Make sure that all added charges are included on invoices to your customers. This is an often overlooked area of receivables. You must have a method of indicating on the order what added costs were incurred in the production and delivery of that order. If you do not, you will be missing legitimate billings unless you discover and bill those charges later. If you do this you are increasing your costs since you are now billing the same customer twice and waiting longer for your money.

In many cases your customers will not even pay a second billing for the added charges. This may cause them too much bookkeeping trouble and they may feel that it is your problem. These are costs such as overnight shipping, custom samples, overage shipping, overtime, and any other added extra charges incurred as a result of the customers actions. You cannot afford to suffer increased costs on behalf of your customer and not charge those added costs back to your customer.

Don't offer a reward for complying with your terms. This will conflict with another strategy I will give you in the section dealing with accounts payables but that's too bad. My interest is in helping you improve your business and reduce your costs. If it benefits you I'll suggest it, but if not, I won't.

You will not hear me preach the nonsense that so many non business people will spew out. Things they teach you in the academic world for instance. Business is about making a profit. Consider this like winning. Don't be held to someone else's standards of what is good, bad, right, or wrong. Set your own standards and live up to them.

In Pursuit of Profits. How To At Least Double Your Profits Without Increasing Your Sales.

This strategy is not to offer discounts for early payment. You have a right to be paid on time, why should you pay for it by offering a discount. You expect your customers to live up to their obligations, you should not bribe them to do it.

On the other hand, later on I will tell you to take advantage of early or prompt payment discounts even if they are not made in accordance with the terms they are offered under. If someone tells you this is not fair I suggest you tell them where to go. You are in business to make money not to meet the standards of someone who never had to meet a payroll in their life.

How dependable are credit references? Be very careful about granting credit to new customers based on credit references provided. Even a company on the verge of going out of business will have a few suppliers they are keeping current simply to keep the business running on a day to day basis. Always try to get money up front instead of just credit references. Try to get at least enough to cover your costs so that in the event of a bad debt you will not be out money.

I personally place little value on credit references. Furthermore, I would not suggest you place your total confidence in information provided to you by many of the well known business rating companies. I know first hand that much of the information given to them by privately held companies is never verified. The same information they give you as a reference about the business you are inquiring about. Besides the questionable value of the information you might be getting, there is also a cost to secure the information. Keep the cost and risk down whenever possible and get money up front.

What do you do when a slow payer wants to place another order? If you have a valuable customer who has proven to be a slow payer but always pays, you may find it very difficult to turn down their business or to demand up front payment. If this is the case, I suggest you at least build an added cost into the selling price of the order to cover the added cost of your collection efforts and the lost income.

An important customer who always pays, but always takes 60 to 90 days to pay, is someone who can still be a valuable source of sales. However, you do not want to sell at a normal price and suffer reduced profitability due to the higher collection costs and lost income during this 60 to 90 days. Therefore, add a finance charge to the selling price. This does not have to be an obvious line item charge that might anger your customer.

If you are not selling from preprinted published price lists just factor in a finance charge based on carrying this past due for 90 days and add this amount to the selling price, and present a bottom line price for the job. I would suggest 2% or 3% of the cost of the product as a finance charge. Then do not start collection activity until the invoice hits 60 days past due. This will keep your collection costs to a minimum. If you do not wish to, or are unable to, add the cost to the customers price, it can be recovered in the form of a reduced commission to your sales representative. This is fair, profits are lower so should the commission be.

I do not suggest this strategy for any account that consistently goes over 120 days. There are however, many large companies and hospitals that routinely pay only between 60 and 90 days. In many of these cases it is not a cash flow problem or a sign of a high risk account. Instead, it is a policy to maximize the float of their money or it may simply take this long to flow through the bureaucratic laden departments of a large organization.

What do you do when a past due account wants to place another order? If you have an unproven customer with no history of always paying but paying late, like I have outlined in the last strategy, consider this strategy. Take, but don't produce orders on 60 to 90 day past due accounts. You want the orders but you don't want the risk of having two non paying orders for this same customer. Aggressively soliciting sales is one thing, stupidity is another. Don't be guilty of the latter.

You already have a problem which represents a potential loss. Don't make it worse by processing more business from this same company until they have paid the past due bills. By taking the order you are demonstrating that at this point you still value their business but by not processing the order until the past due bills are cleaned up you are sending them a message and providing them incentive to bring their account current. I would also suggest in this case you demand prepayment of the new order until a proper payment record has been established.

Make sure your AR department and your sales department are keeping each other informed on past due accounts. Otherwise your sales department will never even know if that customer is past due.

Let your customers provide their own envelope. If you sell business to business do not send a stamped envelope, a business reply envelope, or for that matter, any envelope with your invoices. I have never seen any study that indicated providing a postage paid envelope or any envelope increased payment response time or cut delinquencies. I would also suggest not sending a postage paid envelope to the consumer market and would further suggest that you test to see if it is even cost justified to send an envelope at all.

Let me show you how much money can be saved by not sending out postage paid envelopes with your invoices. If you send out 5,000 invoices per year and with each one you include a postage paid return envelope you would be spending over $1,450 per year just in postage costs at today's first class postage rate of .29. This is not even including the cost of your envelopes.

If you have a pretax profit ratio of 2.5%, you would need to increase sales by $58,000 just to add this $1,450 back on your bottom line. $58,000 x .025 = $1,450. If you send out 5,000 invoices per month your cost in this area is $17,400 not including the cost of the envelopes. You must think like this. This mentality is what total cost control is all about.

If you currently provide postage paid envelopes and you do not want to follow my suggestions here, at least do yourself a favor and conduct some tests to find out if your costs are justified. Many postage paid envelopes will not even be used and you have wasted the money completely.

You may think that by using BRE this non use problem will be neutralized but remember, these envelopes cost you more in postage when they are sent back. Remember, you are trying to find justification to cut costs and control costs, not increase costs. It is a way of thinking. It is a way of acting. It is a way of life.

Sending envelopes but not prepaid? It is still costing you money, at least in the business to business market. Depending on how well you purchase envelopes it is probably costing you about .015 per envelope. Therefore if you are sending out 5,000 invoices per month with envelopes you are spending $900 per year for which you are most likely getting no return whatsoever since most businesses will use their own window envelopes when remitting payment.

If they provide an envelope use it. Of course if your suppliers provide an envelope to you use it. You would be amazed at the number of companies who throw away postage paid and non postage paid return envelopes provided to them by their vendors. Throwing away an envelope that has been provided to you with or without postage and using one of your own instead is the same thing as throwing away money. That is to say, it is stupid.

They sold it, let them help collect it. Get your salespeople involved at the 60 day past due stage. Advise them of the delinquent status and inform you would like assistance in collecting this past due amount. I do not suggest you turn your salespeople into collection agents. They are there to sell. However, if you have put the other policies in place that I have suggested they will most likely want to be involved, or at the very least, be informed.

After all, if the account goes bad they will lose their commission on that account (or at least they should) and if they stay past due you will not process further orders from that customer. Considering these facts it would be unfair of you not to involve the salesperson. They have a vested interest in the payment status of this customer.

Furthermore, you do not want your salespeople spending time and effort selling to an account that is past due. How happy do you think they will be when they turn in an order they have worked hard to get and you reject the order because of the past due status of this customer? If they were not informed of the problem they will be very unhappy. By not informing them, not only did you cause them to waste time selling an account that you won't accept but they have lost the chance to address the problem.

Some salespeople will not want to get involved in collections despite what I have outlined above. To provide this group incentive to assist you in the collection effort don't pay the commission until the order is paid for and reduce their commission each month the account is past due. Each month the account is past due your profit is lowered. Lowering their commission therefore is justified.

Not only will this get your salespeople very interested in collections, but it will also go a long way to helping ensure a quality sale from the beginning. You can be sure your salespeople will not sell an account they know has financial problems if it is going to cost them in the long run. When a sale is made they share in the reward so is it not only fair that they also share in the risk?

I hope you are not typing envelopes. Use window envelopes for all your statements and invoices. Cutting down on the labor involved in processing invoices and statements reduces your costs and improves your profitability as you now will get out more invoices in the same time.

When is payment due? In addition to clearly indicating your payment terms on your invoices (and on your sales orders) you should also indicate the exact due date of the payment. Don't give them any chance to misunderstand your payment expectations. Give them a strong reminder of the exact date payment is expected. This will result in more accounts paying on a timely basis.

Late payments should be penalized. Always include a late service charge on your invoices. Actually, this should also be indicated on your order form if you use one and your credit application. The purpose is twofold. First, you want to provide an added incentive to pay your invoice on time. If your customer is a slow payer and they have the option of paying an invoice that will incur a late charge if not paid on time or an invoice with no late charge, which do you think they will pay first?

The second reason is because you incur added costs when you must pursue past due bills. From statements sent to phone calls made, you have higher costs on past due bills. A late service charge is a justified way to recover some or all of these costs and thereby lower your collection costs while restoring profitability to the order.

Find out what the maximum amount you can charge per year is in your state and add this as a monthly late service charge fee. For example, if the laws in your state allow an 18% annual rate you would charge 1.5% per month.

The exact date on which the past due account will incur the finance charge and the amount that will be assessed should also be on your invoice. Don't just say it, show it.

This should be done even if you will waive the charge or have no intention of forcing payment for the charge. The goal is to provide an incentive for prompt payment. Indicating a fee will be assessed for late payment is a strong negative incentive and costs you nothing. Offering a discount for prompt payment is a weaker incentive and costs you money. If you do not charge a late payment fee you are rewarding your poor payers and punishing your good payers.

Protect your interest every step of the way. Your credit application, order form, and invoice should contain the following:

A venue provision. This is targeted to customers out of state who place orders with you. The venue provision allows you to adjudicate any dispute or suit in your own state. This will not only save you time and travel when compared to taking your customer to court out of state, but it will also provide added incentive to your customer to pay as clearly they will incur added costs by having to come to your area to defend any legal action.

A customer inspection obligation clause. This clause informs the customer that it is their obligation to inspect the goods upon arrival and notify your office of any problem. Very often customers will claim problems cropped up later that they did not know about at the time they got the order. This is a defense often used by past due customers. They claim that there were problems with the order they did not find out about until much later when they examined the goods. By including this clause you will effectively neutralize this usually bogus argument.

A clause indicating that all Attorney's fees will also be assessed to the customer should legal collection activity be needed. Again, not only will this help you collect some of your legal fees should legal action be needed, but it will also serve as an incentive to your customer to pay well before the delinquency reaches that stage.

A non transfer clause. This will help protect your interests should your customer's company be sold or restructured and change their name. The non transfer clause simply indicates that your customer cannot assign or transfer any account relationship they have with you without your approval. You always want to stay in control.

Get it signed on the dotted line. Whenever possible you want a signed order and a purchase order. The order is your contract with the customer. The signature validates the contract. If you have followed my advice and included the various clauses on the order form that I have suggested, this signature will also convey acceptance of those terms. These clauses can, and should be, in small print and worked into the design of your various forms so as to be unobtrusive. Not hidden, just unobtrusive.

Get a guarantee. If you are selling to a customer who is a sole proprietorship, partnership, or even a corporation whose fiscal stability is questionable, ask for a personal guarantee. This will, in effect, make the individual responsible for the debt regardless as to whether the company can or will pay. In most cases a debt that has a personal guarantee will be paid and paid first regardless of the fiscal condition of the company. If you personally guaranteed a debt incurred on behalf of your company wouldn't you make darn sure that debt was paid by the company no matter how close to closing down you were?

Do not reward your sales force for selling a deadbeat. If you have an account that has been turned over to a collection agency, attorney, or written off, make sure you are charging back all commissions paid to your salesperson. This is only fair. You have lost much more on the account than this.

This will also send a message to your sales force that the credit worthiness of the customers does impact them. You don't want them selling accounts that are high risk or accounts they can see are poor risks or have knowledge of that you do not. Salespeople will at times know a customer is in trouble based on what they see or hear while in the field. If they have no risk they may sell these accounts anyway. If they have a risk they will think twice.

I know the risk is only the amount they earned and you might feel that they will still feel they have no risk. After all, if they don't make the sale they did not earn a commission so what is the difference if they make it. The worst that can happen is that you take back that commission. The best that can happen is that the customer pays and they keep the commission.

I can't argue that this can and does happen. I will simply say that it is much harder to give something back once you have it. This is especially true if you have spent it already. Most often this prospect will make a salesperson think twice.

While I do not suggest it, you could go even further and make your salespeople share in the total loss. This would certainly make them much more cautious about selling a customer they have doubts about. However, I do not recommend this for two reasons. First, you don't want your salespeople to be too cautious. Only a very small percentage of customers will ever reach the point where drastic collection activity is needed or they are written off as a bad debt. If they are too cautious you will lose out on sales.

Secondly, you as a company must share in the responsibility and risk. You have a responsibility to establish and implement a strong credit policy. A policy that is adhered to. You have the risk of losing money, just as the salespeople lose commissions, if the customer goes bad.

Why worry, after all how much can it be costing you? How costly are bad debts to your business? A lot more than most people suspect. Don't just look at the bottom line amount you have written off, look instead at how many sales you must make to recover this lost income. If your net pretax profit is 2%, for every $1,000 you write off you will need to generate sales of $50,000 simply to recover this loss. If you write off $3,000 this means you must increase sales $150,000 simply to make up the $3,000 loss. If your net profit is 4%, for every $1,000 you write off you will need to sell $25,000 of product or services just to recover your loss. If you write off $5,000 you will need to increase sales $125,000 simply to recover your losses.

I trust you see my point. Don't be afraid to be aggressive with your credit and collection policies. You must develop stringent policies and you must force adherence to them.

Guilt can be your best collection technique. If your customer has not paid by the first statement send one more. After waiting for 15 more days they now have not paid for 40 days, the first 10 (you did make your terms net 10 didn't you?) plus 15 for each of the statements. It is now time to send them a letter. The most useful letter I have found to use at this point is what I call a guilt letter.

You simply want to remind them that their account is past due and that you worked very hard to produce and deliver the order in good faith and fully expect them pay the same way. I go on to tell them we work very hard to provide a quality product, delivered as requested, at a competitive price. I further point out that past due accounts are very costly to us and we simply cannot afford them.

I am trying to make them feel guilty. I want them to pay me over anyone else. I am treating them nicely and I am not threatening. At this point you want to get paid while preserving the option of doing business with this customer again. This approach may sound corny but who would you rather pay, me or someone who sends you a nasty threatening past due notice and who would you be more apt to do business with in the future? Try this approach, it works and it works well.

Blame others and ask for help. If this guilt letter has not produced results within 10 to 15 days you must next write a stronger letter to the owner of the company, the buyer, or the head of the department. They are often the reason payment is delayed and they will find it easy to issue instructions to others to delay or avoid payment but they will find it much more uncomfortable if they are being approached directly.

In this letter you want to blame someone else and not them for this delay in payment. You want to ask for their assistance in getting this invoice paid and you want to stress the point of urgency you have reached. Remember, most often everyone likes to make decisions and have control. You are giving him or her the chance to do both.

"Never arbitrate. Arbitration allows a third party to determine your destiny. It is a resort of the weak."

Wess Roberts Ph.D. from Leadership Secrets of Attila the Hun.

The last steps internally. If no arrangements for payments have been made you are now reaching the point where you are risking losing this account to outside collection activity. Collection agencies will take up to 50% of the amount owed (of course you should shop collection agencies just like any other supplier) and therefore should be a course of last resort.

If your collection efforts have all been unsuccessful you may be at the point where you must issue an ultimatum. I say may because only you can decide based on the response you are getting to your efforts. If you feel you are at this point, write a letter indicating that if the amount you are owed is not paid in full you will have no choice but to turn the account over for outside collection / legal action. At this point you do not want to state what that action will be. You want to leave your options open while pressing hard for payment. My other strategies will outline some of your options.

Use a collection letter service. These are collection services that will send a series of computer generated collection letters to your debtor over a period of a few weeks automatically. These services are very effective and claim a collection rate of over 50%. They will cost you pennies on the dollar as they are charging only for the letters sent and not a percentage of the amount collected. They send these letters at a much lower cost than you can and they have the added intimidation factor of being an outside collection service. This tells your customer how serious you are.

In Pursuit of Profits. How To At Least Double Your Profits Without Increasing Your Sales.

Small claims court, a possible option. If the account is in your state look into filing for payment in small claims court if the balance due is under the maximum you can file for. I will tell you in my experience the value of small claims court is primarily the scare value. Most of those receiving the notice from small claims court will pay at this point if they are going to pay. If you can get them to pay under threat of small claims court your cost will be about $25.00. Weigh this against the cost of your attorney or collection agency.

The power of a letterhead. When you feel you have exhausted all efforts to collect a past due account and are ready to send it to a collection agency, before you do, have your attorney send them a letter. Work out an arrangement with your attorney whereby they will send, at your request, a standard letter that informs your customer that legal action will by taken if they do not pay within 10 days. The legal action can be further action by your attorney or placement with a collection agency.

The power of an attorney's letterhead never ceases to amaze me. Just seeing a lawyer's letterhead will spur many of your customers to action when all previous calls and correspondence from you accomplished nothing.

Do not allow your attorney to collect a fee for collection at this stage. Instead, pay them a $15 or $25 fee for sending out the letter. They deserve no fee as all they are doing is sending out a standard letter. It would be fiscally foolish to pay them a 25% or 33% fee. Paying your attorney a percentage of the total amount of the bill, for collections made from one letter makes no sense.

If you turn a $1,000 past due account over to an attorney and allow them to collect on a contingency fee it will cost you $250 or more. In many cases the $25 letter will get the same results. Many lawyers will ask for this and tell you their collection efforts justify this fee, but let me tell you many past due accounts will pay off the very first letter from your lawyer. Pay for the letter only and then decide how to proceed if payment is not made.

Remember, this should cost you no more than $25. This is what I pay my attorney. Of course, this was after he tried to charge $125 for the same letter. We quickly reached our current arrangement of $25 per letter once I explained to him I knew exactly what was involved and that the letter was simply pulled up on his computer by his secretary and the required names and figures dropped in. The attorney never even handled the letter and it takes about 3 minutes.

If they tell you anything different they are lying to you and you should find another attorney. The goal here is for you to continue aggressive collection efforts but to do so in the lowest cost manner possible. The $25 or so you spend for this may very well save you thousands, or depending on your size, hundreds of thousands of dollars per year when you consider the percentage the collection agency will take.

The intimidation value of an attorney's letterhead is strong and tells your customer you are very serious. This technique had been extremely effective for me and has saved me tens of thousand of dollars over what I would have paid to a collection agency. Always take this step before you turn past due accounts over to a collection agency.

Don't chase a loser. I have seen companies spends thousands to collect hundreds or nothing at all. Why would they do this? Simple. Ego. The attitude of "I'm not going to let them get away with not paying me". Satisfying your ego in business will always be at the expense of your bottom line profit. Cut your losses when it becomes obvious you are not going to secure payment and turn it over to a collection agency or a lawyer on a contingency basis. Let them chase the debtor. They can do it a lot better than you can and it will only cost you if they collect.

When you are ready to give up. Your final step of course is to turn the account over to a collection agency or have your lawyer file suit. After all, losing some of the money is a lot better than losing all of it. Always assign past due accounts based on a contingency fee. Simply put, when you turn an account over to a collection agency or lawyer, do so on the basis of payment being rendered only for results. No collection, no payment.

You should get references from the agency to verify their effectiveness and tactics. And remember the percentages they list as their charges to you are nothing more than list prices. If you can reduce those fees even by a few percentage points you will have reduced your losses on this account and reduced your costs. Depending on the size of the accounts you are turning over to them, a reduced fee of even a few percentage points can add up to significant amounts of money. Make sure you select a collection agency just like you would select any other supplier. Seek out the best value.

Are you paying and billing the right amount? You must pay very careful attention to what you are billing and what you are paying. A decimal point out of place could cost you thousands of dollars. I know this sounds ridiculous. After all who would be stupid enough to pay a bill for the wrong amount? Well, I hate to tell you, but it happens all the time. I have received hundred and hundreds of incorrect payments from customers. The vast majority of these are overpayments on correct invoices. Most came from banks.

I have also known many bookkeepers who have paid incorrect bills. The errors can occur at your end anywhere from the writing of the purchase order to not catching an incorrect bill. It can occur at the supplier's end from the misreading of a P.O. to the issuance of duplicate invoices.

For example, if your P.O. says you are buying 1,000 widgets at $1.00 each and it should be 1,000 widgets at .10 you might overpay by $900. Many companies will bill you what you have agreed to pay even if they know it is wrong. Do not count on another company to correct your errors in any area that benefits them. Certainly some will but others will not.

At the time this was written, just yesterday a company under billed us by $1,080. The bill should have been for $1,200 and they billed us $120. This was done even though our P.O. was for $1,200. We have issued bills in error for thousands of dollars higher than they should have been simply because the person billing put the decimal point in the wrong place. Many of these were paid.

Check and double check and then check again.

How often does your company pay for products and services you never ordered or never received? Always be on the look out for bogus invoices. These are invoices for products and services that you did not order, did not receive, or do not want.

Throughout the year we receive dozens of invoices from companies that are trying to cheat us by billing for such items. I have read articles about companies that do nothing but send bills each month out to companies. They sell no products or services. They simply send bills out all month long. Apparently, as unthinkable as it is, many accounts payable people never bother to check the validity of the invoices they receive for payment, they just pay them. This costs companies billions of dollars each year.

The creativity of those who go through life trying to steal and cheat others never ceases to amaze me. What a waste of talent. How many of these do you think get paid? Studies have shown that somewhere between 25% and 50% of these bogus type bills are promptly paid without a question ever being asked. If you follow my strategies and put the proper controls in place, you won't be among this group.

In Pursuit of Profits. How To At Least Double Your Profits Without Increasing Your Sales.

Thanks but you've already paid me or did not even owe me. Watch out for duplicate payments to your vendors. Not a month goes by when we do not get at least one duplicate payment from a customer of ours. Many months we receive dozens of duplicate payments. We have even received payments in the thousands of dollars for products that were never ordered from us. How a non existent bill is paid I have no idea. But there are many ways the same bill can be paid twice or even three times.

One way this can happen is if a duplicate bill is received and paid twice by your payable people. Another way is if they pay from a statement and an original invoice. Either way they are paying for the same job twice. You should have safeguards in place to ensure this does not happen in your company.

Just today I received a $2,700 payment from a major supermarket chain who had no current order or outstanding invoice with me. I sent this back but many companies will not. This week I received 5 duplicate payments from companies who paid both the original invoice and the statement.

A guaranteed 36% return on your money? Pay your bills according to the terms offered that are most favorable to you and not according to dates received or due dates. It never ceases to amaze me when I see companies that pay all bills at the same time each month, pay favorite suppliers first or pay based on date received or date due.

You must pay your bills according to the terms that save you the most money. Simply put, you should first pay the invoices that offer you the largest discount to do so. If a supplier is offering 2/10 this is a 2% discount if paid in 10 days. Why would any company pay a bill with no discount ahead of a bill that offers a 2% discount? It happens all the time. Does your company?

You must prioritize your payment schedule so you are gaining the largest discounts you can. To help convince you as to the importance of this, let me give you some examples as to how profitable this can be. The formula to determine what the discount for early payment is worth is shown below:

$$\text{Effective rate of discount} = \frac{365 \text{ days in year x rate of discount}}{\text{Number of days early you must pay to get realize discount offered.}}$$

So, if a 2% discount is offered for payment in 10 days and the normal terms are 30 days (2/10 net 30) the effective rate of return would be determined as follows:

$$\frac{365 \times 2 \text{ (discount offered)}}{20 \text{ (paid 20 days early)}} = 36.5\%$$

The effective annual rate in this example would be 36.5%! Even a 1% discount for payment in 10 days instead of the normal 30 days (1/10 net 30) would equal an effective annual rate of 18%. This is a significant rate of return on your money with no risk at all.

Compare this to any rate you are going to get in a deposit account. Even if you are borrowing short term at 10% annual rates you are going to be way ahead of the game. If you could get this rate of return on your money all year long you could start thinking of retiring early.

What could this strategy mean to you on an annual basis? Lets look at an example. Let's assume you pay $300,000 in bills every 30 days and two thirds of those allow a 2% discount for payment in 10 days. This means that $200,000 per month of your payables can earn a 2% discount. This equates to a risk free return of $4000 per month or $48,000 per year. In this example you have added nearly $48,000 to your bottom line for doing nothing. You have made no added sales. You have not produced any more products or provided any extra services. This is total cost control. If your normal pretax profit ratio is 5%, you would need to make $960,000 in added sales to add this same $48,000 to your bottom line.

Early payment discount for late payments. Take discounts offered even if you are paying past the due date allowed to earn the discount. Of course, you must use good judgment here and not try to take a discount when you are seriously past due, however if the terms are 2/10 and you are paying after 14 days I would still take the discount.

Don't ask, just take it. I have found that 99% of the time it is still allowed. The supplier does not want to risk hurting relations with your company, they still got their money earlier than 30 days and it is often not cost justified to bill you for the amount involved anyway. I must confess that I have even successfully taken discounts much later than a few days after the allowed time. The worst that can happen is that they do bill you for the amount you have taken as a discount. Even when this happens you gain since you have delayed payment on this amount for a bit.

No incentive to pay early? Don't! Invoices with no discount should never be paid sooner than 30 days. Even if you are cash rich you should not pay these invoices any sooner. You have nothing to gain and will lose income since you have deprived yourself of the opportunity to use that money to make you money even if it is just sitting in an interest yielding deposit account. Every day you pay early costs you money. I know many companies who take great pride in paying bills as soon as they come in. I would rather have that money working for me by increasing my bottom line. Wouldn't you?

Scrutinize your employee's expense accounts as though they were an accounts payable. After all, is that not exactly what they are? Monitor all expense accounts. Padding, overspending, and unauthorized spending is a very common problem. You must always require receipts (preferably charge card receipts) and you must periodically verify the validity of these receipts and expenses.

It is very easy and very common for salespeople and executives to run up non related business expenses and submit them as a business expense. Rules must be established regarding expense accounts and they must be adhered to by all including management. Advice on establishing controls in this area will be discussed in other strategies.

Always verify all payables. Never pay a bill unless you have a corresponding purchase order and unless you have verified delivery. If you follow my strategies dealing with purchasing this will not be a problem for you.

All invoices should be checked against the P.O. and quote to verify what was ordered, who placed the order, what the price was, what the quantity is and the terms under which the order was made are, and what materials, if any, are due to be returned before payment has been made. You want to match up the invoice to both the quote and the purchase order to insure that all billing is proper and based on what was authorized. This may be done by the party that placed the order and then sent to the payable department but, however you do it, make sure it is done.

If delivery has not been verified, including quantity and quality, you do not pay. If the terms of the P.O. are not the same as the items and costs you are being billed for don't pay. This includes added charges, overage, shipping method, or any other charge you did not authorize.

In Pursuit of Profits. How To At Least Double Your Profits Without Increasing Your Sales.

All invoices being paid must be in order prior to any payment being made. Mistakes are made everyday. Intentional over billings occur all the time. These are very clear cut rules you should follow to ensure that you are only paying for what you should be.

Cross referencing always provides added protection. When you do pay a bill check the P.O. # that authorized that purchase and indicate the P.O. # and the check # on the invoice you are paying. Then indicate the check number on the P.O. This will give you a record of payment for all purchase orders and eliminate the chance that you will pay for the same item twice or pay for an item you did not order. I would estimate that I save between $10,000 and $20,000 per year simply by making sure that each and every invoice is checked in the way these strategies outline.

Never, never pay for your supplier's problems. You will always have enough of your own. One example of a supplier trying to get you to pay for their mistakes is in the area of shipping. Often if a company is running behind in production and delivery they will ship using a more costly method and then try to bill you for the added costs by claiming that was the only way they could get it to you on time. If you did not authorize this (and you should not unless you caused the delay) don't pay. You should not pay to compensate for the problems of your supplier.

Prove it. You should also ask for proof of any shipping charges that seem out of line. In this case you should ask to see the actual bill from the carrier. This strategy will be covered in depth in another section but for now I want to reinforce the statements from above. If in doubt ask for proof.

Wait for credits before you pay the invoice. Don't pay invoices that have credits pending on them. Many companies will pay the bill in full and wait for a credit. I do not and neither should you. Why would you want to pay for something you have a credit due on? This means you are paying for something that was wrong or you did not get.

This also means that you will be forced to use that company again to get any value for your credit. It also means more work for you in tracking that credit. All of these things cost you money, time, and control. Each of which is exactly what you do not want.

Instead, you want a revised bill showing the proper amount that you owe. No, I do not suggest you just deduct the amount in question and pay what you owe. If you do this, often you will be dunned for the rest of the money later on since your supplier's records still show you owing an amount. Even if you are told that it is taken care of you will find many times it is not and as a result you can spend a lot of time trying to clear the matter up.

Delaying payment until the proper bill is received will also extend your float which is the amount of time you can delay payment legitimately and you can put that money to other income producing or cost saving uses.

Get credit even if you have cash. I do not care if you have the best cash flow of any company ever known to man. You should always seek to establish an open account relationship with your suppliers as soon as possible. You want to avoid prepayment and C.O.D. for the reasons I have outlined in other strategies. In short, both cost you money and reduce your options.

Remember, money has a cost. If you are paying at the time of delivery, prepaying, or paying COD you are incurring a higher cost. You are either borrowing to cover the amount in question or you are losing the opportunity to use that money to make you money in some other manner. This can be some type of investment or by using one of the other strategies I have outlined.

Remember, convenience always costs you. Make sure that your accounts payable department is not paying invoices based on convenience. This is a very frequent occurrence and a very costly one. Unless you have a compelling reason to pay an invoice before it is due, such as a discount you want to take advantage of, you should not be paying them early.

Despite this, the early payment of invoices happens all the time and you probably do not even know it. How? The most common occurrence is when you receive multiple invoices from the same supplier over a few weeks. Let's say you receive 3 invoices from the ABC company on March 1st. These invoices are due in 30 days or on April 1st. Then on March 15th you receive 3 more invoices again due in 30 days or on April 15th. Then once again on March 25th you receive 3 more invoices from this supplier for other orders and these are due on April 25th.

If you promptly pay on the 30th day, on April 1st you would send this supplier a check covering the 3 invoices from March 1st. Then on April 15th, you would pay the 3 invoices from the ABC company dated March 15th and on April 25th you would pay those 3 invoices from March 25th.

However, your accounts payable people would rather send one check to this vendor instead of three. Therefore, on April 1st they send a check to the ABC company for payment of all 9 invoices. They may rationalize this by thinking of the time they saved in sending one check instead of three. But they are wrong.

What they have done is to pay 3 invoices on time, pay 3 invoices 15 days before they were due and to pay 3 invoices 25 days before they were due. What they have done is cost your company money. What they have done is to lose the opportunity to use the money they used to pay 6 invoices before they were due. What they have done is to needlessly and unjustifiably diminish your cash flow. If you borrowed to cover these invoices what they have done is pull down your credit line while increasing your borrowing costs.

Depending on the amount of the invoices that were paid early, this could prove to be very costly and damaging to your cash flow. All this simply to make their job a bit easier. Convenience always has a price. Don't pay the price. Do not allow this practice to exist in your company.

If they have your property do not pay their invoice. Do not pay any invoice until any and all materials of yours have been returned by the party billing you. For example, if you have sent artwork to a printer and the artwork was not returned you should not pay the invoice for the job. The artwork cost you money to produce and it will cost you more time and money to replace it if you need it again. The printer will want to keep it to help ensure that you will place any orders for reruns with them. You want it so that you can have the job rerun wherever you want without having to reproduce the same art again.

The best leverage you will ever have is when you have a bill to pay. They want payment and you want your materials back. You will be amazed at how many times artwork or, any other materials you have given someone to use, gets lost or is damaged if it is not returned before you paid the bill. If this happens before you have paid the invoice you can deduct the value of your lost materials or damaged property from the suppliers invoice.

I suggest you stamp all materials that you provide to a supplier with a message that clearly states all materials must be returned upon completion of the job or no invoices will be paid. I would also add this to your purchase order form.

The final step is to make sure that your accounts payable people understand this policy and that they check to make sure that all material has been returned before they pay any outstanding invoice. By stamping your purchase order with a message that materials have been sent to the supplier in conjunction with this job and by having a box to check that indicates the materials have been returned you should be well covered.

Late payments? Charge for them but do not pay them. Never pay late charges. Charge them, but never pay them. I know this sounds contradictory, but my goal is to reduce your costs and improve your profitability and not that of your supplier.

You must control the use of your petty cash. You must monitor and control your petty cash accounts and your miscellaneous expenses. These accounts have a strong tendency to be misused in most businesses and small consistent drains can cost you thousands of dollars each year. You must have set procedures in place as to who can access these accounts, for what reason, with whose approval, and as to what documentation is needed. These accounts are very commonly used for small, unapproved, and often unnoticed, expenses and purchases.

You must have set guidelines in place. Do not put your bookkeeper in the position of having to decide what they will reimburse or pay out of petty cash and what they will not. Do not make them have to tell an executive or salesperson no. If exceptions are made they should not be left to the bookkeeper to make. This is unfair and unwise. This is your responsibility! Do not pass it on.

Where did you post that expense? Make sure you know what should go on your income statement and what should go on your balance sheet. I know this sounds obvious and I know you will be asking isn't that why you have an accountant. But it is very important you know your way around the financial reports. You have a responsibility to understand what is happening in your own business. To do otherwise is fiscally irresponsible and down right stupid.

You do not need to be an accountant, but you damn well better have at least a basic idea of how to read your financial reports, how they are constructed and what they are telling you. A couple of hours with a basic book on the subject will tell you this information. There is no excuse that you could ever give me that would justify your not knowing at least the basics about your financial reports. **None.**

I have seen many companies put expenses on the income statement that could, and should, go on the balance sheet. An expense that goes on the income statement is a 100% cost to the bottom line of that fiscal year. If you can put that expense on the balance sheet and depreciate it instead, it will have only a fraction of the effect on your bottom line.

Yes, some expenses have to go on one or the other by law but in other cases you have some flexibility.   What if you purchase $1,000 of furniture? Where should it go? Where must it go? Well, if you put it on your income statement you have just added $1,000 to your costs for that fiscal year. If you put it on the balance sheet and depreciate it you will incur only a fraction of that cost in the current fiscal year.

You should always discuss the pros and cons of any questionable posting with your accountant. In areas that you have options you can effect a strategy to minimize or maximize your costs in a given year. Improper posting or, posting costs without a strategy when you have options, can have a negative impact on your IRS liability for any given year. You must know what you are doing, what your options are, and what impact each will have.

Proper fiscal planning and strategies can be a very effective tool in your battle to control and reduce costs. The end result of your actions or inactions can make a significant difference on your bottom line and your tax liability.

Sign the checks yourself. One of the best ways for you to see what you are buying is to sign all payable checks yourself . I know you can't do this all the time but by doing it every few weeks for a day or two you will see first hand where your money goes. At the very least spot check a number of invoices from each department every few weeks. This will be a real eye opening experience for you and it is one that is sure to make you ask many questions about what you are buying, why, and for what purpose. Few things will bring the reality of the need to control and reduce your costs home faster than signing check after check for things you did not even know you bought. This strategy will also serve to keep your people on their toes.

If you use budgets each year establish the new budget lower than the old budget. Budgets and financial management are often a contradiction of terms. Budgets often encourage abuse and waste. The goal of those saddled with budgets is always to get more. They will always seek ways to spend the entire budget. They are afraid if they come in under budget they will be rewarded with a smaller budget. They just do not make sense to me for most small and medium sized businesses.

Frequently budgets are nothing but a way to avoid the fiscal responsibilities of management. Establishing a budget is often nothing more than a way for management to transfer financial responsibility to someone else. If you give people a budget to work with you are giving up control and responsibility.

With this said, if you continue to use budgets lower the budgets you establish each year or at the very least, do not increase them. It makes no sense to reward those who use the entire budget up with a higher budget. This does nothing but send a message that reinforces the idea that the goal is to use all money in the budget. This type of thinking will cost your company a great deal of money. You must stop it. You must give people incentive to reduce budgets without reducing effectiveness.

As a rule I don't like corporate credit cards despite the fact that they do offer some benefits and there are valid reasons why you might use them. I don't like them because they make spending money too easy for the cardholder. Money that you are paying back. Credit cards are like poker chips, they separate the holder from the reality that they represent money.

They may not think twice about using it liberally and they may not think at all about what they are paying. However, when they are forced to use their own money, even knowing that they will be reimbursed, they will indeed think twice before they spend it and they will think about the value and necessity of what they are purchasing. They may not want to front the money and they may shop out better buys. Using one's own money just has a way of making people think more.

If you do use a corporate credit card, or allow your employees to have one, shop around for a low rate, no annual fee, and no interest charges during a grace period. Do not pay extra for status cards like gold cards, silver cards, or platinum cards.

Charity begins at home. There is a big difference between being a good corporate citizen and supporting every charitable organization around. You must be very selective and you should only donate when you are fiscally able to. When you do donate, donate directly to the organization itself and not through a fund raising organization. This way you will know who you are dealing with and that the intended party actually gets your donation.

Not only are there many bogus charitable organizations and solicitations, but in many cases even the legitimate ones often never see your money. The problem may be that the fund raising group the charity hires may be so costly that very little, and perhaps none, of the money they raised ever reaches the actual charity. This happened just recently with the "Toys for Tots" charity.

Over $10 million was raised and not a dime of it was used to buy toys. Hard to believe but true. The costs of the direct mail company used to raise funds was so high the $10 million raised did not even cover their costs. This is ridiculous, but it happens. In other cases, or even in cases where an outside firm hired to raise money does raise enough to cover costs and give the charity money, the money may not end up in the hands of the individuals the charity is raising money for. The administrative cost of the charity itself may be so high that very little, if any, of the money is used for the stated purpose of the charity.

Be careful and be selective. When you do donate, donate directly to the charity. At least this way there is a greater chance that some good will result from your donation.

Consider donating goods and services directly to the charity instead of money. You may get a larger write off and the charity will be just as grateful. For example, instead of donating $500, donate goods or services that may have a selling value of $500 but cost you only a portion of that.

Chapter 16. Customer service.

*"If you don't take care of your customer,
rest assured someone else will."*

Anonymous

Would you want to be one of your own customers? It has been my experience as both a customer and an employer that the area of customer service in too many companies is one that is often under appreciated, overlooked, and somehow taken for granted. This amazes me and I will have more to say about it in other strategies, but here I just want to ask you if you would like to be a customer of your company?

I hope you did not answer that because there is no way for you to answer that question unless you are a customer of your company. I strongly suggest you become one, at least to the point of calling or visiting your own company on a regular basis or if you are too recognizable, have someone close to you do it for you. Ask questions, ask about prices, hours, delivery, service, and anything else that applies to your business.

Speak to as many departments as you can. I think you will be disappointed with the results. At the very least I can almost guarantee that you will feel you can do better. How quickly was your call answered? How many times were you put on hold? How many times were you transferred? How were you greeted? How friendly were the people? How helpful were they? How accurate was the information they gave you?

Is the way you were treated the way you want your customers and prospects to be treated? If you are a retail business I suggest you spend time periodically visiting your stores or again, if you are too recognizable, have someone close to you do it.

If you have someone do it for you, make sure you prepare them for the call or visit with questions and the knowledge of what you are looking for. Make sure you use someone who will not be afraid to give it to you straight. Sugar coating feedback like this will be of no use to you. In fact, it could be very harmful to your organization as it may lead you to believe things are great when in fact you may have some serious problems. Problems, that are costing you customers.

We would all rather hear good things about our business, our people, and our efforts, but the negative things will normally be much more valuable to us as they indicate any weaknesses we have and problem areas we need to address. Like a visit to the doctor's, we may not enjoy the diagnosis but it may be vital to our long term health.

You can't afford to alienate one single customer or prospect. Few things will drive your customers and prospects away faster than an attitude of indifference, incompetence, or inaccurate information.

It has been estimated that it costs 5 times more to get a customer than it does to keep one. The cost of getting someone to call your company or visit your store is simply too high to lose out on business because of poor customer service. This is inexcusable and should never be tolerated.

The most important element in your business is your customer. Don't take your customers for granted. Who does this? Many, many companies. They will work very hard to get a customer. They will spend hundreds or thousands of dollars to get a customer and then ignore them or take them for granted.

In Pursuit of Profits. How To At Least Double Your Profits Without Increasing Your Sales.

Your existing customers are your best prospects for future and ongoing sales. You have already spent the time, effort, and money to get them. Now work to keep them. Don't invite your competition to take them from you.

Like any relationship, you cannot neglect it if you expect it to work. You must stay in touch with your customers and you must provide the type of service and product that you used to get them in the first place. The cost of getting a new customer can be very high. **It will always be much cheaper to keep an existing customer than it will be to get a new one.**

What good does it do to lose one customer and then go get another one? No good of course. It only costs you money. You have not gained any more customers. You also know your existing customers can be your best source of sales, new customers, and word of mouth advertising. Do you think a customer who has left you is going to help you in these areas? You will be lucky if they don't cost you other customers.

Come on Welch aren't you overstating the importance of customer service? Why do customers leave you? Do you spend time and money trying to find out? Do you know it is far less expensive and much easier to sell more to an existing customer than it is to find a new one?

Do you spend time and money trying to find new customers? A great deal I suspect. How much could you cut these costs if you were able to keep more of your current customers? Do you worry that your prices are too high and this is costing you customers? **Think about this. A customer is nearly 5 times more likely to leave because of poor service than because of price or even poor quality.**

If I could show you a way to keep more of your customers without lowering your prices do you think you could find ways to reduce costs in a number of areas? I hope so because you should be able to do this very easily.

According to a study conducted by the American Productivity and Quality Center, 68% of all customers are lost solely because they received poor service, were treated indifferently, or received discourteous treatment. Not because of price. Only 9% left because of price. Blaming price is an easy way to ignore the real problem. Not because of competition. In fact, only 5% of your customers are likely to be stolen away by your competition. **No, face the facts, it is far more likely that you or your people are driving them away.**

If you want to eliminate the overwhelming reason why you lose customers it will cost you nothing. All that is required is that you treat your customers as though they are the most important thing in the world to you. This should not be too hard because this is exactly what they are to your business. Let me tell you, if you don't treat them this way someone else will!

In case you were wondering, of the remaining 18% of all customers lost, 14% left because their problems were not satisfactorily resolved, 3% moved, and 1% died. When you consider the problems that caused the 14% to leave, you can really say 82% of all customers who are lost, are lost as a direct result of a failure in the area of customer service and customer appreciation.

Attracting a new customer cost five times as much as the cost of selling to an existing one. The average company loses 10% to 30% of it's customers each year with the most common cause of losing a customer being dissatisfaction with service. Think of how much money you can save by simply keeping the customers you have.

Double your profits by retaining your current customers. According to a study published in the September, 1990, Harvard Business Review if you could lower your customer drop-out rate by just 5% you could improve your profits by 100%. If the thought of being able to double your profits simply by improving your customer service does not get your attention I don't know what will.

"There is less to fear from outside competition than from inside inefficiency, discourtesy and bad service."

Anonymous

Excellence in the area of customer service can be one of your best marketing tools. Yes, that is right, top notch customer service can be one of, if not your best, marketing tools. Everything about your company that creates a perception in your customer's mind is a tool of marketing. From advertising to the way you answer your phone or greet patrons of your establishment. From clean tables in a restaurant to a pleasant waiting area, every single thing that creates an image in your customers or prospects mind is an element of marketing. Few marketing tools are more direct and personal than customer service.

Smile. It will always be the lowest cost and probably the most important thing you can do to improve customer service. The most dramatic improvement most companies can make in the area of customer service is also the least expensive. What is this miracle you ask? Make sure that your customers are given prompt, friendly service with a smile.

If you think I am joking, ask yourself when was the last time you called or went to any type of business and felt as though you were not only welcome, but were actually important. I suspect you will have to think long and hard to come up with any occasion, never mind a few.

Every day I run into ignorant, arrogant, rude, condescending, lazy people. From employees in retail stores, to receptionists and customer service people on the phone at suppliers we use, most see customers as a nuisance, an inconvenience, and an intrusion into whatever they think their job is.

"There's no great mystery to satisfying your customers. Build them a quality product and treat them with respect. It's that simple."

Lee Iacocca

"Oh great, another damn customer!" If you could read the minds of many of your employees I suspect you would be reading a thought very similar to this. Do not ever, or let anyone else in your company ever, treat your customers as if they are a nuisance. Your employees must understand that without your customers you do not need them. No customer = no company = no job. A very simple formula.

Your customers must be treated as if they are the most important part of your business and that is exactly what they are. Without customers you have nothing else to worry about. Nothing else will matter. You won't need to fret about cost of sales, or profits, or sales. There won't be any business without customers so you need not worry about these things.

A good product and good service? It is a very rare combination today. Most consider themselves lucky if they get one or the other. **This is a disgrace**. A disgrace that exists in almost every company in this country. If you want to beat your competition and retain your customers make damn sure they are treated with courtesy, respect, and as though they are as important as they are. **There is no greater sin in business than spending the time, money, and effort to attract a customer and then losing them for an avoidable reason.**

How much is that customer worth to you? You must start thinking about customers beyond the short term. Think about how much a customer is worth to you in the long term. For example, a customer who may spend $100 a week with you is worth $5,200 a year to you. Over 10 years they are worth $52,000 to you. But only if you can keep them as a customer. If you lose that customer you have lost far more than $100 per week. You have lost tens of thousands of dollars in sales. You must learn to think like this. You must train your people to think like this. Keeping a long term perspective in mind concerning the potential value of each customer will dramatically bring home the point of how important customers are to your business. Thinking long term in this area will remind your people how important their short term customer service actions really are.

Are you involving your customers in your business? Use your correspondence with your customers as a no cost way to conduct market research and improve your customer service. On your invoices, acknowledgments, letterheads, and the like, include a message asking your customers how you can serve them better. Tell them how important they are to you and ask them how you can improve your products or services to serve them better. Tell them you need their input. Ask them what you are doing well and what they think you can do better. Ask them how else you can serve them. What other products or services could you provide that they could use?

Your customers will feel very good about the fact that their input is important to you and that you are seeking ways to improve your company for their benefit. Who could not feel good about a company that cared about them? You will also get input on ways in which you can better serve your customers. This is direct first hand market research. This can point the way for new products or services and cross selling opportunities.

Why did you lose that customer? Whenever you lose a customer try to find out why. You should never assume you know the answer. You should not rely on the input of others in your organization for the answer. They may be the problem and as such will be giving you inaccurate information be it intentional or not.

How can you prevent other customers from leaving if you do not find out why you are losing customers? You can't fix something if you do not know it is broken. Even if you know it is broken, you can't stop it from breaking again unless you know what is causing the problem.

I once pulled $10,000 out of a bank and closed my account out. Not once was I asked why? Not one person in the bank cared enough to ask me if there was anything they could do to keep my business. Not one person even thanked me for doing business with them. No closed account card was ever sent. No follow up call was ever made. No one cared. Yet this bank is a very aggressive advertiser who consistently spends a great deal of money trying to attract new customers.

Yet they let a large one walk right out the door without even asking why or saying thank you. This happens all the time. How many $10,000 depositors do you think they have? How much negative word of mouth advertising do you think I gave them? A great deal I assure you.

It is said that the best type of advertising is word of mouth advertising. If this is true, than it is logical to assume that the worst type of marketing problem a company can have is negative word of mouth advertising. Do you want this? Find out why when you lose a customer. Do all you can to get that account back and take whatever steps are necessary to prevent this problem from happening again.

Review your business hours at least once a year and preferably every 6 months. Just because you have one set of established business hours does not mean that they should stay the same forever. It does not mean that they are the best hours for you to be open. You must ask yourself if these hours are best for your customer. Notice I did not say the best for your company. The customer is what matters. Every aspect of your business should be driven by what represents the best situation for your customer.

If your hours are not the best hours for your customers than you can be sure they are not the best hours for your business to be open. This is pretty simple. Without customers you are not in business. Should you be open later? Should you open earlier? Is the cost of doing so justified by the added sales and service?

Are you paying so much overtime that you should have a second shift or a part time crew working a second half of a shift? Look at all the possibilities. Survey your customers. Study your competition. Examine the costs. Consider the sales you are losing. Your decisions must be customer justified and cost justified.

There is more than one type of customer service you know. External customer service as we have been discussing is important, vitally important. But there is another form of customer service that you must work at improving. I am speaking of internal customer service. Each of your co-workers and employees is an internal customer. Each department is an internal customer to the other. Unless you are able to provide top flight internal customer service you will never be able to provide the best external customer service. Excellence in both areas must be your goal. Any other goal will be very costly. Very costly indeed.

Internal customer service deals with an attitude of assistance. It deals with each employee, no matter how high up or how low down the corporate ladder, making sure they have not made an error or assumption that is being passed on to the next person or department. It deals with each of your people asking and not assuming. It deals with you and each of your employees doing all they can to facilitate the overall objectives of the company and not just individual objectives.

Internal customer service deals with reducing errors in all departments. It deals with clear and effective communication. It means thinking about how you and your employees can make the job of others easier not how to make your own jobs easier. It means going the extra step and striving for excellence in everything you do. It means functioning as a team and not just talking about it. It means treating others as you would like to be treated.

Internal customer service deals with a commitment, a commitment that starts at the top, to doing the best job that can be done the first time. It deals with being careful and not careless. It must start with the initial customer contact and continues through to the delivery of your product or service. The attitude of "it is not my job" or "let someone else worry about that" has no place in a company driven to provide outstanding customer service. **It should have no place in your company.**

Poor internal customer service will cost you money in hundreds of different ways. From quality problems to operational delays and redundancies, poor internal customer service will cost you money. It will also cause you serious morale problems and severely hinders your ability to provide exceptional exterior customer service.

Think of this as a critical piece of the puzzle. The puzzle that makes a bad company good and a good company great.

Chapter 17. Equipment / maintenance / service / service contracts.

"An efficient businessman who found a machine that would do half his work, bought two."

Celebrating Excellence

Get advice from those who know. If you are thinking of purchasing any type of office equipment I suggest you contact a company called "What to Buy for Business". This company is sort of the Consumer Reports of the business world. They accept no advertising from outside sources and they offer impartial recommendations and opinions on a wide range of office equipment. They publish both a monthly (10 months a year) publication on this subject and they offer a book called The Office Equipment Advisor. From fax machines to photocopiers, from laser printers to computer systems, from phones to paper shredders, they can be a tremendous weapon for you in your cost control and expense reduction battle. Call them at 1-800-247-2185.

But the sales representative said it would do that! Get a written statement of performance guarantees you are given in the sales proposal including any verbal statements made by the sales rep. You are, after all, purchasing based upon a certain set of expectations are you not? Don't leave anything to chance. You do not want to hear later on that "I never said that" or "you must have misunderstood" or "oh, we don't know about that he doesn't work here anymore".

If the equipment you purchase does not do what it is supposed to do or what you were promised it would, you must have recourse. This written guarantee must include your recourse options including a refund and payback for lost time, and money, if any.

What do you need it to do? Don't buy more than you need. Don't buy the top of the line model that is loaded with bells and whistles that you have no use or very limited use for. Not only will this significantly increase your purchase price but it will also increase your service and maintenance costs. Many times you can add these options later if you are able to determine that they are cost effective options that will improve your production, improve your quality, and / or lower your costs.

You should only be buying what you need and can justify, not what would be *nice* to have or what you *might* need. The difference between a low end or middle of the line piece of equipment can be 25% to 100% lower than a top of the line fully loaded model. Can you justify this added cost? Remember the domino effect works both ways. A more costly piece of equipment will drive up your payments, increase your interest costs if you are borrowing to buy it, and increase your insurance and maintenance costs just to name a few things.

If possible buy the base model, but negotiate the option to buy the added options you might need at a later date for the same price. As I have pointed out before, you will never be in a stronger position to get the price and terms you want than you are in at the time you are buying something.

By providing yourself this option you buy only what you know you need while providing for the option of adding the options later. You will also give yourself time to learn the equipment and evaluate the performance, costs, and feasibility of the considered options. You give up nothing and gain much.

Take a test drive.   Use the 30 day money back guarantee offered by many companies selling by direct mail to test drive a new product. Try buying a computer at a retail store, use it for a month, then bring it back since it did not meet your expectations. After they stop laughing at you they will probably call security.

Companies selling by direct mail that offer a 30 day money back guarantee will generally take back the product no questions asked. Your only risk will be the return shipping costs. However, if you purchase through the right companies they will pick it up at no charge if you are not satisfied. This is a very good way to test something without commitment. Just make sure the return terms are acceptable to you before you purchase.

If you do not need it year round perhaps you shouldn't buy it. Don't purchase office equipment for short term or seasonal needs. Rent it instead. For example, if you need an added typewriter a few weeks each Fall to help out with last minute billing, rent, don't buy. To decide, determine the length of time you need it and then weigh the cost of buying against the cost of renting. It may be very cost effective to rent for a few weeks but very costly to rent for a few months.

Never leave a lease open ended. If you are going to lease equipment make sure that you have the option of purchasing this equipment at a predetermined price at the end of the lease. The best way for you to set this up would be to have the option of purchasing, but not the obligation of purchasing, at fair market value or a price not to exceed a specific dollar figure such as 5% of the purchase price. This way you will be able to purchase at a preset price if the market value is high and at a lower price if the market value is lower.

You do not want an open end option like "at market value". Who sets the market value? They do of course. You want to know the maximum price you will have to pay if you choose to exercise your option and you want the flexibility of trying for a lower price.

Lease expiring? Play hardball and threaten to give the equipment back. If you already have a lease with a vague unspecified purchase option at the end of the lease don't worry too much. The company does not want your equipment. They are not in business to take back equipment 4 or 5 years old.

Anything they can get from you for it will be better than paying to have it removed from your office and disposed of. Knowing this, you should be able to get the equipment for a song. They may try to hard sell you at first by telling you that you must pay some outrageous price, but if you indicate they can take it away unless they agree to your figure, you should see some very quick price changes.

If an equipment upgrade can reduce labor always at least consider it. For example, we purchased a new typesetter (used) that enabled us to reduce the labor in our art department by 15 hours per week with no sacrifice in production or quality. This typesetter, which cost $50,000 new, was purchased 4 years old for $5,000. It was bought right. It was a brand name, checked out very thoroughly and secured with an extended warranty. The labor savings at $10 per hour was $150 per week or over $7,800 the first year.

How much would you need to increase sales to add $7,800 to your bottom line? In this case we would have had to increase sales nearly $312,000 to add this same amount of pretax profit to our bottom line. The machine paid for itself in one year and as long as we own it, it will provide a $7,800+ profit each year for us. It also saved us about $1,000 a year in consumable materials so the real payback was sooner and the profit greater.

In Pursuit of Profits. How To At Least Double Your Profits Without Increasing Your Sales.

You should always be on the lookout for ways to upgrade your operation while decreasing your overhead. These savings do not even include the savings afforded by the domino effect. Remember, we also saved an added 30% or more on the $7,800 annual payroll savings as all payroll indexed costs are now lower.

Yesterday's technology may do just fine. Following up on the previous strategy, if you do not need state of the art equipment you can get outstanding deals from those who do. The typesetter we bought was a generation below the current state of the art equipment. For us it was a huge step up. For the owner of the equipment it was obsolete. He bought it for $50,000 and sold it to me for $5,000.

One mans trash is another man's treasure. Always consider used equipment before purchasing new equipment. The cost difference can be 100% or more. Trade and association journals are excellent sources for companies offering used equipment as are auctions and liquidators. Don't over look data base sources either. These are companies that list all known equipment for sale by type of equipment and then for a very small fee will provide you with a list of names, numbers, and prices for all sellers.

Look before you buy. Try to check out the service history of any used piece of equipment you are considering. Call the manufacturer's service department and see if they have a service history on that machine. Often they will and they will be more than happy to provide you with repair records and, if feasible, go on site to check out the current condition (there may be a fee for this).

Why would they do this? Simple. They are going to lose a service customer since the current owner is selling the equipment and you may represent a new customer to them.

I was able to do this for the typesetter and by being able to check out the service history I was saved from purchasing a piece of equipment from one seller that sounded very good until I found out the seller was not telling the truth. I know it is hard to believe but some sellers will lie to you. In this case the seller had lied to me about the age and repair history of the equipment.

If you buy the demonstration model make sure you get a full warranty. Consider demonstration models only if offered with full original warranty. Savings here can be significant but you cannot afford to take any chances. A good buy is only good if it meets your expectations.

The total cost is much more than the selling price. When considering any purchase on equipment, new or used, you must consider all factors including selling price, material usage, and service costs. On the basis of selling price one manufacturer's product may seem to be the best buy but once all factors are considered may actually be the worst. They may be coming in with a low product cost and making profits in the area of service or material.

Where will you be able to purchase the materials you need? A strong consideration in the purchase of any piece of equipment should be the option of buying supplies from a source other than the manufacturer. If your only source of materials is the manufacturer they are controlling your costs and availability and not you. You must have options. Before you purchase any new equipment make sure that you have alternative sources for supplies and service. If you wait until after you have made a purchase because you assumed these options exist you may have lost important cost control options. Without competition the manufacturer controls your consumable costs and you have no options.

Special prices at special events. If you are ready to make a purchase of a new piece of equipment (or any capital expenditure) try to time it so that you can attend the annual trade show for the industry selling the equipment. All industries have one and savings of 20% to 30% are common. Participating in these shows is very costly and companies very often offer special show discounts to at least generate enough sales to offset the cost of being in the show.

For example, I had been negotiating for a small printing press. I had a written proposal for a price of $30,000. Two weeks later I went to the regional graphics art trade show and was able to buy that same press for $24,000. The cost of the trade show was $5. The savings was 20% or $6,000 in this case. Not a bad return on my $5 investment. At a 2.5% pretax profit ratio I would have had to increase my sales $240,000 to add the same amount to my bottom line!

What size copier do you really need? When purchasing a new copier make sure you know what your annual copier volume is. Only then will you be able to purchase the proper model based on your usage. Almost without exception, the copiers sales rep will try to sell you a higher than needed volume copier. If you don't know your volume you may be paying for more machine than you need.

Also consider the speed of the copier you purchase. Copier speeds can run from 10 copies per minute to 75 or more. If your usage justifies a higher speed seriously consider buying it. The labor time you save by not having people standing at this machine copying, or waiting to copy, will likely return the added costs many times over.

Where are you going to finance it? Financing of equipment purchases is an area that can be very costly while giving you the illusion of being inexpensive. On most purchases you will a have a number of options on how you can purchase. (If you decide to purchase and not lease.)

Make sure that you get all options from the manufacturer and then look into financing from your own bank. Compare rates, terms, and down payment. Often the manufacturer will attempt to bypass the issue of rates by only talking about monthly payments as though only the monthly payment amount matters. Sadly, this is all many buyers care about. This is bad business.

Yes, this matters, but so does what the total cost of the loan will be. A much higher rate can be disguised in the appearance of a lower payment simply because the loan is spread out over a longer period of time. Flush all the details out, only then will you know which is the best deal. Never automatically finance through the manufacturer simply because it is convenient and you assume all rates are the same. This type of thinking could cost you thousands of dollars in added finance charges.

Some suppliers view financing as a way to make added profit while others seek only to make profit on the purchase and will offer a very good financing package to help them make the sale. If rates or terms confuse you, a quick test is to just multiply the monthly payment times the number of months for each option. From this deduct the cost of the purchase and any money you put down. This will give you a quick and clear picture of what the interest for each proposal will cost you for the duration of the loan.

Do not understand? Do not agree? Do not buy! Remember lead don't be led. If certain conditions of the sale are objectionable to you don't purchase. If any areas of the contract or proposal are unclear, get clarification. If any areas of the contract are objectionable to you don't sign it, walk away, or change the terms to ones that are suitable to you.

Modifying a contract is very easy. Just get a marker, take off the cover, and start lining out the sections that you do not agree to. Have all parties initial and keep a copy. I have deleted whole sections with a large black magic marker. If an addendum is needed to have a written record of things not in the contract then add one.

Just because the rep says something is standard, or that the contract is preprinted, or tells you that is how the company operates, so what? You are the customer, you dictate terms. You must understand the positioning in this relationship. Nothing happens until you say so. The key part of that sentence is "you say so".

Is renting an option? Consider renting with an option to purchase if at all possible. If you can rent for a few months you might pay a bit more at first but if the purchase does not work out you have the option of terminating the deal. Of course, you want any rental payments applied toward the purchase price if you exercise your option to purchase.

Does that cost include everything? Make sure that all delivery and setup charges are included in the purchase price. Better yet would be to get these for no charge as a condition of the purchase. The last thing you want is unexpected charges later on for delivery and installation, training, or anything else unexpected, or overlooked.

Surprises in the business world, as you full well know, are usually unpleasant and costly. Many a buyer has been unpleasantly surprised when, after delivery and installation, they are presented with a bill for hundreds or even thousands of dollars because they assumed these were included in the purchase price.

Before you make any purchase of new equipment make sure that you get estimated material usage and costs in writing, from the manufacturer. Supply costs can eat you alive and you must know what they are going to cost you so you can include them in your evaluation of the feasibility of the purchase.

You also want some recourse if you find out after the purchase that material usage and costs are significantly higher than what you expected based on the sales proposal. This will also provide you with the chance to compare costs with other suppliers before you make the purchase.

Now that I own it, how do I use it? If you have purchased new equipment that requires training of any intensity, consider finding someone in your area that has the same equipment to subsidize any training you get from the manufacturer or distributor.

Depending on the nature of the equipment, you may even want to find someone local to do all the training. Not only will this most likely save you a great deal of money when compared to the cost of the training from the manufacturer or vendor, but you will receive training from someone who uses the equipment day in and day out. They will be able to show you tricks, trouble spots, and shortcuts that the manufacturer or distributor trainer can't or won't. This will be especially true if you can find a person in your industry to train you.

This is not hard to do. Just call around and speak to the operators of the equipment in the companies in your area. You will have little trouble finding a number of people who would love to moonlight after hours, on off days, or during vacation time. These people will also be able to show you less expensive materials you can use from sources other than the manufacturer or distributor who will, of course, want you to buy only from them.

Furthermore, the local user you find to train you will be able to give you maintenance tips thereby saving you service costs and they may have lower cost maintenance and repair sources they can put you on to.

Let me give you a first hand example. I once bought a very expensive piece of electronic equipment. Included in the proposal for this equipment was a fee for one week of training from the manufacturer's trainer. The cost of the training was $4,700. I found this to be an unacceptable price and began calling around to other companies in my area who might use a piece of equipment like this. I could have also ran an ad in the newspaper and if my phone efforts had not paid off I would have. However, this was not needed as within 30 minutes I had found just what I was looking for.

I found a smaller company who had the exact same piece of equipment and offered to train my people at his office for free. All he wanted in return was my word that if his machine ever broke down I would allow him limited use of our equipment in a pinch so he could get his work out until repairs were made. I agreed to this in exchange for his word that we could also use his equipment in a pinch should we find ourselves in the same situation.

Look what one half hour of effort had produced. Not only did I find a source for training at no cost, thereby saving me $4,700, but I also found a back up option to insure we could always get our work out not matter what mechanical problems we ran into. He was happy and we were happy. <u>I would consider this my $4,700 phone call.</u>

I also found another source that would provide the required training during a vacation period at $20 per hour. A forty hour week of training would cost me $800 compared to $4,700. To expedite things and to learn from the experience of two sources, I took advantage of both. I had the one person come in for the week at $800 to train all my people and I sent my key person to the location of the small shop to get more advanced training the next week.

In addition to the benefits I have outlined, my people also got more in depth training at a fraction of the cost. I now also have two sources to draw from should I need short term help. Furthermore, both trainers provided us with alternative sources for supplies and service and both showed my people many time saving tips and techniques.

If you must buy new, and I strongly urge you to think about this, buy last year's model. Not only will you be buying equipment that has a verifiable track record, but you will also save 20% to 40% when compared to the price of the new model. It is rare when a new model has been so vastly improved that you can justify this type of added cost.

For example, a graphic arts image setter comes out in 1993 and is touted as the state of the art, best ever made, blah, blah, blah. The next year along comes a new model. Now this model is said to be the state of the art, the best ever made, blah, blah, blah. The new model costs $100,000. The 1993 model can now be had for $60,000. What happened? The state of the art a year ago is now useless? The best of 1993 is now only 60% as valuable as it was a year ago? **Someone is kidding someone. Guess who?**

Why pay $40,000 more for the new model when you can be sure that next year's model will make this years model obsolete and will be the new state of the art, best ever made, blah, blah, blah? Higher prices also means higher taxes, higher consumable costs, and higher service costs. Don't ever forget that the domino effect works both ways. Your actions, or inactions, determine whether it works for you or against you.

Show and tell. Don't ever buy any new equipment based solely on a demonstration provided by the manufacturer or distributor. You can be sure that any such demonstration, whether in your company or their showroom, will always run perfect and look great.

You must go beyond this. You must get a list of current users of the equipment in question and you must randomly select a number of these users to call and get a reference from. Also contact those in your industry and ask them if they use this type of equipment or know someone who does that you can get a reference from. Depending on the price of the equipment in question you will determine how many to call and if you should go see the equipment on site.

You must be talking to users who use the same equipment day in and day out and preferably for similar applications. You want to ask about performance, service, dependability, consumable cost, ease of operation, and any other applicable questions regarding the equipment you are considering.

Do not allow the sales rep to give you only two or three references. Why? Well, first they could be set ups. Secondly, the ones given may not use the equipment in the same manner or with the same frequency as you will be using it for. Lastly, if they only have a very limited number of references to offer you, you may be considering unproven equipment. If this is the case you better ask yourself why? None of those reasons should be acceptable to you.

On one occasion I called a supplier provided referral and was told the purchase was one they regretted very much and the equipment was once again out for repairs. On another occasion I was told that the new $100,000 piece of equipment I was considering was the worst investment they had ever made. They had owned it for over a year and still did not know how to use it properly.

Don't be a guinea pig for new equipment. Many companies rush new equipment to the market too fast in an effort to grab market share and recover R&D costs. Often this equipment is inadequately tested under actual field conditions. By selling it to you they are in effect charging you to test market their equipment. Not only could this be a cost control nightmare, but think of what this could do to your quality control efforts and productivity. How can your expectations be met if the equipment does not have a performance record?

If this isn't enough to convince you think about this. How can they have experienced service reps for this brand new technology? The answer is of course that they cannot. The only way the service reps can get in the field experience in servicing the new equipment is by servicing it in the field under actual end user working conditions.

They will learn on the job. If you are one of the first customers of this new equipment who do you think will be paying for this on the job training? Who do you think will suffer the down time? Who do you think will pay high service costs caused by full rate repairmen who are learning on the job? Need a clue? Look in the mirror.

Shop very carefully for the computer hardware you need. Unless you have mainframe needs or a very complex system for most, or at least many, of your computer hardware needs you should be able to save 20% to 80% off the retail price of your personal computers by shopping the superstores, computer stores, and direct mail sources.

Resource
The Computer Shopper. A monthly catalog listing the ads from hundreds of software and hardware vendors. You can find this in most bookstores and newsstands or call 1-800-848-8990.

Old advice that is still often overlooked. Buying a computer? Take heed of the very commonly heard, but all too often ignored, advice. Find the software you want first and then buy the hardware. You will save your company a great deal of money and yourself a great deal of frustration by doing this. I know. I went to work for a company that bought the hardware system and then spent the next 5 years trying to customize software to run on it.

You want to buy existing software that you can run and, if needed, adapt your operation to. Trying to build software around your company will cost your company a great deal of money and you your sanity.

Let me give you an example that happened very recently. Our computer has very poor sales reporting features. I wanted to upgrade the software to a more usable system. The computer consultant we use told us it would be no problem. He would just create one for our company at a cost of about $12,000. After the door hit him in the ass on the way out he came back in and suddenly remembered that he had already completed a custom job like ours for another client and he could just mirror it for us with a few modifications for about $5,000.

What a deal, now he was going to resell me a system he had already been paid to create for someone else. This time I held the door open for him. I wanted to make sure he did not come back.

Had we had the right system to begin with I could have upgraded to a very good sales reporting program for about $500. There are several lessons in here did you get them all? Think.

Do not automatically upgrade your computer software every time a new version is released. Modifications made to new versions are not always worth the added cost. Find out what has changed or been added with the new version and then decide if it is worth the added cost to upgrade. Even if the new features sound nice you must ask yourself if you need them and are they cost justified?

Finally, remember that all too often new releases are rushed to the market before they should be and as a result the product has not always been as thoroughly tested as it should have been. This means that the new software is being tested on the market. This can create a very costly and expensive situation for you to deal with. The normal resolution in a case like this is that another new version is created and rushed to the market. A new version that corrects the problems discovered in the first new version.

Guess who is paying for these corrections? Guess who must deal with the frustrations until the second "new" version comes out? Guess who must pay for any costs incurred as a result of problems with the first new version?

You may find it is a wise move to wait awhile before upgrading to any new version so that you can see what happens to other companies who have upgraded.

Don't need it? Don't use it? Sell it! Sell off all unused equipment and inventory. This will generate income, lower your asset base which could help you reduce your tax liability, and frees up space which can be put to more productive uses.

Never buy more protection than you will need. Try to give yourself the option of ala carte maintenance / service contract. If you feel you need to have a service contract at least consider covering only some components. While this is obviously not practical for some types of equipment with many others it will not only be practical but an excellent way to cover yourself while saving serious money.

In Pursuit of Profits. How To At Least Double Your Profits Without Increasing Your Sales.

For example, on our computer system I placed a hardware contract only on the CPU, the main system printer and 1 terminal. This reduced my cost by 60%. I left all other printers and 5 terminals uncovered. The amount of money I saved would have allowed me to buy a new terminal and a new printer every year if warranted. This is in essence a form of self-insurance. Over the last 5 years of doing this I have never had a problem and have saved over $10,000.

When I had a new phone system put in I used the same strategy. I covered the main switchboard phone and 1 back up. I left 19 other phones uncovered. This cut my service contract costs by over 80%. To provide added insurance, when I purchased the system I also negotiated the purchase of 2 extra phones for less than 25% of the list price. I was able to do this of course because at that point the salesman's objective was to sell me the whole system and 2 extra phones meant little to him. Had I attempted to purchase them at a later time they would have cost considerably more.

Now, if an uncovered phone broke down I had a back up allowing me time to find the lowest cost method of repairing it, including sending it out for repairs, which is much lower cost since no on site service call is needed. I bought brand name equipment with a very strong track record of dependability. This was all checked out before the purchase was made and what little risk was left was inexpensively planned for and covered. This proactive strategy allowed me to save 80% of the cost with very little risk.

Please note, that this is a perfect example of proactive cost control. Because I avoided the high cost up front there appears to be no actual savings involved. I did not cut the cost of an existing expense which is very visible. Instead I prevented the high expense from ever existing which is far more effective but not so easily seen.

Do not hire someone to do what you can do yourself. Train your employees who use equipment to handle basic maintenance. This will reduce down time and reduce repair costs.

Should you hire an on staff repairman? Monitor your repair bills. Depending on how much you spend on repairs you may find it worthwhile to consider hiring a full time repairman on staff.

I know one large four color printer who was spending over $250,000 per year in repair bills and travel time with the manufacturer's service department. They also lost a great deal more money in lost production time, forced overtime needed to make it up, and missed deadlines. To solve all these problems at once and to save some serious money, they hired the repairman away from the manufacturer.

They paid him $70,000 per year, which was $10,000 more than he had been making. They eliminated all travel time. They saved over $180,000 and had no waiting time for a repairmen to arrive and, as a result, realized a significant reduction in down time which improved both productivity and customer service. They also had much better maintained presses which extended the life of the equipment.

There is always a better way. For smaller shops look into hiring a retired repair person to work with you on maintenance and repairs. You will get a skilled person who in all likelihood will be delighted to subsidize his meager retirement pay while being back in the game.

If you are unable to locate a retired repairmen for your type of repair and maintenance needs consider hiring someone to moonlight. I have saved thousands of dollars a year in repair costs by hiring a larger shop's foreman to do basic repairs on my equipment after work and on weekends. I pay him $30 an hour which is equal to time and a half for him and I save the normal $94 per hour of the manufacturer's service cost plus I do not pay for the travel time charged by the manufacturer.

This saves me about $5,000 per year. Over ten years this will save me over $50,000 based on current rates. At a pretax profit ratio of 2.5%, I would need to increase my sales $200,000 to realize the same bottom line profit increase of $5,000 per year. Over ten years this would mean I would need to generate $2,000,000 in added sales simply to realize the same bottom line impact. You must learn to think like this. Over and over again you will see me give you examples like this. Learning to think like this will take time and I will constantly remind you of how important it is.

How many copies did you say we made? Employee abuse of photo copies is one of the biggest areas of theft in most companies. You must control abuse and reduce costs in this area. It has been estimated that up to 25% of all photo copying done on business copiers is done for personal use.

Think of the money this is costing you. This is increasing your costs for service, electricity, paper, toner, developer, and oil. It is also causing unwarranted wear and tear on your machine which will shorten it's life and force you to purchase a newer one sooner.

Furthermore, since much of this abuse will take place during the workday, you are also losing time and productivity from employees who are using work time to conduct personal business on your equipment using your materials.

You must take steps to prevent this from happening. One way is to purchase high end machines that have built in volume controls and requires the use of access codes. With these machines each employee authorized to use the machine has an access code or card that must be used to make any copies. Reports are generated that detail the use of the machine by each employee including how often it was used, when, and for how many copies.

These machines will provide you with excellent control and accounting features but they are very costly. Too costly for many small businesses. They are also overkill for many small businesses. You could not justify the cost based on your usage even including employee abuse.

But you still need to control abuses and you still need to make it known that you are monitoring copier usage and that personal use of the company copiers is not acceptable. Start by placing any and all copiers in a very central and visible location. This step by itself will go a long way towards discouraging personal use of the copier.

It will be much more difficult for an employee to use your copier for personal use if it is in a location that has high traffic and is visible by all. A copier stuck in a back room or out of the way will invite your employees to use it for personal use. Out of sight is the wrong place to put it.

You should also monitor your volume on all copiers. Copiers all have counters on them that are easy to locate and read. This is how the service people know what your usage levels are which are used to determine your service contract costs.

Keep a log next to each copier and at the end of each day and the beginning of each day mark down the count. Do not do it just once a day. For example, if you track counts only at the beginning of each day you will never know if someone is coming in the office at night and using the machine or staying after work and using the copier.

In Pursuit of Profits. How To At Least Double Your Profits Without Increasing Your Sales.

By tracking counts in the morning and at the end of the day you will clearly know if someone is using the copier after hours. Remember, after hours your employees can use the copiers not only for personal use but also to copy company files and records.

By taking these steps you will also be providing an added measure of internal security. Also remember, more than one cleaning company has been known to use client's equipment at night for personal projects. Do not let this happen in your company. The daily counts kept in the log will also allow you to see any unusual usage patterns that may indicate abuses are taking place.

If you think that the cost of employee abuse is overstated, think again. Let me give you an example of how to figure out how much personal use of the company copier could be costing you. Let's say you have a copier that you paid $5,000 for. Let's also say that you pay $1,000 in annual service costs and another $500 per year on consumable products such as paper, toner, and developer based on an annual average of 60,000 copies per year.

Assume you keep the copier for 4 years and for the sake of this example assume at the end of 4 years it has no real value. Using these figures your 4 year cost would be $5,000 for the machine, $4,000 in maintenance related costs, and $2,000 in consumable costs for a total cost of $11,000. Dividing this by the 240,000 copies you have made over the 4 years your cost will be just under .05 per copy made. This, by the way, is how you should estimate your actual costs of a copier. At a cost of .05 per copy and 60,000 copies per year, your effective annual costs are $3,000.

If 25% of these costs are incurred as a result of employee abuse, you are paying $750 more than you should each year for every machine you have. Year in and year out. Over the 4 years this is a loss of $3,000 per machine not even including the lost time and productivity that occurs when your employees are using your copiers for personal business on company time. Now multiply this total by the number of copiers you have. Think in these terms. Translate percentages into lost dollars and you will see how much more meaning expenses suddenly start having to you.

How many copies are you being charged for? By totaling the daily counts kept in your photo copier logs you will be able to develop monthly and yearly usage totals for each machine. These should then be used to determine what volume level you should purchase on any service contracts you have on each machine. By knowing that a machine only uses 5,000 copies a month on average, or 60,000 a year, you will not be paying for a service contract based on a higher total. This is a very frequent occurrence.

Many companies have no idea of their usage levels so they either guess or simply follow the suggestion of the copier service company regarding how many copies should be covered in the basic contract. If each year you are taking a service contract out for the same volume as the year before, then it is very likely that you are paying for a copy volume that is too high. By this, I mean that if every year your contract renewal comes in at say, 60,000 copies, you are very likely overpaying by covering an annual copy volume that you are not using.

How can I say this? Think about it. Do you think the service company would keep giving you a contract for the same volume when you kept exceeding the allowable usage? Of course not. They are in business to make money. Any time they get a chance to increase the volume of a contract they will. The higher the volume covered, the higher the cost of the contract. This translates into higher sales.

On the other hand, they are not about to ever suggest to you that you lower the copy volume no matter how far below the covered volume of copies you fall. This would cost them business. If your contract is for 60,000 copies per year and you only use 40,000 per year do you think they are going to suggest a lower volume on your next contract?

You must therefore assume that anytime your renewal volume indicated on your new contract is the same as the previous year, that you are overpaying. By keeping your own log of copy counts you will be able to verify this. You will also be able to verify or dispute any amounts that the service company may bill you for what they claim exceeds the covered number of copies above the contract amount. Your service agreement is almost sure to contain a clause that makes you pay added service costs for any number of copies over a specified amount. If you have no idea of the amount you use you have no way to know if you are being charged for copies you never made.

Remember, even if you are dealing with an honest company mistakes can be made. The service man could very easily have misread the copier counter or an incorrect billing could be made. Knowing your annual volume usage will also enable you to purchase the right capacity copier in the future.

Preventive maintenance can save you a fortune. You must have a program of routine maintenance in place for all your equipment, machines, and vehicles. Proper routine maintenance will save you money and lost time in the long run and will extend the life of your equipment. As pointed out in another strategy your people should be trained to handle this if possible.

Major problems cost you money and lower your productivity. Replacement equipment will also represent a significant cost. To ignore routine maintenance and suffer these problems is inexcusable. Develop a program and make sure it is adhered to.

Do you need a service contract at all? Never automatically assume you do. Many companies assume they should always have one. They are wrong. For many, perhaps even most, pieces of high quality equipment service contracts can be an unneeded and very expensive insurance policy. For lower cost equipment the service contract may cost you more than the equipment itself. Review all the strategies I have listed here and make sure any service contract you purchase is cost justified and purchased properly.

Don't purchase a service contract at the same time you purchase your equipment. Most new equipment will come with a 12 month warranty. This means that if you purchase a service contract it will not even take effect until the 13th month. You have, in effect, prepaid for a service that offers you no protection or any benefit of any kind for 12 months.

Not only is this a very costly use of your money and a very poor example of cost control, but it also drains your cash. Furthermore, it takes away all your options to find lower cost alternative service and you once again run the risk that the company you have purchased the contract from will not even be in business in a year. You may also find that the service is so bad during the first year of ownership that you do not even want this same company to provide your service the next year. If you have already bought the service contract you have a problem.

The only possible justification that could exist for doing this would be if you felt it was protecting you against a large price increase in the cost of the contract a year from now. This, of course, is probably just the feeling the sales representative is trying to give you.

To neutralize this issue, simply make your purchase conditional on you having the option (in writing of course) to purchase the service contract at today's rates and terms at the end of the warranty period. Notice I said the option not the obligation. If they will not agree to this, take your business somewhere else.

In Pursuit of Profits. How To At Least Double Your Profits Without Increasing Your Sales.

When do you need a service contract? As I pointed out in an earlier strategy if you purchase new equipment right you will have very few, if any, maintenance problems in the first few years and you will, as a result, have a number of cost saving options. With this in mind, find out if a full service maintenance contract can be added at any time. Remember, most service departments are run as a separate profit center. This means a sale of a maintenance contract is as important to them as the sale of the product is to the sales department.

Whether the sale of this contract comes at the time of purchase or much later it is still a sale. If you have the option of adding a contract when you want to, you have yourself a tremendous option. You can start by not carrying a service contract, instead only purchasing repairs on an as needed basis paying for both parts and labor as required. When a very costly repair comes along all you need to do is simply call up and have the contract put in place.

Sounds crazy, but I have done it many times. For example, we had a piece of equipment that cost $1,300 per year to cover under a service contract. I waited almost 3 years to put it under contract. When I was given an estimate for a repair that cost over $1,500 I simply called and had it placed under contract. This contract lasted 1 year after which I did not renew until a repair estimate large enough to justify it came up again. Of course, during the covered year I had all basic preventive maintenance done while covered by the service contract.

By doing this I paid for one years worth of service under contract and effectively was able to protect myself for 4 years and even then the cost of the contract was less than the cost of the repair needed. Even after adding in the cost of my time and labor repairs I saved over $4,000 using this strategy with no risk whatsoever.

Are you paying list prices or accepting so called "standard" terms? Remember service contract prices are list prices. All prices are list prices. Don't be brainwashed into thinking anything else. You should never pay list prices. Let me repeat that. You should never pay list prices.

If you feel compelled to purchase a service contract get something in return. I have received lower prices, extended coverage, free supplies, free installation, free delivery, and numerous other concessions whenever I have put a service contract on any piece of equipment I own. Why not, since this is a second purchase with the same company? I am a valuable repeat customer. I expect to be treated as such.

If you know that you are going to purchase a service contract when you purchase the equipment that is the time to make your best deal. First, make the best deal you can on the equipment. At this point the salesman has a very strong vested interest in closing this deal. He or she is close and they know it. They are probably already counting their commission money. At this point you will be able to very easily get serious concessions on the service.

Start by asking for a no charge extended warranty and work from there. If you can get 6 months of added coverage you have already cut your first year service contract by 50%. This should be very easy. Make it clear that you are ready to buy and the only hold up is the service cost. You will be amazed how creative and flexible they will become.

Let me give you another example, I was considering purchasing a new piece of equipment from a company to whom I owed $3,000 in recent repair bills. The new equipment was going to cost about $30,000. So, after getting the best price I could, I started whining and indicating that my anger over those high repair bills was the only thing holding up the purchase.

Well, the next day what do you know, I was advised that if I purchased the new piece of equipment the repair bills totaling $3,000 would be wiped out. I did not have to deal with the service department at all. All I needed to do was express a needed element before I would agree to purchase.

Should you move an outside function inside or an inside function outside? This is a very simplistic viewpoint of a complex subject but I want to at least plant the seed of thought. If you spend a large amount of money on outside purchases for a certain product or function look into doing it yourself.

For example, I know one company that was spending over $250,000 per year in outside printing costs. They bought $50,000 worth of equipment and hired a pressman for $20,000 per year and reduced their outside printing cost by 90%. Along with the resulting drop in cost of sales they also had better control over quality and delivery. Conversely, if too many resources are being tied up internally examine the cost effectiveness of moving that function outside. This is the reason payroll processing companies exist. Ask the questions!

Consider all your options for service on equipment. Look into having your routine maintenance and repair needs covered by a service company instead of by the original equipment manufacturer (OEM) or the distributor. Often they are much less expensive and normally are run by former service people from the OEM who have struck out on their own. This means they have the same training and know what the OEM and distributor rates are. To be competitive they will charge lower rates.

Let me give you a first hand example using that used typesetter I discussed earlier. The OEM offered a yearly service contract on this piece of equipment at a cost of $8,500. I was not going to pay this amount so I contacted other service companies until I found one that covered this equipment.

I found a few of them by reading trade magazines and a few others by contacting companies in the area that might use this type of equipment. The people I contacted were, without exception, very glad to advise me who they used or knew of who covered this type of equipment.

The best alternative to the OEM contract appeared to be a local service company that would provide me with the exact same service for $5,600. This is a savings of $2,900 or 34 %. Over a ten year period this would save me $29,000. I must admit it did take me about 2 hours to find this second source but, at an effective rate of $14,500 per hour I felt it was time well spent.

However, during my conversations with other owners of this type of equipment I learned that their machines were very dependable. In fact, they were so dependable that rarely did these machines require anything more than routine preventive maintenance.

The major parts in these machines were circuit boards that rarely broke down and when they did the circuit board simply could be pulled out and replaced. This led me to think I could save even more money by hiring someone to check my equipment every six months on an hourly basis for a routine cleaning. I then dug a bit more and found a company that would cover all my parts on the machine for $100 per month.

For a fee of $1,200 per year I now had 100% of all parts covered. Since 99% of all repairs would involve the circuit boards I had no need to have a service contract. We could simply conduct any repairs we needed ourselves by popping the old boards out and snapping the new boards in. It sounded simple and it was.

Now we had effectively dropped our cost from $8,500 to $1,200. A savings of $7,300 per year. Over the next ten years, using current rates, this would save us $73,000. Hard to believe but true. Figure out how much you would have to increase sales to generate a bottom line profit equal to this. In my case at that time I would have had to increase sales $292,000 per year or $2,920,000 over ten years just to recover the amount I saved.

The key was thinking and asking questions. It always is!!

In Pursuit of Profits. How To At Least Double Your Profits Without Increasing Your Sales.

Independent service companies usually have lower overhead and therefore can charge lower rates and make equal or even higher profits. Also never forget that the manufacturer is in business to manufacture and sell new equipment. Service is profitable, but they stay in business and grow through new equipment sales.

This sets up a potential conflict of interest, especially on older equipment. If you feel service costs and breakdowns are too costly you will most likely consider purchasing a new piece of equipment. A manufacturer can aid you in reaching this decision by raising service costs, terminating contracts, delaying service, and misleading you on the condition of your equipment. Remember, the service department works for the manufacturer or dealer.

On a smaller scale we were able to find a local service shop to provide service on our photocopier at a rate far lower than the same service that was being provided by the OEM. The OEM was charging us $856 per year. The local service company, who provided much quicker service, charged us only $256 per year. We reduced this cost by 70 % and got better service. **This is Total Cost Control.**

Who are you buying your parts from? If you use an independent service company always compare the cost of buying the parts you need from the service company versus buying them direct from the parts department of the manufacturer. By ordering them direct and providing the needed parts to the service company you may be able to save 25% or more on the cost of the part since you are not paying the service company mark up and you will also be insuring that you are getting a new part, and not a used or rebuilt part, and being charged for a new part.

How fast do you need service? Find out if different response time options are offered and, if so, at what price. Don't assume they will provide you with all options, this may not happen. They may only present you with the most expensive options. For instance, if same day response is offered at a price 25% higher than next day response you must determine if this added cost is justified. Not nice to have, but justified.

Make sure your vendor knows you are paying attention. You should dispute and / or complain about your repair bills every once in a while even if you really don't have a complaint. You want them to know that you are monitoring all bills and that they better not think of padding a bill or cheating you in any way. Keep them on their toes. Be proactive. Never demonstrate complacency.

Are you paying attention? If you are having repairs done and are paying for the job by the hour make sure that you are tracking the time yourself. Padding of hours and rounding off of hours are all too common. If they worked 1 hour and 20 minutes this is not 1 hour and 30 minutes. If your repair rate is $90 per hour you are being charged $1.50 per minute. If they round off 20 minutes to 30 minutes you have just thrown way $15. You have also overpaid by 50% since 20 minutes would cost you $30 while 30 minutes will cost you $45. Do you enjoy overpaying by 50%? Thinking this way will get your attention more than thinking that you overpaid by $15. Either way you are being cheated.

Good customer relations or bill padding socializing? Make sure that any repairman working on your time is not spending time socializing with your people. For example, we had a repairman in working on our equipment for 2 hours one day. After the repairs were done he hung around and talked to my production people for about 1/2 hour. It was near the end of the day and I figured he was just killing time before he went home for the day.

I found out a week later, when I got the bill, that not only did they try to charge me for this time but also another 1/2 hour that he was not even in my building. He was killing time all right, time he expected me to pay for. Of course he was wrong. Keeping a log of the time the repairman was actually on the job will ensure proper billing.

Do not pay to provide your vendor's education. Don't pay full rates for inexperienced repairmen. I fully appreciate the need for new repairmen to gain experience. I also fully understand that due to their inexperience they will often take two or three times longer finding and correcting a problem than a more seasoned man would take. This is assuming he diagnosed the problem correctly.

What I do not understand, and will not tolerate, is that most companies expect you to pay for this training by charging you full rates. Not only is your down time increased, but you have the pleasure of paying for it. Don't let them pull this on you. This is a routine situation, and like so many others, one that often goes unchallenged.

Don't tolerate this! If you have any doubts about the experience and capabilities of the repairman question them. Get a written estimate of exactly what is wrong and what the cost to affect the repairs will be. Then call in another company and get another estimate. You will quickly find out if your suspicions are correct. You can then negotiate a reduced rate or demand a repairman who can complete the repairs in accordance with the time they should take. Or use the alternative repair source.

Two when one will do. Another trick repair shops will use to overcharge you is to send two men for a one man job. They may be slow and just want to bill you double time or one man may be training another man. Either way don't let them charge you for two men and don't let them charge you full price for the time they are there if one is training the other. If this is the case the repairs are going to take much longer since one man must be showing and explaining things to the other. Don't pay for that training.

Are you paying them to get to work? Charging for travel time is another very common and very profitable method repair shops will use to overcharge you. I know firsthand as this scam has been tried on me many times.

Let me give you an actual example. I called the service department of the manufacturer for a service call. This shop was located about 10 miles away. The next day the man came and made the repairs. About a week later I got the bill. Much to my surprise it included 6 hours travel time, tolls, and a parking charge.

Now we do not charge for parking. There were no tolls between the repair shop and our plant and even driving the way a cab driver in New York takes a tourist, I could not understand how 10 miles became 300. Upon questioning the invoice I was advised we had to pay for the repairman's travels from his last job to our plant, not from the repair shop to our plant. In this case they claimed he had been out of state. They expected us to pay for his travel back from that state to our facility.

The company in question by the way is a worldwide company and this is their practice worldwide. To say I was outraged would have been a monumental understatement. I promptly drafted a letter which questioned this practice and sent it to the president of this company. It was clear to me that they were double billing. They were charging round trip travel to the customer out of state and then billing the next customer (in this case my company) for the same return travel.

There was also no way to know if the repairman had even been out of state or if he just came right over from 10 miles away and simply claimed to be out of state. In either case, I questioned both the ethics and legality of this practice. I then demanded to see a written policy that justified this practice and that had been agreed to by our company. Then I asked for proof that this travel had indeed occurred.

In Pursuit of Profits. How To At Least Double Your Profits Without Increasing Your Sales.

Needless to say I never received any such proof of the travel nor of the policy agreement. Instead, what I got back was a letter from the president that stated I would be given credit for all travel time in question and that in the future we would never be charged for more than 20 miles of travel. Imagine that. Do you think they did this under the guise of customer service? Of course not! They did this because they were afraid I was going to sue their butts off and the publicity might prohibit them from overcharging other companies. Using this practice they could, and most likely do, bill out 24 hours or more in an 8 hour day.

If you use a postage meter make sure that it is being read and the usage totals are being recorded every night and every morning. Your postage meter can be a significant source of employee theft. Most companies either do not record usage figures or they only record them at the end of each day. If an employee is going to steal postage from your meter they will very often do it after hours or on the weekend. If you are only recording usage every night you will have no way to spot any theft since all legitimate postage used during the day will cover up any abuses from the night before or early morning that day.

Never pay rent on a coffee machine. If a service charges you rent find another one that will not or buy your own machine. In fact, depending on your time and the amount of coffee, the cheapest way in the long run to provide coffee in your office will be to buy your own machine and coffee. See the next strategy.

Think about what your coffee service does for you. How much did you come up with? Let me think. They lend or rent you a machine and pots. They sell you coffee, cups, sugar, creamora, and perhaps tea. What do you do? You make the coffee, clean the pots and the machines. What is wrong with this picture? Does it seem that you do all the work and they make the profit? It should because that is what happens. One way or the other you will be doing the work so why not at least dramatically reduce your costs in this area.

How? Simple. Buy the machines and pots yourself. Depending on whether you buy new or used and depending on how many burners you need it will cost you from $10 to $200 per machine. O.K., now you own a machine. Big deal right? If the coffee service was providing the machine for free you have gained nothing. If you were renting it you might have saved a few dollars. Great strategy Derrick.

Let's not bad mouth the author just yet. The savings are not in owning the machines, but in buying your own coffee and supplies. Let me give you an example of the savings in one company. They used a coffee service that sold them 120 bags of coffee for $74.60. This is .622 per bag. Each bag yielded 10 cups of coffee. This is about 6 cents per cup.

They can buy this coffee by direct mail from an office supply house like Viking at the rate of $18.89 for 46 bags. This is .41 per bag. Again using ten cups per bag, this costs about 4 cents per cup. They have saved 2 cents per cup. Sounds like an insignificant savings? 2 cents a cup? Wow. Big deal? Well, their people drank 500 cups a day and they saved $10 per day. I know, I know. Hold down the excitement if you can. Get out those blood pressure pills.

Remember, think long and short term. They have reduced their coffee costs by 33%. They are saving $10 per day, $50 per week, $2,600 per year. Now if $2,600 means nothing to you send it to me. I would be delighted to take it off your hands.

If your pretax profit is 2.5% you would need to increase your sales by over $104,000 just to generate the same amount of added profit. How hard is it for you to generate an added $104,000 in sales?

I have shown you how easy it is to save an amount equal to the profit you might make on those sales. For a larger company that might use 100,000 cups a day you are looking at a savings of over $520,000 per year. Over ten years this comes to over $5,200,000. A $5,200,000 savings for doing nothing but ordering your own coffee direct and eliminating the service. All this from a mere .02 per cup savings!

Am I getting your attention now? I hope so. **Never look at any savings as insignificant.** You must always consider the long and short term results, the effort required to realize the savings, and the domino effect. How many ways could you use this $5,200,000 to save and make even more money? I will also remind you no savings of any amount is insignificant. Some are more significant than others but none are insignificant. If feasible, you can purchase your coffee and supplies at a local wholesale club or grocery store. By doing so your savings will be even greater.

This coffee service was also providing soda at $12.50 per case of 24 cans. I can buy the same soda at a wholesale club for $6.00 per case. A savings of over 50%. These types of savings can also be realized for all your paper goods. Most people do not realize that by buying these through a wholesale club, grocery store, or even a direct mail office supply house you can cut the costs of your paper goods by 25% to 50% when compared to the cost of buying them from your coffee service or cleaning service.

On this latter subject I recommend you read my strategies on how to reduce your cleaning costs.

Think small to realize big profits. Do you have bottled water in your office? Do you use a coffee service? Well if you do, and if you ignore my other strategies on this topic, here is a way to reduce your costs anyway. At one point we used bottled water and a coffee service. We used the bottled water because the town water was of very poor quality. (If the water had not been of such poor quality I would have dropped the bottled water and the coffee service and bought our own coffee direct as I have shown you above).

We used 180 gallons per month or 2,160 gallons of water per year. We also used 120 bags of coffee per month or 1,440 per year. The bottled water company charged us $6 per 5 gallon bottle or $1.20 per gallon. They also charged us a monthly rental fee for the cooler of $12. The annual costs for our bottled water came to $2,736. The coffee service charged us .62 per bag of coffee or a total of $893 per year. The total costs of these two vendors came to $3,629 per year.

By replacing both of these vendors with one vendor who provided the coffee and the bottled water, we were able to realize significant savings. How? Simple. This vendor had a coffee machine that connected into the bottled water cooler. At the touch of a button coffee was made instantly. This new vendor charged us $5.50 per bottle of water or .917 per gallon. They also charged us .452 for a bag of coffee. The total annual costs for this new vendor came to $2,726.

The annual dollar savings was $903. We saved 25% on our water and coffee costs with this one simple change in vendors. We made no sacrifice in quality and, in fact, realized a number of secondary benefits. We also now only pay one vendor instead of two. This cut the costs of processing my accountants payable for these services by 50%.

Furthermore, we also saved a fair amount of time each year. Since time is money, I have saved more money. How? Making coffee from a water cooler takes about 3 minutes. This, of course, includes an employee standing by the water cooler filling up the pot. With the new system we just push a button and the coffee is made automatically.

At the rate of 120 pots of coffee a month we saved 360 minutes or 6 hours per month of wasted labor. Annually this is 72 hours. At $8 per hour we effectively saved another $576 per year while at the same time we increased productivity since we no longer had an employee standing around a water cooler filling a coffee pot. We also no longer had a problem over who gets stuck making the coffee as no one has a problem pushing a button. Does the domino effect come to mind?

This one little change improved morale, reduced costs nearly $1,500, and improved productivity. It also did something else. Something very important. It sent a message to the employees. It conveyed to them how serious I was about controlling costs. It told them we were doing all we could to control and reduce costs without sacrificing the quality of our product or the comfort of their working conditions. This is what total cost control is all about. How many departments are in your company that could realize similar savings?

Consider owning your own vending machines. By doing so you can create your own profit center while lowering costs to your employees. If you choose to keep the profits you have made money. Money that can be used to make you more money. If you prefer you can use this money to offset employee benefit costs in other areas thereby reducing your costs in those areas.

Vending machines come in all sizes, both for very large and very small companies. A machine that holds 60 to 80 snacks can cost as low as $650 and are virtually maintenance free. Soda machines can run under $1,000. Look at some of the average profit margins on the products dispensed by these machines.

Cigarettes	$.75 to $1 per pack
Snacks / candies	.35 to .50 per snack
Soft drinks / juices	.35 to .50 per drink
Soup /tea /coffee	.28 to .40 per cup

As you can see, even a small company can turn a cost center into a profit center very easily. Even 10 sales a day at a .40 profit per sale, will generate $4 profit. This is $20 per week and over $1,000 per year. Most companies will average a much higher number of sales than ten per day. At the time of this writing, according to the a study reported in Vending Times, the average candy and snack machine sells 171 units per week. The annual sales per machine is $5,362.

The average price per sale is	.65
The average cost per sale is	.25
Leaving an average profit of	.40 per sale.

This creates an average annual profit per machine of $3,556 per year.

They also reported that for soft drinks and juice machines the average machine dispensed 259 drinks per week.

The average price per sales was	.75
The average cost per sale was	.25
Leaving an average profit per sale of	.50 This represents an average annual profit of $6,734.

These are potential profits per machine. Please note, these are averages and may or may not be an accurate projection of what sales volume in your company may be. Many things affect the sales levels of a vending machine including the number of employees and visitors you have, what the machine is stocked with, and what the selling price is. My point here is not to project profits for you. You can do that yourself. I merely want to give you ideas. Ideas on how to control and reduce costs. Ideas you can explore and expand on. Think. Thinking is always the key.

If you have a vendor who provides your soda machine and soda make sure that if this vendor charges you a deposit for the cans you get a credit or refund for each empty can he redeems.   Why should you pay a deposit on cans that are redeemed by the vendor? If he does not provide a collection bin for these cans and does not redeem them, you should. The deposit money returned for all cans redeemed can add up to enough money over the course of a year to make your collection and redemption efforts fiscally worthwhile.

You will also be doing something good for the earth and you will be reducing your rubbish disposal costs. Since this income was actually generated by the employees who purchased the soda and juice you may want to give the money back to them or use it for some sort of employee benefit.

Chapter 18. Facility related overhead.

"If we are to achieve results never before accomplished, then we must be prepared to employ methods never before attempted."

Sir Francis Bacon

If you own the building appeal your tax assessment. Property values have dropped dramatically in the commercial real estate market and there is a very good chance your property is overvalued for tax purposes. I recently looked at a piece of commercial property that was exactly like a dozen other buildings in the same industrial complex. The price of the property I was looking at was selling for less than half of the price of all the other buildings that had sold only two years before.

The property tax on the building I was looking at would have also been less than half of the property tax the owners of the other buildings were paying. The reason was that the property tax was based on the current value which was reflected in the selling price. Every one of the owners of the other buildings should have been down at city hall screaming for a tax abatement. Perhaps you should be as well.

If you are unsuccessful try again and again for as long as the law allows. Why push so hard? Two reasons. First, commercial property tax is usually very high. To pacify the voters, who are the residential market, those in power will instead raise the rates or the assessment, of the commercial building owners.

As always, those in government find the risk takers of the world as a perfect target. Be it an investor or businessman, they relentlessly seek more ways to separate the achievers of the world from their money. This, of course, removes all incentive for the most productive of our society. But my point is not to discuss business versus the government. My point is to advise you a reassessment can result in significant savings.

The second reason should be obvious. Any amount you save on taxes will be an amount you save every year. Remember the domino effect. A reassessment may also save you money on your insurance.

If you lease the building you operate out of and have paid a security deposit and or last month's rent, make sure that these funds are earning interest during the period they are being held. Leases last years and if you have given them a deposit or prepayment of rent, you have probably given them thousands of dollars. Over a five or ten year period the interest earned on this money can be significant. The purpose you have given the landlord this money for is not to earn interest on it. They should not use your money to make money. Make sure you have an agreement for the money to earn interest and for it to be provided to you.

"The actions you take or fail to take, today, determine the results you will realize tomorrow."

Derrick W. Welch

Think of tomorrow. When things are going well all too many companies think nothing of living the high life so to speak. They move into first class office space and spend a small fortune on furniture and fixtures. They think the good times will never end and that the bottom line will continue to grow. They react by thinking too optimistically and they spend to feed egos and image. Business is cyclical. The bad times will always follow the good ones. You must always look beyond today.

Don't saddle your company with overhead you may have a great deal of difficulty covering one day. More than one company has gone out of business for this exact reason. You must select your facilities, furniture, and fixtures based on need not ego, functionality and not image. You do not need a Mercedes when a Honda will do quite nicely for a lot less money.

When things are good spend your money on things that will improve your company. Liquidate long term debts while you can, upgrade equipment to increase productivity, invest in R &D, and reward key employees. Put your profits where they belong, in making your company a better operation and laying a solid foundation for the difficult times that are sure to come.

Do you need more space? Before you rush out and look for new facilities and incur the high cost of moving and new larger overhead, look within. Find out why you need more space. Find out what space you have that is wasted. Look for every way possible to eliminate wasted space.

Your first objective should always be to find ways not to add to your overhead. In this case the objective should be to find ways to eliminate the need to move into new facilities or lease more space. Once you have eliminated all wasted space and reorganized your office, warehouse, or factory layout in the most efficient manner possible, if you still find you need more space think creatively.

Have you ever seen the ads for companies that manufacture closet organizers? They show a closet before they install their closet organization system. The "before" closet looks like my teenage daughter's room. Which looks like a bomb went off in it. The "after" closet looks so good that you want to run right out and get the closet organization system. The new closet can fit 5 times as much in it and everything is so organized that you couldn't lose that low cut, see thru outfit you do not want your teenager daughter to wear if you tried.

The point is that you have organizational options to create more space that you have not even thought about. Look into shelving, cubicles, partitions, mezzanines, floor to ceiling filing cabinets. A one time cost in these areas will save you tens of thousands of dollars compared to a higher monthly overhead.

You will be amazed at what creatively utilized space will do for you. I mean amazed. Effectively used space can double or even triple the usable space you have in your company for a one time cost that is a fraction of the cost you would incur each year to rent the same amount of space.

For example an 8 x 10 room can easily contain two, 5 x 8 cubicles effectively providing office space for two people instead of one. A 10,000 square foot warehouse with high ceilings can become a 20,000 foot warehouse with the use of a mezzanine.

Modular offices allow for flexibly and maximum space usage. You can also move them as needed and even take them with you if you are forced to move. Moving to, or leasing, new space should be a course of last resort. Call in some companies that specialize in this type of space planning and let the experts give you ideas.

At the end of each year have a set procedure in place to go through all your filing cabinets and either throw out or store all unneeded files and records. Those you need to store should be kept in stackable boxes. Each year you should also look at the files you have stored in the stackable boxes and throw those out that you no longer need. There is no point storing records you no longer need. This simply uses up valuable space and makes it more difficult to access those you do need. All but current files and records should go in storage.

Re-label and reuse all filing cabinets for the upcoming year's records and files. Proper handling of your files and records could make it so that you never need to purchase a new filing cabinet again. In fact, you may find you have more cabinets than you need and can sell some off thereby freeing up space and generating income.

Still need more space? If you need more space determine why you need the space and when. Very often space problems are seasonal and as a result you do not need, and cannot cost justify paying for, year round space. If this is the case, look into leasing space only for the periods of time you need it each year. There are many companies that are saddled with space they do not need year round. Don't become one of them.

In fact, use one of them to solve your temporary space needs. If you need more space on a short, or even long, term basis and the space is for storage of material that you do not need constant access to, consider sub leasing space from another company. Your per foot rate will likely be lower, you will not need to move, and your commitment does not need to be long term.

These companies will be happy to provide you with short term space rentals. Look in your paper and you should find many such companies advertising space for rent. If for some reason you do not, then advertise yourself for the amount of space you need, the type, and the length of time you are seeking it. There is no need to engage the services, and pay the commission, of a commercial real estate agent for this type of activity.

Consider a storage unit. Consider renting a trailer to keep on premises if you have the space. Think. There should be many ways you can solve your short term and seasonal space needs without renting or leasing the added space on a year round basis when you only have sporadic needs.

Remember, renting, or leasing, added space costs more than just the cost of the space. You must also be concerned with added insurance costs, utilities, and maintenance. You simply can't afford all these added costs for a single day longer than they are needed.

Look into executive office suites for a satellite office. These are offices and office suites that provide you with not just offices, but with a full range of support services for a great deal less cost than you would pay to have them dedicated to just your company.

These type of setups share common conference rooms, receptionists, office equipment and the like. Instead of renting your own office and having to pay 100% of these expenses, you rent an office suite and pay a portion of these expenses. You share the service with other tenants and they share the costs with you. You also reduce your capital outlay and avoid any long term cost commitments.

These type of setups can be very cost effective for regional sales offices, offices you are unsure about the feasibility of opening, and companies you are thinking about establishing but are unwilling or unable to commit to on a long term basis. They can be an excellent way to test the feasibility and cost of a permanent office setup without the costs and commitment required to set up your own facilities and hire your own people. This will also allow you to reduce your costs while trying to build up a base of customers or operations that can justify your own office setup and employees.

When you move into new facilities always consider taking less space than you think you need. Normally you will assume you need more space than you actually do Furthermore, I would rather be a bit crowded if the alternative is to be saddled with a higher overhead year round. Overhead that might choke me during tough times. You want to always keep your fixed overhead as low as possible. This overhead may seem fine when sales are high but it can put you out of business when times are tough.

How important is your location? Do not locate in a high traffic, high visibility location unless it is critical to the success of your business. For many businesses location can make or break you. But for others it is nowhere as important. For some it is not important at all.

For example, I moved one company because they did not conduct any retail activity, they had no customers who called on them and labor availability was never a problem. All their business was conducted by sales people on the road, by mail or by phone. Once we determined this, it did not take long to see that a move to the current location was justified and would produce a significant reduction in their fixed overhead. We moved a mere 8 miles away and by doing so cut the facility related overhead by 30%. This move saved this company tens of thousands of dollars per year. Dollars added right to the bottom line.

Consider moving your operations out of state. This strategy has become a very profitable option for many companies. Depending on the size, type of company you have, and your current state, you may find that you can add tens of thousands, hundreds of thousands or even millions of dollars to your bottom line each year by moving to another state.

Many states are very aggressive in soliciting business. They offer tremendous tax advantages and numerous free or low cost services as an incentive to attract new business to their state. These facts combined with what may be much lower labor, operating, insurance, and utility costs, could spell a fiscal bonanza for your company.

I worked with one $3 million dollar company in Taxachusetts that could have reduced their costs by over $150,000 per year simply by moving to another state. This one strategy could increase the bottom line pretax profits of this company by five fold.

With the potential savings involved you would be doing yourself a disservice if you did not at least consider this option. Start by contacting the Chamber of Commerce in the cities or the states you might consider moving to. A hefty bottom line can go a long way to eliminating homesickness.

If you sign a lease make sure you have the option to sub lease the space. This is very important and often overlooked. You always want as many options as you can get in any area of business and life for that matter. Options give you alternatives. Alternatives can sometimes make or break your company. At all times they can help you make more profit.

If you have the option of sub leasing your space you have a number of important options. If you have made a mistake and leased more space than you need you have the option of correcting this mistake by sub leasing the excess space. You may even be able to sub lease it at a profit.

If your business changes or must be reduced in operational size due to business problems, the option of subleasing part of your space may make the difference between staying in business or going out of business. If you find the location you have moved into was a mistake you have the option of sub leasing the entire facility and moving to a more suitable location. Think of what would happen if you did not have this option under these circumstances, and instead, were forced to stay while watching your company go out of business or to pay off a long term lease for space you would not even be using since you had to move elsewhere to survive.

Having the option to sub lease will also allow you the flexibility of moving if you are presented with a much more attractive lease option or a purchase option somewhere else. Imagine having to pass on an excellent opportunity to move into another location at a significant savings simply because you did not demand a sub lease option or you did not think of it.

These are just a few of the scenarios that could develop that would make you very happy if you had the option to sublease. Do not sign a lease without this option. You should have no trouble getting such an option as it matters little to the owner since you are the primary lease holder and as such are the one responsible to him. Also remember, that if you do sub lease part or all of the space you must make sure you are also charging for any other facility related and utility costs that apply.

Negotiate any prepayment clause out of your commercial mortgage. I know that most commercial mortgages carry balloon notes, but nevertheless you want as many options on your side as possible. If you are able to pay off the mortgage early or find a more attractive financing option you want to be able to move on it without incurring a prepayment fee.

If you are unable to get the prepayment clause dropped or if you have a mortgage with this in it and you want to pay off your mortgage early, simply pay all of it off except $1. You will be in compliance and watch how fast your bank changes their tune. The paper work is too costly for them to carry a mortgage for $1.

Add an extra principle payment to your mortgage payment whenever you can. Even a one time added principle payment can save you thousands in interest over the life of your mortgage. Compare that to any other return you can get on this money.

Since this strategy is also suitable for your personal use I will demonstrate this added principle payment concept a bit further by using a residential mortgage as an example. The commercial mortgage works in essence the same way, even on a balloon note. Ask your accountant to run the numbers for you as they apply to your mortgage and see how much money you will save based on your commercial mortgage.

Using a 30 year mortgage of $100,000 with a fixed rate of 9% your monthly payments would be $804.62. The interest you would pay over 30 years would be $189,664. That is right. Your mortgage was only for $100,000 but you would pay back a total of $289,664. Makes you wonder how any bank could run into fiscal trouble doesn't it?

Back to our example. If this mortgage holder paid an added $100 per month toward the principle of this mortgage he would cut 10 years off the life of the mortgage and save $75,792 in interest by doing so. By simply paying $100 extra per month to the principle the 30 year note was reduced to 19 years and 9 months and the interest would be cut from $189,664 to $113,872.

Have your accountant tell you what this strategy will save you based on the amount, terms, and rate of your mortgage. It could save you tens of thousands or even hundreds of thousands of dollars in interest costs even with a balloon note.

Another option for you to consider is for you to make payments on your mortgage every 2 weeks instead of once a month. I am not suggesting you double the payment but instead to pay one half the payment every 2 weeks instead of the whole payment once a month.

You will be accomplishing two things. First, you will be making part of each payment much earlier. The less time you owe the money the lower the interest cost even if it is only being paid a few weeks early. Secondly, by paying every two weeks instead of once a month you will end up making more total payments each year. This enables you to liquidate your loan sooner and save interest.

Always look at refinancing your mortgage if the rates drop 2 points below your current rate. Have your accountant run the numbers for you, but normally, if you will be staying in the facility for at least 2 years and the rates drop 2 points it will be well worth the cost to refinance. Do not ignore this strategy. The savings realized from reduced interest costs can be significant.

Do not always assume that at the end of a lease you must sign a new lease at increased rates if you choose to stay. For some unjustified reason this is the way all tenants think. This is, of course, exactly how your landlord and how real estate agents want you to think. This is the positioning and perception that they want and work very hard to achieve.

This does not mean that this is the way it must be at all. You have the greater leverage not your landlord. You will be able to find new space in most cases much easier than the landlord can find a new tenant. If you move the landlord must deal with finding a new tenant, perhaps remolding, hiring a real estate agent, and many other costly and frustrating factors.

Yes, there may be times where these are not a factor for the landlord. Yes, you must deal with finding new space and moving. But remember the goal here is to change positioning and perception. You must understand it is a give and take situation. The power in a landlord tenant relationship is not all in the landlord's favor. I would always prefer to negotiate from a perception or position of strength. How I think about the roles and how I make the landlord think about the roles, is the key to getting the upper hand or, at least, a hand of equal strength.

I would come into the negotiations not expecting to pay a higher rate or hoping to minimize the increase, but instead seeking a lower rate and facility modifications. This is not a course in how to negotiate but by taking this positioning you cannot lose. At the very least you will walk away with a smaller increase than the landlord might be seeking and you could very easily come away far better off than when you went in, especially when the market is down for commercial property.

If the commercial property market has dropped don't wait until your lease is up for renewal, ask for a lower rate now! If other tenants in the building or the surrounding areas are paying a lower rate due to a declining market, you should be getting a lower rate as well. Why should a new tenant be getting a better rate than you? At the very least ask for it and ask aggressively. If they want to keep you long term you will get their attention.

Always seek to secure a long term lease that is broken up into shorter terms that can be exercised at your option. This will give you the security of a long term lease with the flexibility of being able to break it every few years should the situation arise that benefits you to do so.

It also gives you a chance every few years to renegotiate your deal if circumstances or market conditions have changed. How would you feel if you sign a ten year lease and three years later the bottom falls out of the market for commercial property and you find yourself stuck for seven more years in the lease that has you overpaying based on the current market by 20%, 30% or more?

Give yourself all the options. Break a ten year lease into at least 2 five year periods. This will protect you in the long run and give you options in the short term. Make sure you have caps on the increases you will allow the landlord. This is what will protect you in the long run.

Ignore NNN when it comes to leasing property. Consider this clause a list price. List prices are the enemy of total cost control and expense reduction. **I do not care, and neither should you care, what the self-serving customs of any industry are. Who do you think establishes the customs? Who do you think they benefit most?**

Leases that are NNN have you paying too many added costs that you can't control or verify and being responsible for too many areas. Landlords and real estate agents would have you believe that NNN leases are the only option you have. Nonsense. From common area maintenance to utility related maintenance, NNN leases have you paying for all kinds of things that you have no control over.

Normally the landlord has the work done and you pay the bill. You have no input into what work is done, by who, and at what price. I know first hand that many landlords overbill for work done and charge for work that was never done.

According to an article in Real Estate Review "Improper expenses charged to tenants included such incredible items as snow removal for a southern Florida mall and a miscellaneous expense allowance for cigars for a building manager and his 100 closest friends.". You foot the bill. Some will use NNN rates as an added profit center. None have an incentive to do the best job they can at the lowest cost. Why should they? After all you are paying for it not them.

I have never signed one and never will. Get an all inclusive rate. This is the only way you will know what your costs are each month. In many ways a NNN lease makes you the landlord. You are the tenant not the landlord. Put the responsibility back where it belongs.

If you are leasing property do yourself a favor and have your attorney arrange for a Letter of Attornment. This is basically a non disturbance letter from the mortgage holder of the property you are leasing that protects you in the event of foreclosure. This is a proactive step.

Many companies wished they had protection like this during the last five years as commercial properties around the country ended up in foreclosure. Do not take a chance on the fiscal stability or intentions of your landlord. Do not take a chance on allowing circumstances beyond your control to disrupt or destroy your business. Before you sign any lease get your attorney to arrange for this. Think of this as one of the cheapest forms of insurance you could ever buy.

If you lease make sure that you have a self-help clause in your lease. Forget the standard lease. Modify it to protect your interests. Who do you think writes the so called "standard lease". Your landlord may appear to be the greatest guy in the world during your negotiations and even after you move in. He may even be the greatest landlord that ever lived. But what if he isn't? What if he falls on hard times?

What are you going to do if you have a problem and your landlord won't, or can't, take care of it? Can you afford to spend months trying to get your landlord to correct the problem? What if it is a problem that severely disrupts your business?

Can you take the risk? Do you need the frustration? Can you afford the cost? Get a self-help clause in your lease so you do not need to deal with this type of very common problem. The self-help clause should clearly spell out that it is your option to undertake any needed action that your landlord has not taken care of within a preset period of time and that all related costs will be deducted from the next rent payment. How much time is up to you to put in the clause, but I strongly suggest you keep the time you are giving him to respond to a minimum. How long would you like to wait in the winter for your heat to be fixed or in the summer for the air conditioning to be repaired?

If the landlord violates the clause you can have the needed work done on your own and deduct all the costs from your next payment. Have your attorney draft up the clause for you and make sure it protects you.

Verify every aspect of your lease. Millions and millions of dollars are being overpaid by businesses in this country every year to their commercial landlords. You must verify everything in your lease that you are paying for. This includes common areas charges, miscellaneous expenses, administrative costs, and the actual square footage you are paying for.

Have you checked any of these? Do you have any idea if that 150,000 square foot building you are leasing really has 150,000 square feet? Of course you don't. You have simply taken the landlords word for it haven't you?

Do you know how much you are overpaying each year if you are being overcharged for even a few hundred square feet? Well, if you are being overcharged even 1,000 square at $10 per square foot you are over paying by $10,000 per year. Over a period of ten years you will have overpaid by over $100,000 not even including rate increases and all costs that are indexed to the amount of square feet you lease.

According to Shopping Center Digest, "Many landlords believe they have been given a blank check and can bill any extra charges as they see fit.". According to a St. Louis company called Leasehold Analysis, Inc., which specializes in auditing lease agreements, "clients have been overcharged as much as 12 1/2% of the entire cost of the lease". Isn't it time you started verifying what you are paying for?

If you are considering purchasing any type of commercial property contact the RTC. This is the Resolution Trust Company and they have thousands and thousands of pieces of commercial property all over the country that they are trying to sell. This is their function. They must liquidate property that has been placed with them by the government who has obtained it mainly from failed banks who had been the mortgage holder.

They offer excellent prices and rates. It is not uncommon to be able to pick up property from the RTC for 50% less than what it had been worth. I was offered 15,000 square feet of very nice commercial space for a full 50% less than the business owners on either side of this space had paid for the exact same amount of space only 1 year earlier.

They paid $60 per square foot or $900,000. I could have bought the space for $30 per square foot or $450,000. This was a bottom line dollar savings of $450,000. I would have also been able to secure a much more favorable rate and terms.

If you are looking to purchase property, commercial or residential, include the RTC in your search. Do not count on a Realtor to bring RTC deals to you. Contact them directly. Contact your banker and ask for the number of the local RTC office.

The RTC also has many commercial properties to rent. What they can't sell they will rent or lease. Many times you will also be able to get an option to purchase at your discretion and at a preset price. As far as the rent or lease rates and terms go, you will find similar savings to those I have outlined above.

In Pursuit of Profits. How To At Least Double Your Profits Without Increasing Your Sales.

It has also been my experience that you will find the RTC extremely flexible to work with. They make no commission on the properties they sell or lease. Their job is simple. Get rid of them or get someone in them. This means that even a poor negotiator should be able to walk away with an excellent deal.

Do not forget bank owned properties. For the exact same reasons I have outlined above you should include bank owned properties in your search for space to purchase or lease. Contact all the banks in your area and ask them to send you a list of all available properties they own. Since your search will take some time ask them to also include you on their mailing list for notification of any properties they foreclose on in the future.

Let me also remind you that it is up to you to go out and find the deals. Banks and the RTC do a very poor job at promoting the properties they have. You can't sit back and wait for the deal to come to you. Money on the ground won't jump up into your pocket. You must pick it up.

Remember, everything is negotiable. In few places is this truer than it is in the commercial property field. Never take the asking price for a purchase or lease. This is simply the list price. You never pay list price. Think of what you need and what you are willing to pay to get it.

For example, most prices for purchase or lease include a basic build out or building modification factor included in anticipation of some work being done for the new owner or tenant. Find out how much is included for build out. Normally it seems to be that a 10% build out is included. This means that they will conduct a basic build out in the facility equal to 10% of the space. If you need less, get a lower rate instead. If you need more make the deal contingent on a larger build out being conducted.

I was able to get a build out equal to 33% of the space in one building for no added charge. This saved me between $75,000 and $100,000 in up front build out costs. Think. You will never be in a stronger position to get what you want than you are at this stage.

Forget standard contracts they will not serve your best interest, they will serve the landlord's best interest. Who do you think made up the standard?

Make sure you understand what you are agreeing to. Follow my other strategies for dealing with agreements. Make sure you clearly understand what you are agreeing to. If you do not, get clarification. If you do not like certain terms or conditions do not make the deal until they are modified in writing to your satisfaction. Watch out for built in escalation charges for rates, taxes, and anything else. These can cost you dearly.

Find space on your own. There are other ways to find the space you need than just dealing with real estate folks. The best deal I ever made on a piece of commercial property came from my own efforts. After spending months dealing with real estate people looking for a 15,500 square foot building I found myself nowhere closer to finding the space I needed at the rates and terms I was willing to agree to.

I decided to run a blind ad on my own indicating what I was looking for and what I was willing to pay. Within two weeks over 15 property owners had responded to me with information about their properties. Not one of them had their buildings listed with a real estate firm. In each case they were trying to sell or lease the property on their own.

Of course, not one of these properties had been brought to my attention by a real estate agent. Three of them were exactly what I was looking for. By dealing direct with the building owner and eliminating the middleman I was able to put together a deal within a few days that cost me 30% less than anything I had seen in the months before. Saving 30% on a building of this size saved me tens of thousands of dollars a year and hundreds of thousands of dollars over the life of the lease.

Are your computers expensive paperweights? Do not provide personal computers or network terminals to people who cannot justify having them. Many people in many offices have computers on their desks that are nothing more than status symbols and are effectively giant paperweights.

Ego and status symbols have no place in a total cost control program. Quite the opposite in fact. They can be deadly to a total cost control program. If they do not have a valid use for at least 4 hours a day they should not have a terminal. Don't waste your money on hardware and software that is not cost justified. You are also wasting money on maintenance, supplies, and service contracts.

Let me also point out another all too common problem with giving computers to people who don't absolutely need them. They will use them for personal projects and to play games. Think I am kidding? I know of a number of highly placed executives, as well as a number of staff members, in a variety of companies who have a library of computer games installed in their office computer. They would not be there if they were not being used.

I also know of a couple of companies who sell programs that you can load into in your computer so that by simply hitting one key the screen that you were on is replaced by any one of a number of very businesslike professional looking screens. Depending on the key you hit, up pops a spreadsheet, or a word processing screen or a customer maintenance screen. You don't suppose that the purpose of this program is to cover up that game of golf your employee was playing when you walked by do you?

Look into using a dumpster instead of barrels or loose trash. They cost less, free up space, look nicer, are safer and more sanitary. For example, a major disposal company in my area charges $12 per yard to pick up and dispose of loose trash and trash in barrels. By switching to a dumpster they will charge you only $6 per yard or 50% less for the exact same trash.

Dumpsters come in a wide variety of sizes from the very small to the very large. Dumpsters also are available for inside or outside placement so depending on your needs, space limitations, lease terms, or local regulations, you will have no reason not to get one and take advantage of these savings.

If you use a dumpster make sure you are using the right size. One that is too small will require more frequent pick ups. Each pick up costs you money. One that is too large will result in you paying a dumpster rental fee that is being partially wasted. If you are consistently having your dumpster emptied when it is only 1/2 or 2/3 full you can save 20% to 30% in rental costs by switching to a smaller unit.

Make sure you shop around for the best deal on picking up your rubbish and make sure pick ups are not scheduled any more frequently than needed. Very often trash disposal costs are higher than they should be because less than full barrels or dumpsters are picked up. This means you are incurring a pick up charge when you did not need one.

This happens all too often when a regular pick up schedule is used and your trash disposal needs fluctuate. When this happens you should simply change the schedule to reflect your disposal needs.

In Pursuit of Profits. How To At Least Double Your Profits Without Increasing Your Sales.

For example, if you are a business that has heavy disposal needs during part of the year and lower disposal needs during the rest of the year, why should you pay for a pick up schedule based on your heaviest disposal times? This is exactly what happens all the time.

You should monitor your disposal needs and adjust your pick up schedule to match any seasonal changes in your disposal demands. Do not count on the disposal company to suggest this. It won't happen.

It is up to you to dictate this to them. Most often this never happens. A schedule is set based on the heaviest needs you have and never thought about again. Trash disposal is very costly but by combining proper scheduling with other strategies you should easily be able to reduce your costs in these areas by 50% or more.

Make sure that all material, including boxes, that you put in barrels or your dumpster is broken up or crushed down. Your trash disposal is charged for by the yard, which is a space measurement, and not by the pound. The more you can cram into the barrel or dumpster the lower your disposal bill will be.

Shop trash disposal companies just like you would any other vendor. In my area I have found prices for bulk pick up to range from a high rate of $12 to a low rate of $6 per yard for the exact same service. If you have 200 yards per month picked up and disposed of with the higher priced service it will cost you $28,800 per year. By switching to the lower priced service your cost would only be $14,400 per year. A 50% reduction in cost that saves you nearly $15,000 for the same service.

Look into getting a trash compactor. Your rubbish is picked up and charged for by volume or the yard and not by weight. The less space your trash takes up the more of it you can dispose of at a lower rate. A trash compactor could cut your disposal costs by 50% or more.

Keep old scrap paper in bins and distribute as scratch paper. Reduce your costs of paper and trash disposal.

Make sure that all areas of your company are kept clean and presentable. Do this regardless of whether or not you have customers come to your business. If you have customers who visit you in a retail setting it goes without saying this is important. If you have customers who visit your company at any time it also goes without saying how important it is to keep all areas of your company clean and presentable.

However, even if a customer never steps foot in your doorway this is important. It makes for a safer, more productive, workplace. It fosters a sense of pride in your employees and this is reflected in their efforts. This in turn is reflected in the quality of your products and service. Would you want your daughter to go out with a guy who looks like he slept in a dumpster?

Don't even consider new furniture until you look into used furniture. Office furniture has a very long life and, as a result, furniture a few years old can look very new. The trade off is a 50% to 80% savings over the cost of new furniture. However, if you shop right there will be no trade off at all. In fact, considering the quality of much of today's furniture you might even be able to improve on the quality of your furniture by purchasing older previously owned furniture.

Don't take my word for it. Shop both new and used furniture and see the difference in cost and quality between both then decide. I bought a like new chair for $25. The exact same chair was for sale in my local office furniture store for $300. By shopping right you could furnish your entire office for less than some people pay to furnish one room.

Remember, if you are buying anything by direct mail, especially furniture, you must factor in shipping costs as part of your price evaluation.

Don't hire an interior design firm or use the design services of an office furniture supplier (in exchange for purchasing their furniture). Instead, visit showrooms and look through all the catalogs you have collected (you have saved them haven't you?). You will find a tremendous number of design ideas, most of which have already been designed by professionals. Here you will find not only excellent options for aesthetic designs but also excellent space saving and effective space utilization ideas.

"Satisfying your ego in business will always be done at the expense of your bottom line."

Derrick W. Welch

Don't let ego empty your pocket book. Unless image is vital to the success of your business (in most cases only you think that) don't spend a lot of money on ostentatious furnishings for your office.

Never buy a new filing cabinet or storage unit of any type until you: 1) Know exactly what it will be used for. 2) Find out what is in the ones you already own. Many times you will find out that you do not need a new one at all if you just clean out the old ones.

Even records that you need or want to keep but rarely access, can be stored in low cost boxes designed to be stacked 6 and 8 high. They cost about $4 each and can be purchased from any one of the office supply sources I have listed. Four of these can have the same amount of storage space as a 4 draw filing cabinet. Four of these storage boxes will cost you under $20 while a new filing cabinet will cost you anywhere from $100 to a few hundred dollars depending how well or poorly you buy it.

Look around, are you one of the masses of companies that saves old records when they are no longer needed or accessed? Are you saving old records you need or want in metal cabinets? If so, you may be wasting a great deal of money and space.

If you ignore my advice to purchase used furniture at least purchase the lowest cost new furniture you can. Often this will be from high volume lower cost direct mail sources. Depending on what and where you buy, you may save 50% or more even after shipping when compared to the cost of buying from a local office furniture store.

Again, don't assume this, shop both and compare. Make sure you factor in any shipping costs, set up costs, and taxes so you have an accurate comparison. Also check out return policies including who pays for shipping if you must return an item and consider warranties offered. These factors must all be considered. Sounds like a bit of work? It is really very little when you consider the possible savings you will be realizing.

In Pursuit of Profits. How To At Least Double Your Profits Without Increasing Your Sales.

Don't confine the idea of used furniture to the front office. Consider used furnishings for other areas of your company. You must think. For example, I solicited prices from 2 local companies for warehouse shelving. One sold new shelving and one sold used. The new shelving was priced at $2,990. The used at $1,300. Excuse me, actually there was another difference. The used shelving price included installation.

This is over a 50% savings. As soon as I put something on it the new shelving is used. Even if I didn't like the color or had to buy different colored sections, I could pay someone to paint them a different color or all one color and still be over $1,000 ahead.

The same strategy as above applies to filing cabinets. Used cabinets will save you up to 80% of the cost of new cabinets. In this case you have the added option of placing different colored cabinets away from each other and therefore you can eliminate the need to paint them.

When you purchase office furniture make sure that you are not putting appearance above comfort and functionality. Proper furniture can have a significant effect on employee productivity. If productivity suffers your costs go up.

If you use a cleaning service be very careful about letting them provide supplies. Often they will mark these supplies up 20% to 30%. Make sure you get prices on what they are charging you for these supplies. Don't let them bury the costs in one overall bill. You must have these costs and then price these items out yourself. Most all of the direct mail office supply companies I will give you will carry very low priced supplies of all types for office cleaning.

If you are letting your cleaning service overcharge you by 20% or more for supplies there is no other reason for it other than laziness. Convenience always has a price tag. Please note this also goes for all paper products such as toilet paper, Kleenex, and paper towels.

Something to think about. At our office we have a cleaning company come in once a week. They empty the waste baskets, clean the rest room floors, and vacuum the front office carpets. Of course during the week the waste baskets get full and the people empty them themselves as needed until cleaning day arrives. How could I save money here? Think?

How about having the cleaning done once every two weeks and keep a few carpet sweepers around in case the carpet gets dirty during this time? This would cut my bill by 50% a year with little impact. If your employees are sharing in costs savings you will find your office will be cleaner than it ever was.

How about paying one of my employees some overtime once a week to do the job. It costs me $50 per week. An employee making $8 and hour would cost me $12 a week considering it would take about an hour and a half each week. This would save me over 75% a year or a total of $1,976.

How about combining the two options and having an employee clean every other week? How about assigning this function as part of someone's normal job? You get the idea.

Don't buy brand name cleaning supplies. Buy generic supplies at a cost savings of 20% to 50%. If you can't find a source (this should be easy) call a chemical supply company in your area and ask them where you can get them.

Purchase multi colored, multi patterned carpets and rugs. They will wear better which reduces the need for cleaning due to dirt or stains. In addition to lasting much longer you will reduce your carpet cleaning costs by 50% or more. Just a vacuuming will suffice 90% of the time. The details do matter.

Use mats in high traffic areas and entrances to protect your carpets. This will reduce wear and tear on your carpets which reduces your cleaning costs and replacement costs. Replacing carpets can be very expensive. You want to do what you can to extend the life of your carpets. Consider this a form of preventive maintenance.

Use fake plants instead of real plants. I know, I know, there is some politically correct term for fake but who cares. Fake plants will eliminate your maintenance and replacement costs. If you feel you must use real plants to decorate the interior or exterior of your building at least make sure you use low maintenance and long lasting plants. This is simply being proactive.

Don't hire landscapers, including grass cutters, under an annual contract. It may seem to be more economical but contracts of this sort are usually based on weekly maintenance needs. If you think about it you will find that very rarely will you need weekly maintenance or need the grass cut each week. By purchasing services as needed you determine when it is needed.

If you are buying a contract based on service 52 weeks a year and you really only need service 30 weeks you can be darn sure you are overpaying. If the weekly contract rate is $200 or $10,400 per year and the as needed rate is $250 you may think you are saving 20% or so. However, if you only need service 30 weeks a year the as needed rate only costs you $7,500. You have saved nearly $3,000 or 30%.

If you engage the services of a landscaping company on an "as needed basis" make sure that you are monitoring their work very closely. You do not want work to be done when it is not justified. They may schedule work every week when it is clearly not needed. The grass may only need to be cut once a month in the summer months and they may cut it every week to get their billings up.

Do not buy expensive interior corporate art. Do not rent or lease it either. Instead go to a local department store and purchase inexpensive reproductions or display motivational posters. Better yet, display pictures of your own products and services. This will create a sort of company showroom throughout your company reminding your employees why they are there and showing your customers what you have done and what you can do.

A lesson I learned. As with most things in life, many of the things I have learned over the years were learned at a cost. This is one of those. I once engaged the services of a company to install and maintain first aid cabinets in my production areas. They looked great and contained everything you could ever think of. The company installed them, set them up, stocked them, and came around each month to check and restock. I never had to think about the first aid needs of the company in any way shape or form. It was extremely convenient. One less thing I had to worry about. **But, as you and I know, convenience has a price. Sometimes a big price.**

The price in this case was that I was overpaying for the supplies in the first aid cabinets by up to 600%. That's right 600%. Let me give you some examples of what your shrewd author was paying compared to what I could have been paying.

In Pursuit of Profits. How To At Least Double Your Profits Without Increasing Your Sales.

Item	Stocking company	Drug store	Overcharged
Box of 50 bandages	$4.50	$1.99	226%
Box of 25 large patches	$5.95	$1.89	314%
Box of 10 antiseptic swabs	$2.75	$1.40	196%
Box of 20 alcohol swabs	$2.90	$ .99	292%
Bottle of eye drops	$4.15	$1.88	221%
Bottle of pain reliever	$9.60	$2.39	401%
Blistex	$4.40	$ .69	637%

The list goes on and on. In almost every case I was overpaying by 200% or more. Much more in many cases. I also had no control over the inventory process. We did not check or stock the cabinets. We let them do it. We had no way to know if what they claimed to have been restocked was even legitimate. I have strong suspicions that much of what they claimed to be restocking was never restocked. Either that or my employees were filling up their medicine cabinets at home from the one at the office.

After looking at a few wholesale supply sources for these first aid products it became clear to me that I could have refilled the entire contents of each cabinet each month on my own and still have saved close to 50%.

Don't make the same mistake I did. Many office supply stores and direct mail sources will carry what you need.

Energy Section

Please note that at the time of this writing these strategies represent some of the best ways to reduce your energy usage based on the technology at this time. You should contact the EPA to find out what advances have been made in these areas.

The EPA has estimated that lighting for industry, stores, offices, and warehouses represents 80% to 90% of a company's total electric costs. They have furthermore suggested that by switching to energy efficient lighting electric costs for business lighting could be cut by up to 50%. This would not only add up to significant savings for business, but would also dramatically lower lighting related pollutants such as carbon dioxide emissions, sulfur dioxide emissions, and nitrogen oxide emissions. The EPA claims that the typical investment in energy efficient lighting yields a 20% to 30% rate of return. My experience in this area would validate these claims.

Whether you contact the EPA or not I strongly endorse the conversion to as many of the high efficiency lighting fixtures as possible. The United States Department of Energy's National Appropriate Technology Assistance Service has been established to provide answers and solutions to your energy related questions. Call them at 1-800-428-2525 and see how they can help you.

To promote these benefits to business the EPA has established a program called "Green Lights" which has been set up to work with companies. Call to get the details on how you can help your bottom line and the health of the earth.

Contact your utility company and ask them to conduct an energy audit of your company. Find out if there is any cost. In my state there is no cost. They do not advertise it in my state but there are a number of state and federal funded programs that finance most, if not all, of the cost of any energy saving steps you take. The energy audit identifies the steps you can take to reduce your energy usage, the cost of the steps, and the projected savings.

It took a number of calls for me to find someone who knew of these programs but the effort was well worth it. Why they are not promoted I do not know. Why so few know of the programs and how they work I do not know. Unfortunately, this is typical of so many government funded programs and government run agencies. They would have trouble selling water in the desert.

However, since we are not at this point in time going to try to fix all the problems with the government, let me just restate that the frustration of wading through the government BS paid off. I was able to secure a no cost energy audit that provided me with a very detailed breakdown of my energy uses and listed a number of steps that could be taken to reduce our energy demands.

This audit was then given to a government sponsored contractor who told me how much the improvements would cost and how long it would take to recoup my improvement investment. The bottom line in my case was that by spending $3,987 one time, I would cut my energy use to the point that I would save 26% of my energy costs or $2,174 per year off my rates at that time.

Furthermore, the utility company would pay 65% of the costs of the improvements thereby reducing my one time cost to only $1,361. This meant that my payback would be complete in about 6 months. However, it got even better. The state would finance this $1,361 over an 18 month period at 6.5% interest.

This left me with a monthly payment of $83 against a projected savings of $181 per month. In other words, my payback would be immediate and I could improve my monthly cash flow by nearly $100. $100 that I could put to use in a number of ways to save even more.

The short term benefits were clear. I could save money and help the environment by reducing my energy usage. The long term savings were even more impressive. Over a ten year period, not even factoring in any rate increases, I would save over $21,740.

My cost was only $1,361 and even that was set up to be self-funding. A $21,740 return on a $1,361 investment. Think about this. Perhaps a savings of $181 per month may not excite you, although it should, but how about $21,740. Think of how much you would need to increase sales based on your current pretax profit ratio to add this much to your bottom line over a ten year period. How much would you save with a 26% reduction in your energy costs?

Remember, this is net bottom line money for doing nothing but reducing your energy demands. You have not altered the way you do business one bit. You have sacrificed absolutely nothing. If you don't put the publication down right now and call your utility company, in fact all utility companies, you might as well stop reading. You are just not serious about controlling or reducing your costs. You are just kidding yourself and wasting time.

Consider using reflectors on the outside of your windows during the summer. These can be in the form of reflective peel off plastic or even metallic curtains. By deflecting the sun's rays you will keep temperatures down and by doing so reduce the demands on your air conditioning system.

Consider alternative cooling methods to air conditioning. Systems that can replace, or at least subsidize, your AC system include absorption chillers, store cold and ice chillers. Each of these systems store water or antifreeze and chill it during the night. Then, during the day, the air in your building is filtered through the unit and released chilled into the building. These units generally expend most of their energy during the evening when energy costs will normally be lower.

In Pursuit of Profits. How To At Least Double Your Profits Without Increasing Your Sales.

An audit you do not need to be afraid of. One of the hottest business opportunities of the 90's is said to be utility auditing. This is a business that anyone can start for very little money. A number of companies offer the training and support for prices ranging from $500 to $10,000.

Why is it so hot? Simple. The vast majority of utility bills have been shown to contain errors. According to Ralph Nader "Rather than getting better as a result of computerization, utility bills seem to be getting worse. They are indecipherable, lack itemization, contain inflated or phony charges, and cost customers billions of dollars a year.". Representative Robert Matsui of the House Ways and Means committee has estimated that "utilities over billed $19 billion in energy and telephone charges or incorrect taxes alone.".

Most companies assume that all bills of this type are accurate and therefore never even review them much less question them. Do you? Errors occur as a result of miscalculations, overestimating usage, misreading of a meter, and defective or broken meters just to name a few obvious ways. Even if you did question them you would have no idea how to read them, how to spot errors, and how to file for a rebate.

Why not find out if your's have errors and, if so, why not get a rebate? Most of the people running these utility auditing programs will come to your business and conduct an audit of your bills. They will do this at no cost to you. Their only fee will be a percentage of any errors they uncover and secure a rebate for.

This is a can't lose proposition. If they find your bills are proper you owe nothing. If they find errors they share the savings. All you need to do is contact one of these companies, verify that they will work on contingency, and have them come in.

How do you find them? Simple. Pick up a copy of Inc. Magazine or Entrepreneur Magazine and look for the ads from companies looking to sell the training. Contact them, verify that they work on contingency and ask to be referred to an agent covering your area.

Now here are a few points you should remember. The contingency fees they ask for are not written in stone. They may want you to think they are but they are not. They are list prices. Each agent can structure the fees any way they want to. They will be seeking 50% of any savings they secure for you and this is fair. However, they may want a percentage of these savings for future billings for up to 5 years. This is not, in my opinion, fair.

Some only ask for 50% of the first year's savings. This is what you should agree to with any such company you deal with. Agree to this up front. If they will not agree call another company. You have the leverage not them. Without you they have no business. You can negotiate any split fee arrangement you want and as long as they agree to it you have a deal. You can agree to only 25% of the savings for the first year if you are able to get them to agree. Remember, the deal you strike is entirely up to you and the agent.

If you so chose, you can even purchase the auditing training yourself and keep 100% of any savings for yourself. This is your choice. For a larger company spending $500 on training as an auditor could end up saving you tens of thousands of dollars. Think about it. The risk to reward ratio is very strong.

Do not overlook this cost reduction option. The savings that are possible here can be significant and will cost you nothing to obtain. You will also find that similar services are provided by many companies for many other areas of your business including lease analysis, phone, property tax, cellular phones, and freight costs.

You should consider looking into each applicable one but only after you have done all you can to reduce these costs on your own and only after you have applied and adapted as many of my strategies as possible. You only want to look to outside sources like this after you have saved every cent you can on your own. Don't give money away!

Monitor kilowatt hours yourself. Check at the beginning of the billing period and at the end of the billing period. This way it will be easy to verify if your actual billed or estimated usage appears to be miscalculated. I would also recommend that every few months you keep a daily log of usage by reading and recording the meter totals each day. At the end of the month total these up and compare to both your monthly log and actual billing.

Have your utility meters checked every 6 months. Meters have problems much more often than you would expect and if overcharges are occurring you want to be able to spot the problem right away and get a rebate. There is a three year statute of limitations on utility overcharges so you should also examine past billings and if you find any overcharges you should seek to recover your overpayments.

Look into using dimmer switches in as many areas as possible. Many people would prefer to work in lighting that is a bit lower than it is in many modern buildings and you may find that you can cut your lighting costs by 5% to 10% while providing a more comfortable workplace for your employees.

Look into the cost and payback of installing energy efficient lighting throughout your facility. As I have indicated in an earlier strategy, this should be done only after you have attempted to work through your utility company and the government to secure these types of improvements. Why pay for these improvements yourself if you can get someone else to pay for them or at least assist you in paying for them? This may be one of the few chances you have to receive some direct benefit from the many taxes and fees you pay.

If you do not own the building ask your landlord to consider each of these options for you. After all, it is their facility that you will be improving so it is reasonable to expect that they pay for, or at least share in, the costs of any improvements that make the facility more attractive, economical, and valuable.

Make sure that you have blinds or shades on all your windows. This is especially important in modern buildings with larger windows that do not open. Windows like this can create a greenhouse effect. The sun can cause internal temperatures to rise significantly. In the cool or cold weather you want to open the blinds or shades to reduce the demand for heat. In the hot or humid weather you want to keep them closed to reduce the demand for air conditioning. Use the blinds or shades to make the greenhouse effect work for you and not against you.

Use ceiling fans, desk fans, window fans, and standup fans to subsidize your cooling needs. The cost of running a fan is far less than the cost of running an air conditioner.

Use ceiling fans in the cold weather to drive down the heat and your heating costs. Heat rises. Let the fans push it back down. Unless you are mighty tall, heating the air near the ceiling of your office or warehouse is a costly and wasted effort.

Do not allow the use of small floor heaters. These are very costly to operate, represent a fire hazard, and are very commonly left on all night long or all weekend long by an employee who never thinks of turning them off.

Assign one person in each area to make sure that all lights are turned off, all windows and doors are shut and locked, and all machines are turned off. You would be amazed at how often I have found typewriters, computers, printers, and adding machines left on, windows left open, doors unlocked, and lights left on.

Too many employees assume that someone else will take care of these things. I have even found my shipping doors left open at the end of the day. Not only are you running higher than needed energy costs, you are also running a security risk, wearing out machinery needlessly, and risking damage from inclement weather. Remember, the domino effect works both ways.

Turn lights off in all unused areas and offices. It is also a good idea to have the lights in the offices of those out to lunch turned off. Not only does this save energy, but it also lets others know that this person is out of the office so time is not wasted looking for them. Furthermore, requiring this reinforces the desired attitude and mind set of total cost control. You want to reinforce this in as many ways as possible.

What are you cooling? Make sure any individual air conditioning units and the central air conditioning units are turned off or, at the very least way, down at night.

Use a timer. I strongly suggest that you install timing devices on your central air conditioning and heating units. These inexpensive units can cut your heating and cooling costs significantly. They can be programmed to turn the heat and air conditioning on and off, and to turn the temperature up or down at preset times on predetermined days. This will eliminate the need to worry about whether the heat or air conditioning was left on or whether or not the building will be too hot or too cold in the morning when you come in. If you rent, request that your landlord put these in. They are very inexpensive but why should you pay for anything that improves his building?

How effective? Let me give you an example. When we first moved into a new building during the winter, each night we turned the heat down. The next morning it was always cold and it took an hour or so for the heat to reach a comfortable temperature. The whole hour of course I had to listen to everyone in the company tell me how cold they were and ask me if I knew it was cold.

We finally stopped turning the heat down at night and instead left it at 70 degrees. This meant that for 24 hours a day, 7 days a week, we kept the heat at 70 degrees. This is 168 hours per week. When we finally figured out that there must be a better way we discovered timers. A real bright group we were. It only took months for us to figure out that we only worked about 50 hours per week and we were heating the building at 70 degrees 168 hours per week. Hmm, what was wrong with that picture?

Once we discovered timers we estimated our heating and cooling costs would fall by up to 30%. We set the timers to drop the heat an hour before we closed and bring it up again an hour before we opened. An hour left plenty of time for the building to heat up in the morning and during the afternoon lowering it an hour before we closed has never been a problem as it takes much longer than that most nights for the building to cool off.

In the cooling season we use the same strategy and let the temperature rise an hour before we leave and drop an hour before we come in. A simple timing device that cost us under $200 installed saved us thousands of dollars each year without sacrificing one bit of comfort.

Fresh air can reduce costs. If you have a building that has windows that open use them whenever possible to reduce the need for air conditioning. Do not open them when the air conditioning is on and remember to check to insure they are shut and locked each night.

Not only will this cut your air conditioning costs but you may find your employees prefer the fresh air. Also remember the less you use your air conditioning equipment the longer it lasts and the lower the maintenance costs. The domino effect once again comes into play and affords you secondary benefits.

Keep your heating and air conditioning systems well maintained. By keeping the systems well maintained your efficiency will be higher which means your energy costs will be lower. An efficiently running heating or cooling system can reduce your energy demands and costs by 10% to 20%. The equipment will also last longer and will be much less likely to break down causing you disruption and repair costs. Remember, if you rent make sure you try to get it in your lease that the owner must do this.

Is it time to upgrade? Periodically conduct an analysis to compare the efficiency level of your current cooling and heating systems versus the cost and efficiency savings of installing a new one. All too often heating and cooling systems are never replaced until they simply will not work at all any more. A low efficiency older system may be costing a great deal of money in the form of high energy usage. An older system may be less than 75% efficient while a new system may be up to 95% efficient. A new high efficiency system may be cost justified long before you reach the point of having your current system not work any longer.

Have two or three contractors come in and evaluate both the current system and the cost and projected savings you could realize by installing a new system. Of course these should be free evaluations and all costs and projections should be in writing. The monthly savings may more than pay for the monthly payments of the new system and the payback period may surprise you.

Also remember, that the cost of a new system is a capital improvement and as such will have a reduced effect on your year end profit and loss statement. In fact, depending on your profit levels and your current base of depreciation, capital improvements such as this may be a welcome vehicle to use to get those paper losses to shield taxable profits. **But never make a capital improvement or purchase without making sure it is 100% cost justified!**

Little things can make a big difference. Clean the filters on your heating and cooling equipment a couple of times a year. Clogged filters are very common and cause your equipment to work harder. This results in increased energy demands, more wear and tear which increase your repair costs and will decrease the life of the equipment.

Lights out. Put your night lights, inside and outside, on a timing device or a photo electric activating device. This way the lights will turn on and off according to your preset schedule or the level of daylight. In both cases it will reduce energy demands and costs when compared to you turning the lights on and off as you come to work and leave work.

Think about this. For example, you may leave work in the summer at 5 p.m. and turn the night lights on at that time. However, it may not get dark until 8 or 9 p.m. during the summer months. You may then turn them off when you come in the next day at 8 a.m.. However, in the summer it may be light out by 7 am. If you leave the lights on from 5 p.m. until the next morning when you come in at 8 a.m. you have left the lights on for 15 hours.

If you have them on a timing device or a photo electric eye they would come on at say 8 p.m. and go off at 7 a.m.. This results in having the lights on for only 11 hours.

What you have done is reduce your energy demands, during this time as it relates to night lights, by 27 %. This does not even consider when you leave the building Friday night and turn the lights on leaving them on all day Saturday and Sunday. Not only are you wasting 12 to 15 hours of energy each weekend day, but you are also sending a clear signal that no one is in the office by having exterior lights on during the day. The domino effect here is that you will improve your cash flow, replace bulbs less frequently, and improve security.

If you are in a multi tenant building and you pay your own utilities make sure that you are only paying for your own energy usage. I know this sounds foolish, after all who would pay for someone else's energy usage, but you would be surprised. This is a very common problem. It can be an intentional situation or an unintentional one. I have seen many of the former and a few of the latter.

How could this happen? Very easily. The building may have not been wired for separate utilities and may have since been divided up to hold a number of tenants. The building owner may not have separated the utilities in an effort to keep costs down or he may not have separated them out completely to reflect the number of tenants now in the building. In this case one tenant may be paying for the utilities of another or a few tenants may be paying for the utilities of the rest of the tenants.

I know of one building in which the tenant on the second and third floors was paying for all the energy usage of the tenant on the first floor. This happened because the building owner had previously split up the utilities for one tenant who had the first three floors in the building.

When, years later, the tenant of the first three floors reduced the space he needed down to just the first floor, the building owner rented out the second and third floor to a new tenant. He did not, however separate the utilities to reflect this and for a number of years the new tenant on the second and third floors was paying for the energy usage of the first floor tenant.

The landlord did not care and apparently the first floor tenant never bothered to mention that he was no longer paying for any utilities. This was only finally realized when the second and third floor tenant had an electrician in to do some office wiring for them. He was the one who questioned if they knew they were paying for all three floors. The last I heard of this situation was that it was tied up in a lawsuit with no signs of a quick resolution.

It happens and it happens more than you think. Perhaps not to the extreme of this example, but you may find you are paying for common area lighting or outside lighting. You must verify that you are only paying for what you are using and are obligated to pay for. The best way to do this is to call the utility company in, or if necessary, a private company and ask them to verify this.

If you find a problem you better bring this to your landlord immediately to have the utilities separated properly and to get a rebate for the amounts you have been overcharged. I am not talking about just electricity but also gas and water.

Use high watt low energy light bulbs to improve your lighting while reducing your electric costs. These bulbs also will generally last longer and therefore will save you money since you will replace your bulbs less frequently.

Reduce your water usage by installing low level toilets and low flow faucets. As with a number of these strategies this one will not only reduce your costs but is also environmentally responsible. While you have the plumber on premises ask him what other steps you can take to reduce your costs in the area of water usage. Of course, as with any strategy I give you that involves making modifications to a facility you do not own, you should first try to get the building owner to pay for the improvement and if this fails demand he share the costs with you.

It is always cooler in the shade. Another way you can use the sun to reduce your heating costs or block the sun to reduce your cooling costs is through the use of outside awnings and tinted window coverings. The awning can be rolled down to block the sun and up to let it in. The tinted window coverings are an economical alternative that are placed on the windows during the warm weather to block the sun and peeled off during the cooler months to let the sun in.

Remember who owns the property. On a number of occasions I have encouraged you to look to the building owner first for full payment of any type of building improvements and if you can't get full payment at least get him to share the cost. Remember, you are the customer. He has an interest in keeping you happy. A bad tenant can be a nightmare for a landlord. He should also want you to be a long term tenant. The costs of getting new tenants and preparing the building for a new tenant are very high. He may have a vacancy for months, he must advertise, clean up, renovate, and probably engage the services of a real estate professional.

Furthermore, any improvements that are made to the building may benefit you by saving you money but they also improve the value of his building. If he is reluctant to pay for, or at least share in, these costs I suggest you remind him of these facts.

I will also point out that the best time to try and get improvements and modifications of any sort is before you sign a lease and move in or before you renew a lease. During these times you have the maximum leverage. During these times you want to negotiate as many of these energy savings modifications as possible into the deal. However, if you are currently in a lease go right ahead and ask for the improvements to be done. Do not wait until your lease is up for renewal.

Always have your accountant check to see if there are any tax benefits to any improvements you make in your company. I am not just talking about energy saving improvements, but also about any other type of improvements. The government has so many programs it is always worth looking into. Don't ever assume you can't. If you must assume, assume you can. Working from this position will be much more beneficial.

Consider using a high efficiency gas hot water heater instead of an electric model. The energy costs used by gas will be on average 50% less than that used by an electric hot water heater. Most utility companies will install the gas heater at no charge and you can rent or buy the unit. If you rent the monthly charges are normally very moderate and will normally include all service calls.

Is that computer being used? Are you sure? According to the Environmental Protection Agency the average personal computer is used only 20% of the time it is turned on. That's right 20%. More dramatically put, 80% of the time the computers in your office are turned on they are not being used.

This not only wastes electricity (to the tune of $1 billion a year according to the EPA) but it also results in your equipment needing service more frequently and wearing out sooner than it should. Make sure that anyone in your company that uses a computer plans their work so that while the computer is on it is being used. When they are done using it make sure it is turned off. Do not leave it on all day and do not turn it on and off all day. Make sure the work schedule is planned to properly use the computer.

Use lights switches that light up when on. These are switches that light up red when they are on. These should be used for all areas that you can't always tell if the light is on. Areas like closets, store rooms, basements and attics. I have one of these in my house for my attic and most of the time I find that I have left the light on in the attic and did not even realize it. If I did not have this type of switch the light would have stayed on for days or even weeks before I went into the attic again.

If possible and if applicable to your type of business look into the costs and savings of switching part of your plant hours from peak to off peak. During peak usage times many states allow a form of pricing known as peak load pricing. This allows the utility company to charge significantly more per kilowatt hour (KWH). This type of time-of-day pricing results in a very high cost for any sizable user of power. You may find that by switching as many of your plant operating hours as possible to a second or third shift the reduced energy costs will not only offset the higher labor costs you will be paying for the later shifts, but could even result in a significant gain in overall reduced energy costs.

One company in Wisconsin shifted 250 of it's plant workers to the third shift from the day shift. The added wages cost them $250,000 but the energy savings they realized by shifting power demands to off peak amounted to over $450,000 per year. A net gain of $200,000 per year or over $2 million over ten years.

Replace existing incandescent lighting with compact fluorescents. These are designed to fit into current fluorescent lighting fixtures while maintaining appearance and light levels. They have been estimated to produce up to a 70% reduction in energy usage and the light bulbs will last up to 10 times longer.

Replace 4 lamp fluorescent lights with 2 lamp fluorescent lights and use optical reflectors to maintain needed light levels. These are reflectors that slip in behind lights to reflect light given off by the 2 lamps. The light level that was generated by the 4 lamps is duplicated by the 2 lamps and the reflectors. Not only will you cut your lighting costs by up to 50%, you will also reduce your bulb replacement costs by 50%.

Paint your walls a very light reflective color. Light reflective colors will significantly reduce your lighting needs. This means you will need fewer lights or lower watt bulbs.

Use room occupancy sensors instead of on and off wall switches to control your lighting demands in all sporadically used areas. These sensors turn lights on when someone enters the room or area and off when they depart (after a predetermined period). They can save 25% to 50% of energy costs when compared to manual on and off switches.

Caulk and weather-strip around all doors and windows. Potential energy savings up to 10%.

Seal around all openings for plumbing, heating, and electrical outlets. These let in a great deal of outside air thereby driving up your climate control related energy costs.

At the start of each cooling season check your outside air conditioner units to make sure they clean and free from clogged vents from leaves and other debris.

Use tamper proof covers for your thermostats. If you don't, you will find that all day long they are being tampered with by employees who want it hotter or colder. Before we installed them I watched one day and saw the temperature on the thermostat outside my office adjusted over 30 times by my employees.

Shut doors to all unoccupied rooms and close down all interior heating and air conditioning vents in these rooms. (unless you have a heat pump and in this case check with your installing company to make sure this will not damage the unit).

Make sure you are not providing heat and air conditioning to areas that do not require it. At the very least modify your system to keep these areas at a greatly reduced temperature in the winter and a warmer temperature in the summer. If you are heating and cooling areas of your building that do not have people in them for most of the day, at the same level as the rest of your building, you are wasting money.

Keep the temperature a bit low in the winter and a bit high in the summer. You will never be able to please everyone no matter what temperature you maintain anyway. Someone will always be cold when someone else is hot. This being the case, you should set the temperature with an eye towards cost savings. One note here, do not allow space heaters to be used in the winter by those who might complain about the temperature. Instead encourage them to dress warmer. After all is this not why they invented sweaters?

Insulate your heating ducts. Check all ductwork and pipes once a year for leaks. You will find some and most likely they will be very simple to repair.

Insulate your hot water heaters but first make sure you check with your utility company to make sure that you are not covering any air vents.

Depending on the layout of your building you may find it more economical to use individual air conditioning units instead of central air. Since many people prefer fresh air you may find a reduced energy demand. Clearly this will only be an effective strategy within the right building.

Recycle all your paper. If your office does not generate enough recyclable paper to have a recycling company pay you to take it, look into having them take it for nothing. You will still reduce trash disposal costs and you are being environmentally sensitive.

Resources

"Keeping your company green". A 92 page free book that provides ideas and methods that you can use to start or improve recycling programs on your office. Offered by Rodale Press in Emmaue, PA. 1-212-967-5171.

"Office paper recycling". A 12 page booklet offered free by the National Office Paper Recycling Project, 1620 I Street N.W., 4th floor, Washington, DC, 20006.

For help with your company's waste reduction and recycling efforts contact the Washington State Department of Ecology. They have produced two booklets which they are offering at no charge. These booklets, titled "Success Through Waste Reduction" and "Waste Reduction in Your Business", can be obtained by calling 1-206-438-7586. I strongly recommend you call and get these booklets. They offer you the chance to learn how to save money and help save the planet we live on.

Put recycling bins near your photocopy machines, computer printers, and similar areas to encourage recycling. You should have already contacted your local recycling company and made arrangements for periodic pick up based on your volume. This will reduce your trash disposal costs and possibly generate income for the company.

Co-op recycling. If you do not even generate enough recyclable material to make it worth the while of a recycling company to even take it for free, look into combining your material with that of other companies in your industrial park, strip mall, or area. Combined, you may be able to get a company to pay for your material or at least pick it up at no charge. Think of this as cooperative recycling.

Chapter 19. Insurance including workers' compensation.

"Economy is in itself a source of great revenue."

Seneca

You must shop around for your insurance coverage. Blindly staying with the same company year after year will rarely, if ever, result in the best coverage for the best rates. I suggest that you bring in 3 agents each year or at least every two years to review your insurance needs, recommend coverage, and provide costs.

I would bring in a regional independent agent, a major independent, and a carrier's agent directly. By doing this you are accomplishing a number of things. First, you are shopping for the best costs. But, secondly, and as importantly, you are seeking to find out what coverage each will recommend. This will help you find out if your current coverage is adequate, if you are over covered, or under covered. If all three companies recommend the same levels of coverage then you are probably safe. If two of the three recommend higher or lower levels of coverage you better find out why and see if you agree.

You do not need to be an insurance expert as long as you deal with someone who is. You want to avail yourself of their expertise and by undergoing this process at least every two years this is exactly what you will be doing. You want each to give you a complete written proposal including recommended coverage, explanations for these recommendations, and costs for each. Without costs for each area of coverage you will have no way to effectively evaluate one company against another and you will lose the option to pick and chose policies for different areas of coverage from one company to another.

This process will prevent you from being sold an inadequate insurance package designed to low ball you into working with that company or from overinsuring from a company that thinks they are "the source" and are padding the bill. Make it clear that you are securing 3 proposals. Remember, you do not need to have all your coverage with one company. In fact, unless the individual costs are all best with one company or unless one company has a special package plan for your type of business, you probably should not keep all coverage with one company.

There is no reason why you can't have business coverage with one company and auto coverage with another, etc.. In fact, the only reason that would cause you to by all coverage from one company even though some policies are more costly would be laziness or convenience which is often nothing more than another form of laziness.

Contact the Insurance Information Institute. They offer a wide variety of publications that will be very helpful to you in your quest to obtain the best coverage at the lowest cost. 1-800-331-9146. Call and ask for a listing of all their publications.

Find out what discounts you can get on your insurance costs if you installed security systems. Find out what system would yield what discount and then obtain prices for these systems. If the savings do not justify the prices in a reasonable time it may not be worth it to you to install them on the basis of reduced insurance costs only.

Note: Even if you do not have a system put stickers on the window and doors (also your cars) that indicates you do have a security system. This is an excellent way to deter the average thief. These can be purchased through most direct mail office supply companies and industrial supply companies for a few dollars.

Make sure that any auto coverage you have is not a duplication of what you already have under other policies or one that can be more effectively and economically replaced . For example, if you are carrying a high liability coverage in one area you may not need it on another policy. A general liability umbrella policy may allow you to greatly reduce the liability coverage on your auto policies thereby providing an overall significant savings with no loss in coverage.

You must look at all areas of coverage to make sure what you want is covered at the amounts you want and nothing more is included that you did not want and can drop. Discuss this with your insurance agent.

Make sure you are not overinsuring. It will do you no good to insure something for $100,000 when the replacement value is only $75,000. The agent and company may have no trouble taking your money but they will not pay you more than they have to. They will not rebate premiums if you have overvalued something and therefore overinsured.

It is up to you to know the value. If you cover equipment for $10,000,000 maximum at replacement value and the total replacement value is only $5,000,000 that is your problem. You should know or have a darn good idea as to the real replacement value. The opposite of this is also true, do not underinsure. Make sure you know whether you are insured for replacement value.

This is an area where a lot of gray area exists. This is one more good reason for conducting annual reviews. By conducting these you will get opinions and advice from a number of different sources and an inconsistency is much more likely to surface. Remember, do not just ask agents and companies to provide bids on current coverage but to evaluate your operation and recommend coverage and provide costs.

Look into cost savings offered if you place all policies with one company. You may find that individually one company's prices are too high but when combined with a multiple policy discount they may collectively be the best value. Savings based on multiple policies can range from 5% to 15% when compared to the cost of individual policies. Please understand I am not telling you the best value will always be to put all policies under one roof.

The only way for you to determine this is to obtain proposals from companies on an individual and combined basis. Then you will have the costs you need to judge the most cost effective manner for you to obtain the desired coverage. Please also understand, as I have said many times, that you are striving for the best value for your money. This often, but not always, will be the best price.

Cost should always be a major factor but never make it the only factor. If the cost is close but a bit higher with company B than with company A, but company B has a better reputation and provides better service, company B may be your best buy.

Self-insurance? Worth looking into but be very, very careful. If not planned right, including large claim back up coverage, one large claim could wipe your company out. You had better know what you are getting into, what the costs are, what the risk is and what the savings would be. Even then think about it again.

While I have never been a supporter of self-insurance it is something you may want to discuss with your insurance agent. For the right company under the right circumstances and with proper controls, self-insurance may represent a viable alternative to traditional plans. I strongly caution you to be careful.

As an alternative I would suggest that you look into raising your deductible levels. By raising your plan's deductible level in exchange for reduced premiums, you are, in effect, creating a very controlled and limited liability form of self-insurance. Find out what your rates will be reduced to under various deductible levels.

If you do this for health insurance, depending on the size of the rate drop, your savings may be large enough that you can keep the employees deductible at the current rate and have the policies deductible level raised to a higher level. In this case the company would pay the difference between the two deductible levels in exchange for reduced premiums.

For instance, if your premiums drop by 15% by raising your deductible from $100 to $500 and you keep the employees at $100 you will be paying all claims over $100 up to the $500 level at which time the insurance carrier picks up. You are, in effect, self-insuring with a $400 risk. If your premium savings exceed $400 per employee and the deductible is a one time total of $500 and not $500 on each instance, then you are ahead. Look into this at a few different deductible levels and don't rule out increasing the employee deductible levels as well since they are also sharing in the costs savings via a reduced contribution.

Employee theft. If you have been the victim of employee theft contact your insurance company. Many policies have automatic coverage built in to at least cover limited employee theft.

Make sure any employee you have that handles money is bonded.

Check all equipment leases / financing you have to make sure that you are not carrying insurance you do not need. Often the company financing or leasing the equipment will automatically build in insurance coverage. They will not call your attention to it and, in fact, go to great lengths to avoid discussing it or they make it appear that it is mandatory, routine, or whatever it takes to include it. Instead, they factor it into the monthly payment.

Since the leasing company actually owns the equipment and the financing company co - owns it they want the equipment covered in the event of a loss. Fair enough. What's the problem? Simple, in almost all cases this equipment is already covered under your general business policy automatically. They know full well this is the case.

All you need to do is call and confirm this with your agent and have a binder sent to them (at no cost) indicating coverage already exists. They make a great deal of profit on this coverage as not only is it not needed and almost never collected on, but it is also significantly overpriced. So not only is the coverage most likely a duplication of coverage, but it is also a much more costly coverage.

For example, I leased a new phone system, the leasing company presented me with the contracts that included insurance coverage that ran over $400 per year. No mention of this was made as we reviewed the contracts and when I brought it up I was told it was just routine and required anyway. In print smaller than mice type, the option of getting a binder from my insurance company was printed. This, of course, was never pointed out.

My entire $1,000,000 general business policy only cost me $4,400 per year and they were trying to charge me $400 to cover a $10,000 phone system. Quite a deal. 1/11th of the cost for 1/100th of the coverage. Over the 5 years of the lease I would have paid over $2,000 for coverage I did not even need. The salesman told me that 50% of the people he closes take the insurance without a question. All they are concerned about is what the payment is, not how it is arrived at.

A personal note. This is really a personal strategy and not a business one but it happens so frequently I feel I should present it to you anyway. I don't have exact figures but I would estimate that this cost consumers hundreds of millions of dollars a year. Consumers who think they are doing the right thing.

Most often these are first time home buyers who have enough to do just trying to own that first house and don't need to pay one penny more than they have to. Yet, everyday they are getting ripped off to the tune of hundreds of dollars a year. How? By being coerced into buying mortgage insurance.

Sounds great, if a husband dies he won't leave his wife with mortgage payments she can't meet and that might cause her to lose the house and live in a box under a bridge with the children. If the wife dies they tell you the same thing could happen to the husband. What cad would want this to happen? Of course, you need this insurance they tell you. Your emotions are being played with.

The problem isn't the idea of the insurance. It is the cost and coverage provided by the insurance. This insurance might cost you $500 or $600 per year (of course conveniently built into the monthly payment) per $100,000 dollars of coverage. Coverage payable to the financing company, not the surviving spouse.

Sound reasonable? It shouldn't. Depending on your age and health, you can buy $250,000 of term insurance for as little as $200 a year. If you die you can have the house paid off and leave your husband or wife an extra $150,000. You could cover only the $100,000 mortgage for as little as $100 per year. You might be overpaying on mortgage insurance by 400% to 500% or more.

Still think the people who financed your house are looking out for you? **Remember, they are not helping you, they are not looking out for you, they are not your friend. They are a business trying to make money and you are a vehicle to help them make that money. Don't ever forget this.**

Also, in case you have not realized it, the cost of the insurance can go up each year but the amount of the mortgage it is protecting goes down every year. It gets more profitable for the insurance company every year. If you bought your own term life insurance you could reduce the coverage each year if desired to match the current mortgage balance.

Plain and simple this is a rip off. Just like all insurance coverage offered by any company financing any product or service. You will always be able to do better on your own. Think. Ask the questions.

Ask your agent what you can do to reduce your insurance costs. They won't tell you unless you ask. By asking you are expressing concerns over costs. Dissatisfaction over costs should be construed by the agent as a sign you are going to look elsewhere for coverage. The agent suddenly has a great incentive to try to reduce your costs.

Think long term when you think about ways you can reduce costs. For example, if you install a security system that costs $2,000 and you only save $500 on your insurance costs you might wonder why you should bother. However, if you plan on being in that building for 10 years that $2,000 cost will save you over $5,000 in premiums. You must think both short term and long term and not automatically make a decision based on just short term or long term.

Consider anti theft devices for all company cars. Examine costs versus reduction in premiums both short and long term. Depending on the cost of the system you are considering and the resulting savings on your insurance plan, your payback may be in just a year or two. Be careful here, long term considerations with an automobile must be thought of in a 2 to 4 year time frame at most. However, given the relatively low cost of today's security systems you may find an immediate payback.

For example, a $150 system may save you 10% or more on your insurance. If your auto insurance cost is $1,800 per year (which mine is) and you save 10%, you will have a payback in 10 months. After that you will save $15 per month. Over the next 3 years you will save $570. ($30 the first year and $180 each year for the next for 3 years.) Your $150 cost has turned into a $570 savings. Now multiply this by the number of company cars you are insuring.

Make sure that your auto policy covers towing. Even if you only use it once every 10 years you will be ahead of the game since it only costs about $4 per year and a single tow can be significantly more than that.

Consider taking a higher deductible for both your business and auto insurance policies. Ask for the savings if you take a higher deductible and compare this to the added risk. Compare the rates at 2 or 3 different deductible levels.

Look for agents or carriers that specialize in your type of business. Start by asking any association you belong to for suggestions. Also, ask competitors, suppliers, and even the Chamber of Commerce. If special plans exist for your type of business you should be able realize significant savings due to bundled types and levels of coverage. You will find that needed levels of coverage are built into the plan and that if purchased separately they would cost you a great deal more each year. I was able to save over $1,200 a year by finding a plan designed to cover companies in my industry.

A note of caution however, just because an agent tells you they are offering a great plan for your type of business don't assume this is true. You should still get at least three quotes. The agent with the special plan may be just calling it that to sell you when indeed it is not that special at all, or the plan may be designed for your type of business but it is overpriced, or contains elements that might be germane for most types of businesses in your industry but are not needed for your business at all.

Make sure you are not insuring something already covered by someone else. For example, if you rent a building don't carry insurance on the building. You only want coverage on the components of the building which make up your operation. Make sure the owner of the building carries the insurance not you. As obvious as this sounds this type of situation happens all too frequently.

Make sure that your insurance covers replacement value not current value. It may seem that you are saving money by covering for current value but if you have a claim and need to replace the lost or damaged equipment you will quickly find out that you have been very short sighted. The current value will in most cases be a fraction of the cost you will need to replace the item. Don't cut corners in this area. Make sure you have replacement value or at least coverage equal to what the cost of very good used equipment would be.

Don't risk a misunderstanding and don't fall prey to intentional deceit. If your agent tells you that you are covered for something make sure that you are by checking your policy to verify you are covered for what you think you are and for the amount you think you are covered for. Because most policies are written in an attempt to confuse you over what kind of coverage you really have, you might have to ask for written clarification.

Don't be afraid to ask for a layman's written explanation of any of the coverage you are not sure of. Remember, you are dealing with an industry that goes out of it's way to confuse the insured by issuing policies that are very hard, if not impossible, to understand. This is not an accident. Don't feel stupid asking for <u>written</u> clarification or verification of any or all coverage. If they don't like it, tough!

You cannot rely on verbal statements made by any agent representing the carrier. If you look hard enough you will find a disclaimer in your policy telling you this. Of course, by the time you get the policy it is too late. If you have a claim the only thing that counts is what the policy says you are covered for. You better know what you have. Screaming "but my agent told me ..." will get you nothing but high blood pressure.

<u>Remember, premiums are just another name for payments.</u> Your goal is to control these payments, buy only what you need, and to get the best value for your purchase. Demand written recommendations on coverage and costs and make the agent justify these recommendations to you. Insurance agents are sales representatives. Insurance is their product. Don't forget this. Plain and simple, like any other purchase you consider they should justify this purchase to you.

<u>Whenever you have a claim get your own estimate.</u> Don't do what most companies do and just take whatever they tell you the claim is worth. This is not an open and shut case. Just because they say so does not make it so. By securing your own estimate you can either verify the insurance company's estimate and know you have a fair settlement or you can disagree with their costs and fight for a higher settlement. If you just accept their estimate you may find the actual loss involved to cost more, much more in some cases. Of course, if your estimate comes in much lower than theirs I do not suggest you ask for a lower settlement. I am sure you have better uses for your time than to advise the insurance company of an overpayment.

<u>Make sure you are looking into having one policy to cover all locations and subsidiaries.</u> The goal is to see if you can get lower overall rates based on volume. Do not assume you can or can't. Find out!

<u>Look into renewable term life insurance instead of whole life or universal life insurance to replace any policies you might carry on key personnel.</u> "Key man" or "Key Woman" insurance is designed to pay the company an amount of money in the event of the death of a key executive. The idea behind this type of insurance is that by losing a key person you will suffer lost sales, disrupted operations, or some other business related problems.

The funds from the policy are designed to provide the company with a fiscal cushion while you adjust to the loss, replace the person, and restore profitability. It is not an investment vehicle. Do not buy insurance that promotes itself as an investment vehicle. The point of these policies is to provide short term flow of funds in the event you lose a key person, not to act as a long term investment vehicle.

Under any circumstances I think these types of policies are a dubious investment vehicle at best. If you have a whole life or universal insurance policy on a key person and you lay them off or fire them what happens to this policy? What about if they move on to another company? How about if you sell out?

In these cases and many others you have a policy that severely limits your options. You could be forced to continue payment of a policy solely to retain any cash value you have in it until it reaches a point where you can cash it in and get most, or at least some, of your money back.

Term insurance will give you much more flexibility and if you buy renewable term insurance you will be able to renew it each year. Furthermore, depending on the age and health of the individual you are insuring you may also be able to save a significant amount of money during the early years of the policy, up to 70% of the cost or more.

In years down the road you may not need a policy at all. Think about this carefully and consult with your accountant about the many short and long term considerations beyond those I have outlined that may exist for your company and your employees. However, never assume that the best, or only, way to go is whole life or universal life insurance no matter what your insurance sales person tells you.

"Key man" or "Key woman" insurance, do you really need it at all? Only you can decide this, but do not assume that you must carry it on all or any of your executives. You must ask yourself the questions. How valuable are they to me? What will I lose if they die? How will I replace them? What will it cost me in lost business or income if they die?

Remember, insurance is needed to protect against a fiscal loss. Will you suffer a fiscal loss if they die? How is their death any different to you than if they left for another company? Think it through. Even if you decide that for whatever reason you do need this insurance rethink this decision every year. The needs of the company change and the value to the company of those insured will often change as well.

Perhaps the reason that you felt justified the need for this insurance 5 years ago no longer applies. Do not automatically continue the coverage unless there is justification to do so. This justification could be internal or it could have to do with the policy. If you took out a policy that will cost you money to cancel before a certain time you may be forced to keep it longer than you want to or need to simply to avoid losing money on it. By buying term life as I have outlined you can eliminate this problem.

Again, by thinking out the need and type of policy best for you ahead of time you can build in the flexibility up front that will give options down the road. Think proactive, long and short term.

Are your health insurance costs making you sick? (Sorry, I could not resist.) Health insurance costs are one of the highest costs you have. They literally can affect the fiscal health of your company. You must take whatever steps you can to reduce these costs even if it means increasing your employee's monthly contributions.

If your company has to lay off employees, or even close the doors, due to an inability to pay for health insurance, your employees have lost all coverage and a job. Faced with that as a possible alternative to paying a higher share of their own coverage I would expect you to have few complaints.

I would suggest that you split the cost 50 /50 with your employees. If you have a plan that dictates you pay a higher percentage get rid of that plan. I know some plans dictate that employers pay 80% of the cost. You have enough outsiders in the form of the government telling you how to run your business do you want to let an insurance carrier control you as well?

They seem to have forgotten who the customer is. Don't you forget. The government may pay 100% or 90% of all health insurance costs for their employees (with our tax dollars) but you should not. Quite frankly neither should they, but they do not worry about profits and such mundane things as staying in business. You must.

In Pursuit of Profits. How To At Least Double Your Profits Without Increasing Your Sales.

If you are now paying 100%, depending on the plan's cost, a 50 / 50 split of costs with your employees will save you between $3,000 and $5,000 per year per employee. If you have 20 employees this will save you $60,000 to $100,000 per year. If you have 2,000 employees this will save you between $6,000,000 and $10,000,000 per year. If you have 20,000 employees this would save you between $60,000,000 and a $100,000,000 per year.

This same strategy goes for any other employee benefit policies you have including group life and short and long term disability.

If you are not using an HMO I strongly suggest you look into them today. If you are using an HMO I suggest you compare the cost of the one you are using to all others offered in your area. The savings realized by an HMO when compared to plans such as Blue Cross Blue shield is significant. Let me give you some actual numbers of the type of savings I realized when I switched plans in my company from Blue Cross Blue Shield to an HMO.

In 1991 our rates for Blue Cross Blue Shield Master Medical were as follows:

Individual	Family
$3,892.44	$8,647.92

The average increases we had been hit with over the previous 4 year had been 25% to 35%. That is a per year increase not a total over 4 years. I dropped Blue Cross Blue Shield Master Medical and added the three HMOs indicated below. I have also included the cost of each.

	Individual	Family
HMO Blue	$2,106.96	$5,562.36
Pilgrim	2,124.36	NA
US Healthcare	1,812.00	4,802.40

The average annual increase for US Healthcare and Pilgrim has been about 10% to 15%. Less than one half of what BCBS Master Medical had been each year. Look at these savings. The lowest cost HMO individual plan was a full 53% lower than the BCBS Master Medical Plan. The lowest cost HMO family plan was 43% lower than the BCBS Master Medical plan. The dollar difference on the family plans was a savings of $3,845.53 per year per family. If your company has only 25 employees on the family plan that switched from Blue Cross Blue Shield Master Medical to the HMO the annual savings would be over $96,000.

Using these figures and a pretax profit ratio of 5%, if you are paying 100% of the cost you would need to increase your sales by $1,920,000 to add $96,000 to your bottom line. At a 2.5% profits ratio your sales would have needed to increase $3,840,000 to add the same $96,000 to your bottom line. This is not only a huge savings to your company, but it is a direct addition to your bottom line pretax profit. If your employees contribute a percentage they would also realize a significant savings.

Check all hospital bills. It has been reported that 89% of all hospital bills contain errors. 89%. These errors are always in the hospitals favor. This error ratio is far to high to be accidental. It is up to you to monitor and question these bills. Ask your employees if the services were even performed. I have seen many charges on many bills for services that were never even performed. High hospital costs translate into higher insurance costs. Do not let them get away with this. Ask your insurance company to check all bills and advise them of any questionable or bogus billings you uncover.

Reduce your workers' compensation rates by putting safety plans into effect and by having proper training. This not only will save you money on premiums and reduced claims, but it also protects your employees. This is not only the responsible thing to do, but it keeps productivity up while keeping costs down. As I have said throughout this book be proactive in as many areas as possible not just reactive. Don't wait until you have a claim or a series of accidents. Set the proper foundation now.

Resource

"Workplace Safety Guide". A free 54 page booklet offer by Genum Publishing Company of 1145 Catalyn Street, Schenectady, NY 12303-1836.

Keep an eye on your border line employees. It has been reported that employees who are poor performers and may be in danger of losing their job are 5 times more likely to file a workers' compensation claim. Keep a very close eye on these people. The obvious question here is why have you not gotten rid of them already?

Be involved in your yearly workers' compensation audit. This is the time each year where your insurance carrier will verify payrolls and risk classifications. You must verify all figures to ensure proper payrolls within each risk classification within the period in question and to challenge any risk classifications that you think are wrong.

Mistakes are very common in both these areas. Just because they say so does not make it so. There are hundreds of classifications they can assign. You can, and should, challenge any questionable classifications. You must educate yourself as to what the classification options are and which ones are being applied to each of your employees.

How else will you be able to determine if the assigned classifications are proper and whether or not you have other options? If in doubt challenge. Many are wrong and errors will almost always be in the favor of the insurance company. Errors that you pay for in the form of higher rates. If they will not change questionable classifications look into another company and see what classification they would use.

I did this with one company and saved thousands of dollars per year in premiums by having a group of workers reclassified (correctly) into a risk of under $.40 per hundred dollars earned versus the previous classification of $5.90 per hundred dollars of payroll. An incorrect classification I must add, that had existed for over 20 years. Figure out how much this cost the company in incorrectly charged premiums for 20 years.

Over ten years this will save them tens of thousands of dollars based on rates at the time. Now in my state rates are set by the state. But by being able to find a company who would modify classifications we, in effect, created a form of competitive bidding.

Rates per employee can vary tremendously. You can easily see rate differences of over 1000%. Improper rate classifications can very easily cost you hundreds, thousands, or even tens of thousands of dollars or more per year depending on your size, payroll, and industry. If there is any doubt as to the proper rate classification you can safely bet the insurance company will classify your employee at the highest rate classification they can. Higher risk classifications will result in higher premiums. Their goal is the exact opposite of yours. Never assume otherwise!

You should be involved if at all possible to "help" establish correct classifications up front. Make sure you ask your agent for a list of all possible classifications and the per hundred rate. Payroll assignments are also often incorrect so double check them as well.

If appropriate, request split rate classification. In today's employment world many employees perform multiple jobs. This can result in a number of possible rate classifications. You want the lowest rate classification possible. Your insurance company will try to assign the highest possible rate classification.

But what if your employee spends 40% of his time in a higher rate classification function and 60% of his time in a lower risk rate classification? Why should you be paying based on 100% of his time in the more costly rate function? In this case one rate might be $3.59 per $100 of earnings while the other possible rate might be $2.25 per $100 of earnings. This is a significant difference.

By obtaining a split rate you should be able to reduce the workers' comp costs of any employee who splits jobs by 10% to 50% depending on the rate differential and the ratio of time spent on each job function. If your current carrier will not split rates and your state allows it, look for one who will!

Fight bogus workers' compensation claims. Even though it seems that employers have fewer and fewer rights every year you still have some. Fighting a questionable claim is one of them. Get involved. Dispute it if you have any doubt as to the validity of the claim or if you doubt it was work related.

It has been estimated that false claims of injuries on the job or job related represent 20% to 25% of all claims. In the last ten years alone the average workers' compensation rate has increased 150%. This means huge cost increases to you. You must do something about it.

The workers' comp system was designed to help workers during periods of legitimate injuries, not allow them to take advantage of the system. Every claim will affect your rates. Your rates can triple with just one claim. Fake claims happen every day. Let me just give you one example I know of. A fellow was playing softball on Sunday. He slid into home plate and tore his knee up. He was a quick thinker. He did not go to the hospital. Instead, he suffered through the night and went to work at his job in the warehouse before everyone else the next morning. When the other employees arrived they found him lying next to a pallet holding his knee in pain. What do you know the poor fellow fell off the pallet and wrenched his knee. He was out of work for over 2 years.

Make sure that your employees understand that claims cost you money. Sometimes big money. Often an employee might stay out longer than necessary with an injury because he figures the company isn't being hurt since workers' compensation is covering the costs. Make them understand who really pays.

Monitor medical bills submitted to you for workers' compensation claims. Make sure the bills are legitimate and the service has been performed. It is not uncommon for unperformed services to be billed. You want to make sure the costs are legitimate and that the work was actually done. Check with your employee to make sure they did what they claimed to have done and billed for.

The medical establishment has never been accused of working in the best interest of the business communities workers' comp costs. Some have even been known to take advantage of the worker compensation system. I know first hand of cases in which bills were submitted for treatment and tests that were never conducted.

Remember, higher medical bills mean higher costs and you know who ends up paying for these in the long run. Only you have incentive to drive these costs down. The insurance company recovers their costs from you in the form of higher premiums. They don't care. The medical establishments collects added fees. They don't care. The employee collects the payments. They don't care. Only you care.

When you have a worker out on workers' comp try to get them back on the job as soon as possible even if only in a reduced capacity. This will go a long way toward reducing the claim and reducing the likelihood that a larger longer term claim will result. I know you might not believe this but some employees will milk the system for all they can get. Why, I have even heard that some lawyers encourage this. Some have even suggested that the system encourages abuse, waste, and corruption. I know, I know. These type of skeptics probably even think that there is abuse in the government and that not all people on welfare are doing all they can to get off it. Some people!!

Ask, no demand, that your insurance company investigate suspected fraud. I have done this on two occasions and in both cases the claim was denied. Never assume they will do this on their own. Only you have the incentive. They just pass costs on to you in the form of higher payments.

Cross check to make sure that any employees out on workers' comp are not collecting from unemployment at the same time. Make sure you report to both in writing what the employee's status is. Never assume that a government agency or insurance company will protect your interests. That is your job. Don't ever expect someone to do what you should be doing. You want to make sure they are not double dipping. If they are, you are going to be hit with increased rates from both and your employee is going to get away with cheating unless you have notified them.

Do all you can to make sure a problem employee does not become your problem. As difficult as it is in this day and age of very limited employer rights, you must check out all potential employees as thoroughly as possible. Not just for the obvious reasons, but also for any workers' compensation abuses and prior claims they may have had. I suggest you discuss any potential new hire with your insurance agent to find out what you can do and how they can help you do it. Do the same with your lawyer. Hiring a problem employee will be a very expensive, frustrating, and time consuming process.

Be involved with all claims. Remember, you are without the worker and you will pay the cost in the form of higher premiums. Therefore, you must be involved in the process and not assume your insurance company will protect your interests. You have the vested interest not them!

Find out why the claim occurred and take steps to insure that it does not happen again. Do not ignore the problem.

Make sure your employees do not modify equipment or machines or bypass any safety procedures to accommodate them or to increase production. This happens all too often. Employees can be very creative in ignoring and devising ways to bypass proper safety procedures. I have seen them ignore policy, modify machines, remove safety guards, and devise ways to do things with complete disregard for their personal safety.

Why would they do this? They might want to make the job easier, they may want to increase productivity or they may simply think their way is better. Not only will this result in more injuries which lead to higher costs and reduced productivity, but it could also be leaving you open to liability claims for negligence. Remember, we live in a world in which no one seems to be held accountable for their own actions. If your employee is injured because of something he did and he is not held liable, take a guess who will be.

You must train properly and you must monitor activity to make sure that any manual and mechanical safety devices are not being defeated. You should follow this advice not only because it will save you money and reduce your liability, but, more importantly, because it will protect your employees.

Don't you ever, and don't ever allow your people to, sacrifice safety for any reason. Not for increased productivity. Not for comfort. Not for increased profits. Nothing should come before the safety of your employees. Nothing.

Make sure you monitor all workers' compensation bills for penalty rates you are being assessed. In Massachusetts these are called experience modification rates. No matter what fancy name they call them they are higher rates that you pay due to a claim against you. These are not permanent rates. They are assessed for predetermined time periods after which they must be removed and your premiums must reflect the removal of the penalty rates. Don't expect these to come off automatically. Know how long you must pay these higher rates and make sure they are dropped as soon as that date hits.

It is your job to find out how much your rates have gone up and for how long they will stay up. I am talking about your overall rates. This is not just your basic rate but any type of experience modifications rates, or high risk penalty rates or anything else they may tack on in your state.

Never assume that the insurance company will automatically lower your rates. If you must assume anything, assume they will continue charging you the claim related higher rate well past the point they are entitled to. In other words, you must protect your interests.

I know from first hand experience that the insurance company will at times not only charge you the higher rates well beyond the point they are entitled to but, that you may also have to fight very hard to get your rates lowered. It took me almost a year to get a $7,000 reduction and rebate from an insurance carrier in a case like this. We were being charged premiums that amounted to $7,000 higher than normal as a result of a workers' comp claim. The rates were to stay higher for 3 years. At the start of the fourth year the rates did not decrease. It took nearly 12 months of dealing with insurance company bull to get the rates lowered for the next year and a credit for the $7,000 they overcharged us during the current year.

Train your people properly in all job functions, the safe and proper use of all equipment, all safety procedures and emergency procedures. Document all such training. This is taking both a proactive and reactive stance. Not only are you increasing productivity and helping to reduce the likelihood of an accident, but you are also laying a foundation of responsibility in the event of an accident or injury.

Stay in touch with any employee out on workers' comp or with an injury. You should care enough about your people to follow up with them to see how things are going. They are part of your team. If you do not care enough to be concerned about them then do it for fiscal reasons. You want to show them (or make them think) that you care about them and want them back as soon as possible. If they have not filed for workers' comp your concern and interest may influence their future actions.

Don't think they have not thought about filing for workers' comp or filing a lawsuit. It is very hard to pick up a newspaper or turn the TV on without seeing an ad from a lawyer encouraging everyone to file or sue for everything. Remember, as I have told you, you live in a world where nobody is held responsible for anything and therefore someone else must be held responsible. Guess who that some else most likely would be?

If they have filed, the sooner you get them back the lower your costs will be. If they have not filed a claim, your concern could very well encourage and influence them to the point that they will not file a claim. What do you think they might do if they think you don't give a damn about them?

Furthermore, the sooner you get them back on the job, the sooner your staffing will be back to normal. This is another form of the domino effect. Normal staffing increases productivity and allows you to more effectively service your customers.

Ask your carrier and agent what your company can do to provide a safer workplace and reduce your rates. This lets them know you are a concerned customer. Concerned about both rates and safety. They should be able to come in and provide you with any number of recommendations that will help you save money while improving safety.

Find out if your company has been assigned to a "risk pool" for workers' compensation. If so, most likely you are paying a much higher rate than you would be if you were not in the risk pool. You want to find a company that will take you on and cover you outside of the risk pool in order to get the best rates.

Make sure all outside contractors or workers of any kind that are not on your payroll, but are doing work for you or on your premises, have certificates of insurance. If an injury occurs under these conditions and they do not carry their own insurance they may be able to file against yours. Don't just take their word for it that they have coverage. Demand that a copy of their current insurance certificate be given to you for your files. No certificate, no job. Very simple.

Make sure that both your insurance company and the physician involved in the case are aware of the employee's job duties. You do not want a determination of whether or not an employee can return to work to be based solely on the employee's version of what his or her job entails.

I have seen this happen on more than one occasion. In one case in particular the employee had indicated that the bulk of his job was heavy lifting when in fact the heaviest thing he lifted on the job was his paycheck. Had a return to work determination been based on this employee's description of the job this employee might never have returned to work. You don't suppose that was his objective do you?

As soon as any accident happens make sure that you get statements from all witnesses while the incident is still fresh in their mind. Time has a way of distorting what happened as does a few phone calls from the injured employee. You must have this information if you have any chance of fighting a bogus or questionable claim.

On more than one occasion this has enabled us to stop a fraudulent claim right up front. Don't wait for your insurance company to investigate. This could take weeks or months and may never be done properly. A key witness might forget, quit, have been fired, or have a changed view of what happened.

Chapter 20. Marketing.

"Marketing is simply sales with a college education."

John Freund

The strategies I present here will cover a variety of cost saving tactics that you can use to reduce and control your marketing expenses including your advertising, promotional, media, and research costs. A number of these strategies will also cover ways in which you can reduce your costs when dealing with the "outside experts" that specialize in these areas.

These include advertising agencies, public relations firms, and graphic design houses. In the interest of brevity **I will refer to these "outside experts" in the strategy with the generic term "agencies". However, rest assured that the tactics I give you will most often be equally applicable for dealing with any type of "outside expert". Please also read my strategies in the next chapter on outside experts specifically as many of them apply here as well.**

There are many excellent, highly effective, and honest agencies, but, as you will find in any industry, there are also a number of dishonest, ineffective, and unethical agencies. I will show you how to reduce the costs of working with your agency and how to make sure that you are not being abused by an agency with questionable ethics.

"Let advertisers spend the same amount of money improving their product that they do on advertising and they wouldn't have to advertise."

Will Rogers

<u>Do you need advertising at all?</u> Do not assume that you do. Statistics have shown that two thirds of all United States businesses operate successfully without advertising. You might want to read that again. **Even the legendary adman David Ogilvy has stated "Those in the advertising industry have a vested interest in prolonging the myth that all advertising increases sales. It doesn't.".**

Instead of advertising these companies concentrate their resources on improving their product, process, customer service, distribution, sale force, and every other area of their company. They look within instead of, or at least before, looking outside. They let their products and services speak for them. It is my strong conviction that every company should follow this same strategy. One further thought. It has been estimated that the average consumer is bombarded with up to 5,000 advertising messages a day. Can yours even get through?

"Marketing is the link in the chain between supply and demand."

Derrick W. Welch

Understand that there are two types of market penetration. The first, and normally the only type ever considered, is what percentage of the total market you conduct business with. Even here things are not as clear as some would lead you to believe. It is more complex than just determining that the "market" you are targeting consists of 10,000 possible sales sources and concluding that since you have 2,000 customers you have a 20% market penetration. This is far too simplistic.

Determining the actual "market" can be a very complex issue which must include a definition of the term "market" as it applies to those who you feel are a prospect for your products and services. This definition must include primary, secondary, and peripheral targets. It must include geographical limitations unless your market is worldwide. It must include a time frame definition as to when they last ordered from you. Are you considering a sale from three years ago as a customer? These are a few of the more important considerations that you must take into account when you attempt to define and determine your market and your market penetration.

But my point here is not to teach you how to define markets. It is to make you think about the second type of "market penetration" that is so often neglected by many companies and yet it is the one that offers you the greatest source of immediate sales. Anyone who could use your product or service and does not is defined as a prospect within your market. This includes your customers. Yes, that is right. Your customers are also your prospects. In fact, they are your best prospects. Unless your customers are buying every product and service you offer that could benefit them, they are a prospect for those products and services they are not using.

This is the second, and what I consider most important, type of market penetration. This is also a much easier market to measure. You know who your customers are. If you really know your customers and their operation and needs then you should know exactly what products and services you offer that they could be using. Therefore, since you know how many of your products and services they are using you know what your penetration is with each customer individually and collectively.

The more products and services you can sell them, the greater your penetration will be. The higher the penetration, the more that customer comes to depend on you and the greater the level of customer loyalty will be. All highly favorable situations.

My experience has shown that this is the most neglected market. **Yet, this is the market with the greatest potential at the lowest cost that can be realized in the shortest period of time.** Your customers know you. You should know them. This is the market that has the least path of resistance and greatest level of familiarity with you.

Think about this. If you have 1,000 customers who each buy one item from you a year and you can successfully get even just 25% of these to purchase one more item, have you not just increased your number of sales by 25%? Compare the cost of doing this to the cost of increasing your customer base by 25%.

Consider that it costs an average of five times more to get a new customer than it does to sell to an existing customer. Does it make sense to concentrate the bulk of your efforts and resources in the pursuit of new customers and then spend time convincing them who you are and why they should do business with you when you have a gold mine of opportunity right in front of you now who knows you and trusts you? Of course not.

But this is exactly what many companies, of all sizes, do every day. New customers are targeted while existing customers are simply maintained or taken for granted. Very little, if any, effort is expended trying to develop existing customers. Is your company doing this?

Build on the foundation you already have first. Putting the bulk of your resources in the efforts that will produce the greatest return for the lowest cost is nothing more than common sense marketing.

"Always think about where your advice is coming from. Do you think your barber would ever tell you that you don't need a haircut?"

Derrick W. Welch

Never confuse advertising with marketing. They are not the same thing. Advertising is merely one weapon in your marketing arsenal. The most expensive weapon. Far too many companies think that advertising is marketing. They think everything begins and ends with advertising. They are wrong.

Ad agencies often feel the same way. That is why they are called "advertising agencies". If you deal with an ad agency remember marketing is not advertising. Ad agencies sell advertising. Their whole company is built for the sole purpose of selling advertising. Make sure you understand this. They will recommend what they sell just as you would. Your marketing efforts must extend far beyond merely advertising.

Everything from how you dress and present, to how your customers are greeted on the phone and in person represents marketing. From how you package your product or deliver your service, to the uniforms your staff wears is part of marketing. Each gives your customer an impression about your company. Each is marketing.

There are many more cost effective weapons in your marketing arsenal than advertising. Never forget that anything about your business, no matter how small or how large, that gives your customer or prospect an image or perception about your company is marketing. From the name of your company to the name of your product. From your window display to your corporate logo, you are engaging in marketing.

Don't hire Goliath when all you need is David. Whenever possible use freelance talent to develop your advertising, public relations, and marketing materials if you are unable or unwilling to develop them yourself. Freelance writers, designers, and graphic artists often have big agency experience and are working on their own now or may be moonlighting. You will be able to get big time talent and small time prices.

They have little or no overhead which is a big reason for the lower costs. Agencies on the other hand have high overhead and you might find yourself indirectly paying for a number of services and costs that you do not even use. In the creative department alone of an advertising agency you will find a creative director, copy chief, copy writer, junior copywriter, art director, artist, mechanical artist, layout artist, and on and on.

Even worse, you will never know who is working on your account if you are dealing with a large or even mid sized agency. Unless you are a major account your jobs will be relegated to a lower level writer and artist. These people must get their experience somewhere and your account is as good a place as any to start. Don't misunderstand me here. Many of these people are very talented and will be the big names of tomorrow. However, you may be being charged a great deal more money than you should be based on the level of experience you may actually be getting.

Unless you have a cost justified reason for using the services of a full service agency, don't. These agencies have a very large overhead and this is reflected in the hourly rates they charge you or the monthly retainer they charge you. Why pay for media, production, marketing, creative, administration, and other services which you may never need or use? Many will only work on monthly retainers. Your goal should be to keep costs down and not to incur higher monthly fixed costs. If you think a retainer arrangement is a good deal that saves you money in the long run, think again.

The agency is in business to make money and not to save you money. Any retainer arrangement you have will either reflect the maximum hours they will be expending on your account or it will contain an added billing clause should your demands exceed the projected hours. If the hours they expend on your behalf fall below the projected hours they have built the fee on do you think they will send you a refund? **I'll give you a tip. Don't wait by the mail box.**

As far as buying services from an agency on an hourly rate, be aware the rates will be much higher than the rates charged by a freelancer. A freelancer that may have background and experience that rivals or exceeds that of the agency talent. Another benefit is that you will be dealing directly with the creative talent and not through the account executive. Furthermore, you will be directing the creative effort instead of being directed by the agency people. There is a huge difference here and I will cover this in detail in later sections.

At the very least you should have many projects that can be done very well at a greatly reduced cost by sources other than the large full service agency. Would you call in an excavator to dig a fence post?

Select your ad agency on results not awards. Unless the agency has won awards for increasing sales any awards they have won should mean nothing to you. Your goal in advertising should be to increase sales not to help your agency win awards.

Find out how successful the agency has been with other clients in meeting the objective of increasing sales. Find out what the cost and results of each campaign were and **don't be dazzled by any self-serving awards that the industry bestows upon itself.** Find out what the results were and what the cost to get them was and then contact the client these were done for and find out if the agency is telling the truth.

You want results and you want a commitment to your account by the top people. Normally the best way to insure this is to select an agency in which you will be one of the top accounts.

I would rather be a big fish in a smaller pond than a minnow in the ocean. I would want senior people on my account and I would want to know that my business is very important to that agency. By being a top account in the agency I will be able to control the process better as I am working directly with the principles. I will get better service. I would strongly suggest that you do not deal with a large agency that will consider you a small account just so you can say they are your agency.

Resource
"Selecting an Advertising Agency: Factors to Consider, Steps to Take". Published by the Association of National Advertisers. 1-212-697-5950.

Monitor bills. You should always make periodic audits of **all** your outside suppliers. By audits, I do not mean that you should audit your outside sources books. I do mean that you should request verification of the charges they claim to be incurring on your behalf. No, you do not need to see every bill. But you better see the larger ones and enough of the smaller ones to keep the outside supplier on their toes.

The purpose is to make sure that what they are charging you is what they should be charging you. By this I mean, if a supplier charges you $200 for shipping is this what the shipping costs were? Unless you see proof of the shipping bill you have no way to know this for sure.

What if the shipping bill to the supplier was only $150 and yet you were billed $200? You have overpaid by 33%. This costs you money and most likely will affect the price of your products and services as you raise them to recapture these costs or you will suffer reduced profitability. In the case of items like shipping, in which you can demand and get verification of the costs, I would suggest you have a policy of requesting this proof automatically with the billing.

In other cases you will want proof for every outside cost your supplier claims to incur on your behalf and in some cases you will only want periodic proof. This is especially important with advertising agencies, PR firms, and design houses. I will go into this in more depth in sections covering these areas specifically but let me just give you a couple of examples as to why this is so important.

I know of a bank that was charged $8,000 for a printing job by an ad agency who hired a local printer to do the job. The agency was not pleased with the result and refused to pay for it. The printer, in an effort to appease the agency, agreed not to charge them for this printing. The agency turned around and told the bank the job was fine and billed them $8,000. The agency had paid nothing.

I know of another case in which a design house solicited three bids from printers to print a four color promotional catalog for one of their clients. They received bids ranging from a low of $12,000 to a high of $22,000. They showed the client the high bid and recommended this printer. The client, as they often are, was led and did not lead. He did not ask what the other bids were or if there were even any other bids.

The client simply deferred to the agency. The agency then turned around and had the lowest priced printer do the job. They paid $12,000 and billed out $26,400. This was the highest priced printer's price they had misled the client into thinking they were using, and the standard 20% agency mark up.

Had this client controlled this situation up front and demanded the agency get at least three bids and show them to him this would not have happened. Better yet, the client should have obtained prices on his own and eliminated the agency from the printing process altogether. By doing this he would have had control over the project and the price. He also would have saved the agency's 20% mark up.

At the very least he should have demanded to see the actual bills from the printer to the agency in order to verify these costs. Had he at least done this he would have discovered that they had been ripped off to the tune of $12,000. The printer's bill would have been $12,000. Adding the agency's mark up to this the client should have been billed $14,400, instead of the $26,400 he was billed. This example goes beyond poor purchasing practices and demonstrates how easy it is for any company to become a victim of fraud.

No one will have a greater interest in controlling your costs than you. **No one.** The very nature of the fact that most agency client contracts allow for a mark up of goods bought by the agency and sold to the client, lays a foundation for a conflict of interest on the agency's part. What incentive does the agency have to give you the best possible job at the lowest possible price? None of course. Quite the opposite is true. The higher the cost of the outside product or service they are buying for you, the larger the mark up will be and therefore the more income they will make.

Does this make sense to you? I hope not. They are being rewarded for increasing your costs. They may indeed be paying what they are charging you but this does not mean that they are not spending a heck of a lot more than they need to pay for that product or service. They are spending your money and they have little interest in spending it in the most efficient and economical manner possible. In fact, it could be suggested that the exact opposite is true.

But I am straying from the main point of this strategy. The point is to verify that what you are being charged is what they have paid for on your behalf. **I have used agencies as the main focal point in the above example but this strategy applies to anyone who is working on behalf of your company in any capacity and incurring costs they are passing on to you.**

You must protect your interests. If you have requested this outside work on behalf of one of your customers you have an obligation to that customer to verify all charges are proper. This is yet another reason to make sure that you audit your advertising agency's bills on a regular basis. In fact, I would suggest that all bills submitted to you by your agency be required to have the supplier's bill submitted along with it.

If their contract allows for a certain mark up of all outside material and services purchased or contracted by the agency on your behalf, they should have no problem with submitting the suppliers bill along with theirs for verification of amounts due and mark ups. Just blame the requirement on company policy or a tight fisted accountant if requesting it makes you uncomfortable.

This will not insure that your agency is purchasing products and services at the best price for the quality received but it will make sure that you are not being victimized by a switching tactic that can take place when the agency bids a job out, charges you based on the highest price quoted, and then awards the job to one of the lower bids. Don't kid yourself this happens! And when this is done the agency will still add on their standard markup. What a deal.

"If you don't know where you are going, how can you expect to get there?"

Basil Walsh

What are you trying to accomplish and are your efforts paying off? Your advertising and marketing efforts must have a goal. Far too many companies who advertise simply advertise for the sake of advertising. You must ask yourself what are you trying to accomplish? You must set goals and you must have objectives. You must also remember that advertising is merely one tool in your marketing portfolio.

Without measurable objectives and goals how do you know if your advertising is working? How do you know if you are wasting your money or if your dollars are being wisely spent? Unless you have a way to measure the results of any advertising efforts you have no way of knowing whether or not your money is being spent wisely. If you are working with an agency demand that the agency develop programs that can measure results. This should be part of every plan and program they recommend. If it can't be tracked and measured for tangible results don't buy into it.

Tangible results not some vague promise of long term results or increased visibility or the great coverall, "corporate awareness". Advertising should increase sales. If it doesn't, don't advertise. A very simple formula! Don't try to win awards for creativity with your advertising, direct mail, or printing efforts. This may be a goal of your ad agency or design house but it damn well better not be one of yours.

You must have goals you can track and you must have an established timetable in which you measure those goals. If your advertising efforts are not providing the results you want you cannot afford to keep pouring good money after bad money. Spending more money on bad or ineffective advertising in hopes that by spending more money you will accomplish your goals is stupid. Bad advertising is ineffective advertising. **You spend money on advertising and marketing for one reason only. To get more business. Don't let anyone tell you advertising or marketing has any other purpose. It does not!**

Your goal is very simple. You want the maximum sales at the lowest cost. The bottom line is results. You want proof of how effective the promotional efforts are. This is the only way you will be able to judge how effectively your money is being spent. You also want to make sure that you are not locking into a long term campaign that cannot be terminated without significant costs. By demanding accountability during the campaign and by not locking into unbreakable commitments, you have the option of pulling the plug and cutting your losses. They are your losses by the way. Not the agency's, yours.

Advertising costs money. Big money in most cases. More money than you should be paying in almost all cases. Therefore, this is a very serious matter and a return on this money must be expected and should be demanded.

Selecting an agency? Remember, agency prices like all other prices, are list prices. Once they have taken the time and effort to make a presentation to your company they have a vested interest in getting your account. They not only have a fiscal interest, but they also will have an emotional interest as they have spent time to develop the presentation for you. This is the best time for you to negotiate better terms or rates with them if they are the agency you want to work with. They will know your business can be had and if the alternative to giving a bit is getting nothing, the choice will be a simple one.

"His cardinal mistake is that he isolates himself, and allows nobody to see him: and by which he does not know what is going on in the very matter he is dealing with."

Abraham Lincoln

Giving his reason for relieving General John C. Fremont from his command in Missouri on September 9, 1861.

Control the process, especially the creative process. These comments apply to internal efforts as well, but focus on external agencies. In an ad agency the creative department will very often drive everything. They will control the account management team and the client. You get what they want. This is not always in your best interest. Creative people do not always give your marketing and advertising objectives the weight they ought to. All too often the marketing strategy will be built around the creative process instead of having the creative process built around the marketing strategy.

Set expectations and communicate them to your agency. You are the customer. They will spend as much as you let them. I have watched thousands of dollars spent for illustrations when a stock photo would have worked just as well or even better. I know of photo shoots that took days and cost a small fortune when a stock photo would have been equally effective.

I have seen elaborate four color illustrations and photographs used when a simple black and white illustration would have done quite nicely at a fraction of the creative and reproduction cost. I have watched creative people create campaigns driven by their ego and not the client's objectives. I have sat in creative meetings and seen the process driven by the desire to create an award winning campaign with no consideration ever being given to the client's needs, increased sales, marketing objectives or cost.

Let me give you a piece of advice that may be the single most valuable piece of advice I give you in the area of dealing with creative people. Simply put, control them, do not be controlled by them. Don't let them control you, your project, or your budget. Creative people are often arrogant and intimidating. Do you ever feel stupid around them? If so, I'm not surprised. This is exactly what many of them want you to feel and they work very hard to instill this feeling. I spent 5 years as a VP in the advertising business and as a result I have observed many of these cretins first hand. Some are not like this and are in fact sensitive to your needs, objectives, and, most of all, your budget. However, these quality creative people are in the minority.

At any rate, I have seen hours and hours of time wasted on retakes, set changes, and copy revisions so that the highly trained ego of the creative person is satisfied. The fact that this appetite is satisfied at the expense of your budget matters not one bit.

I have read copy rewrites that would make a sane person scream "enough". I have been in recording studios and watched creative people change copy and concepts for no reason that I could see was justified. I have seen retake after retake with the end result being no better than the first take. I have seen perfection being pursued when it can never be obtained (and does not need to be). I have seen countless hours of recording studio time and talent wasted. Guess who is paying for all this? Do you have a mirror nearby?

You must control the process. If it looks good to you or if it sounds good to you it will look and sound good to your customers. Remember, the creative people work for you. You are in charge or you should be. You are not interested in paying for an award winning creative piece. They may be, but you sure better not be. You are interested in results not awards. You are interested in getting the best job you can at the lowest cost. The lowest creative cost and the lowest reproduction cost.

You are interested in good not perfect. I have never seen and never will see, perfection. I have no intention of paying the high fees of some creative person to try and create it. You are paying the piper, you must be the one to decide on what the tune to be played is.

Prepare right, produce quick, and move on. **In this business time is money and you hold the checkbook.** Remember, when you are dealing with an advertising agency you have art directors, copy people, creative directors, artists, and production people. All with different ideas as to what you should be doing and how you should do it. All have different ideas on what is good and what is not. Think of how much time can be wasted just among the internal people never mind once the process starts. How can any one of them be more right than you?

You must control. In few areas is wasted time more costly than it will be in this area. Remember too that the creative process will determine the extent of your costs far beyond this. It will affect your printing costs, your media costs, your production costs, and costs in numerous other areas. We will cover this more later.

How many times have you read an ad, heard a radio commercial or watched a TV commercial and sat there wondering what the hell they were advertising? Have you ever watched, read, or heard an ad or commercial and wondered in amazement who in their right mind would pay for something like that?

If you have, you may have been seeing the result of the creative process driving the entire marketing and advertising process including controlling the client. I am constantly amazed at the garbage that clients approve and pay for. I am not just talking about the local used car dealer. **In fact, some of the worst advertising I have ever seen has been generated by some of the largest agencies in the world for some of the largest and most powerful companies in the world.**

The next time you see an ad or watch a commercial think about what the advertiser is trying to accomplish. Think about what the strategy might be. Far more often than not you will come away wondering. In my opinion quality and effective advertising is rare. Very rare indeed. With this stated it follows that it is my opinion that the vast majority of advertising is a complete waste of money.

In a recent article that appeared in 2/1/94 The Wall Street Journal echoes these thoughts. Written by Kevin Goldman the headline of this article was "Super Bowl Ads Looked Worse Than Bills". Quite a statement since it was only two days earlier that the hapless Buffalo Bills had set a record unmatched in professional sports by losing their fourth consecutive Super Bowl.

In Pursuit of Profits. How To At Least Double Your Profits Without Increasing Your Sales.

The main thrust of this article was that the quality and effectiveness of the ads that appeared during the Super Bowl were poor at best. Mr. Goldman utilized the results of surveys conducted by a market research firm by the name of Creative Marketing Consultants who conducted their surveys right after the game concluded.

Look at some of the results of this survey. Only 5% of viewers remembered the commercials for Bud Ice Draft. There were four 15 second spots for Bud Ice Draft. Only 16% remember any of the commercials that aired for McDonald's. Only 23% remember seeing any of the Nike spots and only 4% of the people surveyed immediately after the game recalled seeing the spots for Alamo Car Rental.

Let me point out that just the media cost for a 30 second spot during the Super Bowl cost $900,000. Can you imagine paying $900,000 (not even including the cost of creating and producing the ad) for a commercial during the largest sporting event of the year and having less than 5 out of 100 viewers recall seeing your ad? Remember, this does not translate into sales. This is the number of people who even remember the ad, not those that bought the product.

Pepsi ads were recalled by 35% of those surveyed. This was among the highest scores of the survey. It should be since Mr. Goldman pointed out that Pepsi spent $5.4 million on the commercials.

Overall the results were so dismal that I suspect a number of ad agencies will soon be looking for new clients and a number of Fortune 500 companies will be looking for new marketing managers. If they are not they should be.

Mr. Goldman closed his article by stating "Finally, a parting comment that should worry some on Madison Avenue. Mr. Smith of Creative Marketing says the best time to survey viewers is immediately following the game. Why? There is tremendous drop-off in viewer recall of commercials even after one day". Mr. Goldman ended by stating "Nine hundred thousands dollars for that?" Well said Mr. Goldman. The dismal recall rates immediately after the Super Bowl would get worse. Much worse.

Think of the tremendous amount of time and money wasted on efforts suggested and directed by the agency. Of course, the agencies involved made money, a great deal of it. But do you think the goal of the advertiser was accomplished?

<u>Are you getting where you want to go for the price you want to pay?</u> You must evaluate the agency's efforts early and often. From the marketing plan to the media plan, from the creative direction to the production costs, you must stay on top of what is going on, how effective it is, how you feel about it and, in fact, everything about what they are doing on your behalf.

You do not want to allow a big tab to be run up. You do not want to allow the agency to proceed in a direction you do not feel comfortable with or you feel is wrong or even questionable. You need to force corrective action and redirection if any of these things occur. You need to do this as early as possible, or in other words, as soon as it becomes apparent to you. To do otherwise will result in you paying for efforts that will either never be used or that you feel compelled to use even though you don't want to, solely because you let large costs be incurred and now feel as though you must continue in that direction.

<u>The design may be the least of your cost concerns</u>. You must control the cost of any and all designs, printed materials , ads, etc.. I am talking about control at every level from the simplest letterhead and envelope to the most complex and costly six color brochure.

You must understand that the cost of the design is only a small portion of the cost you are incurring when you have a design created. In many cases only a **very** small portion of the cost. You must always understand that the design is a one time cost. Reproducing that design will be a repetitive cost. Every time you run that ad or print that brochure you may be paying for that design in the form of higher bleed costs, multi colors, screens, traps, die cuts, etc.. Every time you reprint your business cards, envelopes and letterhead you are paying for what was created by the design.

You may be paying for special ink colors, fancy stock, and any one of dozens of added costs that may be incurred because of the complexity of the design. Depending on what the item involved is and the level of usage, you could end up paying hundreds, thousands, or even hundreds of thousands of dollars more than you need to in added reproduction and media space costs all due to the design you started with. A design you might have loved and felt was very reasonably priced.

I would suggest if nothing else you pick up a good basic book on the printing and graphic reproduction process. This need not be complex but rather just enough to allow you to feel comfortable in dealing with the graphic arts type so you will better understand why the design is so important.

Let me give you a few examples of how much more your production costs can be increased by design demands. Bleeds can add 10% or more to your cost every time you run an add or print the material, screens can add 10% or more to your costs each time, process color can increase your costs 400% or more when compared to a 3 or 4 non process color job, you will also see large differences in cost for photos, illustrations, line art, and half tones. Each will have a much larger and repetitive cost beyond the basic cost of the design. The design cost is often the very least of your concerns.

Always seek to amortize your design and production costs over as many jobs as possible. For example, if you have paid $15,000 for artwork to use in a folder think of what else you can use it for. Can you use some or all of the art in an ad, a flyer, a direct mail piece, another brochure, or a display? The more uses you can find for that art the lower your per use cost becomes. You should always be thinking and planning beyond your immediate needs.

If you have only used it in the folder it has cost you $15,000 for that use. However, if you can use it in four other marketing vehicles, it has now been used in 5 pieces and you have dropped your cost per use down to $3,000. An 80% reduction. You also accomplished something else, something very important in marketing. By using the same art in a number of promotional pieces you are creating a consistent look for your marketing efforts. By doing this you are sending a consistent visual message and each of your efforts reinforce the others visually creating a type of corporate identity for your company.

Remember who pays for the visit. When anyone from your agency comes to your office demand that they follow the same strategies that I have given to you for reducing costs in all travel related areas including rental cars, hotels, and flights, if applicable. One way or the other you are paying for these costs.

Do you ever feel you are paying too much? Question the billing hours of your agency often. As with any profession that bills on time the potential for billing abuse is huge. Too huge for you to ignore.

Just by questioning and demanding detailed breakdowns of hours spent on your behalf you will stop most padding of bills as the agency knows you are watching and watching closely. They won't like it but what do you care? You are the customer. They must worry about what you like, you should not give a darn about what they like.

In addition to monitoring your hours for abuses by demanding periodic accounting of the time spent on your behalf, you will also be able to see how your money is being spent and at what rate. This will give you the information you need to judge how effectively your money is being spent and to judge for yourself how cost effective the returns on the individual efforts are.

Agencies, like all those who bill on time, seek to drive up the hours whenever possible. Time is their product. They want to sell more of their product. There is nothing wrong with this. This should also be your goal. The question is whether or not this time is actually being spent on your behalf and with what results. Your goals are to get the best product you can from your agency at the lowest cost. This is directly opposite of their goals. Never forget this.

Are they practicing total cost control? If your agency produces your marketing, advertising, or promotional products for you make sure they are looking into all the cost savings strategies I have given you for these areas. Also make sure that they are passing the savings on to you. You must infuse your agency with a cost savings mentality. This will save you huge sums of money and it will reinforce your internal efforts.

Do not pay them to do what you can and should be doing yourself. For example, do not let your agency handle your printing needs. Many agencies will use printers that are much more expensive than needed and will also add a 20% or more mark up to the cost of the job. If the creative product has been properly prepared, there is no reason that you cannot work directly with the printer yourself. You do not need to be an expert in this area. Just deal with people who are and make it clear you expect them to look out for your interests and by doing so it will be in their long term best interests. If you prefer, contact a print broker to work with you in this area for a greatly reduced cost when compared the agency mark up.

Another example would be direct mail. You do not need an agency to handle your direct mail efforts. You can coordinate this yourself or work directly with the direct mail house. The advertising agency offers you convenience but at a price. Convenience always has a cost. In this case it will increase your costs by at least 20% which is the agency standard mark up.

If you must. If you do allow your agency to arrange for and oversee your printing needs as they apply to the agency's efforts, do yourself a favor and spot check the finished pieces with printers on your own. Call a few in and show them or send them a sample of the printed piece and ask them for prices on producing the same thing. Also ask them to give you prices with and without paper. As I pointed out in another strategy, you can often save a great deal of money by purchasing the paper yourself and having it shipped to the printer.

By checking with other printers on your own you will discover a number of things. You will find out if the agency looked out for your best fiscal interests when they selected a printer. If the prices the printers you called in are much lower than the prices charged by the agency you have a problem. A problem you better not let happen again. You will also find out what you might have saved by providing paper to the printer the agency gave the job to. The savings may have been a great deal and the next time perhaps you will choose to supply the paper.

Do your homework. For the same reasons I have outlined previously you should shop printers on your own before you allow the agency to have your printing job. Just have the agency give you the cost they will charge for the job including their mark up. Make sure they provide this cost to you including all specifications of the job. By this I mean have them spec out size, colors, bindery, bleeds, paper, die cuts, and anything else that applies to the production of the job.

Also ask them to provide you with a mock up of what the finished product will look like. Tell them you need this information for some unknown third party in your company if you like. Tell them you are going to compare costs. Tell them anything you want, but get the information.

Then on your own, call in 3 printers and ask them to provide you with written quotes for the exact same job. Make sure the printers you call in handle this type of work on a primary basis. You do not want a four color printer for a one color job and you do not want a one or two color printer for a four color job. Simply ask them for samples of similar quality work and for references.

Compare the prices your agency gave you with those you received from your printers. This will ensure that you are getting the best value for your money. If the prices from your printers are much lower than those of the agency and you do not want to work with the printer directly, demand that your agency find a quality printer who will match the prices you have obtained or make them use your printer.

They will still be entitled to their mark up but convenience always has a price. At least in this case your base printing costs before the mark up will be lower and as a result the dollar value of the mark up will be lower since it will be based on the lower printing cost. If they do the work they are entitled to the mark up. But at least make sure you are getting the best price on the printing that you can with the side benefit of reducing the mark up.

Agencies will very often use a core of regular printers. The printers they use may not be the best priced ones for your job. Since you are footing the bill and not the agency you cannot assume that the best priced printer is being used. Agencies will deal with printers for many reasons. Some of these reasons are good and some bad. Many will not be in your best interest. I will discuss this more in another strategy.

Know what you are hiring them to do and at what cost. Make sure you understand any contract you sign with agencies. If there is anything in that contract you don't feel comfortable with, and there should be many things, don't sign it. Contracts are not written in stone. The agency people will try to convince you it is or that the contract is the standard one used in the industry, don't listen to this self-serving nonsense.

It may indeed be the one used in the industry and it may contain many industry standard customs. So what? Who cares! Any contracts or customs that are industry standard will be designed to benefit those in the industry. Who do you think made the standards up? You are not in the industry, therefore it should be obvious that the contract and customs will not benefit you. Consider them list prices. You know we never pay list prices. Force the agency to modify and / or remove the areas that you do not want and draft a new contract. Lead don't follow. Remember who the customer is.

Listen but never blindly follow. Agency people many times are like doctors and lawyers. They put themselves above you. They expect to be followed without question. You bring the checkbook and follow their advice. Wrong. Change this perception right now. You should be involved and you should lead not follow. You make the decisions not them. They make recommendations and you decide.

Never blindly follow the advice or recommendations of your agency, or for that matter, anyone else. This includes me. Ask the questions. Why are they suggesting this? What other options do they offer? What is the cost? Why so high? Who is going to be working on your account? What are they going to cost you? Why is the ad being shot at night? Why not during the day when a lighting crew is not needed? What is that person or that element going to add? Why are they not shooting in the studio instead of location?

Why are they using photography? Why are they re-shooting? How else can we get the same result for less money? Why are they suggesting that media and not another one? Why radio and print? Why radio and not print? Why is a full page ad needed? Won't a half page ad serve just as well for a lot less money? Do you need a 30 page catalog? Wouldn't a 25 page one do just as well for a great deal less? Why do you need 4 color process work? Won't 2 or 3 colors do just as well? What about black and white? If you reduce your costs by 50% and your return only drops by 15% aren't you far ahead of the game? Why do I need research? How will you be measuring the results of this campaign?

Don't blindly go along with your agency's recommendations. Authorize the ones you agree with and trash the rest. Do not consider programs recommended to you to be an all or nothing proposition. You get the point I am sure. Ask the questions. Make them justify the efforts they are recommending or undertaking, as well as the cost of those efforts.

They must be held accountable. You must hold your agency accountable for not only the results of their efforts but also for how they spend your money. This is not a book on how to deal with ad agencies but if you are working with one I want you to get the results you expect at the lowest possible cost.

You should be spending your money on marketing efforts that produce results and not on wasted agency efforts. What percentage of your marketing dollars are going to the agency? What percentage of your marketing dollars are actually going to advertising that will be seen by your target market? What percentage is going to the agency for internal costs? What return are you getting for your money?

You must know the answers to these and other questions. Would you donate money to a charity that spent 95% of the donations on administrative costs and only 5% on the actual cause of the charity? Don't misunderstand me, I am not saying the agencies will consume 95% of your money to cover internal costs and spend only 5% on actual advertising. I am saying that you damn well better make sure that the majority of the money you spend is spent targeting your market and not on anything else.

Let me give you an example of what I would consider a significant waste of time and money. Agency time and client's money. This goes back a number of years to when I was starting out in the agency business. The event in question is just one of a hundred examples I could give you in which far more time and money was spent than was needed or justified to get the end result.

In this case the agency was looking for an old country store in upper New England to shoot a series of ads for a major financial client. We spent three weeks traveling around upper New England looking for just the right country store. The very first day out searching for locations I saw what I considered a store that was far more suitable than the one we ended up using. Even putting this aside, with proper research ahead of time, we could have identified every country store in New England and conducted the entire location search in three days.

Instead, we wasted tens of thousands of dollars over a three week time period. When we finally found the store the creative people were looking for, they rearranged so much of it that not even the owners recognized it. We could have easily achieved the same result at a fraction of the cost in a studio.

Had the client been involved and controlled the process instead of being controlled, this would never have happened and the end result would have been as good, or perhaps even better, for thousands and thousands of dollars less. Dollars that could have, and should have, been spent on advertising.

Lead the agency do not be led. Would you give any supplier a free hand on how they spend your money and on what? Of course you would not. So do not give it to your agency. They may be an expert in the field, although this is by no means always true, but you know your market, your product, and what you are trying to accomplish better than they ever will. Who is in a better position? Do not give your agency or anyone else a license to do whatever they want. This will cost you dearly. Ask the questions and make them justify their actions.

Never pay for the mistakes of others. Do not pay for mistakes made by the agency or delays that incur added costs which were caused by the agency. They will not, and should not, pay for your mistakes and you should not pay for theirs.

Remember, meetings can be billed. Minimize the number and time of any meetings you have with your agency people. In other sections I have covered in depth the amount of wasted time spent in meetings so I won't repeat this information here. However, wasted time spent in internal meetings is bad enough but wasted time spent with personnel from vendors that sell time as a product is far worse. In this latter case you are paying for the time of your people and the time of the agency people.

Make sure you know what the meeting is for, how long it will last, and who must attend and why. Find out the agenda and objectives, complete your needed participation and end the meeting. Do not let the meeting drag on and on. Do not stay, or let your people stay, and engage in hours of small talk. If you or your people are at the agency conduct your business and leave. I have seen hundreds of hours wasted by employees who think visiting the agency is an all day field trip.

Do not allow this. When I was in the agency business one of my clients who paid by the hour was able to reduce his agency account time, without any sacrifice in agency output, by 5 to 10 hours per week simply by being prepared for needed meetings, eliminating small talk, and eliminating unneeded meetings. At $125 per hour this saved him $625 to $1,250 per week or $32,500 to $65,000 per year.

Lunch can be very expensive. Watch out for your agency wining and dining your marketing people. This includes you. Never forget that one way or the other your company is paying the tab. Not only will the company get stuck paying the tab but you are also paying for the time of both the agency people and your people.

Make sure your people are not scheduling meetings around lunch time. Not only will this increase the billed time but it will also drain your time. A $50 lunch can end up costing you three or four times this as you are paying for the time of the agency personnel at a cost of $125 per hour or more. It has been my experience that clients love to visit agencies around lunch time or at a time that runs into lunch or dinner so they can be wined and dined by the agency.

Perhaps an even more important consideration is that this type of activity will cause your people to lose their objectivity. Their loyalty is being bought. Bought with your company's money. Once your marketing people lose their objectivity your costs will rise and effectiveness will drop.

Spectators should not be allowed. Make sure the agency is only bringing people that have a function to any meeting you have and do not request the agency to bring people whose presence is not needed or justified. The same holds true for people from your company.

In Pursuit of Profits. How To At Least Double Your Profits Without Increasing Your Sales.

Whether you are paying by the hour or paying a monthly fee, you are still paying. Do not think that just because you are paying a monthly fee it does not matter how much of the agency's time or how many of the agency's people you are using. It matters and it matters a great deal.

First of all you should not abuse any relationship you have with anybody. This is just wrong. Treat others the way you want them to treat you. Respect the agency's time, that is their product. Secondly, do you honestly think that the agency will keep their fees at a rate based on a set number of hours each month while you constantly use up more than the projected time? Would you?

If you are requesting people and meetings that are not justified or productive you deserve to pay a higher fee. If they are scheduling meetings and bringing people that are not needed or justified they are running up your hours and will later seek to adjust your monthly fee if you are paying on a fee basis. Do not allow this to happen. I have sat in more than one meeting in which 4 or 5 agency people were in attendance when only 1 or 2 were needed. The same goes for your own people.

How much do you want to spend? Try not to give your agency or anyone else your budget. This is a very common question and will usually be asked early on. They want to know what your budget is. Do you want them to build costs up to your budget? If not, do not give it to them.

Would you buy from a salesman who wants to know what you can afford to pay before he gives you a price? Try buying a car this way. Tell them, as I do, that you believe in zero based budgeting and therefore you expect every expense to be cost and results justified.

You want the agency's recommendations as to what you need to do to accomplish your objectives. Along with the recommendations, which should be part of an overall marketing plan, you want the cost of these recommendations. Give them your objectives and ask them how you can meet these objectives and at what cost.

I do understand that there will be times when the outside source must have some idea of what you are willing to spend otherwise they could waste time and money developing plans or proposals that are not even in the ballpark. In cases like this try always to only give a range. A very wide range of what you might consider feasible.

Just in case you are a blabbermouth. If you ignore my advice for whatever reason, then at least do yourself a favor and give them a budget figure that is at least 20% below what it actually is. Remember, like any another company, you buy products or services from, your agency has different bottom line objectives than you do. You want the most effective advertising and marketing program you can get at the lowest cost. They also want you to be a satisfied customer and to get an effective program but not necessarily at the lowest cost. They want to maximize profits and sales like any other profit minded company. This automatically puts them into conflict with your goals.

Make them keep their promises. Keep all agency estimates and compare them to your actual billing. While an estimate is just that, an estimate, you should still hold your agency responsible for any significant cost overruns. What is the reason for the added cost? Agency mistakes? Creative egos? Whatever the problem was, unless you caused it, do not let it become your problem and do not pay for it.

I hope you are not paying list prices. Remember, agency prices, mark ups, and fees should be considered list prices. For example, if they tell you they mark up everything they buy on your behalf 20%, this does not mean that you must pay the 20% mark up. You can, should, and must negotiate this % down. I would suggest that you shoot for no higher than 10%.

At the very least you should negotiate a lower mark up for higher costing jobs. If you agree to a 20% mark up for a $10,000 job than you should not be paying this for a $100,000 job. Use a decreasing mark up for increasing costs. This is how most businesses in this country work. The higher the cost of the product the lower the mark up. The higher the volume the lower the mark up.

Look at a printing job. If your agency has designed a folder for you and you authorize them to handle the printing of 5,000 pieces at say, $1 per piece your bill will be $5,000. If you allow a 20% mark up on top of this you will pay an added $1,000 to the agency.

Now if this printing job was for 100,000 pieces why should you pay a $20,000 mark up? The agency does no more work. Their work was in the copy and design of the piece. When it comes to arranging and overseeing the printing, whether the printed job is for 5,000 pieces or 100,000 pieces, the agency does not expend any more time and effort on the job.

For 5,000 or 100,000 pieces the agency people still must solicit bids and select the printer. More effort is not required to do this for 100,000 than it is for 5,000 pieces. They may go on press at the printer, or they may not, to approve the run. This time and process is the same whether the job is for 5,000 pieces or 100,000 pieces.

Even if they go on press they do not stay and oversee the entire run. They just arrive for the first sheets off the press and once the job looks good they leave. If they tell you otherwise they are lying to you. I know I started out in the agency business as a production manager and I have solicited thousand of quotes and been on press hundreds of times.

Most businesses lower their mark ups for higher volume and higher priced items. Why should agencies be excluded from this normal business practice? The bottom line is there is no cost justification for you to pay any more for the agency to oversee a larger run than a smaller run.

This is just one example to show you that you should not pay a consistent percentage of a job's cost regardless of the amount of effort involved. Or, for that matter, a fee of 20% at any time.

Watch out for conflict of interest. If your agency is using the same suppliers all the time it may be a tip off that a conflict of interest exists between someone in your agency and their suppliers. This may be a form of single source buying. **Understand that these comments apply to anyone who is acting as a buyer of anything for your company internally or externally.** In all cases it will cost you dearly.

When I started out in the advertising business I was a production manager responsible for buying and hiring all needed elements for all the agency's clients and as someone who handles most purchases for my business I can give you many examples that I have observed first hand that demonstrate buyer greed and conflict of interest. These include letting personal relationships cloud judgment, allowing internal political pressures to influence decisions and the accepting of highly unethical and perhaps illegal gifts.

In my capacity as a buyer, printers, TV representatives, radio sales people, and a dozen other sales representatives from other industries offered me everything from payoffs to prostitutes and tickets to trips in exchange for my business. As sordid as it sounds, it happens very often, especially in a smaller business setting where purchasing authority is often unchecked. I know buyers who accept many of these gifts.

I know one buyer for a former Fortune 500 company that was taken by his primary supplier every year on two major all expense paid trips to exotic locations. This buyer saw no conflict of interest here at all and resented my suggestions that his business was being bought. He must think he is a member of Congress. **Maybe this type of attitude and lack of corporate control is why that company is no longer a Fortune 500 company.**

I personally know of hundreds of jobs produced at thousands of dollars more than they should have been by agency personnel solely to keep the suppliers happy who keep the agency buyers happy. This does not happen in all agencies. In fact, I would say that in most it does not. But I can assure you it does happen and it happens more than an agency will ever admit.

You must be on guard for these types of problems internally and externally. Remember, it is still a human being undertaking the function. A human being with all the frailties, self-serving motives, emotions, and greed of anyone else. Determining whether or not a conflict of interest or an unethical situation exists is not easy, but by following my other strategies, asking the questions and conducting periodic audits or requiring proof of outside costs with the agency billing, you will be taking proactive steps to prevent it.

Recycling your creative efforts is good for your budget. If you engage the services of a professional designer or ad agency to create, write, or design something for you there is no need to recreate the wheel each time you need to create another piece or project. Simply follow the format that has been created by the professional. For example, you pay to have an ad designed, now you need another ad for a different product or service. Don't pay to have this designed simply follow the format already established and paid for.

Not only will this save you money, but it will also keep a consistent look to your marketing materials and advertising. This is like having a professional architect design your house and then using a handyman to make minor repairs around the place.

Test market any and all new products, services, and programs including your advertising, direct mail, marketing, and public relation programs. Insist on test marketing the marketing and creative direction of any program, including ones the agency wants, before you allow completion and roll out of any campaign. The idea is to always be able to kill any ineffective direction or action before you have incurred significant costs or set out on a course that cannot be reversed without great difficulty, high costs, and, possibly, a major embarrassment.

You might like the direction, the agency may love it, but your target audience may hate it. Which of these three parties is the only one that counts? Test market. Yes, you may incur a delay. Yes, you may incur some added cost. Yes, you can definitely expect fierce resistance from your agency, especially from the creative people who will wonder who you think you are to question them.

Too bad. Think of the alternatives. Think of the agency costs. Think of the production costs. Think of the media costs. Think of the problems you will have if you authorize a major roll out of a campaign that falls flat on it's face.

Test marketing will enable you to find out the acceptance level of your idea among those you are targeting it to. If you find the results of your testing to be favorable then you will be able to roll out with confidence. If you find that your idea is more of an Edsel than a Mercedes you might have saved yourself a great deal of money, time, and effort, not to mention embarrassment.

You may find the truth lies somewhere in the middle. You may indeed have the nucleus of a winning idea but simply need to make a few modifications. Test marketing will cost very little in terms of dollars and time to find out how good your idea really is. If it turns out to be an idea a bit ahead of its time then you can console your ego by thinking of all the money you saved. Money that can be used to develop your next idea. So be smart and take a test drive before you buy.

Want to save money on research? Want to find out how effective an advertising campaign might be before you spend a great deal of money or commit to it? Go to the best source you will ever get for the feedback you need. Go to your customers and prospects and ask them. Ask them what they think of this concept. Ask them to look at the agency ideas and how well they might respond to them.

By asking them at the developmental stage you can save a tremendous amount of money in the event the feedback is negative. Show them the layouts or story boards. Discuss the media placement with them. You may find you are on target in all areas or way off target in key areas. You may also save face as you may prevent a marketing disaster in the making.

If you have been running a campaign ask your customers and prospects if they saw any elements of it and if so what did they think. Do their responses measure up to your objectives? If not you have a problem. A problem you can address before you waste even more money and effort.

By involving your customers and prospects you are doing two things. You are getting the feedback from the best possible source, your target audience, and you are showing them that you value and care about, their opinion. Not a bad combination. Furthermore, you will get feedback quicker and the feedback you get will be direct and accurate.

Let your suppliers help lower your costs. Use co-operative advertising whenever possible. If you are selling the products or services of another company every time you advertise your business you are promoting sales of their products. They should be subsidizing your costs. In many cases your co-op ad dollars can amount to up to 80% of your advertising costs.

For example, I know one large food store chain in the area that runs a number of promotions each year for the various departments in the store. In each case they solicit and receive significant amounts of money from the suppliers of the products they sell. A specific example would be a recent super bowl deli promotion they ran in newspapers and on TV throughout the area. The total cost of the promotion ran about $50,000. They were able to obtain co-op advertising from the various deli meat manufactures in an amount in excess of $35,000.

Why not? This is only fair. If they are mentioning Fenway franks as part of a summer cook out promotion then the makers of Fenway franks should be happy to subsidize this cost. They are not only getting visibility but will also sell more hot dogs. I am sure that if they refused there would be many other hot dog companies that would be happy to take their place in the promotion.

You must ask. Don't assume they will offer to provide you with co-op money or any other type of marketing or advertising assistance. You will be surprised how and how much your suppliers can help you.

In Pursuit of Profits. How To At Least Double Your Profits Without Increasing Your Sales.

Get your suppliers to provide you with literature, giveaways, brochures, catalogs, and many other forms of promotional literature. It does not matter if you are a small company, you still should ask, no demand, support from those whose products and services you are selling. Some will offer, many will not. Most, if not all, will provide marketing and advertising assistance if you ask. You can save hundreds or hundreds of thousands of dollars a year depending on your size, by getting this type of support. You will also increase both your sales and their sales.

Are you overlooking the obvious? Every day companies all across the country are missing excellent opportunities to cross sell products and services and to communicate with their customers. All at no cost! How? Simple. Make use of all outgoing correspondence, invoices, orders shipped, and any other type of mail you send.

You are already paying for the envelope or box, you are already paying for the postage (which, by the way in most cases when you mail first class you are paying for 1 ounce and the vast majority of mail sent falls far below this in weight), and you have already paid the labor to label and prepare your outgoing mail. These are costs that you have already incurred. You can expand your marketing and advertising efforts for very little, or no added cost at all, by making sure that everything you send from your office contains promotional literature.

Add in data sheets, special offers, product samples, sales flyers, product line literature, service capabilities, and anything else that you use or can develop to cross sell and to promote your business. For example, if you are sending an invoice out you have prepared the envelope and invoice, and affixed .29 postage. The invoice is a single sheet of paper. The 1 ounce of postage you have paid for will let you include up to 5 sheets of paper depending on the size and weight you use. This means that you can include up to 4 more sheets of promotional literature without increasing your postage costs. Eight pages if you use both sides of the paper.

You are only paying for the promotional materials since you have already incurred all other costs by mailing the invoice. If you are not including the types of material I am suggesting, not only are you missing out on a low cost golden opportunity to increase your sales and improve customer loyalty, but you are also over paying for your postage as you are using only 20% or so of the weight allowed under the first class stamp you have paid for.

You must look at all angles when you are undertaking a total cost control program. In this case you have not reduced your billing costs or shipping costs at all. What you have done however is greatly increase your sales efforts without a corresponding cost in labor, postage, and material. The bottom line is that you are increasing your exposure and cross selling opportunities without a corresponding increase in costs.

Develop your own ads by seeing what others are doing successfully. It has been suggested that there is no such thing as an original idea, but that all new ideas are only old ideas modified. Ideas breed ideas. Since you should already be monitoring what your competition is doing, it is just a simple matter for you to get good advertising ideas. Don't just study your competition become an advertising buff. Keep copies of ads you see you like and direct mail programs that you receive at home and at work. Why do you think most agencies maintain large reference libraries?

If you like a certain style or concept then chances are it is a good one for your market. Don't copy others exactly but rather use these advertising materials as a reference to develop your own. I'm sure you have noticed this trend on TV. A new show comes on, it if it is a hit you suddenly see shows just like it on every channel. You don't think this is a coincidence do you?

By being able to develop your own material you will save most, if not all, of your development costs. Even if you still feel compelled to seek the help of a "professional" you will, at the very least, have a very strong idea of what you want and, as a result, you will be much more in control. Control, you remember, is what you must exert in order to keep costs down when dealing with an agency or design house or with anyone who sells time.

Resource

Wentworth Publishing, 1866 Colonial Lane, P.O. Box 10488, Lancaster, PA, 17605-0488. 1-800-331-5196. They offer a number of publications, including Financial Advertising Review and Healthcare Advertising Review, which highlight advertising efforts and creative approaches used by clients and agencies from around the country. An excellent source for creative and strategic ideas.

Contact your local college or graphic arts school to see if they are willing to work with your company in meeting your creative needs. You will find that most will be very excited about giving their students the opportunity to work on real world projects. You will receive the creative ideas and efforts of a bright and enthusiastic group of young people for little or no cost. The students get real life experience. Who knows, you might also find some who may come work for you one day in an in-house position or even on a freelance basis. Of course, this strategy won't be suitable for many of your projects but for the ones it is you will save a great deal of money while helping a young person get started.

Want to know what others in your industry are doing and why without spending anything? Well, actually you must spend something. About $12 per year for a subscription to the trade magazine for your industry.

One of your greatest sources of competitive information and research about your target market is created when egos and interviews meet. Company executives from any industry will reveal research information, marketing plans, strategies, and numerous other very helpful pieces of information whenever they are interviewed. Helpful to you that is. It is as though when being interviewed they want to demonstrate their knowledge and often the way to do this is to tell the interviewer everything you might ever want to know about what their plans are and why.

I know one company that spent nearly $120,000 dollars conducting marketing research, developing strategies and planning. Any one of their competitors could have obtained the benefit of this research for free and they could have known exactly what that competitor was doing with that research and why.

How? Simply by reading the trade magazine that interviewed the marketing manager representing the company in question. He told the magazine every important detail. I know, it was one of my clients. He told them what we were doing and why, how much it cost and when we were going to do it. He handed them the nucleus of our entire marketing plan and the highlights of the research results. Not only did this provide his competition with a wealth of free research information, but he also placed them in an excellent position to compete against him.

Why should you spend the money if your competition already has and is willing to tell you about it? Study the trade magazines of your industry. If they are expensive see if your local library will carry them for you. Do what you need to in order to get them, but get them.

Read the articles from others in your industry. You will find tips on improving operations, customer service, sales, product offerings, and dozens of other areas. You would pay a consultant top dollar for this information. Information you can get for free.

In Pursuit of Profits. How To At Least Double Your Profits Without Increasing Your Sales.

Do it yourself research. Study the advertising of your competitors. It will tell you a great deal. Look at the advertising of local, regional, and national companies in your industry. It can be a road map to you. It can tell you what works and what does not. It can show you what is selling and what is not. Look at the companies advertising. Look at where they are advertising. Look at the positioning of the ad, the copy message, the creative approach. This can give you insight into what their research and experience has told them.

If you see the same type of advertising or the same advertising over and over again it will be safe to assume it is working for them. Can this type of approach work for you? Can you take advantage of your competition's positioning to counter attack?

You are seeing the execution of your competition's marketing strategy. It must be able to tell you a great deal. Look for it. Remember, this holds true for direct mail as well. Do not consider it junk mail. Consider it research that has been placed in your hands at no cost. Study pricing, packaging, response mechanisms, and every other element. It will give you many ideas that can prove to be extremely useful to you.

Let higher education lower your research costs. A very good source of free or very low cost research is your local college. Contact your local college business department and ask if they would be interested in having their business students conduct a real world research project. You can offer to cover any out of pocket costs. The students get a chance to work on an actual project for a real company and they also have something of value to add to their resume. Most will be delighted. They can conduct phone surveys, customer surveys, competitive analysis, and focus groups just to name a few areas in which they could help.

Let your customers tell you what they need and how well you are providing it. Engaging the services of an outside research company can be very expensive and is often very limiting. Often the surveys conducted by these companies attempt to pigeon hole answers into neat little niches like A, B, C or D. You cannot pigeon hole people. It may be convenient, and it certainly makes reporting results easy, but it simply does not work as well as first hand direct customer feedback.

Furthermore, you are getting second hand information analyzed by someone who does not have, and never will have, the interest in your company or product or the knowledge of your company or product that you do. What they omit in their efforts to present a neat summary you may find very important. What they don't, or can't, record in their limiting survey options may be vital to you.

The best way for you to get information is to get off your butt and go talk to your target audience. There will never be a better way to secure the type of information and first hand feedback that you seek and need, than getting it directly from the people who you are trying to sell. Research companies call this "focus groups" and will charge you a great deal of money to conduct them.

A focus group is a group from your target audience that is gathered together so they can be asked opinions and questions. You can do it far more effectively, you get the information first hand and for a great deal less cost. Research companies will never be as effective as you can be in hearing and understanding what your customers are saying.

Research companies often work with prepared questionnaires and as a result have very little flexibility. They cannot react to the answers with follow up questions the way you can and they often force answers into predetermined response options which can significantly alter the interpretation of the response.

One more very important result you will get when conducting this type of research yourself is that you are demonstrating to your customers and prospects that you actually give a damn about them and their needs. How many businesses do you know that you think give a hoot about what you want, need, or think?

Go to the source. Have you ever purchased something from a major manufacturer and had to send in a warranty card? Along with this warranty card have you ever been asked to respond to a series of questions about your income, education level, gender, marital status, occupation, and the like?

Do you think this has anything to do with the warranty? Of course not! What this is, is a no cost way for the company to conduct research by tying the questionnaire in with a needed and required function. A very effective way to gather useful information from existing customers at no cost.

How can you use this same idea? Think. Don't tell me you can't because your products do not require or offer warranties. Think. Expand and adapt. Is your product a consumable that needs to be reordered? If so, how about a reorder card strategically placed in the product or packaging that not only reminds them it is time to reorder and tells them they got the product from you and how to reorder, but also asks them questions or cross sells related products?

You must think "how can I use this strategy or a version of this strategy", not "this won't work for me or that does not apply to my business". Think how, not won't or can't. Other ways to get direct first hand valuable research for free or low cost, is to have customer survey cards and questionnaires in outgoing mail or at your place of business if you are a retail business.

Put away that computer game for a minute and save some money. If you have a computer and belong to an on-line service you will find a great deal of low cost or no cost research available to you. If your current on-line service does not have what you are looking for, check out the other major on line services until you find one that does.

Resources

Dow Jones News / Retrieval Service.	1-800-223-2274
CompuServe.	1-800-848-8199
America Online.	1-800-827-6364
Delphi.	1-800-695-4005

Would you like an excellent source of no cost research that is available to nearly everyone of you no matter where you live? The public library is one of the most overlooked, under used, and under appreciated resources we have in this country. Every year millions of dollars of our tax money goes to stock and staff these libraries and yet they are usually the last place on earth most people would think about as a resource, or heaven forbid, actually go to.

Get out your phone book and find out where your local library is. Then go down and make friends with the reference librarian. Now don't be surprised if she or he feels a little suspicious at first. These days they don't get many visitors. When you consider that 50% of the population of this country does not even read a book a year are you surprised? These wonderful people must feel like the Maytag repairman. The reference librarian can be an invaluable resource to you and your company. Dust off a few publications, you will be amazed at what you might find.

In Pursuit of Profits. How To At Least Double Your Profits Without Increasing Your Sales.

If you need research it may already be done. Contact your local Chamber of Commerce, they very often conduct, or have access to, a large number of market studies. Don't reinvent the wheel. You may also find out that information is available that points you in a whole new direction or gives you entirely new ideas. Remember, a great deal of research conducted by research companies is not primary research. It is secondary research which is simply research that has already been conducted for someone else. Where do you think they get much of this secondary research? They get it from many sources including many of the ones I am suggesting here.

Research Resources

Business Information Sources. University of California Press.

The Insider's Guide to Small Business Resources. Doubleday.

Bureau of the Census. Washington, DC 20233. 1-202-763-4100. Call and get a list of all their publications.

Department of Commerce's International Trade Administration. 1-800-872-8723. Call for a catalog.

Findex Directory of Market Research Reports, Studies and Surveys. Put out by Cambridge Scientific Abstracts, 7200 Wisconsin Ave, Bethesda, MD. Fax 1-301-961-6720. This directory lists over 8,200 already published market research reports, studies, and surveys covering almost every industry. It indicates where to get the reports and at what cost. It comes with a 30 day money back guarantee.

The Information Catalog. Published by Find/SVP a worldwide research firm. This company puts out thousands of reports on "every imaginable topic" including marketing intelligence studies, competitor reports, and business and marketing sources. The catalog list topics, content, length of each report, and the cost. Their address is 625 Avenue of the Americas, New York, NY 10011. 1-800-346-3787.

Get something for your membership. Contact the trade associations for your industry. They very often will be able to provide you with a great deal of very valuable information on your market and your competition.

Academia. A haven for research. Contact University Micro films. They can be reached at 1-800-521-0600. At last count they had over 1 million Ph.D. dissertations.

Get to know your competition. If possible visit, or have someone from your company visit, your competitor's place of business. Shop their stores, buy their products, compare prices, service, and facilities. You will never get better competitive research than this and it won't cost you a dime. Find out what they are doing that you should be doing. Find out what you are doing that they are not. If possible get on their mailing list.

Look for in store displays, signs in the window, and counter flyers. How are you greeted? How was your call answered? Ask questions. Find out what strengths they have. Find out what weaknesses they have. By knowing this you can plan accordingly to take advantage of them. Your competition may be doing this to you now. You do not need to pay an ad agency or research firm to do this for you.

Do you even need to do research? Do not always assume you do. <u>Try a little common sense first.</u> As David Ogilvy the advertising guru once told us, if you go out and ask 6 of your customers or prospects what they think of an idea and all 6 say it stinks you do not need to hire a research company and spend 7 months and several hundred thousand dollars to find out that it stinks. The reaction of the 6 people you asked clearly indicates there is a real good chance it is a dumb idea. <u>Start taking a very close look at what you are spending your research money on. Start dropping unneeded research projects and research projects that are not cost justified and see how much money internally and externally you will save.</u>

"Statistics are like a bikini. What they reveal is suggestive, but what they conceal is vital."

Aaron Levenstien

<u>Understand your media costs.</u> If you are placing print media buys directly make sure you understand what it is really costing you. You should be determining your costs based on paid circulation only. Not on total readership or mailed copies or anything else the space sales representative tries to tell you.

The cost you pay to reach a 1,000 people is called the cost per M or CPM. This is simply the total cost of your space buy (the size of the ad space you are buying) divided by the total number of paid subscribers. Unless you understand these facts you are going to misjudge your cost of reaching each thousand subscribers and, as a result, pay a great deal more than you think.

For example, if your ad costs $3,000 to run and the actual number of paid subscribers is 300,000 you are paying .01 for each person you reach or a CPM of $10. If you base it on total readership this figure will change dramatically. Total readership is a figure used by space sales representatives to demonstrate a higher number of readers and therefore a lower CPM. Total readership is the total number of readers they claim read the publication.

This is usually stated as a figure 3 to 4 times higher than the paid subscription base. They base this figure on studies they claim show that 3 or 4 more people than just the subscriber read each issue. How they have arrived at this very self-serving figure I do not know.

I advise you to completely ignore it. If you estimate your CPM based on this figure using the same $3,000 ad cost and a total readership of even 3 times the paid circulation of 300,000, your CPM will appear to drop to $3.33 and the cost to reach each reader appears to be .0033.

Wow! Have you dropped your CPM by 66%. Think again. You have done nothing but fall into the trap of thinking your costs are lower than they are on a per thousand basis. Unless you know the real costs you cannot plan accordingly. Knowing the real costs may cause you to alter your plans, change the size of the ad, reduce the number of insertions or otherwise modify your plans.

Of course the real measure of cost effectiveness is the cost per sale or cost per inquiry that results from your advertising efforts. However, you won't know this until after you have run your ads. So CPM is the best measure in evaluating media costs for publications under consideration.

"There are three kinds of lies, lies, damned lies and statistics."

Benjamin Disraeli

In Pursuit of Profits. How To At Least Double Your Profits Without Increasing Your Sales.

Make sure paid subscription figures are verified by a recognized independent agency. Many magazines aggressively offer free subscriptions for the sole purpose of boosting circulation to inflate advertising rates. I receive a number of magazines each month that I have never subscribed to and have little interest in reading. Do not include these free subscriptions when determining your CPM. Consider only paid subscriptions and verified newsstand sales.

There is fiscal strength in numbers. Plan your media efforts, or force your agency to plan these efforts, so that you can produce multiple ads, radio spots, or TV spots, all at the same time. By doing so you will realize economies of production which will result in significant cost savings. Producing two ads at the same time will cost you less than producing two ads at different times. The same holds true for all other forms of media.

Educate yourself. Make sure that you have media kits for all publications that have anything to do with your target audience whether you advertise in them or not. It is not enough for your agency or media placement service to have them. Having these will enable you to verify costs and circulation and not just take the word of someone who is placing space for you.

Having these will also allow you to see other selling and merchandising opportunities that may be offered by the publication and that have not been brought to your attention by anyone placing space for you and even if they have made you aware of these opportunities they may have done so with a different price tag or presented them with a different slant.

Another reason for having these kits is that they are a very good source of free research. These publications conduct research and often include the results in their media kits if this research aids them in selling you on the magazine or newspaper. Lastly, these kits are free and contain a free publication.

Keep the commission. Whether you place just a few help wanted ads each year or whether you place advertising on a regular basis you should look into setting up your own in-house advertising agency. Why? Simple, you will get a 15% discount on every ad you place. This is what the advertising agencies and recruitment agencies get. They get a 15% discount and bill you for the full amount.

Why are you not taking these discounts for yourself? If you know the media you want to be in you should be. Even if you do not know the media you can hire a media planner at an hourly rate and incur a one time cost that will result in ongoing savings.

Over the course of the year the savings can add up quickly if you are even a moderate advertiser. If you buy $10,000 of space or time a year you will save $1,500. If you buy $100,000 of space or time a year you will save $15,000. If you buy several hundred thousand dollars of space or time each year you could afford to hire an in-house media expert on a part or even full time basis and still realize a significant overall profit. The larger your media budget, the larger your savings.

I know first hand that very often you need to do nothing more than say you are an in-house advertising agency for your company. I have done this and earned the 15% discount from major statewide newspapers, local papers, and national trade magazines. But while many publications, newspapers, radio stations, and TV stations won't require anything more than your word, I still advise you take a few simple steps to lend creditability to your claim of being an ad agency.

Don't listen to that nonsense about media sources not recognizing an in-house advertising agency or media placement group. Nonsense is exactly what this is. Despite what they may state for public consumption, they will often deal with an in-house agency. After all, they get the same rate whether the ad or spot is placed by the advertising agency or you. Do you think they will turn down your business? My experience and your common sense should give you the answer to this.

How do you set up an in-house agency? It is not a very complex procedure. You simply pick a name that sounds like you are in the agency business and have it printed on separate letterhead and envelopes. While not always needed, you may also want to open a separate checking account with this matching name.

Don't hide what you are doing. If your company is the ABC company your agency can simply be the ABC agency. As I have told you, many times the media source will never even ask for verification of your agency status. I have placed numerous ads for various companies simply by telling them we had an in-house agency. It seems as though the payment for the space or spot is quite frequently proof enough. What a surprise. What is that old saying? Something about money talking? Hmm, it seems as though there could be some truth to this statement. It sure causes many to listen.

Media Resources

Standard Rate and Data. Lists addresses, rates, and circulation figures for magazines and newspapers around the country. Carried by most major libraries or call 1-800-323-4588.

All-in-one Directory. Gebbie Press Inc., 1-914-255-7560. Lists over 21,000 newspapers, magazines, and publications along with over 7,000 radio stations and 900 television stations.

Can't do it yourself? Hire some help. If you are concerned about your ability to create your own media plans hire a media consultant to come in every six months and review your media efforts and make modifications as needed. This will be a great deal less expensive, while giving you professional guidance, than placing your media through an ad agency and losing the 15% discount. You can hire the media consultant to do it for you on an hourly rate.

For example, if they develop a media plan that takes 40 hours of time and they charge you $75 per hour it will cost you $3,000. If the media placement costs $100,000 and you save the 15% agency commission you have saved $15,000. Your cost to save the $15,000 was $3,000. Your net gain is $12,000. Not a bad return on your $3,000 investment. How many more sales would you need to make to add this much to your bottom line?

If you do not wish to establish your own in-house agency, look into working with a media placement firm instead of having your advertising agency place your media. The media house will perform the same function that the agency will but for half the cost or less. While negotiable, they will give you at least 1/2 of the 15% commission and keep the other 7 1/2 %. This will cut your media placement costs by 50%.

You can easily see how significant these savings can be. If you placed $10,000,000 of media through a media house instead of the agency your costs would be $750,000 instead of $1,500,000. A savings of $750,000. If you placed $100,000 of media through the agency your costs would be $15,000. But by placing it through the media house your costs would drop to $7,500. A savings of $7,500 for the exact same work. Thousands more on your bottom line with virtually no effort whatsoever. If your pretax profit ratio is 2.5% you would have to increase your sales by $300,000 to add the same amount to your bottom line. Think about this.

In Pursuit of Profits. How To At Least Double Your Profits Without Increasing Your Sales.

To find a media house simply pick up a copy of Ad Age or your local advertising trade magazine. If your newsstand does not carry it contact the advertising club in the major city nearest you and ask them how you can get the industry trade journal for your area.

Who says the agency must keep the commission? Work a deal with your agency to split the media commission. There is no law that says the agency must get the entire 15%. Demand a 50 / 50 split. Even a 60 / 40 split will save you thousands or depending on the size of your media budget, hundreds of thousands, or even millions, of dollars. If this agency won't go along with this, find one that will or use any one of my other strategies to place your media. It will be much easier for you to find another agency than it will be for the agency to find another client.

Leftovers can save you a fortune. Whenever possible purchase remnant space for your ad placements. Remnant space is available in both regional and national editions of most magazines and newspapers. Never heard of it? I am not surprised. You will not see remnant space listed on the rate sheet and if you inquire about it the publication may even deny that it exists, but rest assured it does indeed exist and if you are able to purchase it you will save 40% to 60% or more of the published rate for that space.

Remnant space is just what the name implies, space left over or not sold by the publication by the time it must begin production. No, you don't see blank pages in the magazine. What they do is either sell this empty space at the last minute as remnant space or if unable to sell it, they will fill the space with a public service ad, a self promotional ad, or with copy filler. They would much rather sell this space even at a significant discount.

Buying remnant space is not without disadvantages. First, you must make it known that you will be willing to purchase this space at the last minute. They will not sell it to you until they know they are unable to fill it at full rates. This means that you must either be able to send a completed ready to go ad on very short notice or have a set of films for the ad at the publication that they can use if remnant space becomes available.

However, if you leave films at the publication do not give them blanket authorization to run your ad any time remnant space becomes available, you must maintain control over insertions and costs. You must have it in writing that they cannot run your ad unless you provide authorization. This way you can determine at the time if the rate is favorable enough and if the timing is right and if you can afford it.

This may not sound like much of a problem but you must remember that this also means that you will have to pay for space that you have not planned on since you did not know when the remnant space would become available.

The second disadvantage is that most often this space will become available in the form of full pages. You see magazines are printed by using what is called a signature. This simply means that multiple pages are printed at once as part of one large form. The form is then folded and cut to produce separate pages. If a publication has reached the production stage without selling all space the open space will most likely be a full page since they want to have all the rest of the publication laid out and ready to go.

However, when you consider the savings of 40% to 60% or more, these should be problems that you will be happy to work around if these publications are part of your normal media plans or ones you want to be in but don't want to pay full rates to be in. Depending on the publications involved, your savings can run from a few thousand to tens of thousands of dollars per insertion.

Instant credibility. One good strategy to develop a higher level of credibility and perceived recognition is to use the credibility of someone else to create your own. For instance, if you run a small ad in the regional edition of a well known and well respected magazine or newspaper you are borrowing their credibility. By being seen in a publication such as this you are perceived as bigger, better, and more credible.

This also opens up the door to other tremendous marketing possibilities. You can now get ad reprints and enlarge them to use in your lobby as counter displays with the caption "As seen in ". You can reference this in other advertising and marketing efforts. The words "as seen in" carry a great deal of weight when you are not known but the publication you have "been seen in" is well known and well respected.

You have heard the saying before "You are known by the company you keep". Perhaps your mother mentioned it to you one or two hundred times as you grew up. You know what? She was right. This strategy is a business version of mom's words of wisdom.

How impressed do you think your customers and prospects will be when they see your ad reprint or other marketing material that states "as seen in the Wall Street Journal"? They do not need to know that is was seen only by a classified ad you ran in a regional edition.

If you have run a larger display type ad or have received editorial space then get reprints from the publication. These will cost little and provide a valuable perception for you. The only one who knows you are only in the regional edition is you and, of course, the magazine or newspaper. To the readers of the ad it seems that you are running a national campaign. If high profile visibility is important to your business this is an excellent way to get it.

Furthermore, companies like MNI (1-212-661-4800) can place you in a grouping of regional editions of national magazines giving you tremendous visibility at a cost far less than the national edition of only one magazine is likely to cost you. MNI also brokers remnant space.

The biggest is very often not the best. Larger is not always better and longer is not always better. Don't always assume that a full page ad is more cost effective than a half page ad or that a 60 second commercial will be more cost effective than a 30 second one. You should test both. If your agency tells you otherwise don't listen to them, test instead. Remember, the larger the ad or longer the commercial the higher their production costs and commission (unless you are placing it).

A full page ad may cost 50% more than a half page ad and only pull 25% more response. You must test and weigh the cost of each response and each sale. Simply divide the cost of the ad or commercial by the number of sales you realized as a result of that effort. This will give you the media related cost to secure that sale. This is how you determine your media cost per sale.

If you find, as I suspect you will, that the cost per sale or inquiry of the smaller ads and shorter commercials is much lower than those of the full page and longer commercials, you will be able to save 30% to 50% or more of your media costs.

Standard rates published in media kits are nothing more than list rates. You should never pay list rates. You should be able to get at least 25% off these rates. One very simple way to do this is to identify the publications and /or stations you wish to advertise in and send each a letter indicating that you wish to place an ad or run a commercial but only at a much lower rate.

If you indicate a rate at which you are willing to advertise, make sure you start at least 25% lower than the published rates. I would suggest that you first wait for them to offer you a lower rate, you may find that it will be lower than you had hoped.

You will always pay less than the published rate and almost without exception you should end up saving more than 10% off list prices just by asking for a better price. If you are having your ad agency or a media house place ads for you must make sure they are trying to get you the best rates. I will discuss this more later.

Share the risk and the rewards. Buy radio / TV time or advertising space on a per order or contingency basis. If you can buy time or space based solely on the number of products you sell you will have, in effect, eliminated all up front costs and risks. To do this you will have to offer a % of the selling price of each item you sell as payment for the time or space. For example, if you are selling an item for $50 and you make a deal to pay 20% of each sale and you sell 100 you will have to pay $1,000 in fees.

If this type of arrangement proves mutually beneficial to all parties involved you will have a solid selling proposition to approach other media outlets. This will be important because not all media sources will be receptive to this idea. They do not want to share any risk and it will be very helpful to be able to show them how this has successfully worked with other publications or stations.

Also remember that the publication or station may very well have unsold space or time left and you can offer them the opportunity to fill that space in a manner that could result in more income for them than if they had sold it for normal rates.

This brings up something you should be very careful about if you choose to try to advertise this way. You must monitor the amount you are paying under the per order basis and compare these to the best rates you could get if paying for the ad under traditional terms. If sales are strong you might be paying more in "commissions" than you would be under normal terms. Of course, if this is the case you want to make darn sure that the next time you advertise you do it in the normal way.

Other things you must do are create an effective tracking system to ensure that orders received are credited to the right media source. You cannot afford to pay the wrong sources and you do not want to pay a fee on a sale that came in from none of the media sources you might be using.

Finally, make sure that any arrangement you work out limits the fees you pay to the first sale only. If you sell other products or services to the same customer you should not pay a fee to the media source for them.

You are the customer. What can they do for you? Make sure that you are always asking about no cost services offered by the publication, radio station, or TV station that you are using. Almost all media sources will have a menu of incentives that they use to attract and keep advertisers. The sales representative may not always inform you of these if they feel they are not needed to make the sale. Your agency may not advise you of these either if they don't fit in with their plans for your account or for any number of other reasons.

The media source you use can help in your overall marketing efforts. Always ask for a merchandising allowance when you negotiate the rates for your advertising program. A merchandising allowance can be used to purchase low cost promotional materials directly from the media source that can, in turn, be used to further your marketing and advertising efforts at little or no cost.

These type of items include point of purchase displays, ad reprints, and video or audio tapes of your commercial. If they don't offer the types of items you want, push for them anyway. If they want your business they may be willing to provide you with what you need or offer some corresponding compromise.

You will never get noticed if you sit in the back of the room. To get the most response and attention you should always try to get placement on the right-hand page of any publication (and above the fold if a newspaper) and you want to be towards the front of magazines and in the appropriate section for a newspaper. These placement areas are proven to have a higher readership level. Higher response levels will mean higher sales and inquiry levels which will result in a lower per inquiry or per sale cost. You must always seek to control the placement and, in turn, control your cost per sale or inquiry.

Try all you can not to pay for this placement. If you cannot obtain the placement you seek inside the magazine or newspaper then don't run the ad. They will often attempt to try to get you to pay more for premium placement but your goal is just the opposite. You want premium placement at no added cost and you want a written guarantee of this placement. Please understand I am not talking about exact page placement but rather front half of the magazine placement in magazines. I am talking about a guarantee for newspaper sections and for right hand placement.

Believe me enough advertisers have no idea as to the benefit of placement and therefore will not ask for it so as a result the space can be had. The bottom line is that you control the process because unless you get the placement you want you simply do not place the ad.

It you are a regular advertiser you should accept nothing less than premium position and should not pay any extra for it. If you are unable to negotiate top position for ROP rates (run of paper) then you should test your advertising both ways to see if the added cost you have to pay to get premium position is justified by a higher level of quality responses.

Opposites may attract, but should they? Match your print advertising with issues that feature articles that are compatible or will attract interest from your target audience. This also goes for special issues that are likely to attract a higher readership from your target audience and increased newsstand sales. Higher readership will result in more sales or inquiries and will therefore lower your per sale media cost.

To plan this simply ask for an Editorial or Features calendar from the magazine or newspaper. Then you simply need to schedule your advertising in those issues that fit the bill. For example, if you are selling computers or computer related products, you will do much better running in an issue that will cover computers in today's business world than you would running in an issue dealing with recycling in today's business world. All issues are not of equal value to you but they will all cost the same.

Media discounts are often available but not always offered. Always ask about them. Always ask for any and all discounts offered. These can include discounts for first time advertisers, direct mail advertisers, and test advertisements to name just a few. As an example I have listed below the discounts available from Sky Magazine the in-flight publication of Delta Airlines.

A 30% discount for the first test ad.
A 20% discount for mail order advertising.
A 20% discount for publishers.
A 15% discount for non profit organizations.

A 30% discount for destination retail advertising.

How much would one of these discounts save you? Well, using a full page black and white ad as an example, the normal list cost for a one time insertion is over $24,000. A 30% discount would save you over $7,200.

If you are buying your media from an agency or placement firm make sure they are asking for, and getting, these discounts and that they are being passed on to you.

Are you being billed for your media costs based on what they are being billed? If you are having your media placed by your agency or by a media house make sure that you are verifying the actual costs billed to the agency and make sure they are very aggressive in getting discounts, merchandising allowances, incentives, and anything else they can for you as I have outlined in other strategies. Also make sure that these are all passed on to you. You do not want the agency getting a 20% discount and a 15% commission and billing you full list prices.

To verify that this is not occurring you really only have two choices. You can either request written verification from the media source of actual costs and any incentives or you can request a copy of the actual bill from the publication showing what the agency had been billed.

Make sure you are getting the media placement rates you deserve. Always make sure you are getting rates based on total space or time purchased regardless of the size of your ads or the length of your commercial. These are called combined rates. If you are running various size ads or various length commercials you should still get lower rates based on volume. You will realize a significant cost savings by doing this compared to the cost of individual placements of ads in different sizes or commercials at different times.

You must know where your sales leads are coming from. Unless you establish a way to track and evaluate where your sales leads are coming from you will never be able to determine which of your advertising efforts are working and which are not. Unless you know what is bringing you leads and sales and what is not, you will continue to waste money on unproductive efforts.

You may be spending money in promotional efforts that are doing nothing for you or at the very least are not cost justified. By knowing where your leads are coming from you can effectively funnel your limited marketing dollars into those efforts and away from the less productive efforts.

For example, if you spend $10,000 in a media vehicle that produces 100 solid sales leads this has cost you $100 per lead. If the same $10,000 was spent in a different marketing effort that generated 200 solid sales leads you have just cut your cost per lead by 50% to $50.

There are many ways to track where your sales leads are coming from depending on your marketing efforts. A few obvious ways include keying ads with a code, having customers request a certain extension when they phone in, and coming right out and asking the lead.

Your market in microcosm. Trade shows can be another excellent source of low or no cost research. What do you think about when you go to a trade show? Boring, waste of time, sample grabbing? Well, you should view trade shows as one of your best possible sources of ideas. All under one roof you can see what your competition is doing, view new products, see hundreds of new ideas for products and services, and review marketing approaches.

Think of trade shows as your research department. You will also have an opportunity to see how your competition sells, what they use to promote, what they give away, and how much they charge for various products and services. Don't just look at your competition either. New ideas will come from every field. If you can't go to a trade show and come up with at least 3 or 4 new ideas on what to sell or how to market more effectively, you just aren't using the gray matter in that space between your ears.

You should not limit yourself to attendance at trade shows for your industry only. Any trade show you attend is an opportunity to view millions of dollars in ideas for a small $5 to $10 admission fee. You will get ideas on marketing, products, displays, selling techniques, incentives, and dozens of other valuable areas. Marketing ideas and concepts are often interchangeable. What works in one industry may very well work in another with slight modifications.

Even if you are a small company you should consider, if your product is applicable, participating in local and regional trade shows in your area. Hundreds of potential buyers may attend a local trade show and thousands will attend a regional show. Not only will you receive significant visibility but you will also have a chance to see what others in your industry or related industries are doing. This can be an excellent source of ideas for you as I have pointed out before. Trade shows are not just for big companies.

Are your trade show and convention costs justified? This may sound contradictory to what I have told you in the last few strategies but it is not. Trade show attendance can be taken too far and, depending on who goes and where, it is not always productive. You must monitor all trade show and convention expenses. The very first thing you should be asking is -- does anyone need to go? National trade shows and conventions can be very expensive when you consider not only the cost of attending, but also airfare, hotel, time away from work, and dozens of other travel related costs. If you feel someone should attend consider local or regional shows or conventions instead of the national ones.

By attending regional or local shows you can eliminate travel costs and significantly reduce time away from work for all involved. Don't ask those that have gone in the past and take their word as gospel. Of course, they are going to say it was worthwhile since they probably enjoyed the trip and regardless of the worth to the company want to go again or at the very least are unlikely to honestly tell you that you have been wasting your money.

You must evaluate what you are getting out of attendance at these events. They can drain time, money, and very often are not justified by any tangible (translate to $$) returns. You should only attend those that are cost justified, critical to your ongoing sales and marketing plans, and then only send those who must go.

Traveling overnight? If you attend, or send people to attend, any trade shows, conventions or sales calls that require an overnight stay, make sure you are booking a **reasonably** priced hotel within walking distance of the function. By doing this you will be able to eliminate the cost of a rental car and cab rides.

Just one cab ride in a major city could cost you $25 or more and a rental car will cost you over $50 per day. Think how fast this will add up. Even if you only stay two days and only travel to the show or client once and then once back again each day this could cost you well over $50 per day not to mention the lost time and frustration in dealing with cab drivers who might take you on the tourist shortcuts. These are the shortcuts designed to get to your wallet faster not get you to your destination faster.

In Pursuit of Profits. How To At Least Double Your Profits Without Increasing Your Sales.

You will notice that earlier I said reasonably priced hotel. It will serve no purpose to stay at a hotel that costs $200 a night to avoid cab costs and car rental fees if you could instead stay at a $50 a night hotel and incur $50 per day in transportation costs. Think and plan ahead.

If you have a fairly stable product line but prices that change weekly, monthly, or even yearly, keep all prices out of your main selling and promotional literature. Instead have a separate price page or price booklet. This way you will be able to update prices as needed quickly and without spending a great deal of money to change and reprint a catalog or other more elaborate marketing pieces.

The price pages should be a simple one or two color job whereas your other literature will most likely be much more complex and costly. Having to completely update a 4 color catalog each year will cost a great deal of money.

If you are a small company serving the local market, consider putting most, if not all, of your resources into improving your product and service. In cases like this the best type of advertising is word of mouth. If you offer the best service you can combined with the best quality product you can offer, your chances for success are going to be a great deal higher than if you place all your resources in advertising and marketing and offer only mediocre service and products.

Improving your product and being committed to excellent service will, without a doubt, provide you with the most effective and least costly method of increasing sales and keeping your existing customers. **This is advice even the largest companies ought to pay attention to.** How often have you called a large company and been put on hold, incorrectly transferred, lost in a maze of voice mail, or just treated as anything but a valuable customer? I suspect this is the rule and not the exception. Most companies forget that the most important person in the chain of business is the customer. Don't you ever forget this!

Interested in free advertising? If you aren't you should be. Public relations can be one of your most effective and cheapest forms of increased sales, leads, and credibility. The best part of all is that anyone can get it. You do not need to hire a high priced public relations firm. I would suggest you pick up a good book on the subject for basic information on how to go about approaching media people and how to prepare materials.

By writing and properly preparing press releases and sending them to every magazine and newspaper that even remotely reaches your target market you will be surprised at how many will give you a free plug. Don't misunderstand me here, I am not by any means suggesting that most or even many will give you print exposure. But remember the pet rock guy? Newsweek Magazine gave him a full page write up simply as a result of getting his press release. At the time that happened a full page ad of paid advertising would have cost him nearly $30,000.

It cost Mr. pet rock about .30 cents for the paper, envelope, and stamp. This exposure then lead to radio and TV interviews and, in fact, it has been reported that he was written up in over 1,000 papers and magazines around the world. Of course, this is the one in a million exception. But it does happen and, in fact, it happens very frequently on a much smaller basis all over the country every day.

When you get a write up in a newspaper or magazine often you are getting more than a form of free advertising. You are also getting the implied endorsement of the publication. This can give you valuable credibility. Since this is not a course in public relations I will not go into details here about the specifics of writing and preparing press releases but I suggest you visit your local library and pick up one of the many excellent books on this subject.

Resource

Bacon's Publicity Checker. Bacon's Publishing Company. 1-312-922-2400. A 2 volume directory listing over 21,000 outlets for print media publicity. This company also offers many other related products and services. Call for a catalog.

Watch out for yellow pages advertising scams. Every year at least a half a dozen of these cross my desk. They look like renewal forms for your yellow page advertising, some even carry the proper logos and the walking fingers. Many are stamped "renewal". Many people assume these are legit and just pay them. It has been estimated that nearly 25% of all these bogus invoices are paid. Never assume anything and always verify the validity of every invoice you pay or authorize for payment.

Join forces. Remember the days when you could go to the drive-in and pay one price for the whole car load of people? Everyone shared the cost and everyone got in for a lower price. Those were the days!

If you conduct mailings to your customers or prospects consider letting other non competitive companies participate in the mailing. This will reduce your costs since you will be receiving income from these outside companies that you are allowing to participate. They should be responsible for providing all of their own materials in accordance with your specifications on size and weight.

You also want approval of the contents of these pieces to ensure they do not conflict with your sales efforts or with any image you are attempting to convey. They will, of course, also have to pay a portion of the mailing and stuffing costs as well as a fee to you for organizing the project and providing them access to your list of customers or prospects. You should be able to reduce the cost of your mailing efforts by 25% to 50% depending on a variety of conditions including how much play you have in dealing with the weight allowances for each postal rate.

Not quite as much fun as a car load of kids at the drive-in but you might save enough to buy a big screen TV.

Piggyback your products with other companies' mailings. If a company mails to your audience and your products are non competitive, by approaching them and working out an arrangement where you can mail your material in with their mailings, you may find that you can save 50% or more over the cost of conducting your own individual mailings.

You should also find that you will reach some new prospects and even a larger audience than you have been reaching. Furthermore, if the company you are tying your mailing in with is a bigger, better known, or a more credible company you will benefit from the reputation and recognition of that company. Remember, your mother was right, you are known by those you associate with. Of course, you must make sure that the company is reputable and non competitive otherwise you will not benefit by this association but could be "guilty" by association instead.

Also unrelated business in the same mall or building can advertise together to generate traffic to the location. By sharing in advertising and marketing costs you can each receive the full benefit without the full cost.

In Pursuit of Profits. How To At Least Double Your Profits Without Increasing Your Sales.

If you need audio or video recording services for presentations, products, or commercials, consider using a local college or university. Many have excellent recording studios and video production capabilities and would welcome a chance to have their students work on real world projects. You, in return, may be able to have your work done for a very low cost or perhaps even no cost beyond the out of pocket expenses incurred by the school.

Are you paying for the same thing twice? How about three or four times? When buying printed or imprinted promotional items, many times you won't know it, but added charges incurred in conjunction with your order are often buried in the overall selling price. This is very often done by the salespeople so as not to hurt their prospects for getting the sale by listing numerous added charges.

You are much more likely to place an order with them if they give you one bottom line price than if they give you one price for the product and then 5 other charges for other costs. For example, if you buy a custom printed product or imprinted product you might be quoted a price that includes everything or a price that has a charge for the product, a charge for art, one for a proof, one for plates, and another for negatives and so on.

Which would look more appealing to you? Most people don't like seeing a lot of separate added charges so they would feel more comfortable with the one total price even though when added up, the quote listing the various charges may equal the same amount. This is just human nature.

It is an easier sell to give you a quote of 5,000 pieces at .25 each than it is to give you a price of 5,000 pieces at .24 each with an added charge of $10 for setup, $10 for a color match, $20 for art, and $10 for plates. The totals are the same but one makes for a much easier sell.

This can be an effective way to sell but it is not always in your best interest. Why? What difference does it make, after all as I have pointed out the totals are the same? You might even like the one price that includes all because it will look good to your boss or it makes it easier to compare quotes.

But think again. Think about when you go to reorder this item or product. You should not have to pay many of these added charges again if you are reordering from the same source who did the original job for you. Many of the added charges are one time charges that should not be incurred again or charged to you on repeat orders. But if you do not know what the added charges were you may find yourself paying for them over and over again and you might never even know it. You might also be paying higher prices than you should when you actually think you are getting a good deal.

This happens all the time and the customer never knows it. How? Let me give you an example. Suppose you place an order for 10,000 imprinted key chains. You award the job to a vendor who happens to have given you one price. Let's say that price was $5,000 or .50 each.

The order is completed and everything went just right. A few months or even a year or two later you decide to order more key chains. You contact that vendor to get a new price and he tells you the cost is now .52 each or $5,200. You know this vendor was the best value the last time you ordered and it is your feelings that a .02 cent increase is very moderate given the time since your last order so you give the supplier the reorder. Or perhaps you solicit new quotes, as you should, and find this vendor still represents the best value so you give them the reorder. So what is the problem?

The problem is that you may be overpaying and you may not have given the other vendors a fair chance to quote. What if, included in the original order were added one time charges that added $500 to the overall costs? You would not know this because you purchased based on one bottom line total. But perhaps a special die had to be made, plate charges had to be included, ink matches and art work also added to this total. You knew nothing of this since these added costs were never spelled out for you.

Now these added charges were one time charges. They should not be charged again. This means that the original product cost you $4,500 with $500 worth of added charges and not the $5,000 you thought. This also means that the new price from that vendor of $5,200 should be compared to the original product cost of only $4,500. Suddenly your price increase is not .02 per piece but .07 per piece.

The deception has been caused by comparing the new price to the total old price when in fact a significant portion of the old price does not apply at all to the rerun. This means that one of two things has happened. One is that the supplier knows you received a single bottom line price last time and knows you will be comparing this bottom line single price to that one.

Therefore, he has based his new selling price on your total cost from the first order and not the base cost from the original order less the one time added extras. This means that he is making an added profit equal to the total of all those one time charges. In this case if his increased selling price is only .02 your new cost should be .47 or $4,700 not the .52 or $5,200. You are being overcharged by $500.

The other thing that could have happened here is that his price actually has jumped up from .45 to .52 each and you just don't see it since the added .05 increase is hidden from you due to the single price from the first order.

You have no way of knowing what is really happening here since you did not know what your one time costs from the first order were. You also may have been able to get a better deal from other vendors had you known what part of each quote was for the product and what part was for the added charges.

Another possibility is that you placed a reorder a few months later and the vendor tells you that the price will be the same. You think great, after all who can complain about no price increase. You even brag a bit about how you got the vendor to do the job for the same price as last time. But what is the reality here?

The reality here is that this vendor made an added $500 on your order while at the same time he made you think you were getting a great deal. If you paid $5,000 for the first order and this included $500 of one time charges and you paid $5,000 for the second order, you overpaid by $500. Just because you do not know this happened does not mean that it did not happen!

Don't let yourself get cheated by paying for the same one time charges more than once and don't kid yourself into thinking you got a good deal when, in fact, you simply do not know if this is true. Insist that these charges be broken down for you on all quotes. Then next time when you compare costs you will know what is going on, what is the best deal, and how much your product costs have actually gone up.

How to buy promotional products or advertising specialties. These are products that are imprinted with your company's name and logo and are often given away as a promotional item or in conjunction with a promotion. The types of items I am referring to are things such as hats, key chains, calendars, sweatshirts, golf balls, and any one of a thousand items like this that can be imprinted with your company's name and logo. I want to give you a very basic overview as to how this industry works. By having some knowledge about this industry you should very easily be able to reduce your costs of purchasing these types of products by 25% or more.

There are three parties involved in this industry. The manufacturer who makes the products, the distributor who sells the products, and you the customer or buyer of the products. The manufacturer sells through the distributor to avoid having a sales force or to subsidize the sales force they may have. They sell the product to the distributor at a set price and the distributor sells it to you at another price.

In Pursuit of Profits. How To At Least Double Your Profits Without Increasing Your Sales.

In most cases the manufacturer provides or sells the distributor catalogs which they use to sell from and for product research to look for the products you need and to find out the manufacturer's suggested selling price and cost. If you have ever bought these types of products you have most likely seen these catalogs. If you have one around your office get it now. If you do not, get one from your distributor's sales representative the next time he or she calls on you.

Look at the catalog. In it you will find the products being offered and the prices they are selling for. Somewhere on the page, most often next to the selling price, you will see the letters A, B, C, D, E or P, Q, R, S, T. In some cases the prices and codes are in a separate distributor price book, but normally they will be as I am telling you. What these letters do is indicate mark ups and therefore the commission the distributor earns.

The five letters A, B, C, D, E correspond exactly to the letters P, Q, R, S, T. The mark ups mean the same thing, some manufacturers simply use one set of letters instead of the other. The mark up code of "A" means the selling price shown is marked up 50%. "B" means the price has been marked up 45%. "C" means the mark up is 40%. "D" is a 35% mark up and "E" is a 30% mark up. Each higher letter means a 5% lower mark up.

So if you see a selling or list price in the catalog for 100 widgets at $1 each and you see a code of "A", this means the distributor is buying that product from the manufacturer at .50 each (perhaps even lower if they have arranged for special pricing). You may see the codes listed as 2A, B, 3C or the like. This simply means that the first 2 quantities for which prices are shown are marked up on an "A" or 50%. The next quantity or in this case the third one, is marked up on a "B'" or 45% and the final 3 quantities indicated are marked up on a "C" or 40%.

These codes will tell you how much flexibility the distributor has in the price they will give you. In our example of widgets you can see they have a great deal of flexibility since the 100 will cost them only .50 each. This is a very price sensitive industry. In most cases all distributors are dealing with the same costs and therefore, price is a big part of how they are differentiating themselves from the competition to get your business.

For example, if you are looking to buy BIC pens and you call a few distributors and ask for prices, they are all buying and reselling from BIC and, unless they are a very large distributor with huge buying power, they will each be getting the same price from BIC. This means they cannot differentiate themselves on product so they must do it on price and service. As a result this industry is so price sensitive it is very rare you will ever be quoted a list price.

Each of the distributors must decide what they think they can establish as a selling price in order to get your business. This spells cost saving opportunities for you. By knowing the costs and, using my strategies outlined in the purchasing section, you should easily reduce your costs for what you have been paying for these types of items by 25% or more. Very commonly in this industry I see mark ups as low as 5% to 10% and it is my feeling the average mark up falls around 25%. Depending on what you are buying and from whom, your marked up price could be much less.

If you purchase enough promotional type items you should look into becoming an ASI distributor. You could save thousands, tens of thousands of dollars, or, depending on your level of promotional purchasing, hundreds of thousands of dollars or more, over the course of a year. The cost of membership is very low (a few hundred dollars depending on your size) compared to the savings you will realize. On every item you purchase for your company as an ASI distributor you will save up to 50%.

By becoming a distributor you may also find an entirely new line of business since you now are authorized to function as a distributor and sell the products of thousands of companies. Whether you focus on a niche of the market or sell to a wide variety of companies you can increase profits by not only realizing significant savings on your own promotional products, but also by selling them to other companies.

Resource

Advertising Specialty Institute
Bucks County Business Park
1120 Wheeler Way
LangHorne, PA 19047
1-800-669-4636. Ask for the membership information department.

Do not purchase specialty or promotional products from your advertising agency. They are going to buy them from a distributor and they are going to add a mark up. You could very easily pay more than full price for any items like this that you buy from your agency. When compared to purchasing these items in the manner I have outlined you could be overpaying by 25% to 50% on every promotional item you purchase through your agency.

Buy direct and cut out the middleman. Not only will you pay less but you will retain control of the process. Whenever possible buy direct from the manufacturer of the promotional products. The closer you can get to the manufacturer the lower your costs will be and the more control you will have.

If you can't buy direct buy through a distributor. Many manufacturers will sell direct even though they tell their distributors they do not. I do not like the ethics of this as I feel this is a dishonest practice. If a manufacturer promises their distributors they will sell only through them that is what they should do. Some manufacturers will try to get around this by forming a separate shell of a company with a different name and sell the same products direct.

Since my objective is not to teach the ethics of business, but to teach you how to control and reduce your costs, I feel compelled to point this strategy of buying direct from the manufacturers out to you. You can decide on the ethical issues for yourself.

What did we do before money was invented or You help me and I will help you. Bartering is an often overlooked cost control and cost reduction strategy that is used more than you probably think. This can be used in many areas of your business and not just in advertising and marketing.   You have to think. Can you offer your product or service in exchange for radio time, newspaper space, billboards, printing, magazine space, or any other media that might be of use to you?

Isn't much of what passes for charity in this country nothing more than an indirect form of bartering. A company such as McDonald's provides food and drink to a local event. Why do they do this? To be a good corporate citizen? Maybe. To get an image of a good corporate citizen in the local papers, or local radio at the event? Of course.

They are providing something with the primary result being that they are given free promotional time and exposure. Why can't you be more direct about it and offer to exchange whatever product or service you offer in exchange for the exposure you seek? If they have a need you can fill then you have the making of a mutually beneficial, no out of pocket cost, barter.

For example, if you are an office supply house why don't you offer a credit at your store for an equal amount of radio time or newspaper space. You will not only have no out of pocket expense, but you will also be saving money since you are exchanging a credit for merchandise at full price. If you provide a $1,000 credit in exchange for $1,000 of advertising are you not actually buying this space at a much cheaper rate?

Of course you are. The $1,000 credit you gave is for merchandise that may only cost you $600. Therefore you have in effect bought the $1,000 of advertising for $600 which is a savings of 40%. You have also conserved cash which, of course, has a cost associated with it.

Think about what you sell that can be used by other companies who have what you need. Think. Ask yourself the questions. Look in the yellow pages of your local and metropolitan cities under bartering and in the regional business to business book. Here you will find companies that specialize in bringing parties interested in bartering together.

Resource

If you are interested in bartering, contact the trade association of this industry. They are the:

International Reciprocal Trade Association
9513 Beach Mill Road
Great Falls, VA 22066

Your pocket-sized billboard. Business cards are among the most under used marketing tool there is. These should be pocket sized billboards for your company. They do have two sides you know. How many times have you seen both sides used? How many times have you been given a business card that gave you no idea of the type of business the person giving it to you was in? This is a very low cost marketing tool that is rarely used to it's full potential. Getting more for your money has the same effect as cutting your costs. Isn't it time you started getting more for your money?

Check into Postal discounts for any and all of your incoming and outgoing mail. Many companies are eligible for postal discounts. The mailing options you might have could range from the basic first class rate of .29 to a third class presorted rate of .146. This is over a 50% savings on postage costs provided you can meet the requirements.

I strongly suggest you have a representative from the post office come to see you and discuss how you can start reducing your postage costs. With the wide variety of options open to all companies you should find numerous ways to save. If the potential for saving up to 50% does not interest you let me tell you about a company you might recognize. They sure found out how much postal discounts could save them.

Texaco saves over $200,000 per month or over $2,400,000 per year simply by adding bar-codes to their credit card statements. Maybe you should call the United States Post Office today at 1-800-843-8777 ext. 500 and see how much you can start saving.

While you are at the post office get information on adding bar-codes to both your outgoing mail and return mail. Bar-codes facilitate faster automated processing which again can result in lower postage costs and faster delivery. Please notice that I said to look into bar-codes for outgoing and return mail. By adding bar-codes, provided at no cost by the post office, to your business reply mail you will not only receive your return mail faster but you can cut the cost of your return mail by 50% or more. Savings that add up for every piece of mail returned to you. Better service, lower costs. Get down to the post office today.

Resources

"Direct". Billed as "The magazine of Direct Marketing Management". This publication will be sent to you free of charge each month upon request. Write and ask for a free subscription. Direct, P.O. Box 1023, Skokie, IL 60076-8023.

"DM News". This is a weekly newspaper dedicated to the direct mail industry. They will also send you a free subscription upon request. Write them at DM News, P.O. Box 3045, Langhorne, PA, 19047-9145.

Meter mistake? Get a refund. Very often mistakes are made when metering mail. The meter may malfunction or the person doing the metering may make a mistake. In any case, if you have metered mail and it is not being mailed out you should bring it to your local post office for a refund.

Your mailing list. A profit center? Consider renting your customer mailing list to outside companies that are not competitors. You can either run ads to rent the list out yourself or contact a list broker and place your list with them for rental. You must make sure that you maintain control over who can rent your list. You should be able to rent your list for between $50 and $100 per thousand names. Make sure you seed your list with names that come back to you at a couple of addresses so you will know if the usage by the renting party complies with your authorization.

Unless you have a highly specialized list you should have at least 5,000 names before renting the list will be worthwhile to a list broker. If you have at least 5,000 names and you rent it out only once a month at $100 per thousand names you will generate $500 a month or $6,000 per year. You have turned a cost into a profit.

If your pretax profit ratio is 3%, to realize this same added bottom line profit you would need to increase your sales $200,000.

Pocket savings by printing mailing labels yourself. If you buy outside mailing lists you will be able to save up to 50% of the cost of purchasing those names by ordering them on disk and printing them out yourself. If you order them on labels or some other hard copy you will pay up to 50% more.

Whenever applicable use postcards to communicate with your customers instead of letterheads and envelopes or direct mail packages. Not only will you save about 33% of your postage costs but you will also save significant amounts of money on time and material. The cost of a postcard will be about 75% less than the cost of a letterhead and envelope and a fraction of the cost of a direct mail package.

Chapter 21. Outside Experts.

"Farming looks mighty easy when your plow is a pencil and you're a thousand miles from the corn field."

Dwight D. Eisenhower

Let me start by saying right off that I do not think there is any such thing as an expert. The term "expert" denotes someone who knows everything there is to know about a certain topic. I have never met anyone like this and neither will you. The closest you will ever get to an "expert" is someone who knows a good deal about a certain subject and may know more than you. **Never consider anyone an expert in anything**.

I am talking about consultants, accountants, ad agencies, design houses, lawyers, creative people, and anyone who is not on your staff but who you periodically pay to provide you with some sort of service. Your goal must be to reduce and control your costs incurred in conjunction with the use of outside experts while maximizing your results.

As with all my strategies, use those you can, modify my ideas to fit your needs, and think of new strategies on your own. You possess the greatest thinking machine ever created, it resides between your two ears. Use it.

Remember, lawyers, accountants, CPAs, etc., are like anyone else in every other profession. From the local auto mechanic to the doctor at the hospital, some are very good and some are very poor at what they do. Some are ethical and some are not. I have met many so called experts that were borderline incompetent and others who I could describe in no other manner than to say they were incompetent.

Despite what you may think, letters after one's name does not guarantee they are good at what they do. The only thing it will guarantee is that you will pay more. Whether or not it will be worth it is another matter altogether. I am never impressed with letters after one's name, nor am I ever impressed with academic background alone. Honest, capable people impress me, not pieces of paper. If they have these credentials so much the better. When you deal with so called outside experts you don't always get what you pay for.

You must verify qualifications and you must check out these people carefully and completely. You are not just worried about wasting your money on their advice, you also must worry about the cost and implications of following their advice. This could be far worse than any money you lose on their fees. The damage resulting from bad advice that you have followed could be irreparable.

With this said, let me also point out that the right "outside experts", worked with properly, can indeed be an invaluable asset to your company. They can bring a new perspective to your organization. They can provide you with the expertise you need, when you need it, without having to have this type of talent on staff year round. They can be a tremendous source of input and ideas. They can do things you may be unwilling or unable to do. The key here is to use the right people, at the right time, for specific purposes under the right arrangement.

The very first question you should ask is "why do you need the outside expert?". Any use of outside experts must be cost justified. All too often consultants and other "outside experts" are used merely to shift responsibility for an internal party to an external party. In other words, you are paying someone outside of your company to do what someone inside your company should be doing. Every single relationship your company has with an outside expert must be very carefully and frequently scrutinized. Ask the questions and seek ways not to justify the relationship, but to justify not having the relationship.

Pay them for results. Whenever you are working with an outside source who claims to be able to help you sell more, improve productivity, improve quality, or somehow benefit you in a fiscal manner, you should be thinking of a contingency relationship and not an hourly or project rate. The exception to this would be if you are absolutely positive that it is in your best fiscal interest to do otherwise.

A contingency relationship is when someone works with you in exchange for a portion of the profits generated from their efforts. An hourly rate or project rate is paid to the outside expert regardless of any success or failure that results from their rates. If their efforts result in unmet expectations they still get paid. Yes, of course, their efforts could result in a much higher rate of return than the amount you paid them. But in most cases wouldn't it make more sense to insure that they have a more vested interest in the success of the project?

Also think how fast an hourly rate can add up. At $125 to $250 per hour it does not take long to run up a very high bill. Think of all the meetings and wasted conversations. Think of all the time you are charged that you can never verify was ever spent on your behalf. All the risk is on your side of the ledger.

If a sales trainer comes in and tells you he can increase your sales by 20% great. If he is so confident why would he not be willing to earn his fee out of the **net profits** generated from this 20% increase in sales? No increase, no cost to you.

If you do work with someone on contingency you must be fair, you must be honest, and you must agree on a course of action that you follow through with. To do otherwise would be unfair and unethical. The outside expert's income would count on these things. If what he has proposed works he is entitled to your honesty and his fee.

If they over bill you, or did not do the job properly, do not pay. You have got to change your perception when dealing with outside experts. They have spent years fostering a perception that they are somehow above anyone else and as such they should never be questioned. This is bull. Like any other vendor, if they have overcharged you for a job or have not done the job properly, refuse to pay for it. If you have followed my strategies you will have little trouble in this area and when you do have a problem you will be on sound footing when you refuse to pay for overcharges.

> *"No one wants advice -- only corroboration."*
> *John Steinbeck*

I am not a believer in putting any type of outside expert on retainer. I prefer to pay their services only as I need then. I have never known anyone who felt they saved money by paying a monthly fee for services they may or may not even need. Use them and, pay for them, only when you absolutely need them.

Don't pay for the services of a CPA year round. This will generally be overkill. Instead, use a public accountant throughout the year to oversee your bookkeeping or accounting efforts. Then, if you prefer, or if your bank requires it, have a CPA come in only on a quarterly basis or at the end of the year. This will give you the best of both worlds and reduce your outside accounting costs by 50% to 75%.

Negotiate lower rates from your outside experts by offering a long term association. For example, I was able to get my accountant to lower his hourly rate by 25% and to hold it at this rate for two years by agreeing not to review other accountants for at least two years as long as his work continued to be satisfactory. Think of this as a form of volume discounting. This strategy saved me over $5,000 per year without costing me anything in the area of service. Rates are not set in stone. Think of the rates of outside experts as list prices. We never want to pay list prices.

Ask for a lower hourly rate. See the above strategy. The rate they quote you is the asking price. Almost without exception, when I have asked for a lower rate from an outside expert I have received one. Don't tell them what you want to pay. Tell them instead you are hoping to establish a long term relationship and you would like a rate that reflects this. Why should you pay the same hourly rate as someone who walks in off the street? From my accountant to my lawyer, this has worked thereby saving me tens of thousands of dollars per year.

"Make three correct guesses consecutively and you establish yourself as an expert."

Laurence J. Peter

Shift as many duties as possible away from your outside accountant and back to your bookkeeping staff. You should not be paying someone outside of your company to do something you can do inside of your company at a lower cost. To keep your outside accounting costs down it is important that you conduct as many bookkeeping functions as possible inside even if it means hiring an outside accountant to teach someone on your staff to do them. Hiring someone to train a member of your staff, or sending them to school for this purpose, is a one time expense that will yield monthly savings forever when compared to paying an outside source each month.

You should be keeping a log to record the time incurred with all your outside experts. I know that in some cases you are not able to verify the time spent on your behalf as it takes place out of the office. However, in many cases you will be able to track much of the time expended on your behalf and in some cases all of it. By having such a log you will be able to accurately verify or dispute any bills you receive.

For example, if you are billed once a month by your accountant, how will you be able to remember what he has done for you during the month and how much time he spent doing it? If you do not have a log in which you record the time he spent, you will be forced to accept the billing even though you may think the hours are high.

Every once in a while I would question a bill using your records as the point of conflict. At the very least, every once in a while mention "that the hours seem high". This way you will be letting your outside experts know that you are monitoring their time to ensure proper billing. This knowledge will go a long way towards ensuring proper billing of hours. Watch how fast hours start coming down and how much more work you seem to get for your money.

Over billing of time is an all to common and, very often intentional, occurrence. I know many people who bill on time and I have worked for an ad agency that billed on time. I can tell you first hand that over billing of time can be a very serious problem. How does it happen?

Well, sometimes it is intentionally done to increase profits. This is fraud and illegal, but nevertheless it is done. Other times poor records of time are kept and therefore gaps are filled in with any errors benefiting the billing company. Some companies require each employee to bill out a specific minimum number of hours each week. As I will show you in other strategies, the average employee actually only works about 50% of the time they are on the job. With this in mind how do you think these employees are able to generate 40, 50, 60, or more hours each week? Hmmm, how is that possible? Some might suggest hours spent on jobs are puffed a bit. Is that possible?

In other cases, employees lie to the company they are working for regarding the amount of time that they spent with a client on the company's behalf. They will do this to make themselves look like harder workers than they really are, or to set themselves up for a promotion, or larger raise or bonus. There are many reasons and in each case you are the one paying the bill. Do not let this happen to you. Track the time and question the invoice as needed.

Need an expert? You know many of them. Who? Think. How about your suppliers to start? They know a great deal about your market and your competition. They can provide you with a wealth of information and advice. They know sources, they may know what works and what has failed. They may be aware of similar problems to yours and they may know what the resolution is. Don't underestimate them.

Other free outside experts include: Other businesses in your industry, books, trade magazines, many top business people offer advice in the form of columns and interviews, SBA, SCORE, your employees are an often overlooked and invaluable source, your banker they have a vested interest in your success, your insurance agent, and federal and local government agencies to name but a few.

Let me give you an example of what I am saying. I once called my attorney to ask a question regarding hiring a teenager to work part time in our company. The lawyer told me he would have to research the question and get back to me. In the meantime, I called my insurance agent and got the answer in minutes at no charge and he faxed me a copy of the law that applied within 30 minutes. A day later the lawyer called with the same answer and sent me a bill for 1.5 hours of research. This was over $200. He probably just called my insurance agent for the answer.

I could have also called the unemployment department and obtained the answer for no charge. Remember, these sources may not have the answers to all your questions but they can provide many answers and for those questions they cannot answer they may point you to someone who can.

Let me give you another example. I was recently looking into a new typesetter and, quite honestly, did not know where to start. So I started by calling in sales representatives of the major typesetting equipment manufacturers. This only served to confuse me more since they all professed to have the best system and best prices and, of course, all pointed out the shortcomings of each other's systems.

They also got much more technical than I needed or wanted them to get. This, of course, is meant to show that they know all and I, the stupid buyer, know nothing. I decided to ask some of my other suppliers who they knew that had recently bought the type of equipment we were considering or who they might know that was looking into purchasing this type of equipment.

I quickly secured the names of four companies. In turn I called each to see if they would share their knowledge with me. I simply explained that I was looking into purchasing this type of equipment and found myself very confused. I asked if they could help me. This was a very sincere request on my part and since most people are happy to help others and since all people love to talk about what they know, it wasn't very long before I had a great deal of information.

Information that saved me dozens of hours and thousands of dollars to say the least. In fact, it probably saved me tens of thousands of dollars because I might have purchased the wrong piece of equipment as did one of the companies I had talked to.

This one company told me why they bought what they bought and why it was a very costly mistake. This information prevented me from making a similar mistake. Another company had spent a few thousand dollars checking out all the equipment including sending someone to seminars on the subject and visiting shops that had it in place. He was only too happy to share this information with me for nothing.

The end result was that I ended up purchasing a newer used machine for about one tenth the cost of a new machine and it does all I need. I found out the new machines had more capability than I needed and ended up saving over $50,000 on the purchase alone.

Learn from others who have already done what you are trying to do or who have at least already researched what you are considering. This can save you countless hours and a great deal of money. Ask the questions. Who would know this information? Who has already done this or looked into this? You get the idea.

Do not ever allow yourself to be billed in 15 minute increments. This is a standard practice among many who bill on time. Let me give you an example. You call your lawyer and speak to him for 5 minutes. He then turns around and bills you for 15 minutes. You have just overpaid by 300%. You would not allow anyone else to do this would you? Why would you let them do this?

They always round up. You take 20 minutes of their time and you get billed for 30 minutes. You are getting ripped off in a big way. Do not accept this. If you use 8 minutes of time, pay only for 8 minutes of time. Not 10, not 15. Over the course of the year, depending on your size, this can add up to hundreds, thousands, or even tens of thousand of dollars or more. Dollars you have paid and for which you have received nothing in return. Keep a log as I suggested and cross check all bills for these outside experts.

Let me show you how fast this can add up. Using an outside expert who charges $125 per hour as an example, you are paying $2.08 per minute for their time. If you make 12 calls to this outside expert a month and each call last 10 minutes but each time they record it as 15 minutes, at the end of the month you have overpaid by 60 minutes or $125 per hour. Over the course of the year this will cost you over $1,500.

If you allow this to happen you are getting screwed. It happens every day to tens of thousands of companies and individuals. If your pretax profit ratio is 5%, it would take you $30,000 in sales to recover this money you have just given to your outside expert. What have you received for this $1,500? Nothing! You might as well just open up your window and throw it out.

Always be prepared when you call or deal in person with an outside expert who is billing you on time. Ten minutes of small talk will cost you $20.80 at a rate of $125 per hour. Even more if you let them bill you 15 minutes. Know what you want to discuss, be prepared to discuss it, and make your expectations very clearly known. Conduct your business and conclude it as soon as possible. Think of the time as a faucet spewing out $2 bills. Your $2 bills. How quick would you be to turn this off? Damn quick I hope.

When outside experts come to you do not pay for their travel time. I do not care what they want nor do I care how they normally conduct business. Do you get paid for your time in driving to and from work? Why should they? When you go to their offices do they pay you for your time? Why should you pay for theirs when they come to see you? They may conduct business normally any way they like, but if they want to work for you they better conduct business the way you normally do! Remember who the customer is in this relationship.

If you hire outside experts that require any travel, follow total cost control policies. By this I mean make sure they travel the way I have outlined you should travel. From flights to hotels and meals, if you are paying their expenses they must be made to follow your total cost control procedures. Not only will this save you a great deal of money but it will also send your outside expert a message about how you operate.

Unless you must have it in writing do not let them put it in writing. This is a favorite tactic of outside experts. They will give you the answer, advice, or opinion you seek verbally, over the phone or in person, and then they will follow it up with a letter restating the same thing for your records. What is wrong with this? Nothing unless you mind paying for the same thing twice. They will bill you for the confirming letter they send you.

Unless you have a compelling reason for having a written record, make sure you do not get one. If they send you one that you did not ask for refuse to pay for it. I fully understand there will be times when having a written record will be important, in these instances ask for the response in writing to begin with and eliminate the added billing of the in person or by phone reply.

Do not conduct a full audit unless you need one. Many privately held companies pay for a full audit every year when there is no reason or cost justification to do so. A full audit is very time consuming and costly. Unless you have a strong reason to conduct one or, it is required by your bank or by law, think long and hard before you have one done. If your bankers require an audit every year try to get them to agree to a review instead. Very often this will satisfy your banker and, if so, it will cut your costs in this area by 50% or more when compared to the cost of a full audit.

"It is the trade of lawyers to question everything, yield nothing, and talk by the hour."

Thomas Jefferson.

Be very careful about asking outside advisors or experts for advice. By the very nature of their job they are trained to find and create problems not just solve them. This is, after all, how they make their money. Very often you will be paying someone to give you the answer you already know.

You must ensure that your outside sources are utilizing Total Cost Control strategies when buying products and services on your behalf. Demand proof. Did they get multiple quotes for that job? From who? Don't take their word for it. You want to see them. Did they ship in the most effective manner possible considering your delivery needs? Make them aware that this is how you operate and if they are going to work with you they must comply. You call the shots. Remember who the customer is. Follow the strategies I have outlined in other sections.

In Pursuit of Profits. How To At Least Double Your Profits Without Increasing Your Sales.

Make sure that you are demanding and receiving detailed billings for any outside service that you are buying. This is extremely important when dealing with outside "experts" that sell you their time. You want to check these detailed billings very carefully to make sure that your logs of time spent match their billings and to see if any costs for off site work done at their office appears to be priced properly. If you are charged for an hours worth of time for a letter that was written at your lawyer's office and it is two paragraphs and basically a boiler plate form letter word processed by a secretary, you are being overcharged. Not only is the time dramatically overstated, but the work done by a secretary is being billed to you as lawyer's time.

Never ever be afraid to question a bill or a charge and always demand a detailed breakdown of what was done, how long it took, and what the cost was for each invoiced amount. Many times an adjustment will be made with the blame being assessed to a billing department error. Hogwash of course, but the end result is an adjustment.

Never put your entire faith and trust in the hands of your accountant or anyone else. To do so could cost you dearly in a number of ways. This may be the shortest piece of advise I have given you but it may also be the most important.

Hold your outside experts accountable for their advice and for their time. By following my other strategies you will be doing this.

Shop around for your outside experts. For example, shop for a lawyer. Often if you need advice you can get a free initial consultation while getting a good feel for the chemistry, style, and knowledge of the lawyer. After speaking to 2 or 3 you will have a good feel for which you feel most comfortable with and which offers you the best value. Hopefully these will be the same person.

Deal with a specialist when you must seek outside advice for dealing with a specific problem. Yes, you may pay a larger per hour rate when compared to a general practitioner, but in the long run you should pay far less money while getting much more credible and accurate advice. The lawyer who practices general law may charge you $125 an hour and take twice as long to find you the answer to your question. The specialist may charge you $200 per hour but only take half the time to provide you with more accurate information. Which is the better value?

The specialist has years of experience in the area of law that you need help with. The lawyer who practices general law will have far less experience in any specific area of law and may not even have any experience in the area for which you are seeking advice or guidance. This lawyer may take 5 or 10 times longer to research the information you are seeking and even then he may not have current or completely accurate information.

Clearly, the cheapest is not always the best for any particular circumstance. After all, despite the fact that a medical general practitioner costs far less than a heart specialist you would not go to him for your heart problem would you? Well, it is no different than taking an international trade problem to a lawyer who deals mainly in real estate transactions.

Never forget that just because an individual has letters after their name it does not mean that they are good at what they do. It does not mean that they are worth what they are charging. It does not mean that they are right for your needs at this particular time. Just like every other profession, some will be very good, some will be pathetically poor, some will serve you well, some will rob you, and some will be right for your needs at any particular time, while some will not be.

One of the most effective ways to find the outside experts you need is to ask others in your industry to recommend one. Do not ask your competitor, ask others in the industry. I am not suggesting you automatically use who they suggest, but rather that their suggestions can be a very effective way to save time in your search. You are getting both a starting point and a reference at the same time. This strategy can also be used for many other resources you are seeking, from a banker to a supplier, from a Realtor to an insurance agent, people in your industry can prove to be an excellent source of information. They could prove invaluable in helping you avoid making a mistake. The alternative is selecting someone from the yellow pages.

Get an estimate up front and negotiate the hourly rate up front. Outside experts sell time. This is their product. Therefore, it is in their best interest to extend the time needed for projects whenever possible. It is in your best interest to minimize the time extended on your projects, to get this time at the lowest hourly rate you can and to accomplish this while getting maximum results.

When you first approach a firm about doing business with them you have the most leverage. They want your business. If any concessions are to be made they will be made up front in an effort to get your business. Hourly rates may be lowered to get your business. Remember, their standard hourly rate is nothing more than a list price for their product. They are also much more apt to be on the conservative side when estimating the time required to complete various projects. You will hold them to these estimates.

This approach can save you thousands of dollars over the alternative of accepting whatever rate they tell you and having them start working for you with no estimate of time. If they won't work with you on the rate or are unwilling to provide an estimate of time required when you request it, walk away and find someone who will.

Ask for a corporate rate. If they would like to work with you on an ongoing basis instead of on a project basis you should be getting a corporate rate. Why should you pay the same hourly rate as someone who has them do one or two projects and never uses them again? You shouldn't. You should ask for and receive a discounted corporate rate with no minimum guarantee of hours and no retainer or fee relationship. I have done this many times and have secured discounts on rates ranging from 10% to 25%.

"I said that an expert was a fella who was afraid to learn anything new because he wouldn't be an expert anymore."

Harry S. Truman

Change your perception and positioning when you deal with outside experts. I have covered the positioning the outside experts will try to use in other sections so I will not restate them here, but remember they are selling a product and you are the customer. In this case the product is time and knowledge but the formula is still the same. Without you, the customer, they have no sale. You decide what to buy and what you are willing to pay for it.

Do not pay them for time spent with you at lunch or dinner. They have to eat anyway why should you be paying for this time?

In Pursuit of Profits. How To At Least Double Your Profits Without Increasing Your Sales.

Before you hire a lawyer to create a contract or form for you first see if that form or contract already exists in a form you can use as is or slightly modified. Lawyers are often used to provide many standard forms and contracts. This is not only foolish but a waste of money. Most often the lawyer will use a basic form that already exists in their word processor as is or can be slightly modified to give you the impression it has been created or customized for you. You will be paying hundreds of dollars for efforts that may or may not even have been spent on your behalf and any work that was done will most likely have been done by a legal secretary or clerk while being billed out at the lawyers hourly rate.

Many standard forms and documents are available in books at you local bookstore or library. Also, look in the phone book under documents as in many parts of the country you will find many low cost alternatives for your needs in these areas. There are many retail type stores in my area that specialize in handling routine legal needs in these areas at a fraction of the cost of going to a lawyer.

Check with your accountant to find out if you are eligible for a tax deduction or any type of government aid in conjunction with any costs you incur in complying with government regulations. Do not ever count on the government to advise you of anything that benefits you.

You should be meeting with your accountant each year to plan a strategy for reducing your tax liability each year. I have not gone into strategies for that here as the tax laws change so much each year. But rest assured each year the hands of the tax collector get tighter and tighter around your neck. Do whatever you can legally do to loosen this grip.
Resource.
Executive's Tax Letter. Newsletter published by Prentice Hall Tax, Englewood Cliffs, NJ 07632.

Examine how you calculate your quarterly estimated tax payments. If your earnings are much higher at the end of the year than they are during the rest of the year, it will cost you money if you are making equal tax payments throughout the year. By making quarterly tax payments equally when your profits are seasonal you are losing the float on your money which means you are losing the opportunity to use these funds for other more productive efforts.

Yes, the bottom line tax liability may be the same at the end of the year, but by paying money months before you really need to you are hampering your cash flow and you lose the opportunity to put these funds to cost saving or income producing uses. Review this with your accountant.

Make sure you are taking all deductions you are legally entitled to. Very often companies are unaware of all the deductions they may be able to take and, as a result, pay more in taxes than they should. The IRS is sure not going to point this out to you and send you a refund check. It is up to you to find out what deductions your type of business can take. Make sure your accountant is on top of this area.

Even if you have complete accounting personnel on staff you should consider having an outside accountant come in periodically to review their work, insure compliance, and keep an eye out for any fraud. They will be much more able to spot irregularities or discrepancies in the activity of this department.

Chapter 22. Personnel.

"The best executive is the one who has sense enough to pick good men to do what he wants done, and self-restraint enough to keep from meddling with them while they do it. "

Theodore Roosevelt

You must take the time to hire right. Hiring right will greatly reduce your employee related costs, problems, and costly turnover. Unfortunately, this gets harder and harder each year as the government gives fewer and fewer rights to employers. Today they would have a much shorter list if they just told you what you could ask and could check, instead of what you cannot do.

You must be as selective as possible when hiring new employees. You must check out every area of the person's background they list on their resume or application. Many hiring mistakes can be avoided simply by careful screening. Don't hire just on instinct, appearance, or chemistry. These are all important considerations but by no means the only considerations.

Testing can sometimes be a very useful aid in hiring properly.

Resources

Wonderlic Personnel Test Inc., 1509 Milwaukee Ave., Libertyville, IL 60048-1380 1-800-323-3742.

Reid Psychological Systems 1-800-922-7343.

Pinkerton Investigation Services also offers a wide variety of services to companies in this area. Call them and ask for a brochure at 1-800-232-7465.

Have all candidates for employment undergo an initial health screening to insure fitness for the position in question. You must find out what you can about health problems before you commit to hiring. After you have hired, any problems that might have existed could now be your problem. I know of one man who had a hearing problem long before he joined his present employer. Now he has claimed it is job related and is out on disability indefinitely.

If you suspect a claim is fraudulent or if it is even questionable, you must challenge it and challenge it aggressively. Not only for reasons I have outlined before, but also to send a strong message to your other employees who will now think twice before they contemplate similar actions.

Please check with your Department of Employment Training on this as at the time of this writing there has been a movement in the government to restrict health screening prior to hiring. It seems as though some in the government are concerned that employers might not want to hire a high risk employee. Imagine that! They think you should have no right to refuse to hire someone who very likely could prove to be a long term liability. They suggest, and may mandate, that you hire them first and then find out what health related problems the employee may have. Of course, at that point the employees problems would be your problems. Problems that could cost you dearly.

How much should you pay them? Do you have any idea what the pay scale for others in the industry is for each person on your payroll? You had better find out. Overpaying is a very common problem. Harvey A. Goldstein, CPA, the author of "Up your cash flow" tells a story about one of his clients who was paying their bookkeeper $250,000 per year. Yes, you read that right. The owner of the company had no idea what pay scales for his industry were. This salary was ten times higher than it should have been and the bookkeeper who should have been protecting the interests of the company damn well knew it. As hard as it is to believe, admittedly on a much smaller scale, this type of thing happens all too often. Don't let it happen to you.

Pay your people based on performance first and nothing else second. A common problem today is that employees want to be paid more to perform better. The problem is that they have this backwards. What they are saying is that if you pay them more they will do a better job. This, of course, means that they are not doing the job as well as they could, or should, be doing it now. Mediocrity will be defeated only when this attitude changes.

"It seems to me that if more time was spent developing proper procedures and accepting responsibility and less time was spent lining up excuses, most managers would have no need to try and justify failures."

Derrick W. Welch

Make sure you have complete written procedures and policies. This sounds like a lesson in human resources but personnel costs are among your largest fixed costs. You must handle your affairs in this area very carefully. Make sure all employee activity is documented. I am talking about records of attendance, tardiness, warnings, injury claims, performance appraisals, and anything else you can think of. If in doubt record it and keep it in the employee's file.

Have all appropriate documents signed by the employee and their supervisor. These procedures could save you thousands or even hundreds of thousands of dollars or more in legal fees and settlement costs if you are hit with any type of wrongful termination or discrimination lawsuit.

Even if you are 100% correct and justified in your actions you must be able to prove it. Without accurate records you run the risk of losing. This type of record keeping will also help you in disputing unjustified, or questionable, unemployment claims and workers' compensation claims.

Make sure that all policies and procedures you use are legal. Laws change frequently and in most cases the change does not favor the employer. Every year the employer has fewer and fewer options and less and less control over his own business. The government takes more and more of the employer's rights away. It seems to me that we are on a rapid and unrelenting path to a version of socialism in this country. The government has no need to own the means of production if they have control over those who do own the means.

However, since this is not the time or place for a continuation of that topic, I will simply point out that you need to make sure your actions and, intended actions, are allowed and legal. Controlling your costs will accomplish little if you are hit with a lawsuit or government penalty along the way. If in doubt, check it out!

At least once a year review all the policies outlined in your company handbook. We live in a "suit" happy society. Because of this, unfortunately, you must think in terms of a predator prey relationship. Think of your company as the prey. Predators are all around you. The predators include lawyers, the government, and yes, even some of your employees. We live in a society that fosters the belief that no one is responsible for their own actions. It is always someone else's fault.

Business is often the target. Your policies must be consistent with current government regulations and they must be written in a manner that protects your company's interests. You can't afford mistakes here. <u>Do not consider your company handbook to be a vehicle to communicate policies and benefits to your people. Consider it to be a front line defense strategy against those predators who see your business as a target and those individuals who wish to shift all blame, for all things, to you.</u>

Just fighting a wrongful termination suit or any other type of employee claim can easily cost you tens of thousands of dollars. This does not even consider the costs if you lose the suit.

Work with your state department of employment and training in conjunction with both new hires and ongoing personnel issues. This department is paid for out of your tax dollars you should strive to keep your costs down by taking advantage of the many services they offer. Contrary to what most businesses think, this department is not just for the unemployed to go and pick up checks and be treated rudely. Yes, they do that, but they also have other more useful purposes.

You as a business, can also experience this same commitment to customer service at no added charge. Seriously, the DET can be a valuable resource and an excellent way to reduce your personnel related costs. Some of the areas they can assist you in at no charge are:

• Things you can and cannot ask in an interview.

• Things you can and cannot include on your job applications.

• Finding employees that meet your specifications including, in some cases, prescreening the applicants.

• They can keep you abreast of the current laws regarding hiring, termination's, employee warnings, procedures, and disciplinary actions.

• They can inform you of steps you can take to protect your company against discrimination suits and other types of wrongful termination issues.

Using these services at no charge can save you thousands of dollars a year in legal fees. Why call your attorney every time you have a question? They usually don't know, or pretend not to know so they can run up research fees at $125 to $200 per hour. Instead, develop a relationship with the DET office in your area.

Many offices actually have calling officers on staff whose sole job is to work with companies in their area on problems such as this. I suggest you put all questions in writing and request all replies in the same manner. This not only eliminates confusion but also gives you a written record of the advise you follow should any problem arise later on. Being able to fall back on the advice given to you by a state or federal agency is a nice cushion to land on.

Don't overlook the DET for other projects as well. They are an excellent source of research for a wide variety of topics. The government spends more money on research (most of which is probably never acted on) than any other organization in the world.

In Massachusetts I can get comparative wage information for companies like mine in my area. This helps me see if I am overpaying or underpaying. I can get statewide employment and payroll data. I can get occupational profiles of various industries. They will provide me with an analysis of employment trends. These are just a few of the useful statistics and research results I can get at little or no cost.

They also maintain a full library of personnel related resources including information on:

• How unemployment rates are determined.

• How to fight unemployment claims.

• How to reduce unemployment rates.

• How the unemployment system works. (This one seems simple to me. They give money to anyone who requests it regardless of the reason they are unemployed, although somehow I doubt their publication states this.)

• How eligibility claims are determined. (See above)

Put the DET to work for you, instead of against you, for a change.

Always strive to hold your payroll costs down. When you increase payroll you also increase all payroll related costs. Each and every year these seem to get higher and higher. Local taxes, states taxes, federal taxes, workers' compensation costs, unemployment taxes, the list goes on and on. Whenever you are increasing payroll you are also adding fixed costs to your company's overhead. If you are like most companies, your payroll costs are among your largest fixed costs. It is paramount that you do all you can to control these costs. I will give you a number of strategies to accomplish this.

Consider taking advantage of the Targeted Jobs Tax Credit program offered by the Federal Government. The TJTC program is a program that enables you to receive tax credits for hiring economically disadvantaged job applicants from targeted groups of individuals. Like so many government programs this is nothing more than a special interest group program that costs the taxpayer money. However, as a company, it is one that could save you a significant amount of money each year.

You should also realize that this program, as is true with most government programs, is not as limiting as the description would lead you to believe. This program, as with all government programs, is always subject to revision or termination so you should discuss this with the IRS, your accountant, and the local Department of Unemployment to find out the current status.

As of this writing the way the plan basically works is that you can earn a tax credit equal to a dollar amount of up to 40% of the employee's first years wages not to exceed $6,000 for each eligible individual you hire. At this time there is no limit to the number of employees you can hire under the TJTC program. This can be a tremendous source of savings and one that you should not overlook. The potential for annual savings in the thousands or tens of thousands is common. Your personal and corporate taxes are wasted by the billions each year by the government, don't snub a chance to put some of your tax dollars to good use right in your own company.

Whenever possible use independent contractors instead of hiring employees. There are many fiscal benefits to doing this, however, the IRS has been slowly closing off options for companies and independent contractors. Their effort is to force an employee designation. Be very careful to make sure you are in full compliance with the IRS rules in this area. As they frequently change it would serve no purpose to list the current ones here. Contact the IRS and have them provide you with a copy of them. As the rules do change you should keep up to date with the current regulations in this area to ensure ongoing compliance.

Contact your Local department of Unemployment and inquire about all State and Federally funded work programs that are now being offered. There are many out there and few are brought effectively to the attention of the business that can benefit and who are, of course, the target for the program participants. You may find that programs exist in your state to subsidize a wide variety of costs incurred in hiring new employees. We have one in my area called the Private Industry Council which provides a 50% reimbursement to companies for the first 6 months salary paid to all employees hired from their program. If I were to hire someone earning $20,000 per year I would be paid back 50% of the first 6 months earnings or $5,000. This is 25% of the payroll cost of that employee for the first year.

You will never find out about these programs unless you ask. Like so many programs created and / or sponsored by the government they are not properly promoted to the group they need to make them work. In many cases even employees within the department do not even know how they work, or in some cases, that they even exist. Don't let this stupidity stop you. Keep asking until you find out the programs that are available. A few hours of frustrating phone calls could save you tens of thousands of dollars, or more, a year.

Examine your eligibility requirements for benefits. You want to keep key employees. After an employee has been with you only 3 to 6 months you have very little indication as to whether that employee is key or even if they are going to work out. While health insurance is very important for all employees to have you should seriously consider much longer eligibility requirements for other insurance and benefits such as Long Term Disability, Short Term Disability, and Group Life Insurance.

I would strongly recommend you move eligibility for many of these back to at least 12 months and preferably 5 years or some combination in between. These are very costly coverages and you should only be incurring these costs on behalf of your key people and your long term proven employees.

Talk to your accountant about Section 125 Cafeteria Plans. These plans offer important tax advantages to both employees and employers. Basically what Section 125 allows is for employees who participate to pay for specified expenses such as eligible out-of-pocket medical charges, medically related premiums paid under employer sponsored plans, and eligible child care expenses, on a pretax basis. Since employees are paying these expenses on a pretax basis their taxable income is lowered and the employer's gross payroll is reduced. This can result in lower tax bills for both parties and for the company added savings will be seen in other payroll indexed areas such as Workers' Compensation. Like every other government allowed plan the rules and regulations are complex and ever-changing so review this with your accountant or human resources people.

In Pursuit of Profits. How To At Least Double Your Profits Without Increasing Your Sales.

Don't pay outside recruiting firms to do what you can and should do yourself. For 99.9% of all jobs you should do the work yourself. There are many ways you can find the right candidates beyond the traditional method of advertising although, despite what many would have you think, this is still a very effective way to locate the right prospects for most positions. Those that have poor recruitment results when advertising can usually blame themselves. They have usually written a poor ad, placed it in the wrong media, or a combination of both.

Beyond advertising, consider contacting larger companies in your area who are down sizing. There is a lot of talent out there. Just because someone has been let go does not mean they are not a very talented employee who was the victim of a corporate restructuring. These employees are already screened and trained by larger companies and therefore should be much less risky to you. Also look into local colleges, employee referrals, state and local private industry councils, and unemployment offices. Remember, the cost of a recruiter will run you up to 33% of the employee's first years salary. This can cost up to tens of thousands of dollars a year.

If you have not established your own in-house advertising agency have a media recruitment agency place your ads. These are agencies that specialize in placing recruitment advertising. They will help you select the right media, write the ad, design the ad, and place it for you. Your cost? Nothing. They earn their money by keeping the commission from the newspaper.

Watch out for a new scam I recently became exposed to during an effort to recruit a new employee. The way it works is as follows. You run an ad in the help wanted section of your major daily paper. The scam company sees this ad and reproduces it exactly in a so called special help wanted paper. This is actually printed on newsprint and is made to look just like what you might expect a special help wanted paper to look like. Now mind you, they don't print a whole paper. They print just one page. They then send this one page to your accounts payable department as though it is a tear sheet along with an invoice.

A "tear sheet" is what newspapers send along with invoices to verify the ad you placed actually ran. The invoice of course carries some legitimate sounding name like "Professional Employment News". Your accounts payable department sees the bill, probably knows you are running ads to hire someone and automatically pays it.

The only problem here is that you never heard of this newspaper and never authorized placement of the ad. How could you have? The newspaper does not even exist! The bill sent to our office was for $933. The tear sheet sure looked like a page from a real recruitment newspaper. It even had many other ads from recognizable companies, a current date at the top, and the bogus, but official sounding, name.

How many of these do you think get paid? Studies have shown that somewhere between 25% and 50% of these bogus type bills are promptly paid without a question ever being asked. If you follow my strategies and put the proper controls in place, you won't be among this group.

Hiring employees who do not require benefits can save you 30% to 50% or more on overall employee costs when compared to an employee who requires benefits. I am not suggesting that you base your hiring decision on a prospective employee's need for benefits. I would not let this be the main criteria by which I ever hired anyone. You always want the best person for the job regardless of their need for benefits.

However, if all else is equal you can save significant amounts of money by hiring the candidate that does not require benefits. The United States Chamber of Commerce has indicated the added costs of employee benefits can amount to 30% or more of the employee's base pay. Health insurance alone can cost a company $8,000 to $10,000 per year depending on the plans you offer and the company's contribution percentage.

If you hire an employee making $10,000 a year and spend another $10,000 per year on health insurance your costs are $20,000. Hiring the same employee without health insurance will cut this cost by 50% and will save you $10,000 per year. How much would you need to increase your sales to add $10,000 a year to your bottom line profit? Well if your pretax profit runs at a ratio of 2.5% you would need to increase sales $400,000 to recover this cost.

"He was so learned that he could name a horse in nine languages; so ignorant that he bought a cow to ride on."

Benjamin Franklin

Do not be blinded by academic credentials, or your desire for academic credentials, when you are evaluating employment candidates or considering compensation. People get the job done and not pieces of sheepskin hanging on the wall. People with heart, determination, drive, commitment, and loyalty.

Some of the most competent employees I have ever had have had little or no formal education beyond high school. By the same token some of the least competent people I have ever worked with have had college degrees and MBAs.

Look at the person and not their academic credentials only. It is not my objective to minimize the value of education. As you will see, I feel quite the opposite. But it is my objective to stop you from putting too much emphasis on it. Do not ever confuse education with intelligence. I assure you they are not the same thing.

"Among all the legions of lawyers, financiers, bureaucrats, and masters of business administration strutting into the American economy from the nation's leading schools, nothing has been so rare in recent years as an Ivy League graduate who has made a significant innovation in American Enterprise. "

From Recapturing The Spirit of Enterprise by George Gilder

If you think book smart people are more intelligent or more likely to succeed than others I will ask you if you have ever watched the TV show Jeopardy? Most people that watch that show are always amazed at how smart these contestants are. But the next time you watch the show listen to what these contestants do for a living. Listen to the levels of success they have reached. I think you will see my point. If I needed the type of smarts these people had I would buy a set of encyclopedias. I would not hire them to work for me.

Have fewer employees, producing more and earning more. I would rather have fewer, higher paid, more capable and productive workers than more, lower paid, lower producing workers.

For example, I worked with one company that had 5 production workers making an average of $8 per hour. The total payroll each week averaged $1,600. Over a period of time I changed the staffing to 2 full time employees making $11 per hour, 1 part time worker making $8 per hour and working 20 hours per week and 1 floater working as needed up to 15 hours per week making $7.50 per hour.

In Pursuit of Profits. How To At Least Double Your Profits Without Increasing Your Sales.

The payroll dropped to $1,152.50 per week and productivity went up 10%. They saved $500 per week or $26,000 per year while improving both productivity and quality. They had fewer people, earning more and doing more. As you will see later, most employees can easily improve productivity thereby allowing you to have fewer employees doing more.

Consider using retired employees as temporary help during busy periods and periods of staff shortages such as times of vacation, sickness, and leaves of absence. These people are seasoned experienced workers who would probably be delighted to come back and work for the company for brief periods of time. You will not only save 30% to 50% of the cost of a temporary employee hired from an agency, but you will also be getting an employee familiar with your company, product, procedures, and personnel.

For example, if your company has busy periods of billing and your current staff can not keep up with billings this is costing you money. Who better to come in and quickly help out than a former bookkeeper or accounts receivable person?

Outside temporary help agencies can be helpful at times but they should be considered a last resort, not a first choice. In the very short term it might be better off to pay your own people some overtime, or better yet, offer to give them an equal amount of time off during the slow season for some added time during your busy period or current shorthanded circumstances.

These people at least know the job that needs to be done and, despite the higher overtime wages you might have to pay, you should see an even level of productivity which might not be present with a temporary person who must learn your procedures.

Consider leasing your workers. This subject is too complex to go into at length here, but leasing workers has become a very viable option for many companies around the country. Basically the way this works is that another company hires your employees and leases them back to you. They take responsibility for all payroll, payroll taxes, insurance, and benefits. They handle all record keeping. They do this with many other companies and, by doing so, realize economies of scale that each individual company cannot.

Each month you pay them one check to cover the cost of leasing your workers. It has been estimated that it costs the average company up to 40% of it's gross payroll to handle this administrative work and to provide the benefits. The leasing company with it's economies of scale and size, can provide the same effort and benefits at a reduced cost.

There are clearly many benefits and significant cost savings that could be enjoyed by leasing workers, but this is an industry in it's infancy and as such it has limited regulation and a limited number of legitimate established companies working in it. If you consider leasing employees be careful.

Resource

For further information contact the National Leasing Association at 1-703-524-3636.

Consider using interns. The use of interns can represent a low cost, or even no cost, way to subsidize your labor needs on a temporary basis. Many local colleges and universities have formal programs established to place their students into business environments to help them gain valuable on the job experience. Many times the students will also earn college credit for their efforts. Contact the schools in your area and let them know you are interested in accepting interns.

If allowed in your state, check the credit history of any employee out on workers' compensation or unemployment. Credit history often will list employment. You are looking for any moonlighting activities of any employee collecting. This is all too common. Discuss modifying your employment application with your lawyer to include a clause that allows you to do this. If this is not possible in your state, or if this is done after the employee in question has been hired, find out from your lawyer what your options are.

Whenever possible hire a part time employee and not a full time employee. The reasons for this are numerous. I have listed a number of them below:

♦ It will be easier to increase a part time person's hours if needed or to hire another part time person, than to reduce the hours of a full time person when you are slow. You gain a tremendous amount of flexibility by having these options.

♦ You are not saddled with a higher fixed overhead that may not be needed as time goes on. It is always easier and less costly to add staff or increase hours than it is to decrease staff or hours.

♦ If you don't pay benefits you will save an added 30% or more over the cost of an employee with benefits. This is what the cost of taxes, insurance, retirements, etc. add up to. Part time employees are less likely to need benefits.

♦ As pointed out in another strategy, employees do not work at anywhere near 100% of their capacity. A part time employee will work less hours and will have less time to waste.

♦ If you hire with the understanding that added hours are occasionally needed you can offer the employee added hours as justified but without your paying for hours not needed. For example, hire for 20 to 25 hours per week with the request that if more hours are needed they will try to work them. This way you gain the option of increasing hours as needed but do not have a full time person on staff for those slow periods when you do not need 40 hours per week and, as a result, have to find fill in work.

♦ Part timers are usually paid less than full time employees. They should save you anywhere from 10% to 30% in wages on a per hour basis.

♦ If you use two part time people instead of 1 full time person you not only will realize all the benefits shown above but you will also have two people who know the job, providing added protection and coverage for the company. You will have coverage during periods of vacation and illness. You will also have added flexibility in deciding on terminations, cut backs, and shifting of responsibility since you have a greatly reduced concern over leaving a void.

♦ When you employ two part time employees instead of one full time employee you should save 30% or more, depending on whether or not you offer benefits and due to the lower wage scale. Even if you provide benefits to your part time people you should still save money since many will already have at least health insurance through their spouse who most likely will have a full time job.

Don't underestimate the savings potential here, it is significant. For example, if you have a full time employee earning $10.00 per hour and you are paying 75% of their health insurance under a family plan this employee is most likely costing you over $26,000 per year not including the many added payroll tax costs and workers' compensation costs indexed to this payroll.

By hiring two part time people at $8.00 per hour without health insurance you will be paying a base cost of $16,640 per year. This is a $9,360 savings or a 36% reduction in costs. This does not even include the added savings for all state and federal taxes, workers' compensation, and any other benefits you offer. Never forget the domino effect. Reducing this payroll by 36% while gaining all the added benefits outlined is an excellent example of total cost control. This is a very proactive strategy.

"There are an enormous number of managers who have retired on the job."

Peter Drucker.

Do you have too many managers, supervisors, or employees? Most companies do! According to Tom Peters the management guru and best selling author of such books as "In Search of Excellence", "A Passion for Excellence", and "Thriving on Chaos", most companies in corporate America are over staffed at the management level by 600% to 700%. This is not a misprint. Mr. Peters feels most companies of mid and large size have 6 to 7 times more managers than they should have.

Do you know what each and everyone of your employees does each day? Does someone in your company know this? Can they tell you? I mean exactly what they do each day, not an idea. How do you know if you are over staffed unless you know this information? You should put together an organization flow chart of all company personnel. Then list detailed job descriptions for each position. Now look and see where you can effectively eliminate layers of supervision, management, and even routine functions.

This exercise should very clearly show you overlaps in job responsibility and therefore help you locate areas where jobs can be effectively combined. Less middle management will not only save you money, but will also result in more direct and therefore improved communications. You need more workers and less supervisors.

"Middle management and, in fact, overstaffing in general, in a company is often like an added roll of blubber around your waist. It is unhealthy, might kill you, and yet is much easier to keep than get rid of. "

Derrick W. Welch

For example, do you need a production manager, a production supervisor, an operations manager, a general manager, a plant manager, and a foreman? I doubt it. If you think you do please call me. I think you might need to use my services.

You can probably operate more efficiently with a significant cost savings by simply having a floor supervisor and a plant manager. Look internally and externally. Do you really need a regional, district, east coast, west coast, and national sales manager? Again I doubt it. Another very effective way for you to find out exactly what your people do each day is to have them write their own job description. Find out what they perceive their job to be and how much time they spend on each part of it each day. Have the supervisor do this as well, but not only for their jobs. Also have them provide this information for their people. I think you will find out some very interesting information by doing this.

Glaring overlaps and inordinate amounts of time spent on certain functions should show up here very clearly. Most workers do not work 8 hours a day. Not even close to it I am afraid. They might try to justify their jobs and prove how they do work a full day but almost without exception they do not.

This means that without much effort you should be able to trim payroll by reducing the number of employees you have and / or the number of hours they work. You will be amazed at how fast others absorb the work that had been done by the former employee or with the added hours. Thinking about job security is an amazing motivational tool.

I would be very surprised if you could not easily effect a 10% to 25% labor reduction, or more, with no negative impact in productivity. Instead, you will most likely increase productivity. This reduction will add tens of thousands of dollars or depending on your payroll, hundreds of thousands or even millions of dollars, to your bottom line, not only in reduced payroll, but in reductions of all payroll associated costs. Remember the domino effect.

Look at every position in your company and ask the questions. Ask the who, what, when, how, where, and why. Questions such as " can you combine two jobs?", "can you shift from full time to part time?", "can you shift jobs outside?", etc.. This should be done both during good times and bad times.

Make sure you have those job descriptions updated at least once a year. You need these not just for the reasons I have outlined in the last strategy, but also so that any employee who must fill in for another will have a very good idea as to what they must do each day. These detailed descriptions will also be very helpful with training in the event you do have a turnover and deem it necessary to rehire for that position.

"It is more than probable that the average man could, with no injury to his health, increase his efficiency fifty percent."

Walter Dill Scott

Find ways to justify not filling that opening. If you have a position open that you feel you must fill the first thing you should do is not start recruiting, but instead sit down and write a detailed job description of the position you think you need to fill including the amount of time it should require each week.

Then ask yourself the questions. Do you need the position? Must these functions be done? Can you assign these duties to other employees? Are other employees doing these now? Can you shift some of the duties to existing employees and thereby hire a part time person instead of a full time person?

Of course, since you have followed my earlier strategies you know exactly what your other employees do and will have no problem pin pointing employees who could take on added duty or who are already doing this type of work. As I have shown you, there are very few employees who could not take on added work each day. Can the responsibilities of this job be split up and assigned to a number of employees? You must think of all options.

Do not automatically assume that every time an employee leaves you must fill that spot with a new employee or with a new employee working the same number of hours. You must make damn sure that the job must be filled and must be filled full time. The objective is to find ways not to restaff that position. Not to justify rehiring for it.

In Pursuit of Profits. How To At Least Double Your Profits Without Increasing Your Sales.

This works and it works very well. I have been able to reduce staff by over 15% simply by not assuming I needed to restaff all vacated positions. I have replaced full time people with part time people and in other cases I have simply reassigned job responsibilities and not hired anyone.

This is among the easiest times you will ever have to tighten up your staffing since the termination has already happened and you are not being forced to lay off. Lest you think this can only be done in slow periods let me assure you this is not true. With one company I was able to decrease staff by 15% while we increased sales 15%.

This means that payroll costs dropped during a period of growth with no resulting loss in productivity, quality, or delivery. What this really means is that the company had too much fat in the past, had too many people working on non productive or non income producing projects and was able to perform better with fewer employees. Remember, work will always expand to fill available time. Your people will never tell you that they have nothing to do or that they have excess people.

You say you can't reduce the number of employees or reduce employee hours? Think again. According to a report in Today's Office, a study of United States Personnel Directors from both large and medium companies indicated that "the average on the job performance of American workers is only fifty three percent of their total capacity".

Yes, you read that right, 53%. This means that 47% of the time the average American worker is engaged in non productive or non job related activity. A non productive or non job related activity means a non income producing activity. In another study, a private research company in New York conducted a survey among employees to find out if they felt they gave their maximum effort at work each day. The results of this survey indicated that 77% of the employees surveyed by their own admission, did not. Furthermore, nearly 50% indicated that they put forth no more than the minimum effort each day.

Finally, Business Week has reported that over the last 18 years factory productivity has gone up 51% but individual employee productivity has gone down 7%. This, despite the tremendous advances that have been made technologically during this time. So if you think you can't reduce staff, think again.

"Nothing is particularly hard if you divide it into small jobs."

Henry Ford

The key to being able to eliminate a position, or of being able to not replace a departed employee or replacing a full time worker with a part time worker, is to assign a piece of that eliminated job to a number of other employees. If you break a job up into 10 functions and give 10 different people one of those functions, you have covered all the functions of the eliminated job while only adding a small amount of added duties to any one person. This should be very easily accomplished when you consider the overall productivity of most workers. I do not know of one worker in any company who could not handle at least a bit more responsibility.

Your people will fight you on this as they will be thinking only of the fact that if you do not replace that terminated employee they will have to do more work. But try this sometime, ask your people how much you would need that full time replacement if you took the money saved by not rehiring for that position and shared it with them. Watch how fast they find ways to absorb the duties that person had been doing.

What they are telling you is that they could, in most cases, easily absorb the added work as long as added compensation came along with it. While this may anger you it is also something you should consider. If you have a 6 person department and one of these people leaves you may want to offer to share **a part** of the salary savings with the remaining people if they can prove to you that they can pick up the slack without any loss of operational quality or service.

This is something you must decide. But I think you will be amazed at how fast most employees will change their mind from how critical it is to replace that outgoing person to how easily they can do that person's job, as long as you provide added compensation.

> *"When building a team, I always search first for those people who love to win. If I can't find any of those, I look for people who hate to lose."*
>
> *H. Ross Perot*

When you are seeking ways to cut out as much blubber as you can from around your corporate waistline, don't overlook the human resources department. They do little that you can't do and should be doing yourself. You don't want them hiring for you do you? Your managers do not want them hiring for them. Managers want to hire people they feel can do the job not someone human resources tells them to hire. You can screen the people yourself. This department often represents an example of paying someone else to do what you and your people should be doing yourselves.

Robert Townsend, author of the best sellers "Up the Organization" and "Further Up the Organization" and former CEO and President of Avis Rent-A-Car, echoes my thoughts on the value of the human resource department. As a matter of fact when Mr. Townsend became CEO of Avis one of the first things he did was to eliminate the entire human resources department with the exception of one person. This one person functioned as the human resources department for the entire Avis corporation.

If you feel you absolutely have to have a personnel department to screen large numbers of applicants down to smaller more manageable numbers of applicants or to handle government compliance issue or benefits, please do yourself a favor and keep the staffing as small as possible.

If Avis can do with one person can't you? You do not want people creating work and reports to justify their job. This is very costly not just in the human resources area but throughout your company as needless paperwork and reports are generated for consumption by others. If it were not for government regulations there may never have been such a department.

> *"Had there been a computer in 1879, it probably would have predicted that by now there would be so many horse-drawn vehicles it would be impossible to clear up all the manure."*
>
> *K. William Kapp*

Next look to your MIS department, research department, and your accounting department. MIS people, research people, and accounting people are notorious for generating reports and conducting studies that have little or no value and undertaking needless analysis. This is one way in which people in these areas justify their jobs. These areas are always excellent places to review in conjunction with your cost cutting efforts.

Ask the questions. Will the information provided by that report, or study, add to my bottom line? Is the effort cost justified? **Not nice to have. Not something you might like to know. Cost justified!**

Examine every study. Find out why that study is being done? What is to be gained by doing the study? Will the answer help you add to your bottom line? Will it increase productivity? Will it do these things at a level that exceeds the cost of doing the study?

"This report by it's very length, defends itself against the risk of being read."

Winston Churchill

Examine every report you generate. Review the frequency of which you distribute reports. If you are issuing a report once a week is twice a month just as effective? If so, you can reduce the time, materials, and labor associated with that report by 50%. Find out why it is needed? Who uses it and for what purpose? Do they need it? Do they need it as often? Will a summary report suffice instead of a detailed report? Can a summary report be given to most recipients and a detailed one to only a few parties?

I once read of a company who produced a 200 page report each month and distributed it to over 30 departments. This was over 6,000 sheets of paper each month not to mention the hours involved in the preparation and distribution of the report or in the disposal and storage after the report was read. That is, if the reports were read. They did a study and found that 28 of the 30 departments never even read the report each month as it was too long and contained mostly information they knew already or did not need to know. The remaining 2 departments could have easily managed with a few simple summary sheets each month.

The savings realized by the discontinuance of this report counted in the thousands of dollars each year. Even if this information had been needed, they should have found much more efficient, less costly ways of distributing this information such as electronic transfer of the information through network computers. Think of the waste in time and materials that existed here until someone finally asked the questions about who needed the information, why they needed it, and how much did they need.

You must ask the questions! Millions of dollars are wasted each year in these departments. **Start dropping needless reports, studies, and analysis and see how fast you can lower your MIS, research, and accounting personnel and equipment costs. Never forget that cost accounting will never replace common sense, the "what if" provided by spreadsheets will never replace what is and, nice to know is not need to have.**

<u>**Get good people around you and let them do their job.**</u> Hire the best people you can afford and get out of their way. This will allow you to cut out layers of middle management, improve communications, and operations while saving a great deal of money. If you cannot cut out middle management then most likely you either have the wrong people working for you or you are not giving your people the responsibility of doing the job. Instead, you are giving someone else responsibility for your people. Too many supervisory people in your company means you have a problem with the quality of people working under them or you have poor management. Which is it?

Make sure all new hires are properly trained. Proper training will get your employees productive sooner, at a lower cost, with fewer errors. Whenever possible this training should include personal instructions, written procedures, and a detailed job description.

"Never tell people how to do things. Tell them what to do and they will surprise you with their ingenuity."

George S. Patton

When you hire new employees and begin to train them make sure that while you are showing them how you do things that you encourage them to find new and better ways to do the job. Encourage innovation don't discourage it. Let them know you are an open minded company that is constantly seeking ways to do things better. Make sure they know you are seeking ways to increase service, decrease costs, reduce waste, and increase quality. Set the tone now and you will often reap big dividends down the road.

Give written statements on this topic to all new employees, post them in appropriate areas throughout your facility and include them in your company handbook. The more you can reinforce these values and remind your people of them, the better your results will be.

When you hire new employees make darn sure they understand your corporate philosophy as it pertains to total cost control. In fact, better yet, express this during your interviews with potential employees. Set the tone right up front. Set the expectations before they step in your door. To insure this message gets through I would strongly suggest a written statement that reinforces your objectives in this area. It is also a good idea to have such a statement regarding your overall corporate objectives.

"The one real objective of education is to have a man in the condition of continually asking questions."

Bishop Mandell Creighton

Make your people think before they do something to incur a cost not after. After you have already incurred the cost it is too late. You are forced to be reactive. Be proactive. Put signs up around your office, factory, or warehouse reminding people to think before they act to incur a cost. An example of this would be a sign near all your photocopiers that asks questions like:

Do you really need this copy?
How many copies do you really need?
Can you reduce the number of copies you need by using both sides?
Can you use fewer copies and instead send one around and have it routed to all who need it?

Don't review new employees more than once in the first year. It makes no sense to me to review a new employee the first 3 months and then again at 6 or 9 months and then once more after 1 year. All this succeeds in doing is rasing your payroll costs and all costs associated with your payroll.

In Pursuit of Profits. How To At Least Double Your Profits Without Increasing Your Sales.

If you have an employee you hire at $20,000 per year and after three months give them a 5% raise this salary has now gone up to $21,000. If again in another 3 or 6 months you once again review them and give them another 5% raise their salary is now $22,050. Then upon reaching their one year anniversary you review them one more time and raise them a final 5% their salary is now $23,152.50.

Had you instead given them only one review after the first year and even given them a very generous 10%, their salary would have gone up to only $22,000. You would have saved $1,152.50 or over 50% of the increase realized by 3 reviews at 5%. Additionally, you would have saved on all payroll related costs.

The employee would be very happy with a raise the size of 10% (I am not suggesting you give raises out this size, this is simply an example to demonstrate the costs involved) and you would have reduced the cost of the raise by over 50%.

<u>You must think at all times.</u> If you are serious about controlling costs you must think both short term and long term. Had you followed the example shown above and increased the employee 3 times in the first year the next raise would have been based on percentage increases from a salary of $23,152.25. Had you instead only given one sizable raise after a year you would have been basing the next raise on a base of $22,000. Had the next raise been 5%, based on $23,152.50 it would cost you $1,157.63. Had it been on $22,000 it would have cost you $1,100. This is almost a 5% reduction.

I am trying to tell you that with most decisions, including this one, the action you take today will affect you positively or negatively for years to come. In the case of raises it will affect you for as long as that employee works for you. This is an example of the domino effect. You must consider both long term and short term. What you might be able to afford easily today could be much harder to digest next year.

Do you automatically give annual pay increases? If so, I will ask you why? Are your profits automatic? Are your sales automatic? Is your desired profitability automatic? Of course not. Then why should raises be automatic each year? Raises should be given based on merit and profitability, not automatically issued once a year.

If you give annual raises, and again I would ask why, keep the annual raise to a minimum. Issue 1% to 3% raises at most and compensate in other ways during the year. The effort here is to keep the fixed payroll down every week and, by doing so, keep the many costs indexed to payroll down as well.

By holding down annual increases you will be producing long term savings. By this I mean that if you have an employee making $20,000 a year and you give her a 7% raise this year her new base salary is $21,400. If again next year she is given another 7% raise this is based on the new base of $21,400 and would raise her total salary to $22,898.

If instead, you held the annual raise down and awarded bonuses based on performance and profitability, this year you might give that same person a 3% raise. This would raise her salary from $20,000 to $20,600 saving you $800 the first year. The next year if you again give her a 3% increase her new salary would be $21,218. She is now being paid $1,680 less than she would have had you given her back to back 7% increases.

Even if in the second year you had decided to award her a 7% increase after the first year increase of 3% you have still saved money. This second year 7% increase would have been based on the base pay of $20,600 instead of $21,400. Therefore, a 7% raise under this scenario would be $1,442 which would bring the new base salary to $22,042. Compare this to the effect of back to back years of a 7% increase and you have saved $856 on just this one employee. <u>Now multiply this by the number of employees you have and see if I don't get your attention.</u> This does not even consider the added savings in all other areas of payroll related costs.

It will make more economical sense to issue bonuses each year based on the profitability of the company and the productivity of the employee. This way if the company has a good year the performing employees benefit. If the year turns out worse than expected you have avoided being saddled with higher salaries and bonuses are either not given or are reduced according to the company's ability to pay them.

This also gives the employees added incentive to produce top output year-round since they will be reviewed both for a possible moderate annual increase and a bonus based on profitability and individual productivity.

Remember that for every increased dollar of payroll you are also increasing all costs indexed to payroll costs. These added costs include workers' compensation insurance, short and long term disability insurance, possibly group life insurance premiums, retirement pension costs, and a variety of other state and federal tax costs.

> *"All successful employers are stalking men who will do the unusual, men who think, men who attract attention by performing more than is expected of them."*
>
> *Charles M. Schwab*

<u>**If you have an employee who is not making it cut your losses as soon as possible**</u>. Too many companies are quick to hire and slow to fire. You want to be the exact opposite. When an employee is not working out get rid of him or her. Procrastination in any area is harmful but it can be deadly in this area.

<u>**You must not tolerate absenteeism. Period**</u>. It reduces your productivity. It hinders your ability to service your customers. It hurts your quality management efforts. It hurts your business in dozens of different ways. It costs you a great deal of money. It hurts morale. It drives up overtime costs. It forces you to carry more employees than you can justify.

You must take hard and firm action to convey that these problems will not be tolerated. These actions should include verbal warnings, written warnings, suspensions without pay, and ultimately, termination.

Do you know that statistics have shown that on average every one of your employees will take 9 sick days per year? **Think of this as someone stealing from you because they are**. They are stealing time. I know from personal experience that many so called sick days are bogus. Sick days are one of the biggest areas of abuse among your employees.

It has been projected that during 1993 every week over 4.5 million American workers were absent from their jobs at least one day. That's right 4.5 million lost days per week. This translates into over 1.8 billion lost hours per year to American companies. Think about this. These are stunning totals.

If you have 50 employees and each takes nine sick days take a few minutes and figure out how much this lost 450 days of labor is costing you. If you have 50,000 employees and each averages 9 sick days per year you have lost the equivalent of 450,000 work days.

Think of the lost productivity. Think of the increase in productivity you would realize if you could cut this average in half. Increased productivity means lower costs. Think of the added staff you must carry to compensate for this lost productivity. Think of the overtime you are paying to compensate for these absent employees.

Think of how much you could reduce staffing and payroll if you could cut your per employee average absenteeism from 9 days per year to 2 or 3 days per year. If you have 50 employees who are out an average of 9 days and you can lower this average by <u>even 5 days</u>, you have just picked up the equivalent of 250 work days a year. Since the average work year, excluding holidays, is 249 days you have just picked up the equivalent of one full time worker. This means you could reduce your staff by 2%. Depending on what the pay scale was for the position you eliminated your savings could easily run in the tens of thousands of dollars per year.

But how about our example of a company with 50,000 employees? If this company could reduce their average absenteeism per employee by the same 5 days per year they would effectively recapture 250,000 work days. This means they have picked up the equivalent of 1,004 full time workers based on 249 working days per year (250,000 days effectively gained, divided by 249 working days per year, per employee, is equal to 1,004 employees).

Think of how much money this company would be saving if they could reduce staff by 1,004 employees with no loss in productivity. If their average worker earned $25,000 per year they have just saved $25,100,000 in payroll alone. When you factor in the added 30% it has been projected the average employee costs a company in payroll indexed taxes and benefits, this company will save another $7,530,000.

Imagine that. A savings of $32,630,000 without any sacrifice in quality, service, or productivity. At a profit ratio of 2.5% you would need to increase sales, while holding costs level, by $1,305,200,000 just to add the same amount to your pretax bottom line! Yes, that is billion, not million. This is how you must think to understand the impact total cost control can have on your bottom line.

Do you have a problem in this area? Do you know how many sick days each of your employees takes on average? Do you know how many fall on a Monday or Friday? If you do not know these things you have a problem. You are being neither proactive or reactive.

You must track, monitor, and take corrective action as needed. Whether you use a manual system to track it, or a computerized system, you must track absenteeism and attendance related abuses. If you do not, you had better start getting control of this area now.

The best place to set the tone for your expectations in this area is when you hire. The two primary things I have always looked for when I hire anyone at any level is attitude and attendance. If they have the right attitude they can learn the job and do it well. Unless they have good attendance no matter how well they do the job they won't do me much good if they have poor attendance.

<u>Do not pay your people twice for the same thing.</u> You will notice that in the above strategy I did not mention the idea of paying employees for sick days they did not use. This is a favorite benefit of unions and employees in most companies. Their rational goes like this "if I was paid for the days I did not use I would not use as many days". Think about that. Read it again.

This is a prime example of why this country is being driven to mediocrity. They are saying very clearly that they stay out sick when they could be coming to work, that they are calling in sick when they are not, and simply that they are abusing the benefit you have provided to them.

My response is very simple. Why would I pay them not to be out sick when I am already paying them to be at work? Isn't this paying for the same thing twice? If they can manage to come to work more often if I pay them twice then they can sure as heck come to work more often without any hardship if they want to keep their job. Remember, every relationship is a two way street. If you are giving more than you are getting or if you are being taken advantage of, end the relationship.

Do you pay your employees weekly? If so, change it to every other week. You will cut the cost of your payroll processing down by at least 25% and you will enjoy a longer float on your money.

Have firm policies regarding overtime. In all too many companies employees view overtime as some sort of entitlement. They expect it when they want it regardless of whether or not it is really needed. To you overtime represents a 50% increase in labor costs without an accompanying 50% increase in productivity. In fact, you most likely will see reduced productivity.

Seek to increase productivity instead of overtime. When overtime is justified make sure it is approved and monitored closely to ensure you are getting your moneys worth and it is terminated at the earliest possible time. Never give a free reign to your employees to work overtime or to your supervisors to assign it. If the work cannot be completed within the normal 40 hours per week find out why before you just start authorizing overtime. Remember, overtime also increases your costs for all payroll indexed expenses.

Employees will often stretch work out to justify overtime or to keep overtime. It is up to you to control overtime. Even if added labor is needed during times of the year look to other strategies I have given you before you authorize overtime.

"Waste of time is the most extravagant of all expenses."

Theophrastus

One of the biggest thefts an employee can make from an employer is the theft of time. Long breaks, extended lunches, personal phone calls on company time, standing around the time clock waiting for it to click to the punch out time, faking sick time, arriving late, and socializing during work time are just some of the many ways time is stolen from your company.

You must have effective controls in place and you must make your expectations known. I do not suggest you run a military type of company. You want good morale and you should allow some degree of flexibility, but your people must know when to draw the line.

I have already outlined the problems that are caused by absenteeism and many of those comments apply here, but also consider this. An employee making $12 per hour is being paid .20 per minute, not including payroll indexed costs. At .20 per minute even 5 minutes a day of wasted time is costing $1 per day. This is $5 per week or $260 per year.

Big deal you say? Well then think about this. If you have 5 employees who waste 5 minutes a day this is costing you $1,300 per year. If you have 50 employees it is costing you $13,000 per year. If you have 500 employees it is costing you $130,000 per year. If you have 5,000 employees this mere 5 minutes a day of wasted time will cost you $1,300,000 per year. With 50,000 employees you are effectively losing $13,000,000 per year. I assure you most of your employees waste a great deal more than 5 minutes per day.

As you can see, it does not take long for small amounts of time to add up to serious money. You should also walk through all areas of your company a couple of times each day. You want to be involved with your people and you want them to know you are around. Your supervisors should also do the same thing. By doing this you will also quickly spot patterns of time theft. Start eliminating wasted time and see how fast you can reduce staff while increasing productivity.

Keeping track of employee time. We are rapidly approaching the year 2000. I think it is time you looked into replacing the old time clock or honor system with a computerized time keeping system. It will help you in numerous ways. Time is one of the most important cost areas you have. You must control it and you must effectively use it. A computerized time keeping system may be your best method of accomplishing these goals.

A computerized time keeping system offers you many benefits. It offers your employees confidentiality from other employees regarding hours worked. It provides for accurate documentation of time. It eliminates the need to prepare time cards. It automatically calculates all time worked down to the second and applies it to the employee's rate of pay. This eliminates a great deal of bookkeeping time and it eliminates any human error factor.

This will also go a long way to cutting down on the theft of time as long lunches, tardiness, and leaving early will automatically be recorded and not paid for. These computerized systems will also generate reports of employee attendance and adherence to work schedules.

Industry estimates have indicated that a firm with 100 employees paid an average of $7.50 per hour would save on average $27,974 per year. They have stated that even a company with 25 employees would realize a payback on their investment within 4 months.

Estimates of the savings realized from the installation of a computerized time keeping system range from an amount equal to 2% of a company's total payroll to 6% of a company's total payroll. This represents significant amounts of money. How much would you add to your bottom line if you are able to reduce payroll costs by an amount equal to 2% of your total payroll? Many such systems also offer job costing options to track time spent on a particular job or application.

From software that can run on your existing PC based system, to a free standing computerized system, a wide range of options exist. Spend some time looking into them. You will find a number advertised in any office or manufacturing management magazine.

"A company's business would increase by 50% if you cleared the conference room of chairs."

W. F. Heneghan

The biggest time waster of all? The Wall Street Journal conducted a study among CEOs throughout the country. A key question of this study was in what area did these CEOs feel that the most unproductive time was spent. The resounding answer was that the most unproductive time was spent in meetings.

Furthermore, The Wharton Center for Applied Research has reported that senior managers spend an average of 23 hours per week in meetings and that middle managers spend an average of 11 hours per week in meetings. These are stunning statistics. Think about how much wasted time is spent in these meetings. How could this time in meetings possibly be justified? What the hell are these people doing? Apparently not much. You can't be productive when you are sitting around in a meeting. If your people are meeting they are not producing. Why is so much time spent in meetings?

It has been my experience in working for and with both large and small companies that the vast majority of time spent in meetings is wasted time. Meetings make a great place for people to hide from responsibility. Some want others to make decisions. Some want to test the waters and see which way the corporate wind is blowing before they set sail. Many want to be shielded from both responsibility and decisions.

"A cow is a horse designed by a committee."

Abraham Lincoln

Very few people demonstrate leadership, decisiveness, and commitment. All too many want to make decisions and take action by committee.

Many meetings are simply not needed and many others should be much shorter in duration and held much less frequently. The Wharton Center concluded that up to 30% of all meetings held could be more effectively handled by a memo, a face to face meeting, or by phone. I think this is a very conservative estimate. Very conservative.

Before any meetings are held in your company you better make sure they are justified. Why is the meeting needed? What is the objective of the meeting? Who needs to be in this meeting? Why do they need to be in the meeting? What is the agenda for this meeting? Why do you need a meeting every day or every week? What is the scheduled time to start this meeting? What is the scheduled time to end this meeting? Unless you have a time frame meetings will drag on far longer than they are needed. What will be done as a result of the meeting? Who will do it?

Ask the questions. They are always the key. Start eliminating needless meetings. Start limiting the attendance of those not needed. Start reducing the time and frequency of these meetings.

How costly could this be? Think about this example. If you have 15 senior managers spending 23 hours a week in meetings and 30% of this time is wasted, think of how much money this is costing you. Let's say each of these manager works 50 hours per week and earns $100,000 per year. This is equal to a rate of $38 per hour.

If they work an average of 50 hours per week and spend 23 hours a week in meetings, it seems to me that you are paying them $38 per hour to spend nearly 50% of their time in meetings. If I were you I sure would wonder why so much time is needed to be spent in meetings. I must have some big problems somewhere if my key people need to spend that much time in meetings. They may be the problem.

But back to my point. At $38 per hour and 23 hours per week in meetings you are paying these people $681,720 per year just for the time they are in meetings. If indeed 30% of this time is wasted, and again I think this is very conservative, you are wasting $13,634 per year, per senior manager in these meetings. Based on the 15 managers in our example you are wasting $204,516 per year. It would seem to me that perhaps you are way over staffed in this area of management.

In Pursuit of Profits. How To At Least Double Your Profits Without Increasing Your Sales.

"A committee is twelve men doing the work of one."

John F. Kennedy

Perhaps this is one reason so many meetings are held. These people must do something with their time and must find some way to justify their jobs. Meetings have always been a great place to hide. How many managers do you have and how much time are they spending in meetings?

How many management people do you have spending 23 hours a week in meetings? If you have 150 you are wasting at least $2,000,000 per year and most likely a great deal more. Remember the domino effect works both ways.

Employee theft of time, materials, and services cost companies in this country untold billions of dollars each year. The United States Chamber of Commerce has conducted studies that indicate 75% of all employees have stolen at least once from their employer. Excluding the theft of time, they estimated in 1990 alone employee theft cost U.S. businesses over $40 billion dollars. One insurance company has even stated that 1 out of 3 small businesses fail as a direct result of employee theft.

These are alarming statistics and they better command your attention. Employees are often trusted when they should not be. They are often given access they do not need. They can be among the most creative of all thieves.

Instances of internal theft are 15 times more likely to occur than external theft. You had better do all you can to prevent this problem from getting in your front door. The proactive approach here is to hire right. Be as thorough and aggressive as you can in the screening process. Not only for this reason, but also to avoid those high workers' compensation costs.

Make sure you are up to date with the current laws in this area and you may even want to consider the services of an outside company to help you. There are many available. From providing written tests to conducting extensive background checks on possible new hires, to drug testing and undercover investigations of current employees, these companies may be invaluable to you. One such company is Pinkerton Investigation Services 1-800-232-7465.

You must have strong written policies to deal with employee theft. These should be clearly spelled out and made part of your employee handbook. All employees should be given a copy of the handbook and each should sign an acknowledgment indicating they have received the handbook and when.

This should be repeated each time the handbook is updated or reissued. From minor thefts of pens and paper to major thefts of petty cash, stamps, and other materials and products, employee thefts cost companies billions of dollars each year.

Your employees must know this will not be tolerated. You must be very aggressive in conveying this and you must take immediate action if necessary. Proactive polices, clearly and aggressively communicated, will go a long way towards reducing this problem within your company. This is a strategy that will save you money in many areas that will not be visible per-se, as it will help stop employee theft from happening. Stopping the problem from happening is a far better alternative than dealing with a theft problem.

Give your honest employees an option to tell you about your dishonest ones. Many of your employees will be 100% honest and very loyal, assuming that you treat them the same way. Others will not be. There is no way around it. No matter how well you think you hire and no matter how well you treat your people, some of them are going to lie, cheat, and steal from you.

Don't kid yourself, it will happen. This will cause resentment among those employees who are honest and loyal to you. Give these honest and loyal employees a way to tell you about what is going on so you can address the problem. Very often this is the only way you will know what is happening and who is stealing from your company in any form.

One way to do this is to get an outside voice mail box with an 800#. Many local firms offer this service. You want to set it up so your employees can confide in you and help you anonymously if they so desire. We live in a crazy world and because of this very often the only way a well meaning employee may come forward is if they have the assurance of anonymity.

Send it out ? Always evaluate functions within the company or department that could be more effectively handled outside of your organization. Jobs such as security, payroll, and maintenance can many times be done more economically by outside sources. This is only true, however, if it allows you to reduce payroll or put the internal hours saved to a more productive use.

The major benefit of farming out work is the ability to reduce internal payroll and the elimination of the need to pay all payroll related taxes and benefits on the out sourced expense. By the same token, you should periodically verify the continued feasibility of sending work outside. When the cost of doing so exceeds the benefit of not doing it in house you may find a reversal of this tactic is cost justified.

For example, let's look at doing payroll internally. Determine the cost of doing this each week. Include all costs, not just labor. You must also consider banking charges, materials used, and the added costs of your tax reporting functions. Then call in 2 payroll service companies to give you a proposal for doing this all for you.

You are likely to find that you will realize a savings by going outside with these services but only as long as you can reassign the hours you are saving internally to an equally or more productive function or if you can eliminate those hours altogether.

A very common problem I have observed is that when these functions are removed from the bookkeeping department they do not take on more work and their hours are not reduced. They simply take longer to do less work than they used to do. In cases like this you have saved nothing. Instead you have increased your costs since you are now paying an outside payroll company and you have lowered your productivity since the person that was doing the payroll is not taking on any other work but merely stretching out the remaining work. You must know what steps you will take upon moving the payroll and reporting functions outside so that you will realize a real savings. Think it through.

Get on the mailing list of companies who sell personnel forms. They will send you actual samples of their forms that you can use to check the legality of your forms. These companies spend hundreds of thousands of dollars keeping up with the current laws and regulations in the human resource area. By using or comparing your forms to theirs you can save a great deal of legal costs and eliminate uncertainty.

Resources

Amsterdam Printing and Litho Corporation in Amsterdam, NY 12010. 1-800-833-6231

In Pursuit of Profits. How To At Least Double Your Profits Without Increasing Your Sales.

G.Neil, 720 International Parkway, Sunrise, FL, 33345. 1-800-999-9111.
Personnel Department Store. 325 Lennon Lane, Walnut Creek, CA, 94598. 1-800-942-4494.

Give out W-2 forms. Why mail them? This just adds to your postage costs and increases your labor and materials cost.

Do you require drugs tests? If your company is engaged in drug and / or alcohol testing you are probably paying over $100 per employee tested not including the lost time on the job during the testing. Here are a couple of low cost alternatives you might want to consider.

1) Team Building Systems in Houston sells a product called the Breath Scan. The cost is $1.50 for each test kit. This is not a full test but rather a much less expensive quick test. If this test shows a potential problem then you can proceed to a full blood test. If, on the other hand, the quick test shows negative you have saved time, inconvenience, and at least $90 per test in actual costs. Since the vast majority of those tested are not involved with drugs or alcohol depending on the number of employees you test each year the savings could be very significant.

2) Drug Screening Systems in Blackwood, NJ offers a product that can screen for 4 different drugs at once and costs less than $15 per test. This is at least $85 less per test than the traditional blood test. You should contact both companies and ask for information (and current prices) on these and any other related products they offer to see if they might be an effective cost control option for your company.

Resource

Call 1-800-843-4971 for a free guide to establishing a drug free workplace titled "Drugs don't work in your workplace". This guide and many other related resource materials are offered by the Partnership for a drug free America.

If your employees pay a portion of their benefits such as health insurance consider reducing their weekly salary by the amount of this cost and paying it for them in full. Tax laws change all the time so discuss this strategy with you accountant and your insurance agent. What you are doing here is reducing their gross salary by an amount equal to the added costs you are picking up. I know you are wondering how you are saving money since you are still paying out the same amount overall just to different sources now. You save because you have reduced your gross payroll by the amount equal to the benefit payments you are now paying that the employee was paying for.

This will reduce all your payroll taxes including FICA, FUTA, workers' compensation, and many, if not all, state and local taxes. How? Simple, these taxes are all predicated on the gross payroll of the company. You have reduced this payroll by the amount of the added benefits you now pay. Your employees earn less but, if anything, they will gain in net pay. Now, they may be in a lower tax bracket since they earn less. They do not take home less since they previously paid this out in their portion of the benefits.

One note here, keep close track of the increased costs you incur each year as a result of the higher benefit costs. As you would now be paying 100% of these costs you are justified in factoring this added cost you are now bearing as you consider annual wage increases.

Offer direct deposit services to your employees. These services are most often perceived as a benefit to your employees and they are definitely an excellent cost saving tool for you. Direct deposit has been estimated to reduce the cost of check processing and check distribution by up to 50%.

Depending on the number of employees you have and how frequently you pay them, the savings can be significant. Including the cost of writing checks and the applicable bank charges for each check, the average savings should be between .50 + .70 per check that you do not have to write. If you direct deposit 10,000 checks per month you will save $5,000 - $7,000 per month or $60,000 to $84,000 per year. You will also save stamps, envelopes, and the related labor for all the checks you would have normally mailed out.

Less time spent in these areas by your payroll people can lead to increased productivity in other areas as this freed up time can be put to other more productive uses or it can be eliminated in the form of reduced hours. Not only is time saved, but so are materials and postage. Direct deposit services can be used for paychecks, pensions, annuities, dividends, and any other type of recurring distribution of funds.

There is a negative side to direct deposits that I feel compelled to point out. You lose the advantage of the "float". The float is the time between when you issue the check and the time when it clears back to your account after the recipient cashes it. During this time your funds are earning interest for you. This is a hidden cost that must be considered as you evaluate the cost savings you can realize by using direct deposit.

Establish "use them or lose them" policies. Allowing your employees to carry over and accumulate vacation time and sick time is a very costly policy. Why do you think the government allows it? Tracking accumulated vacation and sick time is an added cost. You are also letting them take time later when it costs you more.

By this I mean, an employee making $400 a week this year might be making $500 a week in a few years when they use this year's accumulated time. You are also losing control when you allow employees to accumulate time and use it all at once later on. This could severally hinder your ability to operate smoothly when a key employee decides to use 8 weeks of vacation all at once.

Furthermore, you are increasing temptation for abuse by your employees. It will be awful difficult for an employee who has dozens of sick days accumulated not to take a few fake ones from time to time. Finally, if you allow them to cash in unused time, you could be looking at a serious drain on cash when you can least expect it as employees leave and demand payment for this time. Time they want compensated at current earning levels despite the fact the time was earned at lower rates.

All and all, in my opinion this is a losing policy. Convert your policy to a use them or lose them policy in which your employees must use the time they earn within your current fiscal year or they lose it.

Remember, vacation time is earned during the year. Make it clear in your policies that when you award an employee vacation time it is actually earned during the year. Each month they are with the company that year they earn a part of the vacation. For example, if they are eligible for two weeks vacation per year they are actually earning .83 days per month. This is a very important policy to establish.

By not having such a policy millions of dollars are lost to companies each year. How? Well, let's say you have an employee who is eligible for two weeks of vacation this year. The first month of the year they quit. If you do not have a policy as I have outlined you will have to pay them two weeks vacation time. This could be several hundred or even thousands of dollars.

However, if you have a clear policy that spells out how this time is earned you will only owe that employee .83% of one day's pay. If an employee tries to get around this by quitting after they have taken their vacation, they now owe you since they have taken time they have yet to earn. This also should be clearly spelled out in your policy. This is only fair. Since you have allowed them to take time that was technically unearned, they should be liable to pay the value of this time back.

A policy such as this is fair and can save you thousands, or even hundreds of thousands of dollars a year or more, depending on your size and employee turn over rate.

You must stay on top of the unemployment claims filed by former employees. The more former employees collecting, the higher your rate is going to be. A higher rate can cost you significant amounts of money. You must monitor all charges to your account to ensure only legitimate claims are being made. The unemployment system is regularly abused. According to the US. Department of Labor "claimants were overpaid by 1.4 billion dollars in 1990". Who do you think pays for this? The government? Come on wake up. The government pays for nothing. How could they? They have no money. They produce no income. They simply take money from you via taxes and redistribute it.

Why are so many claims paid that should not be? Simple, the people that work in the unemployment department are in the business of giving away money, not the other way around. If they start doing their job and only pay on legitimate claims they could be putting themselves out of a job.

If I were to offer my opinion on what is wrong with the government and how I think we could correct these problems it would take volumes by itself. Suffice it to say, I have seen numerous cases of claims paid that were questionable at best. I know of many others that were out and out wrong. They will sign up anyone and go out of their way to make it hard for you to fight it.

Don't count on the people at unemployment to pay only the proper claims. Why would they do this? After all it is only their job. You must monitor. You must dispute and you must fight. I know this is a disgrace. I know that you should not have to do this. But you must remember who you are dealing with. The government.

Resource

One source of possible help and clarification is The Association of Unemployment Tax Organization. They can be reached at 614-224-7221.

If you have former employees on your insurance through COBRA, make sure you are charging the allowable 2% processing charge. At this time employers are allowed to assess a 2% processing charge on all former employees who are still on their insurance under COBRA. Charge it. These people are no longer income producing individuals and as such they represent a drain on your organization. You have cost in handling their COBRA insurance so at least reduce this cost by charging the allowed 2%. This is 2% of the cost of the insurance that is paid to you directly by the former employee.

You should have a check list to use in conjunction with all terminated employees. This includes employees who have left on their own and on good terms. You must make sure that all company materials are returned. Trying to remember to get them all, during what will often be a period of upheaval, will result in errors.

You must list all things that must be done and must be returned. They should be checked off as done or as received. These things should include all company credit cards, phone calling cards, uniforms, files, price books, selling material, and any other company material. You should also alter security system access codes and locks if appropriate considering the circumstances. More than one company has been badly burned by not taking the proper steps when terminating an employee.

Make sure all former employees are removed from your insurance plans (except COBRA as appropriate). This is an often overlooked area. Many companies leave employees on health, life, and disability plans for months and, in some cases, years after they have left the company. Get them off and check to make sure they have been taken off.

Don't count on the insurance companies to remove anyone. Many insurance companies don't even list covered employees they simply send a lump sum bill each month. Why do they do this? Could it be because they don't want to remind companies that former employees are still being carried? No, that couldn't be it, that would be sneaky and unethical.

Be very careful here. Premiums that are paid for former employees are very difficult to get back. Once they have your money they will do all they can to keep it and to keep it as long as possible. They will say you never sent in the paperwork or never sent in the forms they sent you or anything else they can do to blame you.

If you did remember and did send in the paperwork make sure that you have kept copies to prove you did comply. Don't just send them in and assume it will be done. Check each month to make sure the person in question comes off your bill and credits retroactive to the date of termination are given. If you sent in the proper notifications and did not keep a copy or if you forgot to send in the notification you have a bigger problem. You are still in the right and simply need to prove the date of termination and insist you did indeed comply.

I know of one company who had forgotten to remove an employee for over a year. Since employees covered were not listed on the bill for the insurance company each month they simply never thought about it. The amount of money involved was over $8,000. The insurance company refused to refund the money paid. In response, this enterprising company simply back dated forms to the date of the termination and wrote a few follow up letters bearing various dates over the last year. They then demanded payment on the basis of proper notification and consistent follow up and claimed they had been ignored. The insurance company paid.

"When you stop learning, you might as well stop living; You are among the walking dead."

Derrick W. Welch

If you wish to continue your formal education, but have neither the time or desire to sit in a traditional classroom setting for two or three nights a week, look into non traditional educational opportunities. Not only will you find the non traditional educational experience as valuable or more valuable, than any education you receive in a traditional setting, but it will cost you a great deal less and it will allow you to accelerate or decrease your studies based on your time demands.

This is also an excellent idea for your employees to consider especially if you reimburse them for their work related educational efforts. I am not talking about the infamous diploma mills that will send you a Ph.D. if you send them a check for $5.99. I am talking about some of the finest schools in this country. Fully accredited schools that have created learning opportunities for the adults in this country who do not want to go back to a classroom or simply do not have a consistent schedule of time they can allot or do not wish to pay the outlandish costs of a traditional program.

In Pursuit of Profits. How To At Least Double Your Profits Without Increasing Your Sales.

A non traditional program of study is simply an off campus program of study that allows the student to work at his or her own pace and <u>costs a great deal less</u> since the student is not on campus tying up college resources. Non traditional programs leading to complete degrees or simply for selected courses are offered at such schools as:

Brigham Young University	City University
Harvard University	Indiana University
Ohio University	Northwood University
Syracuse University	University of Alabama
University of Maryland	University of North Carolina

These are just a few of the hundreds of well known and lessor known, fully accredited institutes of higher learning that offer non traditional programs and courses in most any discipline you can think of. From at home study, to video taped courses and cable courses, a wide variety of course formats are available to you. To find out more about these schools and programs I recommend 2 books which you may find in your local bookstore or order directly from the publisher. They are:

Bear's Guide to Earning College Degrees Non Traditionally
Jon Bear, Ph.D.
Costedoat and Bear Book Sales
P.O. Box 826
Benica, CA 94510

Campus Free College Degrees
Accredited off campus college degree programs
Marcie Kisner Thorson, M.A.
Bob Adams Inc.
Holbrook, MA 02343

The above books will give you a good overview of what programs are offered by what schools. I can personally recommend Northwood University. This is an excellent school that teaches based on the free enterprise system. I highly recommend them. I should, I have a degree from this fine school and I am very proud of it. Of the five colleges I attended Northwood was by far and away the best and the most demanding. In fact, in 1993 US News & World Report magazine rated Northwood University the #3 small university business school in the country.

<u>If you reimburse your employees for outside educational activities do so only with clearly spelled out limitations.</u> Ongoing education can greatly increase the value of an employee but it can also prove to be very costly. I have known many employees who had continued their education with the sole goal of being more qualified so that they can find another job. There is little you can do about this but you can take some steps to at least make sure your dollars in this area are well spent. Only pay for courses that are job related and that have been satisfactorily completed. Make sure you have proof.

I know of one employee who claimed he had been taking a class one night a week for over 10 years. Each semester he would submit a handwritten bill for a class he was claiming to be taking. Proof from the school was never requested of the cost, his enrollment, or his grades. As you might suspect, it turned out that he had never taken a college class in his life.

Also make sure that you are setting a cap on the cost of each course taken and the number of courses you will pay for in a given year. If they choose to attend a more expensive school or take more courses let them pay the difference. Remember, the cost of the school or course is by no means a reflection of it's value.

Rather than pay overtime consider allowing your employees who work extra hours to take off an equal amount of time whenever they would like during your slow times. Your employees will welcome the chance to have some flexibility in their schedule, even at a later time, and you will be able to reduce you overtime labor costs by 50%. You will also have the flexibility of increasing hours during your busy time and decreasing them during slower times.

You must cross train your employees in other areas of your company's operations. This will accomplish a number of things. First, it will give you great flexibility during times when one department is busy and another one is slow. You will be able to shift people as needed to match the flow of your work. It will also allow you to shift trained people from one department to another to cover during periods of vacation and absenteeism without losing productivity or the ability to service your customers.

Furthermore, cross training your employees provides them with a much greater appreciation for each other's job which will go a long way toward improving your level of internal customer service. Internal customer service, if you recall, is the service each of your employees provide to each other. The more you can improve internal customer service the more you will improve productivity, quality, and external customer service. All of which result in lower costs and higher profits.

Despite what some people think I feel that bonuses are indeed an excellent way to reward people for individual performance and to motivate people. Excellence should always be rewarded at a level above mediocrity. But individual bonuses are not enough. You should not just give out bonuses for individual accomplishment or effort. Bonuses should be based upon some measurable basis. They should not be arbitrary. They must be targeted to individual, measurable goals.

Do not give annual bonuses across the board. This would accomplish nothing except you would be rewarding mediocrity and you would be setting an expectation of bonuses regardless of performance. In short, people would come to expect them and consider them as part of their compensation. This is foolish.

Individual bonuses that are earned based on established performance levels should be awarded to employees regardless of your company's fiscal position. I know this may sound fiscally irresponsible, but your employees must know that any bonus they qualify for will be given to them and not held back due to other issues beyond their control. If they did their part, do your part.

But I strongly suggest that part of the bonus formula be predicated on the overall performance of the company. By this I mean that you should break their bonus up into two tiers. Part of it is earned based solely on exceeding individual performance standards and the rest of it is earned based on the company meeting certain performance levels.

This accomplishes a number of things. It is more fiscally responsible. Your employees will indeed get a part of their bonus if they meet individual objectives, but unless the company reaches it's fiscal objectives the second part of the bonus is not paid.

This also will foster a team attitude with each employee since the only way the company would be able to meet it's goals would be for each individual to do their part. This makes all employees more concerned with helping each other so that overall goals can be reached as well as individual goals. You are rewarding individual efforts while encouraging and rewarding team efforts. You do not want individual accomplishments to come at the expense of others or of the overall goal for the company. This will make them think of not just themselves but of their co-workers and the company as well.

You may even want to consider breaking the bonus formula down into departmental goals that must be met as well. This depends on your type of company. The point is to compensate for individual efforts while maintaining a level of fiscal sensibility and tagging total bonuses to the accomplishment of overall fiscal goals.

To get the maximum bonus your employees must be concerned with, and driven to accomplish, both their individual goals and the corporate goals. This is how the best teams win.

Make sure that any bonuses you give out are predicated on profits, not gross sales or gross savings. This goes for all employees and sales people. Giving bonuses based on gross sales or gross savings makes no sense at all. The question is not how much you sell, but rather how profitable those sales are.

Look at sales people for example. If I have one sales person selling $1,000,000 a year in goods or service and they average a 20% gross profit ratio, they are earning me a gross profit of $200,000. If I have another sales representative selling $2,000,000 of my products or services but they average a gross profit ratio of only 8%, they are only producing a gross profit of $160,000.

If my bonus schedule is based on gross sales and not gross or net profits, I would be rewarding the sales person who made the least with the highest bonus. This makes no sense at all. This goes for employee ideas and suggestions as well. Do not kid yourself. **Gross sales or savings mean nothing. Bottom line profits are the only acceptable measurement of any activity.**

Want a quick way to reduce staff or hours without having to resort to laying people off? Try calling your employees together and asking them if any of them are thinking of leaving or if any of them would like to reduce hours. While few may tell you they are thinking of leaving, you will be surprised how many would like to reduce their hours but have been afraid to ask for fear of losing their job. You will find a number of people who may want to convert from full time to part time and you will find some who would like to reduce hours when things are slow and increase hours when things are busy.

Try it. You will be surprised. Not only could you reduce payroll without resorting to layoffs, but remember the domino effect. You will also reduce all payroll indexed taxes including workers' compensation and unemployment taxes.

When you promote people, promote based on ability. Do not promote based on seniority. Do not promote based on politics. Do not promote based on academic credentials. Education is, at best, a very poor measure of potential for success. Of course, if all things are equal factor these areas into your decision. Otherwise, promote on ability.

This is a real pet peeve of mine and I see it all too often. To me this is very simple. Promote the best person for the job. Man or woman. Black or white. High school graduate or MBA. Two years on the job or ten years on the job.

The only thing that matters is that you promote the most capable individual you can. If no one is capable in the organization look outside. You must always strive to put the best person you can in each position. This will always result in the best performance you can get, which in turn, will produce the lowest cost in the long run.

Give each of your employees their own coffee mug. This will eliminate the cost of buying Styrofoam cups. It will also cut down on your trash and demonstrates that you are environmentally sensitive. If you give them mugs with your company name and logo on it you will also generate good internal PR. Before you buy promotional mugs or any promotional imprinted product do yourself a favor and read my strategies on that subject.

If you are considering attending a seminar find out first if they offer a video tape of the seminar to those who are unable to attend. Many times seminar promoters will offer a video or audio tape of the seminar at a cost equal to, or even below, the cost of the seminar itself. For example, the seminar may cost $99 for the day but the tapes may cost only $75. Even if the tapes offered cost the same as the seminar, buy the tape, don't attend the seminar.

The primary reasons for this are that you will have a chance to view the tape over and over, stopping it to take notes or reinforce a certain point whenever you need to. This is a tremendous learning advantage that does not exist when you are at a live seminar during which you may have missed a point, or been confused and are unable or unwilling to get clarification. You will also be able to allow others within your organization to effectively attend the same seminar by viewing the tape without incurring any added cost.

The domino effect also provides us with a number of secondary benefits. You do not have to travel to the seminar. This saves time and money. You do not need to lose a day of work as you can view the tape at home or after work hours. This also saves time, money, and keeps productivity at a normal level.

If you do send someone to a seminar do not prepay. Many seminars will require registration weeks or months in advance. If you are paying when you register this far in advance it is costing you much more money than the cost of the seminar since you have lost the use of that money. Instead, simply issue a purchase order to lock in your space and have the seminar company bill you at the time of the seminar.

Notice I said send someone. If you choose to attend a seminar, and I understand there will be times when this makes the most sense, send only one person if possible and not multiple people from different departments. Have the one person prepare reports and make a presentation to the others upon their return outlining the key points of the seminar.

Monitor all subscriptions that the company pays for. You will be amazed at how many times 3 or 4 or even 30 or 40 more people will be getting the same magazine or newspapers. Make sure any and all subscriptions are needed and authorized. Never have more than one subscription for any publication. If more than one person needs to review the publication in question, simply pass it along from one party to another. Then place them in a common area for others to read as needed and desired.

You will also most likely find that you are paying for a number of subscriptions that are of no use to the company and have been ordered for personal use and enjoyment by employees. Cancel these. Duplicate and personal subscriptions can cost a company thousands of dollars a year.

In Pursuit of Profits. How To At Least Double Your Profits Without Increasing Your Sales.

<u>**Make sure that any organization that you or your employees join is worth the investment and the time.**</u> If you get nothing out of it, put nothing into it. Drop it. Many employees, managers, and owners belong to organizations for unacceptable reasons. It may be a matter of status. It may be a way to get away from the office. It may be for social reasons. None of these are acceptable if your company is paying for them.

Make sure that any organizational membership you pay for is cost justified. Many are nothing more than monthly meetings that last about 30 minutes and then end in 2 hours of socializing. Socializing on your tab, your time and your money.

Decisions to join an organization or purchase a subscription should be evaluated just like any other purchase. You must ask the questions. What is the value to the company? Are you getting something for your money? Who should attend meetings? Why? Is the return greater than the cost?

I know people who go to meetings once a week and do nothing but drink and eat. They are costing the company money in many ways. They are nothing but company paid and company sanctioned 2 hour lunches once a week. You must find out what tangible benefits you are getting from your membership. Not what you think or not because you hope to make contacts and generate business. The question is what are you really getting for your investment?

Are you getting added business? Are you getting competitive information? Are you learning from others in your industry? What are you getting for your money? It had better be more than a few happy employees who love the once a week, all you can eat, luncheons.

If you deem any to be worthwhile and cost justified don't let 4 or 5 people join. It will be highly unusual that you could justify this many memberships, but if you can then look into corporate memberships which will be much less costly than a number of individual memberships.

<u>**Never forget that time is money.**</u> Think of every wasted minute as a wasted dollar. Time wasted not only means money wasted but it also means lost productivity. Always be on the lookout for ways to conserve time. Let me give you one example. For a number of years we used to back up the data on our computer system onto floppy disks. I never gave it any thought until one day one of my bookkeepers mentioned to me how long this took each week. I know, I know. I should have paid attention. It turned out to be very costly not to.

The back ups to disk took almost 4 hours per week. This is 208 hours per year. This is equal to 5 weeks of full time work wasted. At a rate of $10 per hour this was costing me $2,080 per year to have someone feed disks into a disk drive. Once I became aware of this I immediately set out to do something about it. Since I had not been proactive I was left with being reactive. In this case I had a tape drive installed for backing up at a cost of $500. It took about 60 seconds to start the back up and stick the back up tape in the drive.

My first year savings were effectively $1,580 not even including the cost savings from the eliminated disks. The second year and, each year after that, my savings were effectively $2,080 per year based only on the per hour wage from this first year. Of course my actual savings would be higher each year as this base per hour wage went up.

But what else did I accomplish? OK, besides doing something that should have been done a long time before that. Was there a domino effect? Yes, there was. I now had 4 added hours of labor to use each week. Labor that was used to get our invoices and statements out faster. This meant we got paid sooner. This led to increased profits.

"Act! And you won't have to react."

Jeno Paulucci

Do you have an emergency disaster recovery plan? From the death of the owner to a natural disaster, every company is at some degree of risk and should have a contingency plan in place to deal with this risk. Think the unthinkable. What would you do if your building burned down or was washed away in a flood or you die or an earthquake hit? Are you prepared to keep the company going? After it happens is too late. The plans must be made ahead of time. This is a proactive step that will allow you to properly react when the emergency occurs.

This is often an overlooked area in many companies and with small business in particular. Not only will such a plan save you a great deal of money but it can, in fact, make the difference between your company surviving or dying. A full disaster plan is well beyond the scope of this writing and much needed planning depends on your business. However, I strongly urge you to spend the needed time to develop one or if you have one review it periodically and update or modify as needed.

From the safety of your employees to the preservation of your records, you should have a plan to react to any disaster. From the death of the principal to your insurance coverage and claims, you must have an actionable plan to deal with any emergency. From how you will operate if the facility is destroyed or damaged to where you will operate, you must have a plan you can put in place and act on.

This plan should be in writing and your key people should be aware of it. You cannot wait until the disaster strikes. I urge you to begin this planning today. I would recommend you start by contacting your insurance representative and ask them to come out and meet with you on this subject.

They will give you a wealth of free advice, guidance, and written information to help you with this planning. Why? Simple. It is in their best interest that your business survives and continues after any disaster. If they can't or won't help you I suggest that perhaps you should begin looking for a new insurance agent. I also suggest you contact your banker and ask for the same assistance. It is also in their best interest that your business survives any disaster. Both of these sources should be very well experienced in this area and should prove to be of invaluable assistance to you. All at no cost I might add.

Do not copy internal memos and distribute to every employee or a list of employees automatically. Whenever possible post on the company or department bulletin board. Find out who needs to read it and who doesn't. You may be surprised to find that many people you distribute memos to never read them or do not need to read them. Think of the time and money you are losing. You are losing the time and cost of making the copies, distributing the copies, and having people read them.

Cut out as many steps as you can. If you can't post the memo, circulate and have each party initial and pass on. There will very often be a lower cost way to accomplish the same thing in any area of business. All you need to do is to put that fantastic thinking machine you own to use.

Ideas are slippery. You must write them down or record them when they come to you or you may never recall them. Always keep a small pad of paper and a pencil with you or a micro recorder to get your thoughts down when they come to you. You cannot afford to let any ideas slip away. I am not just speaking about cost control or expense reduction. I am talking about all ideas in any area.

Chapter 23. Phones /Fax.

"Whoever admits that he is too busy to improve his methods has acknowledged himself to be at the end of his rope. And that is always the saddest predicament which anyone can get into."

J. Ogden Armour

Don't be a victim of phone fraud. Recent surveys of major phone users around the country have indicated that nearly 70% of all users have been a victim of phone fraud. Based on surveys like this it has been estimated that over 35,000 business phone users will be a victim of phone fraud this year alone with losses exceeding $4 billion per year. This does not even include fraud and abuses by your employees. Don't think this happens to only large companies and don't think it won't happen to your company.

I strongly suggest you call your phone hardware vendor, your local carrier, and your long distance carrier and ask them how you can prevent internal and external phone fraud and abuse. Ask them to send you any published information they have on this subject and ask them to have a rep come see you to inform you of any other information they have.

Make sure you block all access to 900#s and 976#s. Check your system manual to see if you can program this block yourself. If not, call your phone company and find out how much they will charge you to do this. Then look in your local paper for phone repairmen who moonlight. They advertise in most major newspapers. Ask them what they would charge to do the same thing. By doing this I was able to block 900#s and 976#'s on my system for 50% less than the phone company was going to charge me. Be proactive. Don't wait until abuses happen to take action.

Would you like to reduce employee abuse of your phones which cost you money and time? Would you like to stop subsidizing the phone calls of your employees, customers, and suppliers? Would you like to turn an area of costs into a profit center? If any of these areas are a concern to you, and they all should be, look into installing a pay phone in all public areas of your company. From the lunch room to the waiting room, if you have free access phones you are inviting costly abuses by your customers, suppliers, and employees.

Replace these with a personal pay phone. I am not talking about a phone company pay phone, but instead your own personal pay phone. Why give the profits to the phone company? These phones look very much like a normal office phone except they have a coin slot and usage instructions. By using phones like this you are providing access to outside lines but you are not paying for the call. Local and long distance calls can be made from these phones and each charges an applicable rate.

Depending on the number of phones you have in public places and the usage of these phones, you could turn a cost into a significant profit. You will also discourage employee abuse since they now pay for the call they will make fewer calls and stay on the phone a shorter time. This could lead to increased productivity.

At a local call cost of .25, even 10 calls a day will produce profits of $650 per year. At a rate of 100 local call per day this will produce profits of $6,500 per year. This is just the profits and does not include the reduction of your own phone bills which should be even more significant. These profits can be applied to your overall phone bill to lower costs or can be shared with the employees in some monetary manner or perhaps in the form of a company sponsored function. The goal is not to make money from your employees but rather to reduce phone costs and abuses.

Resource

A company called Hello Direct puts out phones like this as well as a number of other excellent products to help you control phone related costs and increase productivity. I suggest you call them and ask for a catalog. 1-800-444-3556.

<u>Don't fall prey to the many phone scam artists that are out there.</u> In other sections I have covered some of the more common ones, here I simply want to provide you with one rule.

It is my policy to never purchase, order, or approve anything over the phone. It should be yours as well. From the charity solicitation to the special good for today only, I demand a written request or proposal before I will even consider whatever it is they have called me about. I do not care if it is the local police department or a nationwide charity. There are simply too many scam artists out there pretending to be someone or something that they are not.

You may find your company sending money to a non existent charity or company. Your money may not end up going to the place or for the cause, you thought is was. This rule will rid you of the majority of bogus phone scams.

<u>Whenever possible call during the lowest rate times.</u> Do you know when the lowest cost time of the day is to make your long distance phone calls? Do you know when the highest cost time of the day is to make your phone calls? Did you even know that there is different times of the day when your phone calls can cost much more or much less than other times?

If you don't know these times how can you possibly think you are using your phone in the most cost efficient manner? Contact your long distance carrier and find out the different rates for the different times. Then, whenever possible, schedule your long distant phone calls and fax transmissions during the times when the costs are lowest.

If you phone or fax internationally you should secure this same information for each country you call and schedule accordingly. Depending on where you call and when, your phone bill savings can be significant.

<u>Don't let people put you on hold.</u> This runs up your phone bills and costs you time. Lost time is lost productivity and this means lost money. Instead, leave a message and ask for the party to return your call. Let them run up their phone bill.

<u>Review your carriers.</u> Call in Sprint, MCI, and AT &T and ask them to review your phones bills and make a proposal to you at least twice a year. Without question one of these three will make you a proposal that will cost you less than the rates you are now paying.

While each of the reps is in your office reviewing your phone activity, make sure you explain to each that you are seeking ways to reduce costs and you want ideas from them on how they can help you. Each will provide you with a number of ideas and programs that they have. Make no commitment to any of them at the time they are in or when they present a proposal to you.

You need proposals from each before you can effectively review and determine which is the best value for you. If you are a smaller company before you sign on with one of the big three contact at least two resellers and ask them to also make a proposal to you. Resellers are simply companies that buy huge blocks of phone time from the phone company and earn significant discounts by doing so. They then turn around and sell this time to individual companies at discounted rates lower than they have earned but often higher than you can earn based on your much smaller overall volume.

Check out any reseller you deal with and make sure you get a number of references. I also suggest you deal only with resellers who allow you to dial direct with no change in phone procedures. In this day and age there is no reason you should have to install separate, or new equipment, or dial any access codes. A reseller may be able to save you 25% or more when compared to the costs of any of the big three carriers although the gap seems to be closing each year.

Check each of these carrier options out and you should easily be able to realize very large savings in this area without sacrificing one bit of quality or service. <u>This strategy enabled us to reduce our phone bills by 27.5% in two years.</u>

Resource

A good resource to keep you up to date on new plans and rates that come out is a newsletter offered by an independent consumer group called Telecommunications Research and Action Center. For a sample copy of the newsletter and information on this group's services send $5 in a self addressed stamped envelope to TRAC, P.O. Box 12038, Washington, DC, 20005.

<u>When you evaluate the various long distance carriers, including resellers, make sure you find out how they charge you and factor this into your overall evaluation.</u> By charging you I am referring to the increments of time they bill you for. Long distance carriers will normally bill you in 6 second, 30 second, or 60 second usage increments. If you are with a carrier who bills in 60 second increments and your call lasted only 30 seconds you are going to be charged double.

If your call lasts 40 seconds with one carrier you would be billed 42 seconds and with the other two you would be billed 60 seconds. Any way you look at it you are getting ripped off since you will almost never talk in increments of exactly 6 seconds, 30 seconds or 60 seconds. The best you can hope for is to minimize the opportunity you give them to steal your money. If all things are equal, and they rarely are, by going with the carrier who bills you in 6 second increments you will accomplish this.

You also want to review the minimum time clause each carrier has. Some will have longer minimum times they charge you than others. One may always charge you a minimum of 60 seconds for all calls under a minute in duration while another may only charge you a minimum of 30 seconds for any call under 30 seconds. Again, anything but an exact count of your usage is a theft in my opinion, but all things being equal select the lowest minimum.

<u>Are you getting maximum volume discounts?</u> Make sure that you are earning total volume discounts on all your phone lines and usage including remote lines, lines at other locations, calling cards, and fax lines. The more usage you can include the larger your overall discounts will be. Do not assume the phone company is including all your lines. Very often this will not be the case at all. Make sure you never assume.

You must monitor your phones bills and employee activity to prevent abuse of your phone lines. This is a very common problem. From friends and relatives calling on your incoming 800#, to employees abusing your outgoing lines for personal activity, the cost of increased phone time and decreased productivity can be staggering. By monitoring your phone bills you will also find numerous instances of employees and salespeople spending far too long on the calls.

For example, I discovered that one of our out of state salespeople was spending 40 hours a month calling the home office. That's right 40 hours per month. Not only was this costing me thousands of dollars per year in the form of higher phone bills but it also made me ask when did this sales person have time to sell anything. She was spending the equivalent of 1 week out of every four on the phone. By forcing a decrease in the amount of calls and in the duration of the calls by organizing a more efficient calling schedule, we were able to significantly lower our phone cost while improving our sales activity.

In another example, I noticed repeated long distance calls coming in on our 800# from the same phone number. Only one of three things could have been happening. We had a customer who was buying a great deal from us and I saw no evidence of this. We had a problem with a customer and I wanted to know about it if we did. We had an employee who was taking a large number of out of state calls from a friend or relative during work hours.

I called the number to find out. Guess which it was? We did indeed have an employee who was running up phone bills by having a relative call on our 800#. We were tying up lines, losing productivity, and increasing costs. One problem almost always creates others. Remember, the domino effect works both ways.

It also became apparent that I had a supervisory problem since this employee was taking these calls during working hours and the supervisor from that department was either allowing this or was unaware of it. In either case it was a problem.

I have often found 5 to 10 hours per month in phone abuses just by reviewing the bills for 5 minutes once a month. This is 60 to 100 hours per year. Just call the number and find out if it is a business and if so is it one of your customers or prospects or is it a personal number? You can also ask the phone company to tell you who the number is listed to.

We are talking about a theft. A theft of time, phone usage, and productivity. The type of theft that costs companies in this country billions of dollars a year.

Monitor your phone bills each month to make sure your people are not overusing directory assistance and incurring added costs. In my area we are allotted only so many free directory assistance calls per month per line. Once we exceed that allowance we are charged for the call at a rate of .50 each.

A great deal of directory assistance calls are made because people are lazy and won't look up a number. At the rate of .50 each you might not think it matters much but think a bit more. If it takes you one minute to look up a number and you pay .50 to call and get it, the effective hourly rate you are paying the phone company is $30.

This is figured by .50 times 60. The 60 came from you being able to look up one number per minute which is 60 per hour. This is a conservative estimate of the real time it would take to look up a number. Looking at this from another angle, even twenty .50 directory assistance calls per day will cost you $2,600 per year or $26,000 over a 10 year period. You must learn to think like this. This is the only way you can determine what things really cost. Translating everything into a dollar value is the best way to drive home the importance of controlling your costs.

In Pursuit of Profits. How To At Least Double Your Profits Without Increasing Your Sales.

Never assume your long distance carrier will automatically apply any discounts you may be eligible for under the various plans they offer. They most likely will not. Why should they inform you of discounts which lower their billings? It is up to you to call a representative in every 6 months and find out about all discount programs that might help save you money. New plans are constantly being developed to attract new customers and keep existing customers. It is up to you to find out about them.

Consider assigning access codes to your employees. These are personal access codes that must be punched in by your employees before they can get an open line. They will allow you to track all phone calls made by each employee. The main benefit is that you can then track the costs for the various phone related functions your people undertake on behalf of your customers. This will enable you to more accurately bill this time or at least track the costs to show you a clearer picture of the profitability of each job.

The secondary benefit is that by using access codes you will be able to very easily pinpoint phone abuse. You will know who is using your phones, when, for how long, and who they are calling to. This provides a strong monitoring tool for you.

Be proactive, have a block put on all phones in your office that have no need to make long distance calls. There are many areas of your company that have no need of a long distance line. Remove the temptation to make them for personal use by simply not providing access.

Make employees pay you back for all unauthorized long distance calls. This will cut your costs but more importantly, it will send a message to your employees that phone abuse will not be tolerated.

Make sure you are aware of your employee's phone activity and make sure your supervisors are as well. Time spent on the phone during working hours robs you of productivity, hinders your ability to produce your products or deliver proper levels of service, sets a bad example, runs up your phone costs, and can seriously damage morale. Do not allow it to happen.

I am not talking about an employee who makes a few brief calls during the week to take care of needed personal business. This is perfectly acceptable and would never be questioned by me. There are occasions when personal things may have to be addressed during working hours. I am talking about the employee who spends more than a few minutes on the phone quite frequently during the week. These are the abusers and thieves you are looking for.

I recommend that you do not participate in phone surveys of any kind. If you are like most companies you will get many calls asking you to participate in a phone survey regarding any one of a number of products and services.

In the last week alone I have been called about participating in a phone survey about my needs and opinions on computers, office cleaning services, direct mail, and phone carriers. Some of these surveys are nothing but come on's to get you interested in the products or services of one company. Others are from companies looking to generate leads by identifying users of certain products and services .

Still others are legitimate surveys being conducted for research purposes. Some will take only a few minutes while others will ask you questions for a 1/2 hour or more. Regardless of the purpose of the survey I suggest you do not participate in them. Why? Three primary reasons. First, they take up valuable time. This means lowered productivity.

Second, you do not know who is really calling and for what purpose. Are they calling to inquire about your computer needs to find out if you have a computer system worth stealing? Is it your competition calling to find out information about your operation? Is the call really a way to make a high pressure sales pitch? Is the caller fishing for names to call and pressure? You don't know and neither do I. If you don't know don't participate!

Lastly, if you have an 800# that is not a dedicated line they may be calling you and making you pay for the call and you will not even know it.

Do not send a letter if a phone call will do. This will save labor, postage, and paper while providing a quick personal response.

If you have an 800# do not give it out to your suppliers. Give only to your customers. Let your suppliers pay to do business with you. My experience with 800#s that are freely given out to all, is that over 10% of your incoming 800# calls will come from suppliers. If you spend $100,000 a year on 800# bills your are probably wasting at least $10,000 of this by paying for the incoming call from your suppliers.

Do not put your 800# on your purchase order or on any correspondence you send to suppliers. You will see later that I suggest you use a cheaper 1 color version of your corporate letterhead for dealing with everyone except customers and other important parties. By using a second version of your letterhead you can delete any 800# that may be on your main letterhead.

Get rid of any private phone lines you or anyone else in your company has. They are needed only to provide status and to satisfy egos. They have no place in a program of total cost control. They demonstrate no commitment by the users of that phone to a program of total cost control. If you are not demonstrating the type of actions you expect from your people you will not get them. Instead, you will get what you demonstrate.

If you need phones that have privacy get a phone that offers you a privacy button to insure no one picks up your line or get a device at your local electronics store that does the same thing. Neither requires a private line.

Dispute any and all questionable charges you find on your phone bill. All too many people assume the phone company is never wrong or can't be questioned. The reality is that they are frequently wrong and can and should be questioned about any possible errors. Look for errors in usage, equipment charges, line charges, and anything else you get a bill for. The more items that you are billed for the more likely it is that your bills will contain errors.

Take out all phones in your company that are not needed. The proper thing to do would have been not to buy them but since the damage is done, pull out any you do not need or cannot justify. Sell the extra phones or store them to reduce your repair bills later on by having your own replacement phones on hand. Phones not needed lead to waste as they represent a temptation and therefore directly encourage abuse. They will also run up your service costs and possibly incur monthly charges. If you are being charged monthly by the phone company or under a hardware service contract make sure you notify the vendor in writing that the phones are no longer on the system. Then check your bills to make sure applicable charges are stopped.

In Pursuit of Profits. How To At Least Double Your Profits Without Increasing Your Sales.

<u>**Place any non dedicated phones in a common visible area.**</u> If you need phones around your office that are for common usage make sure they are located in a central, highly visible location. This will go a long way towards reducing phone abuse. If an employee is taking or making a personal call, do you think they would talk longer or make and take more calls using a phone in a central and visible area of your office or from one that is tucked away out back in your warehouse?

<u>**Do not buy equipment or sign up for services that sound good but are not needed.**</u> Services and capabilities like voice mail, conference calling, call waiting, and a variety of others can be very useful but do not get them if you do not need them or plan to use them.

<u>**Drop any lines you have that are not usage justified.**</u> Very often companies will carry more lines than they need without ever thinking about it. By monitoring your phone bills you can see the per line usage and therefore you can easily determine if every line you have is justified. Each lines costs you a monthly fee. If you need all the lines you have, great. If not, get rid of them. You can always add another line later if the usage in the future justifies it.

<u>**Always use your supplier's 800#.**</u> You are the customer. They should pay for the call you make to them. If you do not have an 800# for every supplier you call, ask if they have one. Just because you do not have an 800# in your files for that supplier does not mean that they do not have one. Find out.

When you get the 800# replace the toll number in your files with the 800#. If you have a speed dial put it in so you will always use the toll free number. Make sure the 800# is circulated to all who might have a reason to call this party.

You will be surprised at how fast your toll calls can add up when you are calling an out of state supplier on a regular basis. We had one that was costing us $50 per month or $600 per year until we discovered they had an 800#. Now instead of us paying to do business with them, they pay for us to do business with them. As it should be.

<u>**Call AT & T and get their 800# directory.**</u> This way you will always be able to look for an 800# for any party you are calling before you incur a toll call. If it is not listed in there you can try to call the 800# information service. 1-800-555-1212.

<u>**Don't pay for convenience.**</u> In my area the phone company has come up with a new service. A service that is the perfect example of what happens when you trade off convenience for cost. Whenever I call information the recording gives me the number and then offers to dial it for me. Sounds great except for the fact that the cost to have the phone company automatically dial the number for me is .35 cents.

If you take the time to figure this out you will find that this .35 cent call equates to a rate of about $252 per hour. Think about it. How long does it take to dial a number? Even if you have bad eyes and arthritis this should take no longer than 5 seconds. In most cases it will take less than 5 seconds.

However , even using 5 seconds you could dial 12 numbers per minute or 720 numbers per hour. At .35 cents each this is equal to $252 per hour. At this rate I could hire the Queen of England full time to do nothing but dial numbers for me. Well, perhaps I could find a better choice than that.

If that is not enough for you, think about how often the phone company gives you the wrong number and now you are paying them to dial it for you. What a deal.

If they offer this service in your area make darn sure that you inform the people in your company that having the phone company dial information requested numbers is an unacceptable practice. Since you monitor your phone bills for other abuses this should be easy for you to spot. You do monitor your phone bills do you not?

Always be prepared when making a phone call, especially a long distance call. Know what you are trying to accomplish and have all needed materials on hand including a list of any questions you want to make sure you get answers to. This will minimize your unproductive time on the phone and keep your phone costs as low as possible. Being properly prepared can reduce your phone time by 10% to 50% and frees up time for more productive activities.

The alternative is to make an unprepared phone call where you are constantly saying "hold on while I get that" or "I will have to get that and call you back". This is rude and time consuming. As a result of being unprepared you will often forget to ask a question or get some information you require. This means you will have to call back again. This wastes more time, increases your phone bills, and is sure to make the other party wonder what kind of company they are dealing with.

Take your calls whenever possible. Of course, you want to have some level of screening done by the receptionist or secretary to insure you are not taking calls you do not want such as phone solicitations, but by taking your calls whenever possible you will be providing better service and reducing your phone bills since the calling party is paying for the call.

You may think that returning all your calls later or, at some specific time during the day, is more productive but I disagree. Yes, there will be times when it simply is not feasible to take a call. But this will not be the case the majority of the time. When you collect all calls until the end of the day or some other preset time you are not demonstrating good service or response to the caller and you are forced to pay for all the calls.

Always take your customer's calls if possible and if it is not possible promptly call them back when it is feasible, but if a supplier calls and it is not a feasible time for you to speak to them have your secretary or receptionist ask them to <u>call you</u> back.

This will keep your phone costs down. You should bear the cost of doing business with your customers but your suppliers should bear the cost of doing business with you. Even if it is only 20 or 30 calls per day at a cost savings of up to $1 to $2 per call, you will be saving thousands of dollars per year. You will also eliminate wasteful time spent trying to connect with a supplier representative who may be on the road most of the time.

Periodically track incoming phone calls for employees. You will find most likely that you have some employees getting far too many personal calls. You may also find incoming 800# abuse.

The first thing you must ask when considering a cellular phone is, "do I need one?" or "does that party need one?". Ask the questions. Why is it needed? What will it be used for? How often can I justify using it? When will it be needed? How many times will having a cellular phone be absolutely necessary? Can I use a beeper instead? In most cases I suspect you will find that you cannot justify the cost of having a cellular phone. Remember, status and ego are not reasons for cost justification. They are the enemy of your total cost control program.

Monitor / audit all cellular phone bills to make sure that all calls made are for justified business use. Many calls made from car phones are personal in nature and many others are made for convenience and not necessity. Cellular calls are much more expensive than regular calls and if they are not warranted they should not be made. You must control abuses and unnecessary calls if you are paying for them.

Do not give out your cellular number to anyone who does not absolutely have to have it. Remember who pays for the incoming phone call. In case you forgot, it is you. Not only are you paying for all incoming calls to your cellular phone but you are paying a very high per minute rate.

Look into having a periodic audit done on your cellular phone bills. I have covered the use of outside auditing firms in other sections so I won't take up your time here. Instead, I will remind you that it will cost you nothing and may save a great deal. I will also tell you that it has been estimated that up to 80% of all cellular phone bills contain errors. Guess whose favor these errors are in?

If your business charges your customers or clients for phone calls made on their behalf make sure your people are keeping a log of all such calls they make. This will enable your billing people to cross reference the cost of the call with the client they should be billed to. Don't forget about faxes sent by your company on behalf of your customers. These are often overlooked but they are also a phone related expense that you should track and bill. Reduce your fax costs by billing them back to your client.

If your company does bill phone time in this manner I suggest you contact your regional phone company and find out what time saving systems they have to help you in this area of tracking and billing phone calls.

Whenever possible use the fax instead of the phone. By communicating via a fax you can save tremendous amounts of time, which is money, and reduce your phone bills. How? Well, you won't get put on hold or switched to eight different people who make you repeat the same thing you told the one before or, get hung up on or, spend 10 minutes fighting your way through an endless array of voice mail menus. You won't even waste ten minutes on unrelated small talk.

A one minute fax could easily replace a 5, 10, or 15 minute call. Plus you can also avoid telephone tag where you leave messages while the party you are trying to reach is out and while you are out that party returns your call.

The fax should state very clearly the nature of your communication and the required course of action or form of response. Since the communication is in writing you are insuring clear communication and by eliminating miscommunication you will cut down on errors and lost time.

Compare the clarity of a written request to that of a verbal conversation, a message left with a person, message service, answering machine, or on voice mail. In addition to a clarity of communication, the fax also provides you with a written record of the communication. Depending on the nature of that communication this could prove to be very important.

Use a fax modem on your computer. By sending any document you need to fax directly from your computer you will eliminate the time and materials involved in printing out the document, possibly photocopying it, and standing by the fax to send it. Since the transmission speed of your computer will be much faster than that of your fax you will also save money on the cost of the call.

Whenever possible fax it later. Most faxes allow you to program multiple numbers in your fax to send documents to different places at different times. Most people do not use this feature but you should as it can significantly cut down on your phone bills by allowing you to send faxes during non peak hours to customers in different time zones or, if time allows, even in your own time zone.

In this latter case, you can still send during non peak hours if the receiving party does not need the fax until the next day send it during the night when rates are lower. It will be waiting for them when they get to the office the next day. If for some reason the fax did not get sent or was not received, you can always send it the next morning and you have lost nothing. By sending your fax transmissions during the hours when your phone costs are the lowest you can cut your fax related phone costs by 30% to 50%.

Do not waste expensive corporate letterhead when sending faxes. If you are unable to use a one page fax form, instead, create any document you are going to fax on a photocopy of your letterhead. Remember, your customer does not get the original. They get a black and white fax.

Your high quality two color letterhead will be wasted. The average 2 color letterhead can cost up to .10 to .15 per sheet. If you buy photocopy paper like I suggest in other strategies it will only cost about .02 each. By photocopying your letterhead onto copy paper and using that you could save .08 to .13 per fax.

If you send even 100 faxes a week and use a photocopied letterhead instead of an original letterhead you could save $8 to $13 per week or $416 to $676 per year. You just made a significant return on your investment in this publication.

Keep a couple of different size fax forms on hand for your people to use. For example, keep 8 1/2 x 11 and 5 x 8 on hand at least. This way the smallest possible size can be used for each fax transmission. The smaller the size the quicker the transmission, which leads to lower phone costs. It also cuts down on paper costs.

Keep a paper cutter next to the fax machine and use it to trim down all faxes you send. The narrower or shorter you make the fax, the lower your transmission phone costs will be. The receiving party will still get a full sheet on their end if you have trimmed off the boarders and the unused bottom of a page.

Every fax you trim down will reduce the time of that transmission by 25% to 50% depending on how much you trim off.   Your phone savings will depend on how well you have shopped for a carrier. By having the shortest billing increments possible and the smallest minimum billing time, you could save significant percentages on the cost of each trimmed fax you send.

Make sure that your people have read the manual that came with the fax machine. Very often a number of time and cost saving features exist on these machines that are never used simply because no one knows they exist, or if they do, how to use them.

Don't buy all the bells and whistles. Find out what each feature of the fax machine you are considering buying accomplishes and make sure they will be useful to you or do not buy them. This is a waste of money and gives you something you do not need. These unwanted options could also result in higher repair and maintenance bills and higher sales tax on the higher purchase price.

In Pursuit of Profits. How To At Least Double Your Profits Without Increasing Your Sales.

If you have more than one fax machine in your company make sure that all supply related purchases are being combined to realize the maximum savings possible based on your combined volume. It makes no sense to have each department order the fax paper, or any other supplies they need, when by combining purchases you can save significant amounts of money.

For your next fax get a plain paper fax. The copies are better. You do not need to photo copy the fax as is usually done with a thermo paper fax, this saves time and money while reducing the operating costs of your photocopier. The paper used is cheaper and the plain paper fax will normally be much faster thereby reducing your phone costs.

Plain paper faxes are much faster than thermo faxes. An old thermo fax can take up to 60 seconds to transmit one page whereas a plain paper fax can transmit the same sheet in 3 to 9 seconds. If you save .10 cents a fax transmission and send 100 faxes a week you will save $520 per year on phone bills alone not even counting time.

In fact, don't wait until you need a new one. Conduct a cost analysis now. You may find the savings so great that a new machine will pay for itself in savings within a very short period of time. After that the savings will continue for years.

Are you using your fax in enough ways? Use the fax to increase sales, speed up collection efforts, improve customer service, and for a wide variety of other low cost applications. The fax conveys a sense of urgency and importance. Use this to your advantage whenever applicable.

Reduce an 8 1/2 x 14 fax on your photocopier to 8 1/2 x 11 before you fax the document. This will reduce your phone related fax costs by 20%. A shorter length fax transmits faster thereby reducing your phone costs, labor costs, and machine wear.

Do not use a cover sheet with your fax. This does nothing but double your transmission time which increases your phone bills, wastes paper, and time while lowering productivity. Drop the cover sheet. Instead, pick up a small stamp that indicates "to" and "from". Other than indicating who the fax is to and from what else does a cover sheet do? Oh yeah, it tells them this is a fax in case they could not figure out why it came from the fax machine. By dropping the cover sheet you will save 30% to 50% of your fax related costs and reduce wear and tear on the fax machine.

Get a reusable fax sheet for all fax transmissions that do not require a permanent hard copy. This is simply a thin wipe off sheet that has spaces for you to fill in the information you need to fax. This is, of course, very informal and therefore will not be suitable for all transmissions. These sheets cost about .50 cents each and are reusable simply by wiping off the information on the board. The use of these eliminates paper and saves typing time.

Whenever feasible send your correspondence by fax instead of mail. Not only will it get there, but it will get there immediately. Furthermore, it will save you a great deal of time and money. Time and money that can be put to more productive purposes. A one or two page fax will cost you far less than a one or two page letter. I would estimate the average fax I send costs .25 cents. If I have an employee sending a one page letter I would estimate the cost to be .74 cents.

I arrived at this as follows. An employee making $9 per hour will take about 3 minutes to type the envelope, fold the letter and insert it. At $9 per hour each minute of that employee's time costs .15 cents. This does not include payroll related costs, this is just based on the hourly wage of $9.

Three minutes at .15 = .45 cents. To this you must add a first class stamp at .29 cents. This brings the total, not including the envelope or more expensive letterhead, to .74 cents. By using the fax I have saved .49 cents per letter. If I send 50 faxes a day instead of 50 letters I will save $24.50 per day. Per week this is $122.50. Per year this is $6,370.

Not a bad savings with the side benefit of knowing my correspondence got there and got there right away. When you consider that your fax provides a printed verification of delivery you could even compare the cost to that of a certified letter. By doing this your savings would be significantly higher.

Also remember, these savings do not even include the money you have saved by not using an envelope and by not using a quality letterhead. At 50 letters a day being replaced by a fax you would save 13,000 envelopes and between 13,000 - 26,000 formal letterheads a year. This provides you with another added savings of thousands of dollars.

Think total cost control. Could you do this 100 times a day and save twice as much while improving service? How about 200 times a week? Can you justify a part time person to do nothing but send faxes? Think. I can only give you the tools. It is up to you to use them or modify and apply them.

Chapter 24. Printing and business forms.

"Pennies do not come from heaven, they have to be earned here on earth."

Margaret Thatcher

Without a doubt the best way to control your printing costs is to control your designer. What, you say? It is true. Plain and simple, the design dictates the printing and production costs. This is something many designers and ad agency creative people have either never learned or just don't give a damn about.

As with all areas of your business, being proactive is the best way to control your costs. Controlling the design is the proactive step when it comes to printing costs. When you are designing or having something designed, the cost of the design process is often by far the smaller cost involved when compared to your printing and production costs.

The design cost will be incurred once, but the printing costs will be incurred over and over for the life of that item. The more complex the design the more costly the printing will be. Don't let anyone tell you otherwise. I can't tell you how many times I have seen artists and designers feed their egos by designing items they love or hope will win them or their agency an award with no regard or consideration whatsoever for the costs that will be incurred in producing that item. Costs you pay for over and over every time you reprint the item in question.

I can't tell you how many times I have watched the client led by the nose during the design process and never question anything, even whether or not the design is what they want. They never even think of the printing costs, production costs, or media costs. Four colors are used when two or three would have been equally effective. Odd sizes are used when a more standard size would do. Bleeds, traps, registration problems are all created in the design phase. Very costly custom illustrations are used when stock photography would be just as effective or even more effective. Well, you get the idea.

Simple is often the most effective and yet designers have never understood this. Don't you fall into this trap. Don't let designers or creative people dictate to you. Don't you pay for the food that feeds their ego.

This area has been covered in other strategies so for now understand the relationship between the creative process and the production process and take the needed steps to control it. Please also understand that I am referring to all printed materials including letterhead, corporate logos, promotional pieces, direct mail packages, ads, flyers, commercials, and even your business cards. This is also true for radio and video productions. Proper control in this area can have a dramatic impact on your bottom line.

Check costs before you proceed. Before you contract to have the actual design completed request a dummy or layout of what the designer has in mind. Make sure they also advise you of stock, sizes, colors, and all other specifications. This dummy should be made to size and include the colors, in position, to be used.

You should then take this to the printers you will be considering using. Give them the dummy and the specifications involved and ask for an estimate of costs. Also ask them for suggestions on how you can reduce the costs without altering the intent of the piece. Even a change in paper stocks can reduce a printing job by 25% or more.

With the costs to produce the piece the way the designer or ad agency wants known, you can now decide to proceed or modify based on the options and suggestions the printers have given you.

Technology can greatly reduce your outside costs. Look into desktop publishing. Between today's high quality photo copies and laser printers you are now able to do many of your own marketing, advertising, and promotional materials including creative, typesetting, and printing. No, you do not need to be an egghead to use today's equipment. Pocket protectors and horn rim glasses are strictly optional.

Today's systems can pay for themselves in a very short period of time. Even the novice user can quickly learn how to create and produce direct mail packages, flyers, sales bulletins, price lists, product and service brochures. You should be able to save 50% or more over the cost of using outside services for these various functions.

Small quantities can be produced right in your office from your printer or photocopier. Larger runs, if you do not have the proper equipment, can be run at your local quick print shop. You do the design and print out the master and they just duplicate. By doing this you will totally eliminate your advertising agency creative costs or design house costs.

A number of sharp companies have started offering what amounts to prepackaged marketing and promotional materials that are creatively designed and printed and allow you to run through your copier or laser printer to add custom copy in certain areas. The end results are very professional looking pieces for a great deal less money than a comparably custom printed piece would cost in small quantities.

A wide variety of stock options and formats are available and for runs of a few hundred to even a few thousand your cost savings can be significant. In larger runs custom printing will still result in the lower per unit costs, however, today's technology provides you with an excellent opportunity to test your promotional materials in short runs before you invest in large runs or major promotional roll outs.

Resources.

BeaverPrints   1-800-923-2837
PaperDirect   1-800-272-7377
Queblo   1-800-523-9080
Idea Art   1-800-435-2278
Premier Papers 1-800-843-0414
Paper Works in RI at 1-800-649-9276 and out of state at 1-800-638-8600.

Don't pay for high priced designs, instead copy and modify existing designs. Every day you are bombarded with thousands of advertising messages, print and broadcast, you see dozens of business cards, direct mail packages, ads, and other types of selling literature. This is your reference library. Furthermore, your local printer will have samples of hundreds or even thousands of different designs from simple business cards and letterheads to complex promotional packages.

In many cases you will be able to save thousands of dollars in original design work by knowing what you want, having actual samples of it and modifying existing designs. After all, how original do you think most designs are? Why do you think ad agencies and design houses keep huge reference libraries and subscribe to publications that display and critique creative work of others in the field? It couldn't be because they "borrow" ideas and designs from others could it? Of course not, what was I thinking?

In Pursuit of Profits. How To At Least Double Your Profits Without Increasing Your Sales.

<u>Don't buy scratch pads, memo pads, things to do pads, or phone message pads.</u> Instead, you should get them free from your printer or paper supply house. They make these by the thousands with their name on them and give them away for self-promotional purposes. If the sales representative doesn't offer them to you ask. If they do not have them they sure will start thinking about producing them.

<u>Don't ever assume that all printers will give you similar prices and quality for the same project.</u> I assure you they will not. You must shop your printing needs just like you should do with any other purchase. You should prepare a written request for a price quote for each printing job you need. You should request a written price quote in return. Verbal quotes should not be acceptable.

Let me drive this point of shopping printers home with an actual example. We work with a number of printers on a regular basis. Some are very competitive on certain projects and not on others. Were we to use the same printer for all our needs we would be greatly overpaying for printing on an annual basis.

One example in particular graphically demonstrates this. I solicited price quotes for a custom 4 color wall calendar from three different color printers. The price quotes I received back shocked even me. They ranged from a low of $35,993 to a high of $108,376. **No, that is not a misprint. There was a $73,000 difference in cost for the same exact job.**

Now I will grant you that this is an extreme case, however, I will also assure you that routinely you will find differences in cost among printers that range from 20% to 100% and more. Why? There are many reasons and these include: the size of the shop, profit goals, equipment (in the example above the lower cost printer had a web press which is made for large high speed high quality runs, the higher priced printer did not), overhead, sales commissions, management, pricing formulas, and union or non union labor. These are just a few of the factors that create a buyers market for you and I. These costs should be among the easiest to reduce and reduce significantly.

On a smaller scale let's look at a difference in costs for printing letterheads, envelopes, and business cards. I called two local printers and gave them both the exact same set of specifications for an order of 1,000 letterheads, 1,000 envelopes and 500 business cards. I then checked the catalog of Viking, an excellent direct mail office supply store, and compared their prices for the same items. Each priced the job on the same stock and same colors. I have listed the costs below:

	Printer 1	Printer 2	Viking
Letterheads	$182.89	$127.25	$84.99
Envelopes	$137.67	$ 95.40	$92.99
Business Cards	$ 50.00	$ 36.00	$24.99
	--------	---------	---------
Totals	$370.56	$258.65	$202.97

Each also charged a $20 set up.

This price comparison effort took about ten minutes. Look at the results. By using printer #2 instead of printer one I would have saved $111.91 or over 30% of the total cost. By purchasing from Viking instead of printer #1, I would have saved $167.59 or 45%. Buying from Viking instead of printer #2 would have saved me $55.68 or 22%.

Furthermore, by purchasing through Viking I would have had the product delivered to me at no charge and I would have enjoyed a 100% money back guarantee if, for any reason, I was not satisfied. I also would have saved sales tax and I would not have had to pay for the order for 30 days. This would save me another 5% to 7%.

Don't misunderstand me here, I am not suggesting that Viking is the best source for these items, I am simply showing you that with very little effort you can dramatically reduce your printing. I have however, used Viking (1-800-421-1222) for years and find them to be an excellent company offering quality products and services at competitive prices.

Check prices with local shops, both large and small, and direct mail sources. Also keep an eye out in your trade publications they often are good sources of leads for low price high quality printers. Remember to find out about shipping costs and factor in to the overall price as you compare costs.

Don't forget loss leaders. For example, you may have noticed ads for The Stationary House in the Wall Street Journal. They regularly offer 500 raised lettering business cards for $10.95. This is a 50% savings off their normal prices. Most printers would charge you $20 just for the set up. This is, of course, a loss leader to get you on the mailing list and hopefully to get you to purchase other things. You have no obligation to do this at all. Taking advantage of loss leaders can save you significant money.

Make sure you are soliciting price quotes and doing business only with the printers that normally engage in the type of work you need. This sounds obvious but it very frequently is not the case. For example, one and two color jobs should be handled at print shops that specialize in one and two color work not four color work.

Ask the printers you are considering for samples of jobs similar to the one you need that they have done for other companies. Then call those companies and verify that the shop did the job for them and find out how they were to work with. Ask about adherence to the quote and quality. Also ask other businesses you know who they use, why, and for what type of work. You are looking for quality and price not just one or the other.

You must be buying right. Much of the cost of printing is in the fixed costs and setup or make ready costs. As a result small printing jobs of almost any type will have a high per unit cost. To avoid this and reduce those per unit costs significantly, you must monitor your needs and buy your printing accordingly.

For example, 100 printed sheets might cost you $50 while 1000 sheets might only cost you $100. If you don't know your needs or buying patterns you are going to be overpaying by 25%, 30%, 40% or more. The more you can buy at one time the lower your per unit cost will be. Of course, you should only buy what you need and can use within a reasonable time period.

I know of one company that sells note cards to banks for closed accounts and new accounts. They sell these starting at a quantity of 100 and go up to any quantity the buyer wants. They have hundreds of customers who purchase small quantities of the same card 3 or 4 times a year. If these customers monitored their buying patterns they would realize this and instead of buying an order for 250 cards 4 times a year they would buy 1,000 once a year or at least 500 twice a year. The per card price would drop by over 40%. I doubt they have very many other uses for their money than using it to reduce a cost 40%.

Are you paying full price for overage? When you have a product printed the printer will always factor in more paper than they need to protect themselves against spoilage, allow for make ready, and to use in the event of a number of other potential problems they may encounter. They also do this so that they can run overage. Overage, they will bill you for.

In Pursuit of Profits. How To At Least Double Your Profits Without Increasing Your Sales.

The amount of paper they factor in can run as high as 20% more than what will be used in the delivered job. In most cases this will not all be needed for make ready and spoilage so what happens to this stock? Stock that could run into the thousands of sheets on a large job. Usually it is run out and delivered to you in the form of overage. Overage is simply an amount over what you actually ordered.

Printers claim they cannot deliver an exact quantity so they have established what they call "printers custom". What this so called custom states is that it is acceptable to deliver a job at a amount up to 10% higher than the amount ordered or as low as 10% under the amount ordered and the job is considered complete. This must be like working for Congress when you can make up your own self-serving rules.

I would guess that 99.9% of the time jobs are delivered with an over amount not an under amount. If a job is delivered short it is probably due to an error on their part since from the very first stage they have planned to provide overage. An error they expect you to pay for!

The reason they do this is very simple, they can, in effect, increase their sales by up to 10% on every job. If they tell you there is any other reason for constantly shipping amounts up to 10% over what you ordered they are lying to you. This, of course, is done at your expense since you are being stuck with up to 10% more pieces than you need with a cost up to 10% higher than you expect to pay. This is highly profitable for the printer as they will be charging you the full per unit price for this overage while most of their costs have already been covered in the base run.

There are a number of ways you can control this. One is to provide the paper yourself. This will be covered more in a later strategy. Another is to state very clearly on your purchase order that normal printing customs do not apply and you will not pay for the overage. Since the purchase order is the contract that you are agreeing to purchase under, these are the terms they agree to if they accept the job. This will be covered more in my strategies on purchasing.

Another way is to negotiate a lower rate for any overage before you award the job. I would suggest a 50% reduction in selling price for all amounts over what you requested. The printer will still make a profit and you will reduce this added cost by 50%.

One more way would be to order less than you need anticipating they will deliver more than you request. Be careful if you do this, since this could be the one time they deliver the correct amount or a shorted amount.

You can use the leftovers. Total cost control is achieved not only by saving large amounts of money, but also by saving a penny at a time. When you have jobs printed, most often the paper they are printed on will not be an exact fit to the item you are having printed. They will be cutting smaller sheets out of a larger sheet in order to print your job or they will be trimming part of the larger sheet off after printing your job. Either way the end result is scrap paper left over. Have your printer make this into pads of scrap paper for your use. The size won't matter and you will be able to reduce an office supply cost.

For many of the printing jobs you do providing paper to the printer can save you significant amounts of money and allow you to better control the overage you receive. Most printers won't like this. That is too bad. You are not in business to make the printer happy, he should be in business to make you happy. The reason they don't like this is because:

• They buy the paper and mark up the cost 20% to 30% on average.

• They combine the paper needs for your job with those for other jobs to get a lower overall per thousand sheet paper cost. These savings are not necessarily passed on to you but instead kept as added profit.

• They can control the overage levels they produce for you.

You can, and should, order the paper directly from the paper distributor and have it sent to the printer. This is a very simple process and the paper distributor will usually only require that the order is at least $200. All you need to do is have each printer give you price quotes specifying the paper (stock), the cost, the size sheet they are using, and the quantity they will need. You need to know nothing about paper.

They, or your designer, specify it and you can now simply call up the paper distributor and request a cost based on the same specifications. Since you have already requested a detailed price breakdown from the printer on the quote you can easily see what your savings are. You can also verify with the paper distributor that the quantity the printer is requesting is the right amount and right size based on the job he is printing.

Depending on the size and type of job you are having done the savings can be significant. For example, I know one company that has an outside printer print 450,000 calendars for them each year. This job requires about 150,000 sheets of paper.

If they let the printer purchase the paper it would cost them $172.50 per thousand sheets. By ordering it from the distributor and having it delivered to the printer their cost is $132.50 per thousand sheets. They save $40 per thousand sheets or $6,000 per year. How much effort does this take? One phone call lasting about 2 minutes.

At a pretax profit ratio of 2.5%, this savings adds a profit amount to their bottom line equal to a sales increase of $240,000. Imagine that. One 2 minute phone call equates to the same profit margin as a $240,000 increase in sales. Since their average sale is $400, this one 2 minute phone call is equal to the average net pretax profit they would make from 600 orders. Furthermore, their average salesperson sells only $240,000 per year. They have effectively produced a net profit with this one phone call equal to the efforts of a full time sales representative. **This is what total cost control is all about. This is how you must learn to think and analyze your costs and profits.**

If you deal with the same printer often enough and provide the paper most of the time, you will find that they will start offering to match the prices that you can purchase the paper for. They will do this because they can still combine your paper purchase with the stock needed for other jobs and get an overall volume discount (paper prices are actually based on total weight bought). They are still able to make a small profit on your job and a larger profit on other jobs.

Once you have reached this point with your printer you no longer have to act as the middleman. All you need to do is verify that they are giving you the same price that you could buy it direct for. If you are a large buyer of printing and use a number of outside printers you may still want to provide the stock since you can get combined weight paper purchases from the paper company regardless of where they are being sent.

You can contact your local paper merchants by looking in the yellow pages under "paper" and "paper distributors". You will find that some paper distributors will have minimum purchase requirements and others will not, so shop around.

If you ignore that advice, at least consider this. For those of you who will not do this, even though you can save tens of thousands of dollars, let me give you an alternative way to save on your paper costs. Just request that the printer provide you with a price quote with and without paper included. They will know that you are thinking of providing paper and are comparing costs. Normally this will result in a much lower paper cost for you. Just by doing this you should save 10% to 15% on the paper cost due to a reduced mark up from the printer.

The strategy of providing paper to printers or at least making them think you might be providing paper, can save you a great deal of money over the course of the year with no sacrifice in quality, delivery, or change in suppliers.

You must be concerned with what is best for you not your printer. As pointed out in an earlier strategy printers have invented their own self-serving policy called "Printers Custom" which allows them to deliver 10% more or 10% less than you ordered and still consider the job acceptable. My earlier strategy showed you how to neutralize this custom and put purchasing control back where it belongs -- in your hands.

If you do not follow my earlier strategies, this strategy is for those times when the printer ignores it's own custom and ships you an amount over the 10% they claim is acceptable. What should you do in cases like this? Simple, refuse to pay for anything over the 10%. They set up their own rules, make them live by them. If you order 10,000 flyers and they deliver 12,000 that is their problem not yours. Do not let it become your problem or your cost. Do not pay for the extra 1,000 flyers and refuse to pay for the related shipping costs. Do not ship them back to the printer, this will cost you time and money.

Simply notify them in writing that you will not pay for them and if they want them back they should come and get them at their expense and by a specific date or you will dispose of them and bill them for the cost. Upon receipt of this notification they will normally do one of two things. They will either advise you to keep the extra 1,000 at no charge or they will try to get you to buy them at a reduced per unit figure. They must do one of these two things since they are of no use to them and if they pick them up they will incur a cost and then another cost to dispose of them.

If these flyers can be used by your company you should be able to very easily, either get them for no charge, or for up to 80% off the per unit cost.

The flip side of the problem outlined above is when they ship you less than 10% under the quantity ordered. This will happen infrequently and when it does it means someone really screwed up at the printer. They want overruns to increase sales not shortages. If this happens do not pay the bill until they rerun at least the amount needed to comply with their own 10% under industry standard.

Do not let their problem become yours. If, for example, you ordered 10,000 flyers and they only delivered 8,000 you are short by at least 1,000 to comply with their 10% under custom. If you must go back on press at your cost later to run such a small quantity it will cost you at least 50% or more per unit than the per unit rate you paid on the first run of 8,000.

This is because the setup costs are now spread out among only 1,000 or 2,000 units instead of the 10,000 you ordered to begin with. Don't put your company in this situation. You have a legal right, and, indeed, a fiscal obligation, to force them to live up to the terms of the order. Do not pay for the amount ordered and then wait for the shortage to be delivered later. This may never happen. By not paying until the order is properly fulfilled you are providing them a tremendous incentive to rerun the order very quickly and deliver it to you so they can secure payment.

Speaking of payment, do not consider the bill due until the order is complete. If they deliver the short amount today and the rerun is not delivered for another three weeks, I consider the entire bill due 30 days from the latter delivery date.

Establish ownership of materials up front. When you purchase printing jobs of any type your purchase order should specify that all artwork and films created from that artwork are to be owned by you and should be returned to you upon completion of the job. You should also have a stamp made up that states this and states that no invoices will be paid unless these materials are returned to you.

Why? You should understand that the ownership of artwork, films, and negatives is often a very confusing one and one that can become a very expensive problem to you.

Another printers custom is that they will often claim ownership to many of the materials created in conjunction with your job. You pay to have the work done and they claim ownership. What a deal. They do this because they have more leverage over you in forcing you to rerun a job with them. If they have possession of the materials you need to rerun a job they have a great deal of control over you. What else would they want it for? What possible use could they have for your materials? None. They want control.

We want control and options, we do not want to be controlled or pay a cost to remove that control. If we do not have the materials we need to rerun the job where we want, then we will either be forced to recreate those materials or to rerun them with the same printer as before.

Depending on the complexity of a job, number of colors, and size of the run, a rerun of a job can save you 5% to 30% over the cost of the first run. But only if you use the same printer or have films or plates. This will eliminate the need for much of the prepress work needed. You want the artwork in case the films and plates can't be used by the alternative printer that you want to rerun the job with, or in case something happens to the other materials, or in the event modifications or revisions are needed.

Don't be held hostage by self-serving printers customs and don't allow yourself to be forced into paying for something twice. You should establish a safe area to store the artwork that is being returned. Artwork should be kept in a separate place than plates and films. This way if something happens to the art or to the films you can still work from the other.

A final note on this issue. If they do not return your art or materials for any reason including claiming to lose it, deduct the value of this off your bill. Hundreds or thousands of dollars will have gone into the creation of that artwork (this includes photos, type, illustrations) if it is not returned to you it will cost you to have it done over again in the event you ever have use for it again. This is not a cost you should absorb. Your purchase order should clearly state the return of these materials as a condition of the order. If they did not comply, this is their problem not yours.

Be careful of what you are signing. Printers will often submit quotes for your approval and ask that you sign and return the quote form as indication of your acceptance. This is exactly what you do not want to do. I never have and never will. By signing this quote form you are agreeing to the terms laid out by the printer including agreeing to all those "printers customs".

Take a look at the quote forms you receive and see what is written on the back or in small print somewhere. You may think that by signing this form you are only locking in the price on the quote. Believe me this is not the reason they want you to sign it. They want your agreement, knowingly or not, to their terms.

What you want is control over this process. You want to alter any terms that are not in your favor. You do this by spelling out the terms you are ordering under on your purchase order which clearly indicates the conditions under which you are agreeing to buy. Their acceptance of this purchase order shifts control back to you. Remember who the customer is and remember what your goals are.

In Pursuit of Profits. How To At Least Double Your Profits Without Increasing Your Sales.

When you pay for artwork including illustrations and photographs make sure you know the terms under which you are buying it. All too often companies paying to use photos or have illustrations made do not understand who owns them and for what they can be used. This can be a very frustrating and costly misunderstanding. The terms of the contract should be very specific and must clearly indicate ownership and uses allowed.

Imagine paying for an illustration to be created that you plan on using for many different projects, you develop a budget and start using the illustrations in ads and flyers or whatever. Then, suddenly, the illustrator contacts you and wants you to stop using his / her illustration or else pay a large added usage fee. Suddenly you are facing a legal battle, unexpected costs or the prospect of stopping your campaign in mid stream. I have seen this occur and a lot worse. It happens because the use and ownership has not been understood or clearly established.

Be very careful when you bid out printing jobs. If you get one quote that is much lower than all the others you may be looking at a low ball quote. This means that the printer is coming in with a very low quote to get your business and may be planning on hitting you with a lot of added charges along the way, ultimately driving your costs up over the others or causing constant delays and headaches for you.

This is unacceptable. To avoid this from happening you must get all costs in writing before you award the job. Understand that the lowest price will not always be your best buy. You must balance quality, service, and price. Price must be a factor, an important factor, but it should never be the only factor when you buy anything, including printing.

Always think about how you use paper when you print or photo copy your own work. For example, an 8 1/2 x 11 sheet of paper can produce four 4 1/4 x 5 1/2 forms or two 5 1/2 x 11 forms. Forms such as credit memos, from the desk of sheets, etc.. One sheet of paper has yielded 2 to 4 times the number of items. Instead of 500 sheets of paper cut down to yield one form, by proper design and use of stock, that 500 sheets of paper can yield up to 500 sheets each of 4 forms.

You must get quotes up front. If you are dealing with an advertising agency or design house make sure that they give you an estimate of all costs from creative through finished product for any printer piece or ad that they are recommending to you.

You must know all costs up front not after the expensive creative process has been completed. You want these cost estimates to be broken down to show the costs for each area separately and not all lumped together and you want the specifications of the job to be included. With this information in hand you can price out the job on your own and solicit modifications to the design as discussed in previous strategies.

By pricing out on your own you are able to see how effectively the agency is proposing to spend your money and how large their mark up really is. You want to control your costs from start to finish.

Make sure that all bids for any product you order, especially printed products and forms, include the delivered cost. Depending on how the products are shipped and from where, the cost of delivery can be a major portion of the job and must be factored into your evaluation of the price quotes.

Paper is very heavy, don't underestimate the cost to deliver it. If you have any doubts as to the validity of a shipping charge from the printer don't pay the bill until they provide proof of the actual costs they incurred.

Unless they used their own truck, this simply means they must show you a copy of the bill they received for shipping your material. We have discussed this in other sections.

You should price out your form needs as custom jobs with a local printer, a printer who specializes in forms, and a direct mail forms house. You should also be aware that many of the companies who sell forms do not print them, instead they just act as a middleman and farm the jobs out to other printers or act as brokers. This may or may not mean that they are more costly, that depends on many factors. This will not be important to you because you are bidding out your forms to a wide variety of sources. By shopping the different sources available to you, you will find prices that will differ by up to 50% or more.

Can you do it yourself ? For all forms that are not multi part, consider photocopying them yourself instead of paying to have them printed. This will allow you the flexibility of running only what you need as you need them and of modifying them with no waste of existing inventory.

Standardize form size whenever possible. This will enable you to gang run form orders more easily, it simplifies filing, and saves time in setting up for your computer processing.

Is that form the right size? This is a very common problem with many companies. All too often the form mentality is 8 1/2 x 11. Many companies have all forms this size. Are you guilty of this? Whenever possible reduce the size of your forms from a larger standard size to a smaller standard size to reduce your paper and reproduction costs. Ask the questions? Why is that form that size? Should it be smaller since you only use part of the form? For example, are you using an 8 1/2 x 11 invoice form when your invoices are all only two or three lines on average? Should it be larger since your are often using two or three forms for the same task? Think and ask the questions. Your goal is to eliminate as much waste as you can.

Another word for convenience is often laziness. Buying forms from your data processing company may be the most convenient way to purchase for you, but it will rarely be the most cost effective way. Like anything else in life the easiest way is rarely the best way. Often your data processing company may include forms in the overall costs they give you for handling your data processing needs. This might be presented as a benefit to you since one cost covers it all so to speak, but what they are really doing is burying the cost so you do not notice or know what you are paying.

Bid out your form needs on a 12 month supply basis. Have your printer or forms house give you prices based on what you use on an annual basis. Then have them ship and bill you only what you need each month or quarter. You are buying on total volume this way but only paying for what you need when you need it. Your savings will be significant when compared to purchasing only what you need, as you need it, and paying prices based on this lower volume. If your current suppliers won't work with you on this basis drop them and bid your forms needs out on this basis with other form providers. You should have no trouble finding many who will since they are locking your business up for 12 months at a time.

Buy standard forms for all you cannot create on your own your computer. Standard forms are offered for any and every type of form you could ever need. You can buy standard forms from local printers, quick print shops, direct mail form houses, and direct mail office supply outlets. These are forms that are already produced and you simply have your company information imprinted onto the existing form.

In Pursuit of Profits. How To At Least Double Your Profits Without Increasing Your Sales.

These are very professional high quality forms and will save 50% or more off the cost of producing your own custom forms. I can think of few reasons to use a custom form today. Maybe you can, but if you follow my advice you should be thinking of how you can use a standard form to save money and not why you should be using a custom form. You must adjust your thinking.

Don't create new forms even if you are unhappy with the available selection of standard forms or if you feel they do not meet your needs. The cost to design and typeset a form can run into the hundreds of dollars. Instead of reinventing the wheel go to the bookstore or library (1st choice) and pick up a forms book. These are books that will include a wide variety of existing designs for almost any type of form you could ever need. They are sold for you to copy and use as you want with no violation of copyright laws. You can also modify the design if it does not match your needs exactly. If you can't use a standard design at least try to use a design from a form book it could save you hundreds of dollars.

Do you even need that form? Review all the forms you use once a year and consider what you use these forms for. Ask the questions. You want to eliminate all unneeded forms and if you are like most companies, you have unneeded forms. As your business changes your form needs will change. You cannot afford to waste money and space inventorying obsolete forms. Look at all your forms with an eye toward reformatting so that one form can do the work of two or more forms.

Look to see if you can alter the forms to make them more efficient. A form that requires less paper or parts will cost less. A form that is laid out in a manner that allows for faster processing will reduce labor costs and errors. A poorly designed form will not only result in more errors, but can also take 3 to 4 times longer to process than a properly designed and laid out form.

Look at what banks have done. Instead of having a separate loan application form for personal loans, auto loans, home equity loans, boat loans, or any other type of loans, many now have one all purpose loan form. They have replaced many forms with just one. By doing this they have reduced inventory by not having to carrying quantities of less frequently used forms and they have improved buying efficiency by being able to purchase one form in larger quantities, thereby generating a lower per form cost.

Think. Ask the questions. Can you use the front and back instead of two pages? Should it have another part to save photocopy costs and time? Ask your forms salesman for ideas if you can't think of any. If you can reduce the number of forms you use or, make those you do use more efficient, you will save on labor, space, printing, inventory, and, depending on the form, postage.

Duplicate, redundant, and inefficient forms negatively affect your labor costs including filing and processing costs, storage costs, and photocopying costs. Beyond the obvious savings in form costs, these peripheral costs can run into thousands of dollars each year.

Whenever possible you should plan your printing runs so that you can gang up your printed pieces. You want to put as many products, forms or promotional materials as you can on the same printer's form. All you need to do is plan ahead so that all materials using the same stock and colors can be run at the same time. The savings in running costs and setup costs can be significant.

Help your printer and help yourself. Contact the printers you work with on a regular basis and ask them to advise you whenever they have space on one of their printing forms that is comprised of the same colors and stocks you use for your various internal and external materials.

You see, printers normally print on large sheets of paper in order to run as many pieces at one time as they can. This allows them to reduce time and materials thereby offering a more competitive price and increased profits. The sheets they run come in precut sizes. The major draw back with this is that rarely does the sheet they are using allow for a perfect fit of the pieces they are printing. This means that a portion of the sheet they are running is not used. They simply cannot fit everything they are printing perfectly on the sheet.

This is where you come in. They have waste and you have a need. They are running a sheet through the press that has empty space on it. A sheet that has already been paid for by another customer. You see, when they price the job they have no choice but to factor in the wasted paper. The main customer is paying for the run through the press and the unusable portion of the paper.

This spells opportunity to you and the printer. An opportunity for you to save huge amounts of money and an opportunity for the printer to make added profit on a run that is already paid for. By running your job on this unused portion you should be able to get your printed pieces completed for pennies on the dollar.

Don't just think of your promotional materials. Think of anything you use that is printed. Better yet, let your printer know ahead of time the types of printed materials you use and they can advise you when they are running a suitable form that has space available.

The more flexible you can be the more opportunities you will have to save money. If you can order ahead of time, or change colors and stock to match those of the run with space open on it, you should have numerous chances to secure cut rate printing prices.

Chapter 25.   Purchasing including office supplies and inventory.

"More people should learn to tell their dollars where to go instead of asking where they went."

Roger Babson

The strategies I will be discussing here apply to all areas of your company. From purchases of office supplies to purchases of inventory and equipment, I will show you how to save money. I will also be giving you a few strategies designed to reduce your purchasing needs by reducing your use of certain items.

Do not be limited by the application I have chosen to demonstrate here. I have said that before and I will say it again. All too often people do not look beyond the obvious. They will read what I have written and think that it does not apply to them since they do not use that product or buy those items. Don't you be guilty if this. Think how can you? Think where can you use that strategy? Improve, adapt, and modify what I have written to apply it to your company. Think can, not can't!

Always try to negotiate better deals with your current suppliers.   Call them. Tell them you are happy with their current service but you must get better prices. If you are not bidding out jobs and purchases, as you should be, tell them you are going to have to start getting bids. Tell them you want to give them a chance to provide better prices rather than just be dropped for a lower cost vendor.

If you feel uncomfortable doing this due to long term relationships or anything else, blame someone else. **Tell them your boss is forcing this or changing policies, blame your accountant, your banker, your silent partner, the Easter bunny, or anyone else you want to, but do it.** Make sure you stress to them that you want to continue doing business with them but forewarn them that changes are coming. You must control prices better and cut costs.

It has been my personal experience that in over 75% of the cases you will get better pricing than you have been getting simply by doing this. Getting a customer is very costly. Most companies will give on price to keep the customers they have. **By just telling your suppliers that you must have better prices you should be able to add thousands, tens of thousands, hundreds of thousands, or even tens of millions of dollars, depending on your size, directly to your bottom line.**

In fact, depending on your volume of outside purchases and current levels of profitability, you may be able to easily double your profits with this one strategy.

Think about this. If you are a company with sales of $1,000,000,000 and you are spending 50% of all your income on some type of outside purchases you are spending $500,000,000 per year in some type of purchasing activity. If you can get your suppliers to reduce prices by only 1% you have just added $5,000,000 to your bottom line. If you can get a 5% reduction you will add $25,000,000 to your bottom line. A 10% reduction would add $50,000,000 directly to your bottom line profit.

Now if your profit ratio was 2.5% last year this means you made $25,000,000 in profits. **The 5% reduction I have outlined above has just doubled your profits and the 10% reduction has just enabled you to triple your profits. It really is this simple!**

Many suppliers take your business for granted. Now that they risk losing some, or all of it, they will use a sharper pencil on prices to your company. The fear of competition and of losing your business will serve to drive prices down in the majority of cases.

Let me give you a couple of small examples. We had a trash disposal contract with one of the largest waste disposal companies in the country. I had no problems with the service. In fact, I had no complaints at all. However, by calling and telling them that I needed to reduce my trash disposal costs and that I was going to shop around for a lower cost disposal company, I was able to secure 20% off our current rate within a few hours.

Using this same strategy I was able to secure discounts from a paper distributor that averaged nearly 20%, which amounted to tens of thousands of dollars per year of added profit!

Stop thinking about minimizing your price increases and start thinking about lowering your current costs! You should use this strategy with every single vendor you have. You should find that 50% to 75% of all your current vendors will respond with price rollbacks of at least 5% to 15%.

A very simple way to reduce costs is to express disappointment over the first proposal from any vendor for any product and service. By the time your discussions reach the point of your vendor making a proposal they have invested time and money. They will also have an emotional attachment to this proposal since it has progressed to this point. When you tell them that you had hoped for better prices or terms or whatever, your chances of getting a rapid concession in the area questioned is very high.

Of course, you can't do this all the time with every proposal and, in fact, you won't need to. By selectively using this strategy you will accomplish your goals with many other proposals beyond just those you question. The reason for this is that your vendors will expect that you will request lower prices and they will build them into your proposal. I know you might be thinking just the opposite will occur. You are thinking that they will make the price higher or the terms poorer so that they have room to move if you object.

However, since you are only raising objections on selected proposals they will never know if they will be given the opportunity to revise their proposal. Therefore, they will feel compelled to come in very favorable right up front. You have set the expectations. You must be fair. You should not do this two or three times on the same proposal. You should only do this when you clearly sense that you can secure a better deal.

Check your vendor or supplier list. If you find that your people are dealing only with 1 or 2 sources for each of your purchases your people are simply not shopping around no matter what they tell you. The only exception to this would be if they are employing a strategy of using one primary supplier to maximize their leverage and a secondary supplier to back up the primary supplier. This will rarely be the case when you find your company is single source purchasing.

It will normally be a case of favoring a supplier, an attitude of "it's not my money", or pure laziness. It could also point the way to a conflict of interest situation that might exist between your buyer and a supplier. If they are using a primary supplier and a secondary supplier to back up the primary supplier, make sure that you are verifying the primary supplier was chosen on the best value for your company and not for any other reason. Also make sure at least once a year, preferably every 6 months, a review is conducted to verify this is still the best supplier for you and if not, change primary suppliers.

In Pursuit of Profits. How To At Least Double Your Profits Without Increasing Your Sales.

Never forget that business is business. It is not personal. Do not take it personally. If you are negotiating with a supplier and you are unable to get the price or terms you are seeking then just walk. Thank them for their time, tell them you simply can't do business with them at that price or for those terms, advise them to contact you if they are able to improve their proposal, and then end the meeting.

Do not argue. Do not antagonize them. Be professional and be polite. Let them know clearly that you would like to do business with them (if this is the case) but you simply cannot at this price or those terms. Explain your objectives and how you must get a certain price or terms. If you feel more comfortable blame a third party as I have suggested in another strategy.

When you do this one of three things will happen.

1) They let you walk and do nothing.
2) They make you a counter offer right then and there.
3) They call later and offer you better terms or a better price.

Two of these three accomplish your objective. A 66% chance of success. I'll take those odds every day!

Put most of your eggs in one basket. For many smaller businesses this will be a very effective strategy. By this I mean use one or, even two, primary suppliers for the majority of all your needs in each area of your business. Up to 90%. Use a secondary supplier for the remaining 10%.

By doing this you will gain significant leverage with your primary supplier in the areas of cost, supply, and service. You will be a more important customer to them. You will also be protecting yourself by having a secondary source. If something happens to the primary supplier and they can no longer effectively fill your needs in the manner you require, you can turn to the secondary supplier.

Under no circumstances should you have one source handling 100% of your purchasing needs for any area of your business. If they can't deliver what you need you may be the one to go out of business. This is single source purchasing and it will rarely, if ever, result in you getting the best value for your money and it almost always places you in a vulnerable situation regarding price, quality, and dependability.

The secondary supplier will be a back up source and will also serve to keep your primary supplier on their toes. Having each know of the existence of the other will result in the primary supplier working hard to eliminate the risk of them becoming the secondary supplier and the secondary supplier will be working hard to replace the primary supplier. Under the right circumstances this can be a highly effective cost control strategy. I have used it in the past in a number of areas with different companies with resulting savings in each case that exceeded 25%.

Don't buy all your routine supply needs from one company. This may seem to be a time saving cost effective way to purchase your office products but it is really nothing more than the lazy persons way of purchasing. This is single source buying. Never single source buy. If you do I will guarantee you that you are not getting the best value for each and every one of your purchases. Remember my earlier comments. Yes, a primary source and a secondary source to keep the primary source honest and back them up can be an effective purchasing strategy, as long as you are verifying their value compared to others in the market at least every 6 months.

But no, buying from a single source only, should never be allowed. Not even for smaller routine needs. Not only will you most likely not be getting the best value for your money but you are also very vulnerable without a back-up. A single source may or may not offer you the best value on some products or services but you can be damn sure that they will not offer the best value on all products or services.

If you ignore my advice and deal only with one supplier or deal primarily with only one supplier you must: 1) Verify at least every 6 months that you are getting the best value. You do this by comparing prices and service. **2)** Use the leverage you have in this relationship to get concessions from the supplier. Concessions such as added products, lower prices, better turnaround, free delivery, extended warranties, reduced service costs, etc..

Who is doing your purchasing and what experience do they have? Let me tell you a story about when I first joined one company. At that time all their office supply needs were filled by a local office supply store. The people at the store, and the reps who called on them, were very nice dependable people.

The products they carried were brand name quality products. Delivery was free and always on time. Over the years the people in the company who ordered these types of products had developed a very nice and very loyal relationship with those at the office supply store. In many ways you might say they enjoyed the perfect customer / supplier relationship. All parties involved seemed to be very pleased.

Other sources were never considered. Why should they be? After all they never had a problem with this supplier and they always had more important things to worry about than where they purchased their office supplies didn't they? A comfort zone existed and purchasing of all office supplies was bought from one source, never even thought about, and buying was based solely on convenience and personal loyalty.

That was the attitude. To compound things, they had people purchasing these products that had no formal training and no qualifications to do so. This would not have mattered as much if those doing the buying had an attitude of total cost control. Since they did not, the situation that existed here was deadly to any cost control and cost reduction efforts. This is exactly the situation that exists in companies large and small all over this country regardless of what the industry happens to be.

When I came in and advised them we would be changing procedures in this area and, as a result, we would be reducing costs for the exact same products by up to 70% you can imagine the reaction. My ears were ringing as I am sure behind my back the mixture of laughter and resentment was spreading throughout the company.

The problem was that people felt I was criticizing them. They felt I was indicating that they had been doing a poor job. They resented this. They, on the other hand felt they were doing a very good job and that I was both foolish and ignorant to suggest that such savings were possible.

They were wrong on both counts. They were not doing a poor job. They were doing a job that was not part of what they were hired to do. They had no skills in this area or training. They had no incentive to do anything but whatever got the job done with the least amount of work involved so they could return to doing what their real job was. You see, the hour or two they spent each week on purchasing related activities was an unwelcome intrusion on their main responsibilities. They received no added compensation for the function and were offered no incentive to seek the best value.

No, I was not suggesting they were doing a poor job. Any deficiencies that existed here were solely the responsibility of management who thought so little of the purchasing function that they thrust it upon people who did not want to do it and had no training in how to properly do it. This is very typical of many businesses in this country today. What I was stating was that the job could be done better. Much better.

By now you are probably thinking what is the big deal? How much could these purchases add up to? Could my time not have been better spent on more important issues? Well, at this company annual office supply purchases exceeded $20,000. If I could reduce these costs by only 50% I would save over $10,000 the first year and $100,000 over ten years. I could also make a statement to the employees about the importance of total cost control.

I knew this type of reduction could be made with very little effort since all purchases were being made out of a catalog from this local office supply store and all prices paid were list prices. I knew this meant that the company was overpaying for each and every item by up to 70%. The resentment lasted awhile as it was difficult for them to severe ties with long time sales reps, but within two years we had reduced costs in this area by over 50% without sacrificing a thing.

This was a savings of over $10,000. At that time that company had a pretax profit ratio of 1.5%. This means that this $10,000 savings added an amount to the bottom line that was equal to an increase in sales of over $660,000. This would have been equal to a 25% increase in sales for them at that time. Think about this. Since the previous year's profit for that company was just over $20,000, the savings in just this one area increased profits by 50%.

It was done by using the same strategies that I am showing you here. Today, these same employees have a great deal of confidence in their purchasing capabilities and find it challenging to find the best value and exciting when they get it.

I know of another company that had a secretary purchasing office supplies for them and she was purchasing all pens and pencils in a special blue color. No one ever questioned why this blue color was chosen. It turns out that the color was chosen merely because the woman doing the buying liked the color.

What was the problem? The problem was that each of these pens and pencils had to be produced as a custom item due to the color the woman ordered and as a result the cost was 5 times as much as the same pen or pencil cost in a standard color. These types of things happen day in and day out.

Most employees and, in fact, owners in small and mid sized businesses in this country, have no formal training in cost effective purchasing, cost control, or expense reduction. It has been estimated that in over 80% of the small businesses most office supplies are purchased by secretaries or administrative assistants.

Employees who have little interest in doing the job, little or no formal training in how to do the job, and are most likely to look to the easiest most convenient way to do the job. Not very conducive to a program of total cost control is it? Don't let your company be among this 80%. It has also been estimated that most businesses overpay for daily and routine purchases by up to 30%. Don't let your company be one of these businesses.

You must provide training. You must establish policies and procedures and you must ensure that they are followed. You must have objectives and they must include best value purchasing goals. Accept nothing less. There is no reason to!

Make sure only authorized personnel can purchase anything. If you allow anyone who needs anything to purchase whatever they need, even if it is small quantities of office supplies, you have a serious problem. All purchases must be authorized and funneled through one central purchasing group or individual, This is the only way you will be able to control the process and this is the only way you will be able to maximize your purchasing power.

Can buying or producing in bulk result in significant savings? Yes, but only if this is the most effective use of the money (see section on this) and if what you purchase or produce will be called for and used in a reasonable period of time. By buying or producing unrealistic quantities to drive unit costs down, without reasonable expectations of use or sales that demand these quantities, you are losing money.

If you think "who would do this?" let me give you an example. I know one company that printed small folders for sale to banks. They wanted to realize a lower unit cost to make the selling price more attractive. They had no basis to project sales on. To realize a low per unit cost in production they produced 250,000 folders. This enabled them to offer the product at a low unit cost.

All sound good so far? Well, over the next 5 years they sold a total of 10,000 folders. The other 240,000 were thrown out. **Quite a savings, don't you think?** They also ran the risk of spoilage and product obsolescence.

They should have found a way to project sales. They should have used that projection to base production and pricing on anticipated sales and then they should have ran run only a small test quantity until projected sales turned into actual sales. Never forget that unless what you are buying is needed and can be used in a reasonable period any price you pay is too high!

Remember lead don't be led. If certain conditions of the sale are objectionable to you, don't purchase. If any areas of the contract are unclear, get clarification. If any areas of the contract are objectionable to you don't sign or strike out that section and have the sales rep initial the change along with you. If an addendum is needed to have a written record of things not in the contract then add one.

Just because the rep says something is standard, or that the contract is preprinted, or tells you that is how the company operates, so what? You are the customer, you dictate terms. You must understand the positioning in this relationship. Nothing happens until you say so. The key part of that sentence is "you say so".

You must analyze all your purchasing patterns at least once a year. You must ensure that your purchasing patterns are the most effect ones for your buying habits. You should be looking at quality, prices, and delivery. The goal is to get the best of all three.

Find out if your purchases are being delivered on time. Is the quality of the items acceptable? Are you buying in the right quantities based on your annual usage? The right quantities are the quantities that yield the lowest price per unit. In other words, are you buying an item every 3 months when instead you could be ordering it every 6 months and realize a 15% to 25% savings based on the higher volume? Ask the questions. They are the key to your program of total cost control!

Don't fall prey to unsolicited phone sales calls. These are the type of scams that costs businesses millions of dollars each year. The calling party will offer overpriced, poor quality products. The sales pressure is very high and can range from pushy and aggressive to very friendly and sneaky. These people could sell a mongoose to a snake. I think many of them must be retired politicians. Before you know it one of your people has given approval for a product that you do not need or want. Tens of millions of dollars are lost in this manner each year.

Think of this as a predator and prey relationship. Guess which one you are?

Your best defense? Hang up. If anything sounds fishy it probably is. They will offer close-out specials, deals on over buys, canceled orders they are liquidating, and any one of a hundred other scams to make their offers not only sound legit, but like a very good deal.

Demand that any and all offers be submitted to you in writing. Since you are following my strategies and you do not allow any order to be placed over the phone, and since you require purchase orders to be written and cross checked before any bill is paid, you should be safe from these types of scams. You are utilizing these type of procedures aren't you?

Even if you needed, or normally bought, such items you can be darn sure the price of these is much too high and the quality is sub par at best. Often they will also offer a free gift just for the party approving the order and will even send it to their home just so it is between your employee and the scam company. They do this for two reasons, first it sweetens the pot in an effort to get the sale and secondly, it gives the sales company strong leverage if your company tries to void the sale by refusing to pay for the merchandise or trying to return it.

If the person who approved the purchase tries to send it back or refuse payment, the first question they will be asked is how did they like the free gift. They are being reminded that they took something to buy something. They are indirectly being threatened that others will be told and they may get in trouble.

Make sure that you get everything in writing. I know that this sounds obvious and is anything but new advice, however, you will be amazed at the number of times your people, and even you, do not abide by this rule. You must know all costs to effectively evaluate your purchase. You must know the performance expectations. You must know the ongoing consumable cost. You must know maintenance costs. You must know training costs. You must know shipping costs. You must know anything and everything that applies to whatever it is that you are considering purchasing.

You can't afford a misunderstanding over what you are buying, how many you are buying, what you are paying, what the terms are, when delivery is scheduled, or any one of a number of other concerns. You must get this all in writing from the suppliers and you must reference these terms on your purchase order or change any terms that are not satisfactory to you on your purchase order.

The only way to know these things for sure is to get them in writing. What you are told by the sales rep means nothing. Don't assume anything. Get it in writing.

Make sure that you read the small print and that you understand all terms and conditions under which you are agreeing to buy anything. Again, this may seem obvious but it is rarely done. Most people do not take the time to read the small print . They take the sales rep at their word (big mistake) or they are afraid to ask for clarification lest they feel stupid. The only time you should feel stupid is if you are buying something without knowing all the details and conditions under which you are buying.

I know of one business owner who signed a contract to lease phone equipment and then 4 years later was shocked to find that he did not own the equipment. He thought he was buying it and not leasing it. He admitted to never reading what he signed and blamed the sales rep for misleading him. The only person he should have blamed was the person in the mirror.

Remember, what is said by the sales person means nothing. The only thing that means anything is what you sign. Also remember, that just because something is written or typed does not mean it can't be changed. I am always amazed at how people feel proposed contracts or agreements cannot be changed.

This of course is exactly what the vendor or supplier wants you to think. This is wrong. Of course they can be changed and most often should be. You should be purchasing on your terms, not theirs. Guess who their standard contracts benefit? You don't care how they normally conduct business or what their terms normally are. Contracts can be rewritten or amended. I have deleted whole sections with a large black magic marker. Modifying a contract is very easy. Just get a marker, take off the cover, and start lining out the sections that you do not agree to. Have all parties initial and keep a copy.

You should request all paperwork that you will be required to sign ahead of time. This will be the best way for you or your people to prevent signing something you do not understand, might not like, or did not even know you were signing. Most often, other than errors caused by just plain laziness, problems occur because the buyer is unwilling to question something at the time they are requested to sign it or they won't take the time to read all details or make changes.

Often the sales rep, and maybe his boss, is there making conversation. You, or the buyer, are distracted and cannot devote full attention to all the small print. Or you might not want to appear ignorant over a term and therefore will not question something. Or you might not be willing to reschedule the meeting so new paperwork can be done as you might feel any detail that seems out of place is only minor and you just want to wrap things up.

There also could be errors made by the vendor in preparing the paperwork. In each case you are put on the spot and feel under pressure. Don't let this happen. Insist that any and all paperwork that will be required during the purchasing process be provided to you well ahead of time so that you can review it, or have others review it, in a non pressure situation.

Remember, what is said means nothing. What is signed means everything. Do not rely on the verbal representation given. I know this is another way of saying what I have discussed earlier but it is so important and I have seen so many people get burned over a misplaced trust in verbal comments regarding price, performance, delivery, and all other conditions, that I feel compelled to restate this point here.

I would strongly suggest that you develop a purchasing policy and written statement to be used for all purchases. Large or small. The elements to be included in your policies have been covered in many other strategies. The written statement would precede all purchases and be given to the supplier to comply with in preparing any proposal. This statement would outline the terms you would purchase under and the items you want spelled out in the proposal they submit to you.

Make all your year-end purchases early in the year if an incentive is offered to do so. If you purchase year-end items of any kind including holiday cards and calendars, make sure that you are finding out the incentives offered to you for purchasing them early in the year. Most companies selling year-end products want to lock your orders up early so that the competition does not. They also want to be able to determine their production schedules and material needs as early as they can so they can realize economies of purchasing and labor.

The only way they can accomplish these things is to get as many orders in as possible early in the year. To do this most companies dealing in the sales of year-end items will give you significant discounts for ordering early. These can be anywhere from 25% to 50% off your purchases depending on the product you buy and the quantity you buy.

Place your order early to get the discounts, but specify that the product should be shipped in the Fall and not billed until then. Do not let procrastination cost you money. Depending on what year-end products you buy and how many, your savings can be significant.

Extra charges - don't pay them. Never pay extra charges unless they are completely justified by changes you have requested and if they had been pointed out to you up front. Many companies will come in with low prices only to bury you with added charges later on. Do not let this happen. If extra charges are not pointed out up front and agreed to by you then do not pay them. If they want to continue to do business with your company they will absorb them.

You must know all charges up front so that you can compare costs among suppliers and so that you know the total bottom line costs involved in any purchase. Hidden charges, or charges that will be tacked onto your bill later, will not enable you to make an informed decision up front about the most cost effective supplier to use.

You should simply get the best price you can and then clearly state on your purchase order that the price you have indicated includes everything. Their acceptance of that purchase order creates a binding agreement indicating the terms you are agreeing to purchase under.

If you switch suppliers for an item that requires set up charges, art charges, plate charges, or any other type of charge that you have already paid for with the original suppliers, do not pay for these again. You have already paid for these items once, do not pay for them again! You have two choices, you can get the material from the original supplier (you did indicate your ownership rights on your PO to that supplier didn't you?) and give it to the new supplier or you can make the new supplier absorb these costs as part of the cost in doing business with you. After all, they now have you as a new customer and they should enjoy reruns and new orders in the future. If they want your business they will gladly do this and will understand your reluctance to pay them again for something that was already paid for by you.

You should be creating a library of sources for each of the items you purchase with any regularity. You must be able to check the basic costs of frequently ordered items in a minimum of time. Having such a library will enable you to search quickly for any item you need on a regular basis. Since items routinely purchased will not be bid out each and every time, the price pages, data sheets, or catalogs you have on hand should be kept current and should be considered a written proposal.

If you can't take the time to look through 3 or 4 catalogs to find the best buy for the product you need then you just are not serious about controlling and reducing your costs. This library should include direct mail sources as well as local companies. You must be able to quickly compare prices for items with three or four sources so that you are not blindly ordering from one source all the time.

Having a library of sources that you can reference will eliminate any excuses about not having time to check for the best deal. For example, on your office supplies you should be on the mailing lists of at least 3 direct mail companies and perhaps a local office super store and warehouse club.

This will enable you to compare costs for all office purchases very quickly. If you sit there and tell me that you can not look through 3 or 4 catalogs to insure that you are getting the best deal on each purchase and that saving 50% or more is not worth the time (because that is exactly what you are saying if you can't do this) then you are just wasting your time and are not serious about controlling and reducing your costs.

Remember, the easiest way to do anything will most often be the most costly way. Laziness, procrastination, and convenience all have steep price tags. Don't you or, your people, pay them.

Take a few minutes right now and test what I am telling you. If you have catalogs from 3 or 4 sources pick out a dozen items that you commonly purchase. Compare the costs of each item and you should see at least a savings of 20% to 50%, or more from one company to another. By being on the mailing lists of these companies you will also be offered monthly specials on many different commonly purchased office supplies that will further increase your savings.

Office supplies should be one of the easiest of all areas for you to save 25%, 40%, or even 50% or more, simply by purchasing the same items from different sources.

Let me also point out, that for any larger purchases you should always call the source or the sales rep for that source, and ask for a better price. Even with direct mail office supply stores the prices on the larger items are not set in stone. I recently ordered a laser printer from a direct mail office supply store. I had checked the prices through other sources including local super stores. The best price I could find was $999.00. I called the direct mail office supply source and told them I needed a better price or I would buy the printer at a local store. They sold it to me for $900 with free delivery. This 1 minute phone call saved me 10% on the purchase price and I did not have to go pick it up. The next day it was delivered to me. I also saved 5% sales tax (on $999.00) since I bought it out of state. The total savings for that 1 minute phone call was $148.95. An hourly rate of $8,937. Do you think this was worth the effort?

Once you go through the process of reviewing suppliers to find the best combination of price, quality, and service you will be saving from then on. You do not need an extensive review each month or each quarter. You only need periodic reviews to determine that the sources you are now using are still the best ones based on your criteria of cost, quality, and service. A periodic review will keep your current suppliers on their toes and insure that you are not falling into the costly trap of complacency and convenience.

"Your answer will determine your actions."

Derrick W. Welch

You must analyze every purchase you intend on making. You must ask yourself the questions. Do we need it? Why? Where are they going? Who uses them? How many are being used? Why are we buying so many? Why are we buying so few? Who else can we get it from? How many should we buy to get the best pricing while making the most efficient use of our cash? What can we use instead? Why do we need that model? Why do we need those options? On and on ask the questions I have outlined. These questions and your answers will be the single most important factor in determining the level of success you have in reducing and controlling costs.

Don't blindly accept the self-described, self-serving, self-established customs of any industry you deal with. While I have covered this in other sections it is so important, and so often blindly accepted, I feel it bears repeating here. For example, I deal with the printing industry a great deal and one of the many self-serving customs this industry has established is that you as a buyer must consider a quantity of 10% too few or 10% too many pieces to be considered as the completion of your order.

This means that if you ordered 10,000 folders and they ship 9,000 you must accept the shortage of 1,000 and consider the job complete. Of course, this is of little use to you if you had to have 10,000 pieces and now must go back and run 1,000 more at a much higher unit cost due to the smaller run. If, on the other hand, they ship you 11,000 this is to be considered acceptable as well and you must pay for the added 1,000 pieces. This will cost you about 10% more than you wanted to pay.

What a deal. They can screw up, ship too few and you must live with it. Or they can increase their sales by shipping you more than you might need or want and you must also pay for it. This must be like working for the government and always knowing someone else will pay for your mistakes.

Don't go along with it. As a tax payer you may have few choices in controlling how your "contributions " are spent, but as a customer of a private business you have a great deal to say about how you are treated and charged.

In the example I have given you I could have indicated on my purchase order that I would pay for only what I was ordering. But wait, some printers have even adopted a "custom" to cover this, they charge extra for exact quantity deliveries. Can you imagine they will try to charge me more for giving me exactly what I ordered?

Don't go along with it. Start your own "buyers custom". You should specify exact amounts and terms on your purchase order at the agreed upon total price. Be very clear that your purchase order states that it supersedes their printers customs. The purchase order is the binding contract. By accepting it you consider the printer to be agreeing with the terms you have indicated on the purchase order.

Clearly indicate this with words to this effect "The purchase order and all indicated terms are the conditions we agree to purchase under and, as such, supersede any and all vendor or industry policies and practices. Acceptance of this purchase order constitutes agreement of this". In fact, a statement such as this should be a standard part of every purchase order and therefore I recommend it be a printed part of the purchase order. If need be, or inapplicable, you can always strike it out. By including it as part of your purchase order you are taking a proactive stance.

If they take your order, as most will, they are bound to your terms. If they do not someone else will. Remember who is the customer. All too many businesses today have forgotten this. Understand I am recommending this strategy for use in all industries, not just with printers. I have merely used printers as an example.

You do not need to be a big company to get big savings. I have shown you many ways to realize savings equal to, or exceeding, those enjoyed by large companies. Follow these strategies, use your common sense and always remember the tremendous impact cost control has on your bottom line and you will quickly find yourself locating top quality sources with low prices for all your purchasing needs.

You should always be thinking of cost reduction in this area not just cost control. Let me show you one way.

Many companies still use loss leaders in an effort to get you to do business with them. You may or may not agree with this type of selling strategy. It doesn't matter. You can use their selling strategy to create an effective buying strategy. Often these companies will sell products at, or even below, cost in an effort to get your business so they can cross sell you other more profitable items or services.

This by no means, obligates or compels you to buy anything else. You can simply buy the loss leader, realize a significant savings and continue to purchase your other products and services from the most cost effective source you can find.

You decide the ethics. While I do not agree with this strategy for the reasons I have outlined earlier, it can be effective and therefore, I feel compelled to share it with you. You can get a price from one supplier (or claim to have a certain price from another supplier) and then inform your other sources of this price. You can then tell them that if they can beat this price they can have the order.

This may indeed help you secure the best price but it does not guarantee the best value. The best value is more important in some purchases than others. The best value remember, is a combination of service, price, and quality. Price is always a factor, a big factor, but rarely should it be the only factor.

I also question the ethics of conducting business in this manner. Would you want your sales people or your company to be treated in this manner? I will advise you this happens all the time but remember the golden rule. Do unto others as you would have them do unto you!

Every time you see the words "list price" ignore them. They mean nothing. Do not ever pay list price. List prices only exist so that discounts can be given.

Buy the steak not the sizzle. You have heard the old adage about selling the sizzle and not the steak. Well, you must do the exact opposite when buying. Look through the hype and advertising and weigh the potential purchase based on the actual benefits and cost. Don't buy just on name and advertising visibility. Purchase based on what it will do for you not what it has been claimed to do for someone else.

Force your suppliers to commit to holding their prices for at least 6 months and preferably 12 months. Consider making this a condition of doing business with your company. This is especially important if you are in a business in which you must hold prices for preset periods of time or if you issue a catalog that forces you to hold prices for a specified period of time. In these instances, unexpected and unplanned price increases from your suppliers will reduce your profit levels. This is unacceptable.

Even if this is not the case with your product line or service it is still very important for you to have your suppliers hold costs to you if at all possible. Constantly changing prices from your suppliers will cost you money in numerous ways and it will hinder your ability to be competitive. For these same reasons you should require advance notice of any planned price increase. This will enable you to have time to find another source or adjust your prices accordingly.

Barter your products and services for those that you need. For example, we purchase the rights to use photographs in one of our products. This product is a 12 page desk calendar. We pay an average of $300 per photo or a total annual cost of about $3,600. We struck a deal with a photographer that he would allow us to use all 12 photos we needed at no cost. In exchange, we would give him 500 calendars printed with his advertising copy on it.

The cost to him for the photos was minimal. The cost to us for the calendars was about $150. We saved over $3,400 and he received calendars he could resell or use for self-promotional purposes. This is a good example of bartering. Look in the yellow pages under bartering or check your regional business to business directory. There you will find companies that do nothing but bring bartering parties together. Please also see my strategies in the marketing section on this topic.

In Pursuit of Profits. How To At Least Double Your Profits Without Increasing Your Sales.

Get angry when you overpay. Damn angry. Do you like getting ripped off? This is exactly what happens every time you or someone from your company overpays for something. And you are the one to blame! You and your people must make it a quest to get the best combination of service, cost, terms, and quality that you can.

"Success consists of a series of little daily efforts."

Mamie McCullough

Don't ignore small savings.   All too often companies overlook small savings. Think of this as money lying all around you and you not bothering to stop and pick it up. This is what is happening when you overlook small savings. If you find 50 ways to save $200 over the course of the year you have saved $10,000. If these savings are in recurring areas of cost over the next ten years you will have saved well over $100,000 when you factor in the increased costs that money you have saved would have incurred.

You must look for large and small ways to save money, cut costs, and control expenses. Small gains in a football game set up the big plays that score the points. Set up the needed mentality with savings in large and small amounts.

Think you run a tight ship? Try this. Put a few boxes around your office and ask all your employees to put any extra office supplies they might have in their offices or desks in these containers. You will be very surprised when you see the volume of things like pens, pencils, paper clips, and the like that gets put in these boxes. In my desk alone I found I had over 30 pens and pencils. Not only will this periodic effort reduce your need to order as many office supplies, but it will also send a message to your employees about how serious you are about controlling and reducing your costs.

Never purchase on price alone. Price should always be a factor in your purchasing evaluation process but never the only factor. You must consider many other costs, including any and all not so obvious costs. I always look for the best combination of price, quality, service, and terms. Without each of these I have not done a very good job in purchasing.

Combine your purchases whenever possible to get the lowest overall price. This may result in no shipping costs or reduced shipping costs, it may result in a lower per unit cost or it may result in some sort of free items. Often you must ask for the discount or benefit.

For example, if you are buying paper, you can combine your purchases of different types of paper to realize an overall lower paper purchase price. Paper is sold based on total pounds bought.   If you look in a paper house price book you will see that the price for each type of paper you buy is priced based on the total amount of paper of that type you are buying. However, if you ask, you will, without question, be able to save 10% to 25% by purchasing paper based on the total weight of all types you are buying.

Looking at office supplies, by ordering a certain level of supplies at one time I am always able to eliminate my shipping costs. If I can reduce $10 of shipping costs when I purchase $100 worth of products, I have reduced my costs by 10%.

Let me give you another example. Often you can get an overall price based on purchasing needs spread out over a certain period of time. Two areas I have done this with in one company are label strips and vinyl cards. They used to buy both of these products based on their needs over a three month time period. This allowed them to realize a small discount, compared to buying as needed, and yet not tie up too much money in inventory.

By suggesting and asking, they are now able to buy both of these products based on a 12 month supply. The manufacturers are able to produce the entire order at the same time and inventory it if they choose. They tie up the business for the full year. They win.

The company wins since they have reduced their costs by over 25% on these items and they only take what they need, when they need it during the year, thereby freeing up cash and reducing inventory and they always have a supply ready for them to take as needed. They only pay for what they take. The manufacturer ships and bills only what is requested each time. If the company has over estimated their needs for that year they simply adjust the order for the next year. If they have underestimated their needs they simply place a small order at the end of the current year.

For the record, this company sells over $250,000 worth of these products a year. By following this strategy they have cut their costs by 25%. Material costs are about 60% of their selling price costs. So they have saved $37,500 with no reduction in service or quality.

At a pretax profit ratio of 2.5% they would need to increase sales by $1,500,000 simply to add this same $37,500 to their bottom line. You must learn to think this way if you are to fully understand the tremendous bottom line impact a program of total cost control can give you!

For over 30 years this company bought what they needed as they needed it. This resulted in a much higher per unit product cost and an ongoing flow of paper work and invoices. The first step to improving their purchasing patterns was to buy based on quarterly usage. This reduced costs significantly. However, you must always be searching for a better way to improve your product and process while lowering your costs. The steps I have outlined represented the efforts to accomplish this for this company in this one area.

Remember the "domino effect of cost control"? If they choose to they can pass some of these cost savings along in the form of reduced prices and still realize a higher profit margin or simply keep the savings as a higher profit. If they reduce the selling price they may sell more and thereby earn an even larger profit. They have also freed up cash since they no longer inventory even 3 months worth of product. They also need less shelf space which means lower facility overhead costs.

Buy out of state? Please check with your accountant on this one as both the federal government and states are always looking for ways to reach into the pockets of business and extract your hard earned profits to fill their pork lined coffers. Your state may have a self-serving law against this strategy. Laws and IRS rules change often. Many times businesses do not even know what the new ones are. You don't think this is intentional do you? Nahh, what was I thinking?

But, if possible, and if it is the most cost effective source, seek to buy your purchasing needs out of state. Often by buying by mail out of state you will not have to pay sales tax on your purchase. This can save you an added 5% to 8%. This can add up to significant savings over the course of the year. For example, if you spend $100,000 per year on office supplies and you can buy them all out of state and save 6% sales tax you have just saved $6,000.

Don't just look at office supplies, look at all your purchasing needs. If you can buy a $3,000 computer in a state with no sales tax you can save $150 to $240 on that purchase.

In my state however, I found out the hard way that a users tax law was quietly passed. In short, this law says that if I buy products out of state and incur no sales tax I must keep a journal of each of these purchases and then remit an amount equal to the current MA sales tax rate. Can you imagine this? I must track all these purchases and assess myself a tax and then remit it. They have forced us to become our own IRS agent. The greed and arrogance of the tax department in this state is perhaps unequaled.

You must check the prices on everything you buy. I mean everything! From fax paper to toilet paper, if you are not seeking to establish the most cost effective source you can you are overpaying. From shipping supplies to computer paper, if you are buying based on convenience, or from the "regular" source, you are overpaying. You must develop and apply purchasing policies to everything you buy. From the once a year purchases to the weekly purchases. Make no exceptions.

Whenever possible buy direct from the manufacturer. It might take a little digging to find the location of the manufacturer but the savings will be worth it. If you are unable to deal directly with the manufacturer try to buy direct from the distributor. Your goal must be to try and eliminate as many middlemen as possible. The closer you can get to the product's origination point the lower your purchase price will be. Each step you can eliminate between you and the manufacturer will save you 15% - 25% or more, compared to the list purchase price of the item in question. This is one reason why so many things can be bought cheaper through direct mail.

Ask any local business you deal with for a discount and an open account. Many times you will deal with a local business for a service or product you might need on a regular basis or even just in a pinch. It is customary for local businesses to give discounts to other local businesses but this will normally not be given unless you ask.

Ask and while you are at it make sure you have them set you up on an open account so you are billed every 30 days for any purchases you made during the month. The goal is to get a discount and have a 30 day float on your purchases. It should go without saying that if they accommodate you and they can use your products and services, you should accommodate them if they ask for the same type of terms.

"Ego will always be satisfied at the expense of your bottom line."

Derrick W. Welch

Always call your suppliers on larger orders and try to get a lower price. I am telling you to do this not only for large orders that you are buying for internal consumption, but also for large orders that involve products, or materials going into products, you will be reselling.

The key here is to let the supplier know (or think) that the order is contingent on them giving you a better price. They must understand that you must get a lower cost from them in order for you to be able to offer your customer a better price. Without this you want the supplier to know that you will not be able to get the order. If you do not get the order they do not get the order.

If the order is for internal use and not for resale or material used in a product for resale, you want the supplier to understand that you expect a better price due to the size of the order and that if they are unable to give it to you someone else will.

Please understand that I am not telling you to do this only if what I have outlined above is true. I am telling you to also do this on large orders as a way of generating higher profits through lower costs. Of course, it should go without saying that in cases where you are trying to sell a large order, price will most always be an issue and this strategy can help you present a more competitive proposal and possibly improve your profit margin.

I have found that 70% of the times that I have sought a price reduction from my suppliers for larger orders and price sensitive orders I have received a better price. Sometimes much better than I had even hoped for.

Business is tough enough. This is a personal strategy. I try never to deal with any supplier that I do not feel comfortable with. If the chemistry is bad or my instincts tell me to avoid a certain supplier, then I will not deal with them. Why? There are many reasons. They may not be flexible with me when I need them to be if our relationship as buyer and seller is strained. It is hard enough to run a business today, I don't need the added headache of dealing with a rep I do not feel comfortable with. I must be able to trust them.

When a problem comes up this sales rep may not work very hard to fairly resolve it in a timely basis. I may still deal with the company but I may request another rep. Do not misunderstand me. I am not talking about being friends with the sales rep. I am not even talking about liking the rep. I am talking only about having confidence in the rep and not disliking the rep.

Maybe this makes no difference to you but it does to me. If I am going to be dealing with someone on a regular basis I damn well want to feel comfortable with them.

The types of salespeople I personally try to avoid? The "it is you and me against them approach" this is when the sales rep tells you that he is on your side and together you will go up against the sales manager to get a good deal. This is commonly used in the automobile industry.

The high pressure reps. The rude, aggressive, and condescending reps. The type of reps who try to dazzle you with techno babble to demonstrate their superior knowledge and intimidate you by making you feel ignorant. I also avoid the reps who use the "gang up on the prospect" sales strategy. This is when they bring two or three other members of their company in an attempt to gang up on you and force a close to the sale. They may bring in the sales manager, a service guy, a finance guy, or any other combination of people they think are needed depending on the sale they are trying to make.

How aggressive do you want to be in controlling your costs? I believe in being aggressive but fair. Business, like all relationships must be a two way mutually beneficial relationship if it is to work. Therefore, I suggest you use this strategy very selectively. I do not use this as a routine strategy nor do I suggest you do. Not only would this be unfair but your suppliers would also anticipate it if you used it all the time and they would adjust their initial prices to you accordingly.

A very effective negotiating strategy is to pull your supplier into the bidding process to a point where they have a more committed interest in the project or order. They may have spent time and money but, as importantly, they have a mental commitment to it.

Much like a buyer who falls in love with a house will never get the best deal, you will have a seller who in a manner of speaking has fallen for this deal and is therefore much more open to making concessions. These could come in the form of a reduced price, free delivery, free set up, extended warranty, or reduced maintenance costs.

In Pursuit of Profits. How To At Least Double Your Profits Without Increasing Your Sales.

This strategy has the most success when you are dealing with less frequent, perhaps even one time situations, and you are dealing with a high ticket item. I have had tremendous success in this manner when dealing with equipment purchases, real estate transactions, and even when dealing with our corporate bank over loan terms and rates.

Make the best deal you can and then ask for a better one. Let's say you are buying 10,000 widgets. The best price you have been able to get for these widgets is .47 each. A good price to be sure, but you think it can be a bit better and a savings on a widget order of this size will add a significant amount to your bottom line.

At this point the supplier you are dealing with has a vested interest in the order. They have spent time and money on bringing you, the prospect, to this point. The salesman has already figured out how to spend his commission. He will be taking his family to Disney World.

Suddenly you tell him that you know that .47 is a good price but if he can give you a better price today you will give him the order. How much better? Let him make that offer to you. If his price comes in lower than what you were hoping for you have saved even more. If not, you can always tell him the price you need to close the deal.

Use the third party strategy if you prefer. It is not you but rather someone else in the company that has authorized the purchase but only at this predetermined price. The third party strategy can be a very effective one in many purchasing situations.

If you can't get a lower price perhaps you can at least get a longer warranty, or free shipping, or special packaging, or a lower cost service contract. Whatever it is you are buying you can be sure that you will get a lower price or something more in return.

Just ask. Just tell the supplier that you really want to give the order to them but you simply can't do it at that price and under those terms. Don't drag this out and don't play games by using this strategy frequently or more than once during the same buying process for that purchase. Be as fair as you can while striving to accomplish your goal.

Depending on what you are buying the concession could take many different forms. This is the stage to press for what you are seeking. Your leverage will be very strong at this stage. They will be much more flexible. Be ethical and honest and don't keep coming back for more but do not alter what you are trying to obtain. Make the best deal you can and close it.

If they offer what you are seeking don't think "hmm perhaps I can get an even lower price or a better package", give them the order. This, of course, assumes all the other elements of the product purchase requirements have been met including service, terms, delivery, and quality. As I have said before, price is a key ingredient of the purchasing decision but only one ingredient.

"In business, the competition will bite you if you keep running; if you stand still, they will swallow you."

William S. Knudsen

Let your supplier's competition do your negotiating for you. By this I mean, let your suppliers know that you are bidding your job out. They will do the rest. They will understand that they must come up with a good proposal or they will not get the job or order.

You can be sure that they will not come back and present you with list prices. Many suppliers know what other suppliers' prices are. They will react to this knowledge to propose lower prices to you and / or a better overall package if other items such as service, setup, and delivery are applicable.

You should not allow gifts of any kind to be accepted by your personnel from outside sources. This applies to both those personnel involved in purchasing and those involved in selling. You do not want your business compromised. You do not want supplier loyalty to exist due to the personal gain of those buying on behalf of your company and you do not want selling prices affected by those selling on behalf of your company.

Both represent a conflict of interest and neither scenario should be tolerated. Each is unethical and each can cost you money. This policy should be a written policy and it should be conveyed in written form to your suppliers, purchasing people, and sales people. This policy, like all others, must be followed by all within the company, including owners and management. You cannot have those in management doing one thing and saying another. **Also see my strategies dealing with conflict of interest in the marketing section.**

Try never to pay in advance for any product or service. If you do you may be kissing your money good-bye. Not only do you run the risk of never receiving the product or service you have paid for, but even if you do, it may not meet your expectations. If this happens you have no leverage. Your best leverage is payment due. If you have not paid up front you have options. If the product or service does not meet your expectations you can simply refuse to pay or you have the option of paying a reduced amount.

If the product has not been delivered on time or the service has not been performed on time, you now have the option of going elsewhere for your needs. You must keep as many options as possible open and you must maintain leverage. This is true both in your personal business and professional business.

If you must (and I can think of no reason why you would) pay something up front make sure you only pay a small amount with the balance being due 30 days after the product was delivered or the service was rendered. Do not pay the balance at the time of delivery or at the time the service was performed. You want time to make sure everything meets with your satisfaction and you want time to pay the bill.

Another reason not to prepay for any type of purchase is that you have lost the use of this money. Remember, money has a cost and you want to always use this to your advantage. If you must borrow to pay you have increased the cost of your purchase. If you could be investing the money until the bill is due you have decreased the cost of the purchase.

Let's say you make a purchase and you prepay $10,000 and you do not get the product for 30 days. You have lost the use of this money for 30 days or you have increased your borrowing costs for the same amount of time. If you do not follow this strategy you actually would be losing the use of this money for at least 60 days. The 30 days you do not need to prepay and the 30 days before billing was due.

Using this 60 day window, if you had to borrow this money at 9% it cost you $150. This has effectively added 1.5% to your purchase. If you did not have to borrow and you paid the $10,000 from funds on hand, you have still increased your cost. You have lost 60 days interest or you have lost the opportunity for this $10,000 to save you money in other areas. This lost income could have gone toward lowering your overall costs. Since it did not, your costs are effectively increased. This is what total cost control is all about.

In Pursuit of Profits. How To At Least Double Your Profits Without Increasing Your Sales.

<u>**Buy local? Buy made in USA? Buy union?**</u> Of course, but only if the product or service you are buying offers the best value. Don't confuse so called patriotism with running a cost efficient business. Don't let special interest group slogans influence you.

Don't let patriotism interfere with profitability. It is not your problem if an American business can't make a quality product and sell it at a competitive price. You have no obligation to pay a higher price so that some union worker can get paid $25 per hour while standing on an assembly line all day doing what someone making a great deal less than that could do.

<u>**Test all new vendors and suppliers on a limited basis to begin with.**</u> No matter how strong the sales pitch or how enticing the product and costs appear, if you do not know who you are dealing with you are running an unacceptable risk. Placing a large order with an unproven source could not only cost you money in the long run, it could also cost you customers. If the product or service you are purchasing does not meet your expectations, arrives late or damaged, is of inferior quality, or results in numerous hidden costs you have real problems. Your product quality will suffer, your ability to service your customers will suffer, and your profits will suffer.

Only by starting small and working into a larger more significant relationship will you give yourself the opportunity to judge both the quality and service of this new vendor. Without quality and service the lowest price is useless. In fact, it may turn out to be a very unwise purchase.

Please understand that I am not just speaking of the small unknown supplier. I am also talking about the Fortune 500 companies. Some of the most unpleasant and frustrating experiences I have ever suffered through have come as a result of dealing with some of the most recognizable companies in the world. Don't be fooled into thinking this is a strategy you can ignore if you are dealing with a large well known company. It is not!

<u>**Never let an outside company determine your office supply needs and fill them**</u>. They may present this as a tremendous time saving practice. They will tell you they will provide the control you do not have. They may tell you that no inventory will be needed and that they will monitor what you need and when you need it and ship accordingly. They will do it all and at a low price. This is the pitch. When you hear this big red flags should pop up in your mind. You are giving someone else control over your purchasing function.

You might want to save a step and just give them your company checkbook. They will determine what you need, when you need it, and what you pay for it. Do the words "conflict of interest" come to mind? Are you thinking "like letting the fox guard the hen house"? You should be. If you let a company do this you are trading off low prices and control for convenience. This is simply another way to say you are too lazy to do the job right. This is an inexcusable situation.

<u>**Don't buy supply contracts or prepaid coupon books for your consumable office product needs.**</u> These are another way to force you into single source buying. They may seem to offer a good value but don't be so sure. Think about the downside.

• You are forced into single source buying.

• You have no options to seek and find lower prices or better products.

• It ties up your money since you have prepaid for the products or services.

• It eliminates your best source for savings -- competition.

- Many of these coupons are never used. They are forgotten (do you think the supplier will tell you that you have some credit left?), others are lost or stolen.

- You may not even keep the machine that uses the product coupons you have prepaid long enough to use them all. Don't sit by the mailbox waiting for an unused coupon refund check.

- The dealer or manufacturer you bought them from may go out of business or sell out to another company who will not honor them.

- Coupons may expire before you can use them.

All and all not one of your better cost control options.

"Ideas without action are useless."

Derrick W. Welch

<u>**Don't just read what I write.**</u> Act on it. These strategies are not theoretical or complex. Use them. Improve on them. Adapt them for your business. Whatever you do, do not ignore them.

<u>**Beware of suppliers who low ball you to get in the door.**</u> This is a very common occurrence. They will offer you very low prices to get the business and after the first few orders they will start jumping up their prices. So what, you say? Think about this. Most companies do not change suppliers that often. There are many reasons for this. Some good and some bad.

But complacency and laziness are often the reasons for such supplier loyalty. In these cases, competitive quotes are not often solicited. Very often on repeat and future orders the company may not even ask the supplier the cost. They just order and assume they are being taken care of. Taken, probably. Taken care of? Very doubtful!

The supplier who uses the low ball price to get in the door strategy knows this. They are willing to forgo profits and, even to accept losses, to get in the door so that later in the relationship, when their friend complacency sets in, they can begin to make up for these lost profits by inching prices up in what is now a non competitive situation.

Don't fall for this. This is unfair to the honest supplier and in the long run will cost you money. The best defense against this is to quote every job of any size with more than one company. I suggest three. I also suggest (especially for smaller non quoted jobs) that you compare current bills to past bills. I do not mean compare today's bill to the last invoice for the same product or service. I mean go back to the last 4 or 5 bills. Rising prices will quickly become apparent. If you only compare to the last bill you may only see a very small increase and you may think this is fine. After all, don't things go up each year? However, by comparing invoices from a number of previous orders a pattern of consistent price increases will be more visible.

<u>**If you locate a sale on a frequently purchased item and the savings is significant you should consider purchasing a larger supply**</u>. Of course, you must consider the savings versus the cost or lost opportunity of the money needed to make the purchase, and you must always be aware of your demand for the item in question, the risk of obsolescence and spoilage. You only want to buy more than your immediate needs when the savings

offered justifies the cost of money involved and these risks are not an issue. In a case like this the overall savings can be very significant.

"There are few things more uncommon than common sense."

Derrick W. Welch

If you don't need it don't buy it. I mean need it, not want it. Don't buy because of a sale. Don't buy it because you might use it. Don't buy it because you think you could use it. This strategy, as with so many of these strategies, is nothing more than common sense. If you do not have a productive plan to use the item, do not purchase it. I have seen countless examples of items purchased that were never used. They sit and collect dust for years until they no longer have any value.

Look around your office, plant, or warehouse right now. Stop reading and look around. How many things do you see that should never have been bought? Look for both large and small items or quantities of items. Take an inventory of these items that are not being used, have not been used, or are used very little.

I am afraid you may be surprised. How did this happen? Who bought them? Who authorized the purchase? What purpose were they bought for? Why are they not being used? Try this at home sometime, you will most likely find the same problem.

Before you purchase anything you must analyze the prospective purchase. Think of each of the items you see on your list from above as money. Think of that unused box of samples as a box of $10 bills. Think of that case of air freshener sitting in the corner collecting dust as a box of $1 bills. Think of them this way because that is exactly what they are. You must change your thinking to thinking of money.

Before you spend your money you must ask why? If it does not have a planned use and a productive purpose don't buy it. Will it increase sales? Will it help prevent a loss? Will it help improve quality? Will it help reduce costs? Will it improve service? When do I need it? Can we do without it and not hurt the quality of our product or service? What will I gain by purchasing this? What other uses of my money can I discover that will give me a better return?

Ask the questions. Don't think you might. Don't think you may. Either you do, or you do not, have a productive purpose for any purchase you are thinking of making. If you do, then you must ask if the price you are paying is cost justified by the benefit you will be getting in return. If it is going to cost X and it will only return Y then perhaps you should not buy it at all. Ask and ask and ask the questions. They are the key. Once you are satisfied the purchase is justified then ask the questions about where can you get it at a lower cost, what will it cost, where else can you get it, how can you save on this purchase?

"Competition is the keen cutting edge of business, always cutting away at costs."

Henry Ford

Since competition is one of the keys to your ability to control and reduce your costs you should have an open door policy for dealing with vendors. By this I do not mean that you should see every sales rep who comes knocking on your door. After all, using your time efficiently is an important factor in increasing your productivity which leads to reduced costs.

What I am saying is, use some common sense in choosing who you see and when, but make sure that you or your people are seeing a revolving base of suppliers and vendors. You want competitive bids for the products and services that your company buys.

If you or your purchasing department are only reviewing prices from the same nucleus of vendors over and over you are never going to approach anything even close to total cost control. If you are only dealing year in and year out with a base of regular suppliers you are not going to know if you are getting the best value from your current sources and you will not know if you can get a better value from another source.

You must develop and instill the mentality of total cost control in the minds of your employees. In order for those that are doing the purchasing to get the best value they must constantly be considering new sources, new products, new services, and new procedures.

What if a new product has come on the market that lasts twice as long as the one you have been buying and costs half as much? If your regular supplier does not offer this product and you do not keep up with the product lines of other sources, you may not even find out it exists.

Don't let your people deal with only a regular base of suppliers and certainly not with a single source. They must keep an open mind and this requires keeping an open door. Remember, competition is a vital weapon in your battle to control and reduce your costs.

Be careful, buyer loyalty can be a powerful tie. Many of your employees who purchase items will do so from one source simply because they like the sales rep. "So what if it costs a bit more, it is not my money anyway" they think. After all the rep is a good guy. This is poison to purchasing at any level in any quantity. Never allow this to happen.

"Never let profits come ahead of your principles."

Derrick W. Welch

Play fair. While not actually a cost cutting or cost control strategy, I feel it is important to include it anyway. If a source, including a new source, comes in with a better price than one of your regular or "pet" sources offers you, you should not turn around and allow your regular supplier to match it.

Make sure they are not low balling you, that the terms are acceptable, and that they are a qualified source for that product and give them the order. If they have worked hard to get your business and their proposal reflects this, they deserve the order. <u>Turning around and giving it to another source who offers to match the price is simply wrong.</u>

By playing fair in the short term you will reap long term benefits. The next time this order comes up the source that lost the order will come in with an even lower bid and you will most likely save even more money. But even more importantly, you and your people must maintain your integrity and ethics. The same thing goes for suppliers who come in and offer to match or go below your current prices. When you have suppliers who do this I suggest you tell them what I do. Don't let the door hit you on the way out.

In my opinion this is an unfair and unethical way to sell a product or service. Yes, you may save some money by letting this source fill your order but if you do, I hope you have trouble looking in the mirror.

If a source wants to bid for your business or present a proposal to you that is one thing, but walking in and offering to match or beat your current prices is not selling or fairly trying to get your business. It is simply a form of prostitution. Don't deal with companies that employ people who use these sales tactics.

There are a lot of good, honest, hard working sales reps out there. More than enough to enable you to accomplish your objectives without dealing with these types of sleaze balls. You do not want to develop a bad reputation and you do not want to discourage new suppliers from calling on you.

A great source of ideas. Another benefit of dealing with a core of normal suppliers and a revolving base of secondary suppliers is that you will be exposed to many other ideas. These suppliers will be an excellent source of input regarding your competition, market demands, industry trends, new products, and new processes. They can provide your people with new ways to look at things and new ways to do things. They may give you ideas that can be used to increase sales, improve productivity, reduce costs, or reduce errors.

It is the business of these people to sell to your industry and related industries. Therefore, in many ways it is their business to know about your industry. Consider the best suppliers and sales reps to be much more than a vendor. Consider them to be a resource and don't hesitate to ask them questions.

They can, and should be, an excellent source of new, creative, and innovative ideas. They can provide you direction, prevent you from making purchasing mistakes by sharing knowledge with you and they can help in many other ways.

Let me give you a first hand example. One of the sales reps that called on us to sell printing material informed us about a new printing plate that provides a better image reproduction, lasted 25% longer, and costs about 15% less than the ones we had been using. We gave them a trial run and found all these claims to be true. We changed to these plates exclusively.

We had many reps calling on us and yet only this one was an authorized distributor of these plates. None of the other reps could have sold us these plates even if they had wanted to. Had we only been working with a single source or small base of regular reps, and had we not asked questions and developed a relationship with this rep, we may never have known about these plates.

This is just one of dozens of examples I could give you. I have secured sales leads from reps, I have been given tips that improved our production and reduced rejects, I have obtained employee leads from reps, and I have been given new product ideas by reps. Don't overlook these no cost sources of invaluable information.

If you routinely bid out projects make sure that you are rotating those you are inviting to bid. Yes, you can still invite your current best value suppliers to bid but make sure you include a rotating base of other suppliers. The reasons for this have been covered in detail in other strategies.

A word of caution, make sure your people are not protecting certain suppliers. This is a very frequent occurrence. As I have indicated, corruption in this area is all too common as are examples of favoritism, laziness, and convenience. Make sure the purchasing decisions are justified. This will require an ongoing periodic review of the purchasing activities by someone outside of the purchasing department.

Make sure you are comparing total costs when you are considering vendors. This must include tax, any extra charges, and shipping. If you think this is not that important think again. The shipping costs alone can represent a significant difference in your bottom line cost if vendor A is shipping from the state next to yours and vendor B is shipping from across the country.

Depending on what you are buying, and how it is shipped, shipping costs may be a minor consideration or one that could cost you more than the product itself.

Let's talk about warehouse clubs and low cost office supply stores for a minute. By these I am referring to stores such as BJ's Warehouse, Staples, Price Club, Costco, Sam's, OfficeMax, and Pace. These stores can offer you significant savings on a wide variety of office products and equipment. In many cases the savings may, in fact, be the best you will find anywhere even when compared to direct mail sources like Viking, Reliable, and Quill.

However, whether or not they offer the best value is another case all together. The answer to that depends on many things, not the least of which is the time and effort required to shop for and get the items needed and the potential lack of return privileges. You may be losing time and options. Since time is money, you must factor in your time involved in purchasing from sources like this.

Some will offer delivery and have a catalog and others will not. In some cases you may have to visit a number of stores to compare prices and in other cases you may not. Some may offer loss leaders and others may not. I simply bring these sources up to you to remind you of all your options and to remind you that you must consider all the costs and not just the listed prices.

In many cases the convenience of shopping by direct mail, or with reps who call on you, may prove to be the best value. Much will depend on what your purchasing needs are including how frequently you buy and what you buy. Since only you know these I cannot suggest a more specific strategy.

If you do shop at a warehouse club that requires membership and you only go a few times each year, try to get free passes so you can avoid the membership fees. These are given out readily to companies thinking of joining and they are normally dispersed very liberally at trade shows. Why join if your usage of the membership does not justify the cost of membership? This will save you $25 to $100. More than you paid for this entire publication.

Don't ever fall for the sales tactic that basically says "this deal is only good for today". If a sales rep ever uses this line on you, after you stop laughing ask them to call you tomorrow. Since this deal is only good for today tell them you expect a better deal tomorrow.

Do not worry if you think that you must be a strong negotiator in order to reduce and control your costs. Sure it helps if you are, but don't be concerned if you feel your skills are lacking in this area. Once you make your suppliers aware that you are looking at other sources and that you are bidding out jobs they will take care of the rest. This knowledge alone will normally be enough to cause your suppliers to suddenly find ways to sell you the same product or service that they have in the past at 10% to 20% lower cost.

Even if this does not occur, your new procedures will help ensure that you are getting these types of savings from other sources. You will, at the very least, find that once it becomes known to your suppliers that you are aggressively seeking the best value be it with them or someone else, annual price increases will drop significantly and may no longer be annual.

In Pursuit of Profits. How To At Least Double Your Profits Without Increasing Your Sales.

The reason for this is that some suppliers may not feel they can lower the prices they have been charging you lest it appear that they have been overcharging you. Therefore, instead they eliminate, or dramatically decrease, their normal and planned price increases in an effort to become more competitive.

When dealing with sales representatives put yourself in their minds. In almost all cases they will have a certain amount of flexibility in the areas of price, terms, and delivery. They will not tell you this and, in fact, many times will indicate just the opposite. This is simply good strategy on their part. After all, would you want to tell your customers that your price and terms are not really what you have indicated and instead tell them "let's make a deal"?

Their goal is to get the maximum price they can with the best terms for their company while still getting the sale. This is good business. Your salespeople should do the same thing. They often will also be reluctant to alter prices or terms as this would affect their commission. Higher prices and more favorable terms often translate into higher commissions.

The key here is to understand that in most cases the sales person will have the flexibility that you are looking for. Don't tell them what price you are looking for. Instead, explain that you always seek the best value and you are securing competitive proposals. Ask them to give you the best price they can. You will find many times the price they give you will be better than the one you might have asked for.

Now, of course, this strategy, like many others, will not work for all types of purchases you make but it will apply to many circumstances. Please also remember that you are educating those salespeople who call on you. They must learn that you are no longer conducting business the old way. They must understand your goals and new policies and procedures. After a few times they will begin to come in automatically with the best package they can which will reduce your need to go through this process every time.

You won't always get the rock bottom price but this is not your goal. Your goal is to get the best value you can and this strategy should enable you to consistently save 10%, 20%, or more, off the normal price offered by the sales rep.

Remember, even if you only save $20 in the two minutes work it takes to request the best price the rep has, you have just saved a rate equal to $600 per hour. You don't think that the effort was worth it to save $20. You think instead that you have just earned a rate equal to $600 per hour. Now do you think the effort was worth it?

Total cost control is a state of mind, a way of thinking, a company culture. Thinking like this is what total cost control is all about. Thinking like this gets my attention and it should get yours.

Remember, both you and the seller have a related goal. You want to buy and he wants to sell. The only real issue is how successful each of you are in meeting your objectives. How hard or intimidating can this be?

Avoid C.O.D. deliveries. Not only do they cost you more normally, but they also deprive you of the opportunity to check the quality, quantity, and performance of whatever it is that you are getting. You also want time to check these things and to match up the delivery to the purchase order. You do not want to feel pressured by having the delivery person standing there looking impatient.

Furthermore, C.O.D. usually means cash or a bank check. Both take time to get and time is money. What else does it do? Think. It eliminates your 30 day float on the payable. This increases the cost of the product by increasing your overall cost associated with that purchase.

You should be using a purchase order for every purchase. The best way to eliminate the possibility of miscommunication is through the use of your purchase order. This purchase order should be designed to clearly indicate all terms under which you are purchasing the item. This should include price, terms, delivery, timing, quantity, and anything else that affects this purchase.

Indicate that acceptance of the order constitutes acceptance of your terms and that no changes or added charges will be paid for, or accepted, unless agreed to in writing by both parties. This also holds true for changes the supplier needs to make regarding anything about the order. You will not be held liable for them unless you have agreed to them in writing.

In this day and age of the fax machine, E-Mail, and overnight mail there will be no excuse for not handling things in this manner. Have you ever heard "I never said that" or "I never approved that" or how about "I did not mean that"? Making these conditions a printed part of your purchase order form will help insure that you never do.

I would also strongly suggest that somewhere on your purchase order it be indicated as part of the PO form that these are the terms under which you are ordering and they supersede any terms or customs of the supplier. See my comments on this issue in the printing section.

The purchase order not only protects your interests and eliminates misunderstandings, but it also serves as a reference to be used by accounts payable in processing and paying the invoice for this order.

These terms should be a standard printed part of your purchase order. Why a printed part and not just hand written when needed? Simple. The person filling out the purchase order might forget to add them. Even if they remember they may not think these conditions are needed for a particular order. The supplier could claim they were added later and that the copy they had did not contain them. In this case they will have, of course, lost their copy. By adding them as a permanent part of your purchase order you are taking a strong proactive step. Finally, adding them by hand takes time and time is money. Think total cost control.

If your supplier balks at this perhaps you are dealing with the wrong supplier. Remember, this policy also protects the supplier against any miscommunication.

Don't ever assume that just because one company offers the best price on a few items that they offer the best prices on all items. This will not be the case and, in fact, it may turn out to be quite the opposite. They may be overcharging on other items to make up for the lost profits on the lowest priced, aggressively marketed items. You may be looking at a form of loss leader products. Follow the proper purchasing procedures and never assume anything.

Ignore the term "discount". When you hear this term think of Honest Joe the used car salesman. Your warning bells should go off. Ask the questions. Discounted from what? Discounted compared to what prices, over inflated starting prices?

Discounted prices may not be at all. They may be establishing the list price and then telling you about the discount off of this price that they are giving you. What do you care about the list price. You should care nothing about the list price. All you should care about the list price is that it is the price that you will never pay.

Don't assume a discount is giving you the best price or the best value. You want to compare the prices and all other factors of the sale as I have shown you. Do not just start dealing with a supplier who claims to give you discounts or calls themselves a discount supplier.

You must compare. A discounted price from one source may be higher than the normal prices of another source. How good is a 30% discount on a product that they list as selling for $100 when you can buy it from other sources for $50. You have actually overpaid for this discounted product by 40%. A 30% discount from $100 leaves the price at $70. This is 40% higher than the $50 you can buy it elsewhere at. Quite a deal don't you think?

You should require dual signatures on all purchase orders over a preset amount. This will give you added protection not only against fraud but also against bad buying practices. Furthermore, if something happens to one of the parties signing you will have a second party available that is familiar with the purchase.

In this case I would suggest that the purchase order form contain a slot for a second signature and the printed words that indicate that all purchase orders over the preset amount you establish are not valid without the second signature.

Examine all products from new suppliers as soon as you receive them. Not only must you verify you received what you ordered and it is in good condition, but you also want to make sure that you have left yourself a margin of error in case there is a problem with the order. You have left a margin of error by ordering early, haven't you? This way if a problem does exist you are not caught short thereby eliminating the risk of disruption and of being forced to restock that product on short notice which would most likely result in inefficient buying. Procrastination has a price. Don't you pay it.

You must have controls in place to control usage and reorder points for all your office supplies. This must be done not only for the reasons I have outlined in earlier strategies, but also because employee theft in this area is very high. From the theft of pencils, pens, and paper, to the theft of more expensive items, employee theft of office supplies costs companies billions of dollars each year.

One very effective way to control and monitor the usage of office supplies is to have all supplies kept in a locked supply closet or supply area and have one authorized person responsible for the supply and demand of this area.

Each person that needed supplies would have to go through this person to get what they needed. A sign out sheet can also be an effective way to monitor usage. If all employees are required to sign out whatever products they take you will have a method of controlling inventory and cross checking against quantities on hand versus quantities ordered and signed out.

Discrepancies would show up very quickly between what you should have on hand and what you do have on hand. This would enable you to determine if more drastic action was required to reduce employee thefts.

The use of predetermined reorder points will insure that you are not ordering items at the last minute thereby eliminating your ability to use proper purchasing procedures. This is being proactive. If you do not have reorder points you will be constantly running out of things that you need right away which will force you to bypass many of the cost control procedures I have given you including comparison shopping.

You must have strong purchasing procedures in place. You must be proactive. If you do not have strong purchasing procedures in place I urge you to go to the library or a bookstore and pick up a few books on this subject. I cannot overstate the need for strong purchasing procedures in every business, large or small.

I have given you a number of procedures and hopefully you will use my ideas to develop even more of your own. I will list a few more for your use or adaptation in the next few strategies but remember, this is not a book on purchasing. It is a book on total cost control. Yes, I do cover a number of purchasing policy issues but there are many more procedures that you should be putting in place depending on the exact nature of your business.

Proper purchasing policies can save a company thousands, tens of thousands, or even millions of dollars, a year depending on your size and purchasing volume.

Think how much of your total costs are made up of outside purchases. In most companies it will be at least 30% to 80%. In many companies it is much higher. If you spend 50% of all your costs on outside purchases and you can reduce these by even 10% you may have just doubled your profits.

Please do not overlook the importance of this area.

<u>Have one source for the issuance of purchase orders and a second source to periodically review the efforts of the primary source</u>. You must control the purchase order. Consider a purchase order a blank check. You must control them just like you control and guard the company checkbook. If you do not you may regret it. A misused purchase order could cost you a great deal of money. You may find yourself paying for unauthorized items, illegal purchases, and purchases made for an employee's own use. You will also find many more mistakes occur when one person is responsible for checking all their own work.

Let me give you a first hand example. A few years ago my company received a rather large order for three products from a mid western bank. Not only did we view the order as large, but it had come from a bank that had a history with us of small orders.

To put it in perspective, this bank normally ordered two or three products from us each year with the average order being 2,500 pieces of each item. This order came into us for 25,000 each of three items. We could have processed the order immediately, but since we felt a mistake may have been made we called the buyer and asked if they wanted 2,500 of each item or 25,000. The buyer confirmed it was 25,000 of each item and we had a confirming purchase order. Since we are not in business to turn orders away we sent the order through but we also sent a personal letter to the buyer at the bank acknowledging the order at 25,000 of each item and thanking the buyer for the order.

Well, as I am sure you suspect, shortly after the products were delivered we received a call from a panic stricken officer at the bank indicating we must have made a mistake. The officer told us it would take them ten years to use all the products we delivered.

I advised the officer that we had suspected the order might have been incorrect so we had contacted the buyer to verify the quantity and then had confirmed the order in writing back to the bank. We also had a signed purchase order. We had done all we could have short of refusing the order or going over the buyer's head to verify the bank's intent. Since the order was custom produced there was little we could do about it.

It turns out that the buyer was going to be let go by the bank and she knew it. As a result she began ordering many items, from many companies, that the bank did not need and huge quantities of other items that they did use, but could never use in the quantity she ordered. She felt she was being screwed by the bank and she did the same thing to them.

The bank had no recourse. Look at all the things they had done wrong. They continued to let a buyer stay on the job after they had made a decision to terminate her. They assumed she would not find out before they took official action. Even if she had not found out, they had a buyer in the position that was doing an unsatisfactory job. After all, that is why they had decided to terminate her.

They had no real purchase order controls. If they had, she would never have been able to order the type and quantities of products she was able to order. They let her issue her own purchase orders. They had no double signature requirements for purchases over a preset amount.

In many ways the bank was inviting this type of employee abuse. Worse than that, they still have not modified the purchase order procedures they had in place at that time. They feel this was an isolated incident and one that will not happen again. Making a mistake once is one thing but making the same mistake again is stupid!

Centralize all your purchasing efforts. This is the best way to realize maximum control and cost savings. It makes very little sense to have each department or division ordering what they need on their own. It makes very little sense for different branch locations to be ordering what they want on their own. It makes no sense to allow each person who needs something to order it on their own.

Not only is control lost, but you are also losing the economies of purchasing. Having one source do all the buying will enable you to combine purchases for the best overall prices and terms. It will also allow you to work with a smaller more select group of proven best value suppliers to further ensure that you are getting the best value and maximum leverage in your dealings with these suppliers. Centralized purchasing will provide these significant benefits to you. Decentralized purchasing robs you of these cost control and reduction efficiencies and replaces them with inefficiencies, waste, and duplication.

Note: I am aware that the costs associated with processing purchasing requests for small quantities and low cost items from various departments or divisions can often exceed the savings realized on the purchase itself. Therefore, you may wish to establish a minimum level of purchasing that you will let various departments engage in to eliminate the internal costs and delays. This topic is too complex to cover in any detail here. I merely mention it for your consideration.

Never tell a supplier who got the order how much lower his bid was than the other bids. If you do you can expect a higher price from this supplier the next time you have them bid. No one likes to leave money on the table. The bidding process always contains a certain amount of educated guessing as to what price to come in at. If they find out they came in at a bid that was much lower than the competition then you can reasonably expect them to increase the price next time.

After all, why come in so much lower than the competition when they can come up in price and still have a good chance to get the job since they were so much lower last time? If they know they underbid by 15% ,the next time they may feel they can come up 10% and still be well under the other suppliers.

Never tell a losing bidder how much over their bid was. You always want them coming in with their lowest price. If they find out that their bid was only slightly high the next time they may only lower it slightly. If they think they came in much too high you may find the next bid they come in with to be much lower thereby providing you with an overall greater savings.

For example, if I know my bid was 5% too high, the next time I bid on this job I may bid 5% less figuring this will match the winning bid last time and this time that winning bidder will come up somewhat. On the other hand, if I think my bid was much too high and I decide to bid again next time I may lower my bid by 10% or even much more. The end result could be that you get a much lower winning bid.

Never tell a vendor what your budget is for anything you are considering purchasing. If you tell the vendor what your budget is do you think they will give you a price below this? Pretty unlikely I would say. It is much more likely that they will build their proposal up to your budget. I have talked to many vendors who have told me that whenever they are aware of what a prospect's budget is they will always build their proposal up to the budget. If their costs are more than the customer's budget they will not normally lower the proposal to meet the budget.

Think about this. If I tell you my budget for a project is $100,000 and you know that you can do the job for $60,000 are you going to give me a proposal for $60,000? I doubt it. You may think I would not give you the job because your bid is too low. Therefore you raise it. You may get greedy and see an opportunity to make some added profit. Therefore, you may bid $90,000, coming in under my budget of $100,000 and still making significantly more profit. I have seen this happen many times.

Never tell a supplier what you now pay for an item. You want a fair process of competition and you want the best possible price. You do not want to give one supplier an unfair advantage over another supplier and you don't want a supplier coming in just under your current price, when without prior knowledge of your prices, he may have come in much lower than this.

To ensure that you are getting all factors in writing including costs, added charges, delivery, terms, quantity, warranty, service, performance standards, or anything else that is important to you and your business, create a quote solicitation form. If in doubt put it on the form. Indicate that all pertinent areas must be completed in order for you to accept and review the quote. Make all suppliers complete and submit this form in order to have their proposal considered.

This is by far the best way to insure that all needed areas are considered and that all suppliers are being considered on the same basis. It will also go a long way toward eliminating any miscommunication. Putting things in written form has a way of creating much clearer communication and eliminates the need to ask or remember to ask. Be proactive.

Any time you are soliciting prices on multiple items make sure you clearly indicate that you reserve the right to purchase any one or any combination of the items being priced. You want all items priced separately with all costs spelled out for each item. The goal here is to be able to pick and choose among the suppliers to get the best deal from each on individual items.

If you simply request bids or prices on ten items you are apt to get a bottom line price for the entire group. Yes, you can still select the vendor that offers the overall best value this way but you cannot select the best value items from each vendor. By purchasing based on the best value for each item and not by purchasing from the overall lowest priced supplier, you will be providing yourself with the opportunity to realize significant savings over the group buy.

This will allow you to save the maximum on each item and not just the maximum on a group of items. You will also be able to reward more than one vendor since you are purchasing a number of products, each based on the best value, and this will mean placing orders with more than one vendor.

By doing this you should be able to realize savings of 10% to 25% when compared to an all or nothing purchase with one supplier.

In Pursuit of Profits. How To At Least Double Your Profits Without Increasing Your Sales.

Always match purchase orders to quotes and to invoices. You want to insure that you specify accurate ordering information on the purchase order and the best way to do this is to refer to the quote. As I have discussed earlier, you also want to match up the invoice to both the quote and the purchase order to make sure that all billing is proper and based on what you authorized.

Buy your copy paper in boxes of bulk packed sheets 5,000 at a time as opposed to buying 10 reams of 500 sheets. If you shop right you will find that you can save 25% to 50% on the cost of this type of paper. The reason is the cost of the per ream packaging will be eliminated.

Be very careful of buying anything from your local office supply store. My experience has been that they generally sell at, or very close to, list price. If they sell at list price this means you are buying at list price. You should never buy at list price. This means that you are overpaying by 25%, 50%, or more. Who would overpay this much, you ask? Somebody must be as there are over 12,000 of these local office supply stores in this country.

All other things being equal I would suggest that you buy from the source that offers at least a 30 day money back guarantee. This gives you options and flexibility. Many of the direct mail office supply sources offer this and a number will pick up any products you wish to return at no cost.

As I have stated, the only way to accurately compare the costs of the products you buy is to compare the delivered costs. Whenever possible the easiest way to do this is to request prices for the products delivered. However, I know this is not always possible. Sometimes you buy from a catalog and must factor shipping costs yourself and other times the supplier, for whatever reason, just doesn't give you the costs.

Because shipping costs can represent a significant added cost to certain purchases you must be familiar with the shipping terminology. The last thing you want to do is to order a product assuming that shipping costs are included and find out later that they are not. These are the more common shipping terms and what they mean.

F.O.B. Factory. This means you pay freight from the factory at which the product was made to your company. The factory may be closer or much further away from you than the company you ordered the product from.

F.O.B. Dealer. This means you pay freight from the dealer's place of business to your company.

F.O.B. Origin or F.O.B. Point of Origin. This means that you pay freight from where the products are loaded onto the truck to your company.

F.O.B. Destination or F.O.B. Delivered. This means that shipping charges are paid for by the supplier. This does not mean however, that the supplier will not turn around and bill you for these charges or that they are not factored into your costs already.

Prepaid. This also means that the shipping company pays the freight. But again, be careful as you may be billed for these charges directly or as part of your product cost.

Prepaid and Add. This means that the shipping company prepays the shipping and then adds it to your bill.

Freight Collect. As it appears, this means that you pay freight to the trucker at the time the order is delivered to you.

Be careful of hidden charges. This is especially true on purchases made by mail order from a catalog. These will often be the types of purchases that you will not be able to use a quote solicitation form for. This leaves it up to you to be aware of all added costs. To find them you must carefully read the catalog and then factor all charges into your evaluation to properly determine the best value. Some of the more common charges you may run into follow.

• Small order charges. Because many companies have high fixed internal costs it will often cost the same, or little more, to process a larger more profitable order than it does to process a smaller less profitable order. To recover some of this lost profitability some companies will add an extra charge for small orders or less than established minimum order size. It pays to know this not only because you need to factor in all costs in order to properly compare the suppliers, but also so that you can combine purchases if feasible to eliminate these added charges.

• Insurance charges. Some direct mail companies add these to your order. They are designed to cover the value of the shipment. At times I deal with companies that charge these types of costs but I must confess I do not like them. Who are they insuring? You know the answer to this rhetorical question. If the product does not reach me, or if it reaches me in a damaged condition, I simply refuse to pay for it. I do not fight with the shipper. That is not my problem. They may try to make it my problem but I simply will not let them. So they are sure not insuring me.

• A handling or processing charge. You may or may not even see this cost. Some companies will tell you they are adding this charge while others will not. These latter companies will simply list your shipping costs as shipping and handling and they include an amount to the shipping costs they are billed and bill you the higher total.

Remember to always try to negotiate both terms and prices. Both are important. If vendor A offers a better price but vendor B offers much better payment terms you must conduct a cost evaluation to determine which vendor represents the best deal. Every purchase you make effects your bottom line so you darn well better take the time to make the right purchasing decision. Proper purchasing practices can make or break your company. Think I am overstating this? Take a few minutes and figure out what percentage of your overall costs are incurred through some type of purchasing activity.

Whenever you are seeking some type of special pricing, terms, or any other arrangements you should go above the entry level customer service or salespeople you might normally encounter with this company. The idea here is not to go over someone's head, but rather to reach someone who has the authority to make the concessions you are seeking. This most often will be the sales manager, or if a small company, the owner. Front line or entry level people very often will not know any other arrangements are possible and even if they do they will not normally have the authority or incentive to authorize them.

When you have an employee that has done an exceptional job in purchasing something at a significant savings give that employee immediate recognition. Also let others in the company know of the employee's fine efforts. Not only should the effort be recognized but you also want to reinforce this type of activity with all employees. You want them striving for this type of sincere, visible recognition. This should be done for both large and small purchases.

Make sure what you are actually ordering is what you mean to order. If you order the wrong product by mistake or through carelessness you could end up paying a 20% to 30% restocking charge plus shipping both ways, if you can return it at all. This could be a very costly error. This happens very often and it is easy to do. For example if you want to order item #942698 and instead you order item #942689. Make sure you are double checking what you are ordering and make sure you completely understand the terms under which you are buying, including the return policies.

Your office supply purchasing options. Today you have four primary sources for your office supply needs. These are, the local office supply store, direct mail office supply houses, office supply superstores, and warehouse clubs.

By purchasing your needed supplies and products via direct mail or from an office supply superstore or warehouse club, you should easily be able to save 30% to 80%, or more, off the list prices used by most local office supply stores. These sources can supply you with everything your local office supply store can and a whole lot more. If you have an office supply need of any type there is a very good chance that you can get it from one of these sources.

Let me just give you a short list of the types of items you can get from a direct mail office supply house, a warehouse club or an office supply superstore. From coffee to computers, pens to paper, cassettes to cases, folders to filing cabinets, forms to furniture, disks to dispensers, binders to batteries, books to bookcases, boxes to buckets, calculators to cash registers, clocks to clipboards, copiers to crates, fax machines to first aid kits, lunch room supplies to laser printers, maps to markers, paper clips to postal scales, telephones to typewriters, toilet paper to tissue paper, well, you get the idea, they will most likely be able to meet your needs.

Listed below are some specific examples of actual price differences you will find comparing the costs of a local office supply store to what the same items cost from a direct mail office supply company.

Product	Local office supply store	Direct mail supply store
2 dozen pencils	$ 6.24	$ 3.78
Computer disks	$ 2.36	$ 1.49
Typewriter ribbons	$ 8.70	$ 5.98
1/2" binders	$ 6.40	$ 3.19
Fax paper per roll	$ 21.10	$ 9.99
File cabinet	$303.70	$189.59
Box of staples	$ 2.50	$ .56
Calculator	$ 85.00	$ 39.96
Manila folders per box	$ 11.30	$ 2.99
PaperMate pens per box	$ 3.60	$ .79

In every case significant differences exist. Savings that range from 10% to 80%. Now let me show you how to secure even greater savings. First, obtain catalogs from the superstores in your area and the warehouse clubs if they offer them. Then request catalogs from at least three of the top direct mail sources. Get on the mailing list of each one of these.

Each time you need to purchase supplies, furniture, or office equipment all you need to do is list the items you need to purchase on a sheet of paper that I call a purchasing comparison sheet. To make a purchasing comparison sheet, simply take an 8 1/2 x 11 sheet of paper and from left to right at the top list the titles Product, Quantity, and then list the name of suppliers you will be price shopping.

It should look something like this:

Purchasing Comparison Worksheet

Product	Quantity	Viking	Reliable	Quill	Other (sources)

Once these headings are setup with as many suppliers as you are looking at, I suggest at least 3 but no more than 6, all you need to do is list the appropriate information under each heading. List all products you will be ordering under the "Product" heading and the quantity needed under the "Quantity" heading. Then simply go through each catalog and list the cost for each source. Make sure you are also checking sales flyers to insure that you are listing the lowest price from each supplier.

Once this is completed you can very quickly spot the best price for each of the items you will be purchasing. Remember to factor in shipping costs, if any, before you make the final determination of which source you will be using for which item and remember the time and cost involved in having to go to or send someone to the office supply superstore or warehouse. These factors may cause you to pay a slightly higher price and, as a result, go to another source as they represent the best overall value.

This comparison purchasing worksheet should be used once a week or once a month depending on how you buy your supplies. It should also be used for infrequent or one time purchases. The time expended to comparison shop will be minimal and the savings will be significant.

How significant will your savings be? Is the added effort worth it? Are you eating up any savings with the time the comparison takes? The answers are, very, yes, and no.

First of all, remember that simply by shopping at one of these discount sources your savings, when compared to shopping at a list price office supply store, will be up to 80%. By then comparison shopping the discounted sources you can save an added 50% to 75%.

With this type of added savings the effort required to secure the best source will be well worth it. Furthermore, the effort required is just not that great. You will be shopping in your office from catalogs and sale flyers. Cross checking the prices on 10 or 15 items at a time with 3 to 6 sources will not take very long at all. In fact, I can think of fewer ways 15 or 20 minutes can be spent once a week or once a month that will yield greater returns for the effort.

Each year for the last few years Inc. Magazine has done just this. They have comparison shopped 12 commonly ordered office supplies among 13 different sources. The sources consisted of 10 superstores and 3 direct mail houses. They looked at the total costs as if they had bought all items from each of the 13 sources.

In a recent survey they found, based on the items and quantities they shopped, that prices ranged from a total cost at the lowest source of $145.82 to a total cost at the highest priced source of $211.54. This is a 45% difference! They did not include sale prices and instead only used catalog list prices from each source.

They found that mail order houses were more expensive than superstores, but this must be tempered by the fact that mail order houses deliver the products to you and you must go to most superstores and buy the product. There is an added cost for this convenience as there will always be.

However, anyway you look at it, a 45% difference in costs equates to a very significant savings. Now remember, I am not suggesting you simply buy all items from the source that offers the lowest total price. Yes, you could do this as the shoppers of Inc. Magazine did and you will realize significant savings.

But I am encouraging you to take this a step further. I am suggesting total cost control. Do not just shop for the lowest total for all items from among the suppliers. Instead, shop for the lowest priced item from each supplier. By comparison shopping on the lowest cost item you may end up ordering from 2 or 3 sources instead of just one.

What you will have accomplished is that you will be getting the maximum savings on each item. The best savings on each item will translate into the best total savings. Had the Inc. Magazine shoppers shopped this way they would have paid a total for all 12 items of $129.25.

Remember, by shopping based on all items bought at one source, Inc. found the lowest to be $145.82 and the highest source to be $211.54. A 45% difference. By shopping for individual items instead of one source for all items, we would have paid $129.25 or 63% lower than the highest total and nearly 13% lower than the lowest total.

Now, of course, this is a simplistic example as we would never shop 13 sources as it would not be cost effective to do so and we definitely would have included sale prices, but it does serve to show a point.

Among the individual product prices shown by Inc. Magazine there were these differences. One source sold 5,000 staples for $.69 while another sold them for $1.69. A 244% price difference. One source sold a ream of 20 lb. copier paper for $2.53 while another sold it for $3.29 and yet another for $3.99. One source sold 6 rolls of fax paper for $27.71 while the highest source sold the same paper for $58.26. A price difference of over 210%. Similar price differences existed on every individual product. Shop around. It pays.

If you have followed my strategy and are keeping catalogs from a number of local and direct mail office supply sources this will only take a few minutes and will be a simple process. Once completed all you or your people will need to do is look left to right on your chart to find the lowest cost supplier for each item. Remember, the only reason for ordering everything from one source will generally be convenience. Convenience will cost you money and is, in most, cases nothing more than another word for laziness.

By comparison shopping the way I have indicated, no matter what form you use, you will find that you will save an average of 20% - 30% on your total purchases when compared to buying from any one source no matter how low the costs of that source are. **One source will never offer the lowest cost for all items.**

Remember to factor in shipping and any minimum order requirements that might be required to obtain free shipping. You may find that you can save even more by purchasing an extra product or two to meet the minimum even though it may be a bit more costly to buy that extra item from this source. The overall total including the free shipping may significantly outweigh the added cost of the one individual item.

Resources

Viking	1-800-421-1222
Reliable	1-800-735-4000
Quill	1-717-272-6100
Staples	1-800-333-3330
Office America	1-804-273-0900
Penny*Wise.	1-800-942-3311
Visible	1-800-323-0628
Wholesale Supply Company	1-800-962-9162

For your basic weekly and monthly purchases you do not need to and should not bid out everything. This would simply require too much time and most likely any savings you realized by doing this on these small repetitive purchases would be negated or worse via the lost time and reduced productivity involved. Instead, for these ongoing purchases review your vendors every 6 months. Select a base of 2 or 3 to work with on an ongoing basis during each 6 month time frame.

At the end of 6 months select 2 or 3 more to review. Then, along with the 2 or 3 you have been using, solicit prices or catalog shop prices for the most frequently used items you buy on an ongoing basis. By doing this you will be able to select your key base of suppliers for these products for the next 6 months. This keeps you with the base of key vendors who have proven to offer the best prices for the types of products you are purchasing.

Then whenever you need to place an order just comparison shop among these key base vendors as I have shown you. Most often, since you have carefully selected the limited base of suppliers, you will be getting the lowest, or near lowest, price for each item you purchase.

This strategy will help ensure that you are always dealing with the best price and best value suppliers without the time consuming process of shopping 6 to 8 vendors for every order you place. You are significantly reducing time and paper work while rotating suppliers as needed to insure maximum savings.

Remember to review all sale flyers. Many direct mail companies such as Viking and Reliable have monthly sale flyers that are used to subsidize their main catalog. The savings in these flyers can be significant. Do not consider flyers from any of your suppliers to be junk mail. Think of them to be potential significant savings and therefore as an important element of your total cost control efforts. Savings on sale flyers can easily add up to 25% to 50% off what you would normally pay for the items.

Make sure any office supply room you have is no larger than it absolutely has to be. Yes, this will conserve space but that is a secondary benefit. The primary objective here is to maintain an efficient level of inventory. Space has a way of filling up. Filling up with things you do not need. Have you looked in your attic, cellar, or garage recently? If you have you know what I mean.

A few years ago I remolded the kitchen in my house. The new kitchen provided 4 times the cabinet, draw, and storage space than the old one did. I had no idea how I would ever use that much extra space. After all, I had the old kitchen for 12 years and while space was at a premium, it was never that difficult to fit what I needed in the kitchen.

Well, as you might suspect, not only have I filled up all that space but now I have trouble finding space to put everything away after food shopping. This is just human nature. We will always find ways to use up the space no matter where it is. We will usually fill it up with things we do not need and will never use. It seems as though the sight of a half empty draw or cabinet or storage room just commands us to fill it up.

In this case of an office supply storage room we will fill it up with items and inventory we may not need or at least will not need for some time. The employees in charge of keeping the supply room stocked and in order may be concerned that the appearance of a half empty room or shelf will give the appearance that they are not doing their job. The end result will be that they will buy more supplies than can be cost or use justified to fill up the space. This ties up needed cash, increases the risk of obsolescence, and increases the probability of theft.

If you make bulk purchases with any consistency consider maintaining two storage rooms instead of one.
Use one for your day to day needs and the other for the storage of your bulk purchases and more expensive items. Both should be kept locked and access should only be allowed by authorized personnel.

In Pursuit of Profits. How To At Least Double Your Profits Without Increasing Your Sales.

Remember, it has been estimated that between 35% and 75% of all employees steal something at work. Don't be naive and think it does not go on in your company. One of the most common areas of theft is the theft of office supplies. In many cases employees do not even think taking pens, paper, tape, folders, and other types of office supplies is theft. I doubt many think much of it at all. But you better be thinking of it.

Employee theft in these areas can easily add 10% or more to your costs for many office supplies. Do all you can to reduce the temptation to steal. By allowing only authorized employees to access your office supplies you will be reducing access which will reduce temptation.

The second storage room that will contain any larger quantities of inventory will serve as added protection. If your main store room is experiencing theft it will be much less damaging since your more expensive items and larger quantity of items are in the secondary, more secure and less accessible store room.

You must know what a good price is. This sounds obvious but what does 20% off mean if you have no idea what a good price is to begin with? How many times have you gone to a store having a 50% off sale and left feeling they marked everything up 100% before they gave you 50% off? See my point. You must know what you are doing or you may think you are getting a bargain when in reality you are being taken.

Look into obtaining a typewriter re-inking system if you have enough typewriters and ribbon usage is high enough to justify the cost. A ribbon re-inking system will cost you about .05 per ribbon. Compare that to the cost of buying a new ribbon. One source for these is a company called Computer Friends, Inc.. They can be reached at 1-800-547-3303. Call and ask them to send you information.

Use ink jet recharging dispensers instead of buying new cartridges for your ink jet printer. You can purchase the refill kits in most office supply stores, direct mail office and computer supply sources and computer stores. Ink jet printer cartridges are extremely expensive at a cost of $30 and up per cartridge. Re-inking your existing cartridge will cost you 1/10th of that amount. Depending on the number of cartridges you use each year this can easily save you hundreds or even thousands of dollars a year.

Remember the domino effect. In these last two strategies, as well as many others, you will see many secondary benefits. You will be reducing trash disposal costs, cutting down on the frequency of which you order these items, and reducing your payable cost since you are buying fewer items. Small savings to be sure, but small savings are the foundation of your total cost control program.

Use recycled laser printer cartridges. They are not only environmentally sensitive but they will also reduce your costs in this area by 25% to 50%. This can add up to significant savings over the course of the year.

"What's in a name? A thirty five percent mark-up."

Vince Thurston.

Don't buy a brand name unless you have to. You can easily save up to 50% or more when you purchase generic supplies instead of brand name supplies. If you are buying paper clips why would you possibly want to spend twice as much to purchase a name brand of paper clip? I do not know, but I do know that millions and millions of boxes of brand name paper clips are bought every day. There are hundreds of items for which you could choose a generic or house brand at a savings of 50% to 100%, or even more, with no loss in quality or usefulness at all.

Always look to purchase generic brands of office supplies. You will almost always pay more for name brands and almost never will this added cost be justified. Always look first to the distributor brand of products or generic name products. How could you possibly justify buying brand name pens, pencils, paper, paper clips, note pads, tape, forms, and any one of a hundred other items that are for internal consumption?

The brand name can cost you up to 100% more. Let me give you an example. At the time of this writing generic copy paper bought by direct mail will cost you under $5 per ream in small quantities and under $3 per ream in larger quantities. Name brand and premium brands will cost you $8 to $12 per ream by direct mail and $10 to $15 per ream at your local office supply store.

By purchasing generic or economy copy paper you can reduce your costs significantly. Savings like this are possible on most of your office supply products. So no matter what is specified to you, always look to the generic or house brand first.

At least be willing to try them. Test them on a limited basis and compare the quality and effectiveness of the product to the brand name equivalent. By testing a limited quantity of generic products while continuing to use the brand name product you will have no risk in the event that the generic product proves to be unacceptable. Of course for many products a testing period will not be required.

In many cases the generic product is actually manufactured by the same company that makes the brand name product. The products are simply distributed and sold under a different label.

Let me give you some more examples of the type of savings you can realize by purchasing generic products. These examples will also serve to further demonstrate the savings you can realize by purchasing your office supply products at direct mail office supply houses instead of at your local office supply store.

Product	List price for name brand	DM house price for name brand	DM house price for generic brand
3 Ring Binder	$ 6.00	$ 3.78	$ 1.76
Legal Pads, 1 dozen	$12.12	$10.98	$ 8.27
Liquid Paper	$ 1.69	$ .99	$ .79
Paper Clips -1,000	$ 4.60	$ 3.89	$ 1.99
Hanging File Folders	$16.21	$ 9.99	$ 5.98
Copy Paper - ream	$10.95	$ 8.29	$ 4.98
Computer Disks, 10	$19.70	$13.21	$11.40

As you can see, buying name brands at list prices from a local office supply store can cost you 300% ,or more, when compared to generic brands and even 100%, or more, when compared to the discounted DM house brand name.

"Assumption must never replace effort."

Derrick W. Welch

One note here, do not assume that a generic name item is always lower priced than a brand name item. In the vast majority of the cases this will be true, but nevertheless you must compare prices to ensure this. There will be times when the brand name may actually cost less than the generic item. This is especially true when a manufacturer or distributor is offering specials or running a sale. Never assume anything.

Do not overlook direct mail office supply companies and office supply superstores as a source for executive and personal gifts. Many of the products they carry will be the exact same products that you will find in retail stores that would charge you 100% more or higher.

For example, if I buy a top grain leather attaché case at a retail store I would pay at least $150 and most likely much more than that. I can buy an excellent top grain leather attaché case from a direct mail office supply house or an office supply superstore for under $90.00.

Make sure you are comparing prices based on equal quantities. By this I mean, you must be comparing costs on an even basis, per piece, per hundred, per thousand, or whatever so long as you are comparing equal amounts. If you make price comparisons on a per case or per carton basis you may find you are not getting a very good deal and, in fact, you will be overpaying many times.

For example, if you buy computer paper and you shop prices based on a per box cost, you may be comparing different quantities and not even know it. You may get a price from one source of $40 per box of paper and from another source you see a price of $50 per box of paper. Thinking the $40 source is the better buy, you purchase from that source. But the real reason the price of the $40 per box supplier was cheaper was that their box contained 2,500 sheets of paper while the $50 per box contained 5,000 sheets.

So, instead of getting a good buy you actually overpaid a great deal. At $40 for 2,500 sheets your cost was $16 per thousand sheets of paper. Had you bought the $50 box containing 5,000 sheets you cost per thousands sheets would have only been $10. You overpaid by 60% for the exact same product. The figures I have used here are actual figures from two different sources.

Watch out for the packaging difference in anything you buy. As I have pointed out above it is a very common problem with paper but it can also cause problems with the cost comparison of many other products you buy. Always make sure that you are making accurate comparisons of product quantities.

If you are serious about doubling your profits here is one book you should go right out and purchase. The title of the book is "Double Your Profits in 6 Months or Less". It was written by Bob Fifer, Chairman & CEO of Kaiser Associates, Inc.. You can find it in most bookstores and it is published by Harper Collins. I recommend it highly.

Co-op costs. I am sure you know how office suite buildings work. They rent or lease office space to a number of companies or individuals within the same building. Each tenant has a specific area of space designated for their exclusive use and they share a number of common areas, service equipment, and personnel.

They may share conference rooms, the receptionist, the fax, the photocopy machine, and any number of other things. The concept is a good one. It allows individual companies access to equipment, facilities, and personnel that they either can't afford to have by themselves or do not need frequently enough to justify purchasing for their own use. This is a form of cooperative tenancy.

Why not consider mirroring this strategy within your building or even building complex? If you have a number of other small companies in your complex or building that have needs similar to yours but cannot justify filling them on their own you have the perfect setup.

For example, let's say you are in a strip mall and you have a need for a copier and fax machine but your need is not so often you feel you want to purchase your own equipment. There is a very good chance that other tenants in the mall also have the same problem. Why not look into sharing the costs of these purchases with these other tenants? Even if you only get one other tenant to participate you will have access to the equipment you need and saved 50% of the cost.

What other areas might this co-op strategy work for? How about cleaning services? If a number of companies use the same service you will be able to get a much lower rate compared to each of you using different cleaning services. The cleaning service will realize economies of scale that can be passed on to you in the form of lower prices.

Consider common purchases? Can you coordinate your purchasing needs on some items to enable you all to enjoy a lower per unit price? By purchasing together on common items your volume buy is higher which should result in lower per unit costs.

What about printing needs? How about your marketing efforts? Can you combine your efforts with other non competing businesses in your area to reduce your costs? A larger media buy will provide lower space costs. The cost of direct mail efforts can easily be reduced significantly by sharing the costs with other companies.

For example, if your company and 2 or 3 other companies are targeting the same audience with non competing products or services, it makes sense to combine any mailings you conduct. This will result in significant savings as economies of scale are realized and as postal rates may not be affected at all by the inclusion of one or two more elements in the direct mail package.

For example, let's say your company is making a mailing to your target audience that contains two pieces of paper. You find another company that wants to reach the same audience and they want to add 3 pieces of correspondence. You would be able to reduce your mailing costs here by 50% since you would not increase your postage, you only need one envelope and one label. You are, in effect, splitting the cost with the second party.

A doctor and dentist may team up. How about a printer and graphic design firm? What about a used automobile sales firm and an automobile repair shop? What about a computer manufacturer or distributor and a computer supply company? Think. Who can you co-op with? Not only will you save significant amounts of money, but your target audience will be better served as they are being offered related, but non competing, services and products from a number of companies at once.

If you have personalized corporate stationary for anyone in your organization, including yourself, get rid of it. Ego has no place in a program of total cost control. Such ego feeding items as personalized stationary not only waste money but as importantly, it sends the wrong message to your employees. Do not kid yourself. You won't be kidding your employees. <u>You are either committed to total cost control or you are not. There is no in-between!</u>

Use erasable bond paper whenever possible. This will cut down on your paper waste and typing time.

In Pursuit of Profits. How To At Least Double Your Profits Without Increasing Your Sales.

Use a lower weight lower cost brand of computer paper for all internal reports and correspondence. Depending on the weight and quantity that you normally buy, you could save 25% or more on the cost by switching to the lower cost lower weight paper. You do not need the most expensive or the heaviest weight computer paper.

Never use corporate letterhead or second sheets for internal, supplier, or secondary correspondence. All communications of this type should be done on a lower grade of paper and should be in one color only. This is also true of outgoing envelopes used for this secondary type of correspondence.

When you compare the cost of a lower grade paper and one color to bond paper and two colors you will find that you are saving 50% to 80%. Over the course of the year, depending on your level of secondary correspondence, your savings could add up to hundreds, thousands, or even tens of thousands of dollars.

But even if it adds up to only $100 or $200 dollars it is a savings. Remember 100 strategies that save $200 each will save you $20,000 a year and $200,000 over ten years. If I told you I could show you how to save $200,000 over the next ten years would you be interested? Of course you would! You must think total cost control. This means small savings and large savings.

When applicable, you can save time and money by responding to correspondence on the same form or letterhead it came to you on. Respond right on the same piece of paper and send it back. If you need to keep a copy, photocopy it. This will save both time and materials. It will also enable you to provide a quick and personal response. The secondary benefits are that you will reduce the amount of paperwork you file, assuming you did not need a copy, and it will reduce your trash as you are sending back the same correspondence you received.

Reuse any large envelopes you receive that have the sender's name and address on a label in the center. Simply use labels a bit larger for your company and put them right over the old label. The trick here is, of course, to open the envelopes carefully so that you can reuse them. Do not worry about the envelope looking used. You should be using a stamp to stamp all recycled materials that indicates you are an environmentally sensitive company and the reuse of materials like this is simply one way you are doing your part to make the earth a better place.

You don't want to hide the fact you are reusing someone else's envelopes you want to get credit for it. You are not being cheap. You are helping to save the planet. Yes, you are also saving money by reducing envelope costs and trash disposal costs but this is not what you want to highlight to your customers.

Turn folders inside out and reuse. After that continue to use each folder by simply affixing inexpensive labels over the old label to designate what the folder is for.

Keep containers around the office earmarked for paper clips and elastics. Do not throw out paper clips and elastics after they are pulled off whatever you are using them for. Recycle them in your office by collecting them in small containers. This may only add up to pennies, but pennies add up to dollars. You should not waste anything. Throwing a paper clip out after one use is waste and waste is costly.

You will also be reinforcing your message of cost control and expense reduction. Even if you only save $50 to $100 a year you have saved more than you paid for this publication. You would stop and pick up a $100 bill lying on the ground, wouldn't you? Over ten years this could add up to thousands of dollars. Your secondary savings are in the areas of trash disposal and less time spent ordering and paying for them. Never feel embarrassed or cheap when you are saving money. Finding ways to save money should be worn like a badge of honor.

You must have strong inventory control procedures and you must have a very good handle on your inventory needs at all times throughout the year. Dun and Bradstreet has reported that 9.5% of all business failures are a direct result of excess inventory. If you are tying up money with products sitting on the shelf in your store or warehouse you are losing money. You are also risking damage or obsolescence.

You cannot afford to have too little inventory and not be able to meet the demands of your customers or factory. You must be able to effectively project. Inventory control cannot be a "guess at it" proposition. I know this sounds obvious but it has been my experience that inventory control is an area that needs improvement in most companies. A great deal of improvement in some cases. Remember, inventory can also have an effect on your insurance and will have an effect on your tax liability.

Consider using EDI technology. This is electronic data interchange. An in depth discussion of this technology and it's benefits is beyond the scope of this book but be aware that for many companies the use of EDI can result in significant savings coupled with greatly improved inventory control. If you have ever shopped at a store that used scanners to ring up your sale you have seen EDI in action. But please understand the use of EDI technology goes far beyond this simple retail application.

Resource
Electronic Data Interchange Association 1-703-838-8042

Inventory can play a key role in your reported year-end profits. In fact, with many companies the amount of money tied up in inventory is more than the entire profit for the year. This means that inventory can make the difference between your company having a profit or a loss. Proper valuation of your inventory is critical. If you value it too low you may turn a profit into a loss. If you value it too high you may pay much more in taxes than you need to. The basis for your inventory valuation should be sound and predicated on proper accounting procedures. Make sure your's is. Don't kid yourself into thinking your inventory is worth more or less than it is. Do it right.

Because the inventory figure in your year-end financial reports can have such a major effect on your reported bottom line pretax profit and because it is very difficult to verify years later what your inventory was years ago, I have heard of many companies who manipulate this figure for a desired benefit. If they have made a large profit and want to reduce their tax liability they will lower the inventory figure to lower profits.

They figure if they ever get audited it will be years later and, in most cases, verifying past inventory will be very difficult, especially in a manufacturing environment. Other companies do the same thing but they do it not only to lower the profit to reduce their tax liability, but also to cheat employees out of bonuses or profit sharing.

I have also heard of private companies who manipulate the inventory figure to make themselves look like a better credit risk to their bank. If they are losing money they simply beef up the inventory on paper and turn the loss into a profit. Unless the bank requests an audit or is deeply involved in the company's operations and books, they would never know.

I even know of one company who prepares their year-end financial reports with all figures posted except inventory. Once they see where this leaves them they simply walk out back into the warehouse, look around and then decide on what inventory figure to use to make the financial reports come out wherever they want them to.

This type of activity is illegal and I urge you not to conduct your business in this manner. I point these examples out solely to drive home the point about how important proper control, tracking, and valuation of your inventory is and to show you the major impact it can have on your bottom line.

If you live in a state, county, or city that assesses a tax on inventory, equipment, or corporate assets, you must find out what the assessment rates are and when they occur. Your goal should be to reduce your taxable assets or inventory to their lowest possible level prior to the assessment date. It would make little sense to delay plans to liquidate assets until after the assessment date, nor would it make sense to beef up inventory prior to the assessment date unless you have no other alternative. The overall objective is to reduce your tax liability.

Some companies have been known to remove assets or equipment from their facilities during the assessment period. I will never suggest any illegal activity to you. But I do strongly suggest you do all you legally can to reduce taxes whenever you can. You have a legal obligation to pay taxes but you have no obligation to pay one cent more than the law demands.

Delete obsolete inventory or revalue inventory of reduced value if applicable. Carrying inventory that has limited or no value is foolish, takes up costly space, and falsely inflates your profit picture. By inflating your profits you will pay higher taxes and, as importantly, you will be distorting your own profit picture which could negatively affect management decisions.

Many companies kid themselves into thinking inventory is worth more than it is or that old items will sell. By doing this you might succeed in paying more taxes. This is certainly not a goal of mine and should not be one of yours.

If you have slow moving items in inventory lower the price and sell them off. They are doing you no good sitting on your shelf. Try to recover your cost and drop them from your line.

Chapter 26. Sales.

"The typical salesman is a man with a smile on his face, a shine on his shoes, and a lousy territory."

Anonymous

Sell solutions and benefits, not products or services. While I touched on this in the marketing section I feel it is important enough to remind you of it again here. The best salespeople (and the best marketing people) do not sell products and they do not sell services. They sell benefits and they sell solutions.

However, before they can sell a solution or benefit they must find out what the problem or need is. The only way to accomplish this is to ask the questions. This applies to the area of sales as much as it does to every other area of your business. You must look beyond what you are trying to sell and find out how your products or services can meet the prospect's needs. Questions will give you the direction for your sales efforts and questions will provide openings to potential sales you might never have known about.

All sales leads must be followed up. As with other strategies this sounds obvious but I could write a book on the number of times I have requested sales information or a sales call and have never heard from anyone. If you are spending money to generate sales leads you damn well had better make sure that every lead is followed up and you must have a way to ensure this is being done. If you do not you are wasting your money.

Let me give you just one example. Recently I attended a local business trade show. There were about 50 businesses displaying their products and services. I went to every single booth to inquire about their services and gave them my business card and signed up for their mailing list. Out of the 50, over the next month I heard from 9. Over 80% of these people wasted their time and money participating in this sales effort. **This is inexcusable.**

Let me give you another example. About two weeks ago I was contacting companies to solicit proposals and bids on a piece of equipment that would cost about $100,000. Among those I contacted was the major manufacturer of this type of equipment. I left messages with the sales department 4 times over a 2 week time span without a single call back before I finally got fed up and asked for the sales manager.

Furthermore, a study by Performark, Inc., found that a full 22% of all sales leads generated by inquiries, response cards, and bingo cards were never answered. A full 22%. Think of the money that is wasted. Effective follow up generates sales and justifies your expenditures of sales money. Anything else is a waste of your time and money.

If you do not have a plan to handle follow ups and a method to make sure they are being done, don't waste your time advertising or promoting. Just open up the window and throw the money out. At least this way you will only waste the money and not the time. Wasting your money on any type of advertising without an actionable systematic follow up procedure is not only stupid, but it also makes your company look bad and can create resentment among your prospects. On the other hand effective follow up will drop the average cost per sales ratio since you will be converting more leads into sales.

In Pursuit of Profits. How To At Least Double Your Profits Without Increasing Your Sales.

"In sales, think of "I don't know" as a yes, "No" as a maybe, and "get the hell out" as promising."

Derrick W. Welch

<u>**How quick do your salespeople give up?**</u> According to a recent article in the magazine "Sales and Marketing Management", 80% of all sales are made after the 5th sales contact. Think about this. A full 80% of all sales are not realized until after you have contacted your prospect at least 5 times. <u>The vast majority of salespeople give up long before the 5th sales contact.</u> In fact, most give up after the 2nd or 3rd sales effort.

"Failure is often a solid foundation for success."

Derrick W. Welch

Those who push on and refuse to give up are the ones that are making the sale. Those who consider "no" a stepping stone to "yes", are the ones making the sale. Those who consider indecision a positive step on the path to "yes" are the ones that are making the sales.

I know from first hand experience as a buyer for hundreds of different products from dozens of different salespeople each year, that this is true. Relationship selling generates the majority of all sales. Ongoing relationships with your customers require ongoing contact. Relationship selling demands that you think in terms of serving your customer's needs and not just in terms of making a sale. **Remember, persistence prevails when all else fails.**

<u>**Understand the difference between a sale and a customer.**</u> A sale is a one time event. A sale does not make a customer. There is a difference. A big difference. A sale is a one time occurrence. An ongoing relationship translates into a repeat buyer which is exactly what a customer is. Repetitive contact in the form of in person sales calls, phone calls, notes, letters, and faxes is what builds the relationship.

Visiting or calling a buyer once a year or every 6 months to sell them a specific product will not accomplish the goal of establishing the relationship needed to turn an occasional "sale" into a customer. Relationship selling is a combination of service and cross selling. By working from a position of developing long term relationships with your customers you will be working to conduct business in a mutually beneficial manner instead of just thinking of short term profits or gains. Don't think of making a short term profit if it could mean you are sacrificing a long term relationship.

This is very common when a customer has a problem and a company sees a chance to capitalize by taking advantage of the situation to maximize profit. This occurs quite frequently and I have been on the receiving end of a company who realized we were in a bind and gave us the shaft. Any short term profit they made was far outweighed by what they lost in long term business and referrals.

"You can't buy a reputation, you must build one."

Derrick W. Welch

Who would you rather do business with or help, someone who took advantage of you when you were down or someone who helped you? It is just that simple. The short term loss of profits will be replaced with a bastion of goodwill that will pay dividends for many years. But you should not do this because you are seeking long term profits. That is a side benefit. You should do this because it is the right thing to do. Wouldn't you want to be treated the same way?

If you sell by catalog, consider sending a condensed version of your catalog until you have qualified your prospects and customers. The vast majority of those who receive your catalog will never buy from you. If you keep them on your mailing list and periodically send them a new full size catalog you are wasting a great deal of money. Instead, you should think about sending out a very condensed version of your overall catalog until they purchase and qualify for the full catalog or, at the very least, until they express interest in buying from you by requesting a full catalog.

If you sell by catalog consider issuing one main catalog each year or every six months and then as needed issue periodic updates and supplements. By doing this instead of issuing a new catalog more frequently you will save significant amounts of time and money as a result of reduced printing and postage.

If you sell by catalog or issue a catalog and your product line stays consistent for long periods of time consider removing prices from the catalog and instead mail along a small one color price list that corresponds to the catalog. This will allow you to issue fewer catalogs and instead only issue new price booklets when your prices change. Why issue a new catalog every few months when the products have not changed but the prices have? This can save you tens of thousands, or even hundreds of thousands, of dollars a year.

If you sell products through sales representatives and you have to prepay for those products make sure this is being factored into the cost of the order being sold and the salesperson's commission is adjusted accordingly to reflect the actual profitability. For example, if you are a distributor of custom made or custom imprinted products very often you take an order, send it to your supplier and have them ship this finished order direct. Once completed and shipped the supplier will bill you and you, in turn, bill your customer.

But most likely there will be times that a supplier will request that you prepay all or part of the order. This puts you in the position of prepaying a sum of money for what could easily be 60 or 90 days. This costs you money and hurts your cash flow. When this happens you should recalculate the cost of the order and adjust the selling price or commission paid to reflect the higher costs you are incurring on prepaid orders. This will normally equate to 1% or 2% of the order's net cost.

If you are selling in a business to business environment you must make sure that all orders you are accepting include a purchase order from the customer. An actual purchase order is best, but at least get a purchase order number with an actual purchase order to follow. Many companies (and yours should be one of them) will not pay an invoice unless it includes a purchase order # from their company. They want to control the accounts payable process and make sure that only authorized purchases are paid and that all terms and prices are correct and in agreement with the purchase order.

If you do not have a purchase order #, or at least some written form of authorization, you are at risk for not getting paid at all, or at the very least, suffering delayed payment. Both can cost you a great deal of money. Imagine having a $10,000 invoice held up because you proceeded without a purchase order. You might not get paid at all on this order. Imagine having a $10,000 order held up for payment because you had a purchase order and did not include the PO # on your invoice.

Get the purchase order and make sure you reference the purchase order number when you invoice the customer. Think of how costly this can be to you if you do not. First of all, you may never get paid since it could be said that you proceeded without authorization. Even a delay can be very costly.

For example, let's say you have an order that cost you $8,000 to produce. To cover this cost you had to borrow the $8,000 at 10% interest. This means your interest cost on this money is $67 per month. Let us also say that your net profit (not gross) on this order is 5%. This means your bottom line profit is $500.

Assuming you have factored the initial borrowing costs into the cost of your order based on the time it took to produce, deliver, and collect payment based on a 30 day due date. If your customer pays within the 30 days your 5 % net profit margin remains intact. That is assuming that you billed the order out without any delays on your end.

But what happens if your customer refuses to pay because you forgot to add the purchase order number to the invoice? If your customer held your bill until you call him 30 days later and ask for payment you have a problem. Your customer will tell you to send a new bill with the purchase order number indicated and he will then consider this a new bill due in 30 days.

This added 30 day delay will reduce your net profit by 13.4%. This is figured by dividing your monthly interest cost of $67 by your net profit of $500. If he takes 60 days to pay it will reduce your net profit by over 26%. Can you afford to give this type of profit away? If your answer is yes, you had better call me quick you could use my help.

Make sure that all proposals are submitted in writing. Allow no exceptions! Most surprises in business are negative. You cannot afford to have any misunderstanding over what you are selling, under what terms and conditions, and at what price.

Make sure that your salespeople are receiving complete and in depth training. Putting an improperly trained sales rep in the field or on the floor is going to cost you money and it is going to give your customers and prospects a crisis of confidence. Make sure they know what they are doing and how to do it before you expose them to your customers and prospects.

Use all forms of communication you can to reinforce your selling efforts. As I have outlined earlier, most companies miss many low cost and no cost opportunities to cross sell and reinforce the selling effort. You must think. From including selling messages on your order forms and invoices to interior and exterior signs, I have no doubt you are missing opportunities to get your message out. You don't agree? Call your own office. What do you hear when you are on hold?

Always look to improve your cross selling efforts to your existing customers. They are your best and least expensive source of increased business. They know you and trust you. You have already spent the time and money to make them customers. Cross sell them whenever the opportunity exists. You have a base to which you can sell more to with a significantly reduced cost and effort. If you have 100 customers who each buy one thing from you and you can sell 50 of them one more thing you have just increased your items sold by 50%.

Compare this to the time, effort, and cost of getting 50 new customers. Just like adding a new room to your house is a lot easier and a lot less costly than building a new house, cross selling to your existing customers is much less costly and much easier than getting a new customer. My next few strategies will help you accomplish this.

> *"There are three kinds of people;*
> *Those who make things happen,*
> *those who watch things happen,*
> *and those who don't know what the hell is happening."*

> *Dr. Robert Anthony*

Are you getting the most for your money? This is a continuation of the last strategy. Let me make my point further by demonstrating a recent experience I had at a local restaurant. Now if you are the restaurant owner you have fixed overhead, you are open, and you are paying your people. The more you can sell your customers the lower your overall cost per customer will be. Well, when was the last time you went to a restaurant and were offered an appetizer? Dessert? An after dinner drink? This is cross selling.

Back to my example. I eat out quite frequently both while on business and for personal pleasure. I find that wherever I go it is very difficult to get good food or good service. It is almost impossible to get both at the same time. I recently went to a moderately priced restaurant in my area. I was not greeted as a welcome customer but rather as one more inconvenience on a busy night.

I had to wait for nearly 25 minutes to get a table. While waiting, not once was I asked if I wanted a drink or an appetizer despite the fact that the waiting area was conducive to the serving of both. During this time I would have enjoyed a drink and something to eat. Instead of increasing sales and keeping a customer happy at the same time, they offered nothing. I sat and waited and watched the clock in frustration.

I was finally seated at a table that had yet to be fully cleared and reset. A very poor tip from the previous patron sat in front of me. At this point my only surprise was why any tip at all was left. It was another 10 minutes before the table was completely cleared and reset. By now my anger was rising and my stomach was in knots. Not a very conducive situation to have a customer in when your only products are food and service.

Another 5 minutes went by before a server came by and asked if I was ready to order. Notice I said she asked if I was ready to order, not would I like a drink or an appetizer. I had now been in this restaurant for over 40 minutes and had been offered nothing. **Do you see a problem here with sales management? Not only did the server not try to sell me anything, she was obviously trying to avoid having me order anything else.**

Despite this, I ordered a drink and my meal. Nearly 30 minutes went by before my meal came and not once during this time did the server come anywhere near my table to see if I would like another drink or anything else. In fact, each time she came near my table I tried to get her attention so that I could ask for another drink. She was simply too good. Her radar must have warned her that a customer was going to ask to buy something and each time she avoided my eye contact and scurried away before I could place my order for another drink.

When the food arrived it was quickly dropped in front of me and before I knew she had been there, she was gone. It reminded me of when I was a child and thought I saw Santa Claus. I thought I had seen him one year but he came and went so quick I just could not be sure. I do know however, his visit turned out much better than my server's had.

Now I had my meal, which was lukewarm, and nothing to drink with it. I had never been asked if I wanted anything else or needed anything else. No one had attempted to sell me anything. No wine, no side dish. Nothing. I quickly finished my meal and sat and waited for the server to return. I was now the waiter. I was waiting and was not being waited on. When this elusive creature finally made another appearance it was merely to deposit my check on the table. The table had never been cleared. I had not been offered dessert, coffee, or an after dinner drink. Not only did she not try to sell me anything, but she did not even try to find out if I wanted anything else or if my meal was acceptable.

The price of this arduous odyssey? It was $38.00. I estimated that if I had been allowed to order drinks when I wanted to and had been able to order an appetizer and dessert, as I would normally do, and finished with an after dinner drink the bill would have come to almost $60.00. Their sales to me alone could have been increased almost 60%. The tip that I left will require 49 more just like it to fill a roll of 50. Had the service been as it should, my tip would have been based on a bill close to or exceeding $60 and therefore would have ranged from $10 to $15 depending on the server. We are talking an increased tip income amounting to 1000% to 1500%.

As important to the restaurant, they would have had a repeat customer that spends close to $5,000 per year to dine out. Instead, they will never see me again and I will negatively influence others regarding their choice of this establishment. They could have received significant word of mouth advertising from me.

This type of poor service and lack of cross selling costs restaurants a great deal. It drives up costs while driving down profits and sales. For example, if the server works 10 hours at $3 per hour and produces tabs of $210 it has $3 in labor cost for every $7 in sales. If however, the server did a better job in selling and servicing the customers the tabs might have totaled $300. This would mean that $10 in sales was generated for every $3 of labor. The labor cost per sale has dropped significantly.

Another example is a shoe store. They have the same base overhead but can lower costs as a percentage of sales by increasing sales. They can increase sales by selling not just shoes but also socks, laces, protective polish, handbags, belts, and any other related item. But these added items will not sell themselves. It is up to the owner of that shoe store to make sure his people are suggesting and cross selling. This means getting more for his money.

The same thing is true of stores that sell suits. When I buy a suit I am spending a few hundred dollars. It would be very easy for the sales person to also convince me to purchase a new tie, shirt, or belt. But they never do. They never bring a shirt or tie over to me and show me what a great match it is. They never tell me what a beautiful shirt and tie combination this is and how perfect it would be with the suit I am buying.

They are not selling. They are order takers. They expect the shirts and ties lying on the counter to somehow sell themselves and jump into my pile at the register. If these people cross sold properly the owner would be enjoying more sales and more sales means lower costs as he is getting a higher return on his investment.

You want salespeople not order takers. Think of anyone who deals directly with your customers and prospects as a salesperson, not an order taker or customer service representative.

Think of real estate people. The owner of the real estate company has a certain level of fixed overhead. The more sales his people make the lower his overhead cost per sale is. But think of most real estate people you have met. Are they salespeople? Of course not. They walk prospective buyers through properties and make brilliant comments like "this is the living room" or "here is the kitchen" as though this is somehow selling. As though anyone over the age of two who had an IQ above that of a flea would not know that the kitchen was the kitchen unless the real estate salesperson told them so. They are merely tour guides not salespeople.

If the owner of the real estate office had salespeople instead of tour guides he would see many more sales and many more sales means he is getting more for his money which, of course, means a lower overhead cost per sale.

What do you have order takers, tour guides, or salespeople?

<u>**One of the most effective and easiest ways to cross sell products is to look for what I call "triggers".**</u> Triggers are purchases made by a customer or prospect that trigger a cross selling reaction on your part. The concept of "triggers" is the same for all type of companies, but to demonstrate what I am saying let's assume for a minute that you are a company selling note cards to banks. If you have a customer who does not use note cards you have to convince them of the value of using note cards and to buy them from you. On the other hand, if you have a customer that uses note cards already you have no need to convince them of the value of note cards or of why they should buy from you, but merely that they should use more and buy them from you.

The job of selling them on the benefits of note card use has already been done by you or someone else. Now let's say you have a customer who purchases only new account note cards. **This is a trigger.** They already use a note card and therefore it can be assumed that they understand the value of communicating with their customers. The door is wide open now for a cross selling effort targeted to selling them other types of note cards.

The sales message is that you know they understand what an important tool note cards are in maintaining customer relations. But you also know that they are using the note cards they are now buying to say thank you only to new accounts. As important as this is, they should also be using many other types of note cards to communicate with their customers.

Thanking new accounts is only one part of what should be a systematic program of ongoing communication with their customers. Since they use the thank you note card to solidify the foundation they have established with the new account holder and generate good will, should they not also be doing the same thing with dormant accounts, paid loans, and closed accounts?

Shouldn't they also be using personal note cards to constantly reinforce the banking relationship by sending birthday cards, good news cards, and get well cards? The foundation of note card use is already established by the purchase and use of new account cards. You are suggesting to them that they should build upon the foundation they have started just as you are trying to build on the foundation you have started.

Since attracting new accounts is just one part of their marketing efforts they should also be using the same tactic of sending note cards to cross sell services, solicit customer feedback, activate dormant accounts, reinforce the bank's caring attitude, solicit new loans, and thank customers for their business.

Their best prospects for increased business lie within their existing customers. Thanking a new account is only the beginning of the process. Retaining the customer and increasing their business via cross selling of other products and services must command an equal level of commitment from the bank. One way for them to accomplish this is to use more of your note cards.

Remember, the trigger to this particular sequence of cross selling efforts was the fact that they already use a note card for one purpose. All you are doing is reinforcing the intelligent decision they made to use note cards as part of their marketing efforts and explaining to them why this same logic applies to a number of other applications. **You are not selling them on the benefits of note card use in general. They already know this since they use a note card.**

You are merely reminding them of the benefits they already get from the new account cards and suggesting that they use more note cards to realize similar or greater benefits from other sections of their customer base. You are simply telling them how to expand their internal cross selling efforts by using the same type of marketing tool they are already employing in another area. You are cross selling by educating them as to how to more effectively cross sell and solidify relationships. You have the same goal they do.

You simply need to remind them that marketing is not a static one time event. Marketing is a program of ongoing communication and reinforcement. Effective marketing is an ongoing process with each subsequent effort reinforcing and building on each preceding effort. By explaining this to them you are selling the benefits of using note cards for many other purposes than to just thank a new account. You are not selling note cards, you are selling a way for them to inexpensively and consistently reach out and communicate with their customers and prospects. A way they already know works.

Yes, I said prospects, even though in this case they are communicating with their current customers. Unless the customer is conducting business with that bank in every area they could be, they are a prospect for more products and services. Just the way it is with your customers. Customers for one or a few products are always prospects for other products or services. The best prospects they or you will ever have.

Triggers are merely one way to cross sell but they are among the easiest ways to cross sell you will ever find. Your customer not only already has an awareness of who you are and what you do, but they also already know the benefits of using the related type of product.

Combine products and services whenever possible. This is an excellent way to build in an automatic cross selling strategy. Instead of selling a suit, sell a suit, tie, and shirt combination. Instead of selling an appetizer, entree, and dessert, sell a compete dinner package. Instead of selling one thing sell two or three related items combined as a package. What you are doing is automatically cross selling with no more effort. You are also eliminating the salesperson from the cross selling effort since your packaging has already accomplished this for you.

Think. Unless you sell only one product, and if that is the case start thinking product line expansion quickly, you have products and services that can be packaged together. A packaging strategy can dramatically increase your sales without a corresponding increase in costs.

"To see what is right and not do it, is want of courage, or of principle."

Confucius

Don't sell your customer poor quality products or something that you know is not right for them. Just because a customer might want something, or be willing to buy something, does not mean that it is in your best interest to sell it to them. I am not suggesting that you decide what they should and should not buy. I am suggesting that if something may not be in your customer's best interest you should at least point this out to them and explain why.

For example, if your customer wanted to buy a lower quality product from you and you know full well this is the wrong way for them to go, I think you owe it to them and to yourself to tell them this. If they still buy it fine, at least you have done the right thing. If they choose not to buy it and you lose the sale they will at least respect you for looking out for their best interests even at your own short term loss.

In either case you are building a strong foundation for a long term relationship. I have talked many customers out of purchases that I simply felt were wrong for them. Normally it involved pointing out things they did not think of or did not realize. In almost every case they were very surprised at this tactic and very appreciative. The long term relationships this type of honesty and integrity have fostered have paid dividends thousands of times more profitable than any short term profit loss would have been.

I have turned jobs away at times because I knew the customer could get the product they wanted much cheaper somewhere else. If I sold it to them and later they found out they could get this at a much lower price how good do you think they would feel about doing business with me in the future? The long term goodwill I receive when I do this couldn't be bought. Goodwill that not only cements the foundation for a long term relationship, but turns into numerous referrals. It is also the right thing to do! Think of serving the best interest of your customer long term even if it costs you in the short term.

"There is less to fear from outside competition than from inside inefficiency, discourtesy, and bad service."

Anonymous

Studies have shown that the price of a service or product is a prime concern to only 14% of all customers. It has been my experience that "price" has been used by so many companies and salespeople as an excuse for sub par performance in other areas that this statement bears repeating. Studies have shown that the price of a service or product is a prime concern to only 14% of all customers. Take this crutch away from yourself and your people.

While price is a factor, as it should be, it is by no means the most important factor to most customers or prospects. In fact, studies have shown that other factors are more important to 86% of your customers and prospects. Factors such as customer service, consumer confidence, and quality just to name a few. Selling on price only will always cost you money. Sometimes a great deal of money. It can also undermine your customers' and prospects' confidence in the areas of service and quality. You must be selling on the whole package. Product, price, service, and quality.

Never sell on price alone. You should not buy this way and you should not sell this way. Doing so will simply cost you too much lost profit and will drive up your cost of sales. Sell based on quality, service, and price. Just the way you should buy. Selling on price only is not selling. Relationship sell. After all, the price is the deciding factor to only a small percentage of your customers and prospects.

The basic goal of every business is simple. To sell your product or service at the highest price you can while providing it at the lowest possible cost. Yes, many complexities enter into this simple equation but don't ever lose sight of the fact that price is only one component of the successful selling formula. A prime factor to only 14% of the buyers.

When you are pricing your products make sure that you are not kidding yourself by basing your pricing on an unrealistic sales volume. The proper pricing of a product or service can be a very complex process which involves numerous tangible and intangible factors depending on the product or service involved, the competition, what the market will bear, and dozens of other factors. As such it is beyond the scope of this book to even attempt to provide you with all the questions and answers you need to properly and profitably price your products and services.

However, I do want to at least point out an all too common problem I see that exists in many companies. All too often sales projections of your products or services are overly optimistic. This leads to a false conclusion regarding the economies of scale you will be realizing. This, of course, leads to a lower than justified cost for producing and providing your product or service. It can also lead to many other very costly problems. Again, my objective here is not to teach you how to price your products or services but rather to caution you about basing your projected sales on reality.

How do you price your products or service? As I have mentioned before, discussing how to properly price your products or services is a subject beyond the scope of this book. However, I do want to make another comment on this subject. Your cost to produce and deliver your product or service should only be important to you to the point that it allows you to know the amount you must charge above to make a profit. Your actual selling price should be driven by what the market will bear, or in other words, what your customers and prospects will pay. Never forget your objective should be to make the best quality product you can for the lowest cost and to sell it at the highest possible price.

> *"There is hardly anything in the world that someone cannot make a little worse and sell a little cheaper ... and the people who consider price alone are this man's lawful prey!"*
>
> *John Ruskin*

Do not be afraid to raise your prices. Remember what I showed you before about price being the deciding factor to only 14% of all buyers. Many companies do not understand this and sell far too heavily on price. **Selling on price alone or as a primary sales tool is often a trademark of a weak sales force. The weak in any endeavor will always turn to the easiest way first**. They cut prices and underprice products and services. They are afraid to raise prices or charge proper pricing. They leave money on the table too often. Are your people guilty of this? What drives the sales process in your company? What drives the pricing process in your company?

Think about how much bottom line profit you could add if you are able to hold costs while raising prices. If your sales volume is $100,000,000 and your costs are $95,000,000 and you can hold costs while rasing prices by even 3%, your income will rise to $103,000,000. This means you have added $3,000,000 to your bottom line thereby increasing your profits from $5,000,000 to $8,000,000. **Your 3% price increase has produced a 60% increase in profits. A 5% price increase, while holding costs level, would double this company's profits!**

I know this is a simplistic example as it does not reflect the possible loss in sales that might occur as a result of your price increases. But even factoring in the possible loss of sales resulting from a price increase you can see the overall potential gain in profits should greatly exceed any loss of sales.

Six primary reasons exist for the failure of a product. 1)A supply is created where no demand exists. Simply put, no one wants the product. 2) Too many similar products already exist in the marketplace and the new product is unable to enter the marketplace and differentiate itself quickly and clearly. 3) The new product is copied and / or improved upon by a competitor and the market is lost. 4) The product is forced off the market due to safety concerns or regulatory action. 5) The product is of poor quality or does not live up to promotional billing. 6) The product is overpriced or underpriced.

While there are many other secondary reasons for the failure of a new product if you can neutralize these 6 concerns you will significantly increase your chances of success in the market.

Are your salespeople asking for the order? Studies have found that nearly two thirds of all salespeople never ask for the order. You might think this is hard to believe but think about how many times a salesperson asked you for the order. This is another example of wasted time, money, and effort. Making a sales call in any type of business is an expensive proposition. If your salespeople are not doing all they can to close that sale they are costing you money in the form of unproductive sales calls and lost sales.

Control salespeople price cuts. They may be willing to settle for a reduced or small profit level but you should not be. There are a number of ways you can control price cutting by salespeople. Here are a few:

• Don't allow price cuts without home office approval.

• Make them absorb all of the price cut or at least the bulk of it in the form of a reduced commission.

• Establish a minimum profit level for the company. If they sell below this profit level the added cut comes out of their commission.

You want your salespeople selling on price, product, and service, not just price. Make them do their job.

Always make sure that you are securing the names and addresses of all your customers. The best, and lowest cost, source you will ever have for added sales and referrals will be your customers. Don't you think it might be a good idea to know who they are and what they buy? If you do not know who they are how can you ever expect to sell them again and how can you expect to get referrals?

You can't, of course. It is a disgraceful situation for a company not to even know who their own customers are. You spend a great deal of time and money trying to get new customers and yet you may not even know who your current customers are. How could you possible justify this?

How can you communicate with your customers if you don't know who they are? How can you send them a thank you card? How can you ask for referrals? How can you advise them of a change in hours, prices, or location if you do not know who they are and how to reach them? How can you advise them of a sale?

Many companies have no idea who their customers are. Think of retail stores. They are among the worst offenders. When was the last time a retail store of any type asked you for your name and address or offered to put you on their mailing list? I suspect you will have to think awhile.

I am sure you see my point. Even if you have no plans to use this information now you should be obtaining and recording the names, addresses and purchasing interests of your customers. Whether it be on an order form, sign up sheet for your mailing list, a warranty card, or any other vehicle you can think of, get this information.

Even if you never use this information, and you should, you may be able to use it to generate added income. How? Sell your mailing list to other non competing companies who are targeting your type of customers and will do what you won't, or don't do, with these names.

In Pursuit of Profits. How To At Least Double Your Profits Without Increasing Your Sales.

Keep your mailing lists clean. You must do this. The cost of sending out direct mail is simply too high. At least twice a year you should provide copies of mailing information on each of your salesman's accounts to them so they can review and update. You should also update every return piece of mail as soon as you get it back. Other steps are to take note of changes on orders and to consider using "return address requested" on your mailings once a year. It will cost you a bit more but it will go a long way to keeping your mailing list up to date.

Look into proactive steps such as tag along notices with outgoing mail and packages that ask your customers to notify you of any move they make or change in mailing information. Think of the cost and time that go into any piece you mail out. Between time, material, and postage you can be spending $1, $2, $3, or more per mailing piece. Depending on the size of your list, the cost of your mailings, and the frequency of your mailings you can be spending thousands, or hundreds of thousands of dollars a year or more, on mailings that don't have a chance to make a sale.

Make sure that your salespeople are using samples and sale literature effectively. You want salespeople not order takers. They should be out selling your products and services not just leaving samples and literature behind. This is not only unproductive, but also very costly to you.

One way to control this is not to provide unlimited samples and literature. Instead, consider providing a base amount to each and then provide additional ones at cost or half the cost. Another way would be to provide a base amount to each salesperson and then provide additional ones at cost or at no charge contingent upon achievement of a specific sales level. In other words, the more they sell the more sales aids you will provide them with.

Drop all products that have a low profit margin and / or a low sales volume. You must use your resources effectively and rarely, if ever, are these type of sales effective uses of your resources. I know this is a book on cost cutting so I'll refrain from delving into this area too much and save that for my next book, however, I will tell you I am not a believer in loss leaders and low profit sales. In most cases I have found that by dropping these types of sales you will realize much higher overall profits as a direct result of the savings realized from the resources no longer expended to create and maintain these types of sales.

You will be able to cut costs (or put these resources to better use for efforts such as selling more high profit items) in labor, inventory, and space among the many areas. The loss of these low profit sales will normally be greatly exceeded by a greater savings in costs. Remember, if you drop $1 in low profit sales you are only reducing your bottom line by an amount equal to your pretax profit ratio not the full $1. This will most likely be only a few pennies on every dollar of sales. However, if you are able to decrease costs by $1 you are adding $1 directly to your bottom line.

By shedding yourself of low profit or no profit sales, you should very easily be able to decrease your related overhead costs by much more. You are now also able to turn your attention and resources to providing products and services that are profitable. This will lead to the sale of products and services that are profitable. This is what I hope you are in business for.

Examine every product and service you are selling or providing to make sure it is cost effective to continue to do so. You will find many marginal profit and low or no profit products or services that you offer. Some may be justified because they are of value in keeping and cross selling your customers but others simply use valuable resources and force you to maintain higher overhead levels than can be cost justified.

Pay your salespeople based on commissions earned and not a flat salary. Salaried salespeople have a greatly reduced incentive. This is just a reflection of human nature. If earnings are not based on performance then you are not very likely to get high performance in return. Simple common sense.

If a salesperson's earnings are based on performance (sales) they are much more likely to perform better (make more sales). This is not brain surgery we are talking about here, this is just simple common sense. Pay them for what they sell. Salary gives them little or no incentive and you take all the fiscal risk. If they are paid a salary and don't perform up to the level you expect or need to recover that salary, you are out the money you paid them.

For example, if you pay a sales rep $600 a week or $31,200 per year and they only make sales that return profits equal to $15,000 you are out $16,200. Had you instead paid them based on actual sales you would have saved $16,200. This does not even include all the added costs involved such as FUTA, workers' comp, etc..

As an alternative you could give them a very low base salary (to provide weekly income) and then a commission override for all sales that exceed the base salary on an annual basis.

If you pay a draw against commissions make sure that there is a cap on how far in the hole your salespeople can go on a draw. Many times new salespeople do not work out and the relationship is terminated or they quit. If they leave owing you thousands of dollars you are going to have a very hard time collecting from someone out of work. If you must take legal action to collect you will run up legal costs and risk the bad publicity of suing an employee you terminated. Even if you do decide to take legal action to collect, your chances of winning the case and collecting are slim and none. Who do you think the judge or jury will sympathize with, you or the person you terminated?

Pay commissions only after you have been paid. This will not only allow you to avoid prepaying commissions which is very costly to you, but it also helps reduce your collection problems since your sales representatives will be more careful of who they sell and will gladly get involved in any collection activity. It will also stop you from paying commissions in advance on an order, having the sales rep leave, and then finding out later you cannot collect on the order or that the order wasn't even a real order.

Consider switching your employee salespeople over to independent contractors. Significant savings are possible under this type of arrangement as you can save 30% or more when you consider the added cost of carrying them as employees. However, before you do this you must check with your lawyer and accountant to insure you can meet the IRS test for the legality of this type of arrangement. Proceed carefully. If this type of arrangement is suitable for your company it can save a great deal of money, but if not, in the long run it could cost you a lot of money and create tax problems.

Never sacrifice the quality of your product or service in the interest of cost control or anything else. Never! I will never suggest you do this and do not ever read any suggestion to that effect into any of my comments. I will suggest that you do the exact opposite. As I have stated in a number of other places, you must constantly seek ways to improve your operations, products, and service. By doing this you will automatically improve efficiency and reduce costs.

In Pursuit of Profits. How To At Least Double Your Profits Without Increasing Your Sales.

"There's never enough time to do it right, but there's always enough time to do it over."

Jack Bergman

Always put quality ahead of price. People will remember a poor quality product or poor service long after they forget the cheap price they paid for it. On the other hand, they will long forget the fact that they paid a bit more for your product or service if they continue to enjoy or benefit from the product or service you have sold them.

If you think quality costs, think about what poor quality costs. I can guarantee you that poor quality in any area of your business is going to cost you customers in the long run and money in every phase of your operation.

Studies have indicated that companies that sell products spend 20% or more of all income from gross sales on correcting quality related problems. From product returns to service calls to customer service costs, think of the wasted time and money that is being spent simply because the time and effort to do it right was not expended at the beginning.

Studies have also shown that 35% or more of all operational costs incurred in service companies goes to correct quality related problems. Think about this. These are stunning totals. Start spending your time and money where it belongs, in making your company a more efficient profitable organization and not in correcting quality control problems.

Resource
One source for quality management materials is ASQC Quality Press, 611 E. Wisconsin Ave., Milwaukee, WI, 53201. 1-800-248-1946.

Establish a minimum profit level for your products and services and do not go below that level. Make sure the level you establish justifies the risk involved. If the order goes bad, or the customer does not pay, you have a problem. The risk should always be justified by the reward. The reward, of course, is the profit.

If you accept marginal or low profit jobs, do so with the agreement that you will produce them as fill in work during your slow periods. This will often require a longer than normal lead time, but if the price is right it can benefit both you and your customer. They will save money and you will be able to keep your staff busy during slower times, or realize economies of scale by working this type of work in with other jobs as it is advantageous for you to do so.

You already have a large amount of fixed overhead, including much of your labor and most of your facility related costs. Therefore, during slow periods, this lower profit work will allow you to recapture some of these fixed costs. You will, in effect, be lowering your per job overhead cost since you are spreading out these fixed costs over a larger number of jobs.

To clarify this a bit I will demonstrate my point using a very simple example. If you have 100 jobs and a fixed overhead of $10,000 your overhead per job works out to $100. This is how much of your overhead is covered by each job. Of course, this example does not include many other factors that must be considered, but please indulge me while I make a point. If you have 120 jobs with the same fixed income of $10,000 you have now reduced your per job fixed income to $83. Even if these added jobs were low profit jobs you have spread your fixed overhead over a larger number of jobs.

Increasing the scope of your product and service offerings will accomplish the same thing while increasing sales and market share. By lowering the amount of overhead covered by each job you are increasing the profitability of all jobs since a smaller portion of the income from each job must cover fixed overhead.

If your product or service involves added charges for added services make sure that your salespeople are charging them. Elimination of these is a very common occurrence by salespeople. You must take steps to recover the lost profits if this occurs and to encourage them not to do this in the future.

One step you should consider is a reduction for the amount of the added charge from the salesperson's commission or at least a partial reduction. Let me give you an example as to how this can add up. I work with one company that has a salesperson who cuts a routine added charge for art preparation about 80% of the time. This is a justified $20 charge. This salesperson sells about 400 orders per year. 80% of this is 320 orders. At $20 per order this has cost this company $6,400 per year in lost income.

By splitting this cost with him by reducing his commission an amount equal to 1/2 of the $20 charge every time he does not charge it, they would recover $3,200 of this cost and provide a tremendous incentive for him not to continue this practice since it also costs him $3,200. If they chose to assess the entire price cut to him they would recover all $6,400 and in all probability end this practice. As a point of reference this company's other salespeople charge this cost 95% of the time. I am well aware that this conflicts with my advice to you not to pay added charges but my interest is to save you money, not to save your suppliers money.

Don't be forced into carrying high cost medical plans for salespeople out of your current plans area. By this I mean, if you can cover all your local people under a low cost insurance plan (see insurance section) but you have a few people out of the area your plan covers, don't rush out and take a much higher cost plan that extends coverage into those areas.

Instead, have the salespeople involved seek insurance in their areas. They can look into private insurance, local association insurance, and insurance offered through the local Chamber of Commerce. Then compare these costs to the added costs you would incur had you added another plan, or changed over to another plan, to accommodate these people. Almost certainly you will see that by having these people purchase their own insurance locally and by reimbursing these people the same ratio as your other employees, you will realize significant savings.

At one time one of our salespeople was causing us to continue a very expensive plan with Blue Cross Blue Shield. This was the only plan we offered that covered his area. By having him join a local association and purchase insurance through them we were able to save 50% of the costs for an equal level of coverage.

He too saved 50% since we split these costs equally. This 50% was after the cost of joining the association. On an annual basis this saved each of us over $4,000 per year. How much would you need to increase your sales to add $4,000 dollars to your bottom line? Think. If your profit ratio last year was 2.5% you would need to add $160,000 in sales to realize this same bottom line impact.

Develop the sales territory before you assign a sales rep to it. I know the conventional method is to put a rep in a territory to develop it but this can be very expensive especially if you are putting a salaried rep into the territory. Try to at least build a foundation of business and awareness for your company and it's products or services in the targeted territory before placing a sales rep into it. If you are a well known visible national firm this won't be as critical, but if you are like most small businesses this will indeed be needed.

In Pursuit of Profits. How To At Least Double Your Profits Without Increasing Your Sales.

At least 6 to 12 months before engaging a sales rep for the target area start conducting highly targeted mailings into this area and aggressive phone follow up and sales efforts. These can be conducted with minimal risk and cost. The goal is to have a foundation built before you put a costly rep into it. If you hire a sales representative in an area that you have little or no sales base and no corporate visibility, you are going to be running a very high risk of a costly failure.

Even if you do not have this person on salary you are running a risk. You will be unable to attract a high quality individual and keep them unless there is a reasonable expectation of success in a reasonable period of time. Constant turnover will be very costly and directly counter to your goals of establishing this territory.

An alternative would be to consider using commission only independent reps, distributors, or manufacture's reps to extend your sales base into markets in which you now have little or no market penetration. By locating reps in these areas who now carry similar, but non competitive products, you can find a ready made market for your products and the reps can expand their product offerings to the customers they already serve. The customers also win since they have access to added products and services.

Make sure that your salespeople are making the most productive use of their time and travel. This is another area that seems obvious, but, once again, I assure you it is not. Remember how uncommon common sense really is.

Make sure that they are scheduling their sales call with economies of time and cost in mind. I know of many salespeople who just get in the car and make calls all day. They never set up appointments and never give any consideration to the availability of the party they are seeking to see. The result is a lot of wasted time and travel. They should schedule ahead of time to maximize their own time and to be more considerate of your customers.

I know others who will cover existing business in one area one day and then later in the week return to that area to solicit new business. If the area involved is hours away they have again wasted time and money by repeating the travel. It makes no sense to travel a few hundred miles to the same territory twice in one week when by properly planning they could schedule current business and solicit new business all on the same trip. This is especially costly if you are paying for time and travel costs. Even if they are on straight commission this ineffective scheduling still costs you in the form of fewer sales due to poor use of time.

You should know the average number of sales that can be expected for your type of business in a given time period, if you have a salesperson falling short of the average this type of activity may be a reason why. By increasing the return on sales efforts you will decrease the cost per sale and improve profits.

How many times do your customers and prospects wish to get the same mailing from you? You must eliminate duplicate names and addresses not only on a regular basis from your own house list but also from outside lists. As discussed in another strategy, you must cross reference all names on your own list against those from the outside list. Since your target market is the same, you will most often find large numbers of duplicate names that are already on your list and are on the outside list that you buy.

When you review your lists you must be careful to look for duplications that are not obvious. To insure a clean list you should run a dupe elimination program each month and you be checking your lists manually at least once every 6 months.

The reason that you should manually check your lists each month should be obvious to you when you consider the number of duplicate mailings you get both at home and at the office. The computerized duplicate mailing elimination programs have serious flaws. They will only pick up exact match duplicates.

If it sees John A. Smith at 211 Old Road, Hanson, MA 02341 twice it will pick it up as a duplicate account. However, depending on the dupe elimination program you use, it may not pick up any variation of this such as J. Smith at the same address. Or John Smith at the same address or John Smith at Old Road.

You get the idea. Unless it is a perfect match, dupes will be left on your files. This can cost you hundreds of thousands of dollars in completely wasted mailings each year. I have received as many as four copies of the same four color catalog from the same company. This means their cost to reach me was 300% higher than it should have been.

You must either use a very sophisticated elimination program or you must make the time to manually check these yourself. You should also set up very specific entry procedures for all names entered into your system. You want to make sure that each person entering a name has checked to verify it is a new name and that they are entering them in the same way. Proper input procedures will go a long way to insure that most potential duplicate accounts never get in the system to begin with.

If you buy outside lists and your system cannot run dupe elimination properly through your computer then you should run a set of labels from your list sorted in the same sequence as the list you purchased and manually pull off all duplicate labels. You must think how can I accomplish something not that you can't accomplish something.

If your market is highly targeted you are going to find a large number of duplicate names. One outside list we rented to target one of our markets contained a 50% ratio of duplicate accounts. This was over 1,800 duplicates on the outside list that we already had on our in-house list. Granted, this was to a highly targeted audience and in most cases duplication ratios will not run anywhere near this high, however, it does drive home the point.

This list we rented was for 5 mailings spaced out over a year to subsidize our house list. The mailing packages we were sending cost an average of $2 each. Had we not eliminated the duplicates we would have wasted 1,800 pieces each mailing times 5 mailings for a total of 9,000 pieces or $18,000. Since our computer system did not allow us to run a duplicate elimination program we ran a hard copy list of our names in the same sequence as the rented list. Then we had a person come in for $5.00 an hour and manually eliminate the duplicate names. This took about 4 hours and cost $20.00. A $20.00 cost to save $18,000. This is serious cost reduction.

Just today I received a very expensive mailing from one of the largest, best known business schools in this country and on the outside of the envelope was written "We use mailing lists from many different sources. Because it is impractical to cross-check every list, you may receive more than one copy of this brochure." I did. In fact, I got 4.

Think about this. This is quite a comment coming from anyone never mind a so called top flight business school. This is clearly an example of academic ignorance. **Is it any wonder institutes of higher learning do not teach how to control costs, they have no idea.** Oh, by the way, the mailing was for a program the university was offering on financial management.

Not a week passes that I do not receive at least 2 or 3 duplicate mailings. From postcards to very expensive color catalogs, billions of dollars are wasted by duplicate mailings each year.

In Pursuit of Profits. How To At Least Double Your Profits Without Increasing Your Sales.

If you rent outside mailing lists make sure that you know your short term plans (short term is 12 months or less) so that you will be able to take advantage of multiple set purchase prices. Depending upon the frequency of use and size of your purchase, you will be able to save 50% to 80% of the cost of your list rental prices for all list rentals beyond the first one. Then go one step further and only have the lists sent to you and billed to you as you need them during the year, not all at once.

This way you are realizing the maximum discounted prices but only incurring the actual costs as you need to. This will also enable you to be getting current lists since by taking delivery as needed instead of purchasing months ahead of time you are much more likely to get cleaner lists.

Make sure that you are including and promoting use of your fax number on all mailings and outgoing correspondence. This will save you postage if you offer business reply cards or envelopes and it will save you labor and time from answering phone calls. If you offer an incoming 800# by providing this alternative method of placing an order or making an inquiry this will also cut down on your phone bills.

If an order is faxed in instead of phoned in on your 800# you have saved time from answering the phone and writing up the order since they are faxing you a hard copy. This will also eliminate errors on the order since you have written proof of what they ordered. This is another example of the domino effect. You have reduced your phone bill, saved time, and improved productivity. All without sacrificing your product or service.

If possible, try to have business lunches at your office. Not only will this save 50% to 80% of the cost of eating out, but you will also be saving time and demonstrating your commitment to maximizing your time and minimizing expenses.

Give your customers as many options to pay as possible. If you do not offer them the ability to pay by credit card consider it. This will not only provide them with another payment option, but can also lead to increased sales, lower bad debts, lower accounts receivables, and will eliminate the need to run credit checks on new customers. Contact a few banks in your area to find out what the best value in your area is.

Never allow one account or one customer to dominate your business. If you have a customer that represents 25% or more of your business you may find that you have a partner. In fact, you may find out the hard way that you are in many ways a subsidiary of this customer. They will be able to exert control over your operations and there will be little you can do about it.

It will be very simple for your customer to find another source for their business in almost every case. On the other hand, if you lose 25% or more of your business you may find yourself out of business. I have seen this happen first hand. At the very least you are looking at tremendous disruptions within your company as you struggle to adjust to the devastating loss of such a large piece of your business.

Is it any wonder that you may find your company acting as a subsidiary to this customer? They can call the shots and you will comply out of fear. You are trading off your independence. I have worked for a company that found themselves in exactly this situation. You would be sickened at the compromises made in exchange for holding on to that business. I was.

If I were the owners I would seriously question whether it was worth it. But when faced with the opportunity to pick up such a large customer or develop a current customer to this size, what would you do? This is a very personal situation. I cannot answer that for you. I merely suggest you think long and hard about what you may be giving up. With this said, I expect you would take the business. I suspect I would also.

With this in mind I would strongly suggest that you do two things. First, aggressively develop and execute plans to increase your market share. By increasing the overall sales base you will be able to somewhat minimize the overall percentage that this one customer represents.

Secondly, I would carefully work out a detailed plan as to what I would do in the event this customer started to force compromises upon my business, and I would work out a plan, and update it every 6 months, as to exactly what I would do in the event this customer left me or went out of business. How would you react? What would you do?

Make these types of decisions now when you are not under the fiscal pressure that you will be when they start. You must know exactly what you would do to react to this loss of income or customer pressure. A knee-jerk reaction when it happens could result in far more damage and cost to your company than it can withstand.

No business relationship is forever. Don't be naive. By taking these types of steps I would at least have been proactive in planning a reactive strategy. It could make the difference in whether or not your company survives.

The same goes for your sales force. For many of the same reasons that I have listed above you must be very careful not to let one sales rep represent a dominate portion of your business. In the vast majority of cases your sales person is the company to your customers.

This means that if they leave to start their own business, or go to one of your competitors, they will be taking many of your customers with them. Develop the same type of contingency plans for this possible circumstance as I have outlined above.

Chapter 27. Shipping & receiving including overnight deliveries, overnight mail and packaging.

"Economy is half the battle of life; it is not so hard to earn money as to spend it well."

Spurgeon

Do you know that in most companies the selection and utilization of an overnight service is made by someone who is not qualified to do so? This could be the receptionist, a secretary, or a clerical worker.

These people see this function as nothing more than an added headache. The boss never thinks about it. They just give the work to them and tell them it must go overnight. The person stuck with the job will send it based on convenience, or because they like the driver or sales rep or for any one of a dozen other reasons. **This is understandable but unacceptable.**

Sometimes decisions made by the people are influenced by gifts or contests directed to people at this level. Back in the early 1980s one of the largest and best known overnight services in the country ran a program that awarded airline tickets based on usage of the service. The more you used their service the more ticket credits you earned. The program was clearly targeted at receptionists and secretaries. The overnight company had conducted research and knew exactly who was making the decision on which service to use.

Plain and simple, they were buying the decision from the customer. They were also the most costly service at the time in most cases.   Beyond the obvious conflict of interest and ethical questions another problem came up. When owners and managers found out, they wanted the tickets. Think about this. They were not concerned that they might have overpaid for the services in question.   They were not concerned with the ethical questions. They were however, very concerned with ownership of those "free" tickets.

They felt that since they paid the bills the tickets should be theirs and not the person's who used the service. What a mess. The decision on what service to use, under what conditions, should be made by someone based on which represents the best buy. No other reasons should be acceptable to you.

This also goes for any courier service that you may use. In fact, while not specifically stated, many of these strategies should be used or adapted in conjunction with courier services. Not too long ago I read a story about a large courier service in Dallas that developed a marketing program designed to increase usage and selection of their services. They also targeted their efforts at the secretary and clerical level.

What does this tell you? The company in Dallas awarded points for usage and the points were redeemable for gifts such as chocolates and roses. The more usage of their courier services the better the gift. Sexist? Clearly. Ethical? Questionable. A conflict of interest? I would say so. Successful? Very.

This company realized a 300% increase in business. The word of mouth advertising among workers from different companies was so strong the courier company had trouble meeting the demand. Do you see what happened here? This company realized who made the decision on what service to use. They targeted these people. But even more importantly they awarded these people for their decision.

They knew the task of sending things via a courier had been passed down from someone who did not want to deal with it to someone who had many other more important things to do. The courier company provided the recognition and award that the employer did not. Ethics aside, you have to recognize the excellence and effectiveness of the strategy.

The worker could have cared less about the cost. They got stuck with a job they did not want and along came someone who would take the problem off their hands and say thanks in a tangible manner. You can't blame the employee. You must blame the company. Use these strategies to help make sure these types of things do not happen in your company. You must take responsibility.

A $3 billion dollar waste. The Wall Street Journal has estimated that 30% of all letters and packages sent overnight do not need to be shipped overnight. This, according to the Wall Street Journal, costs businesses over $3 billion dollars per year.

Does this sound hard to believe to you? It doesn't to me. In fact, if anything, it surprises me that the figure is only 30%. Decisions of when to ship overnight are usually made with very little thought and often by the wrong person and without verification of the need for next day delivery. Another big reason for overnight shipments is procrastination.

You should be using overnight services only as an absolute last resort. All too many think "no problem, we can just ship overnight" or something like this. The thinking should be instead "we are not going to use overnight delivery unless we have no other choice".

Your people should be planning ahead to avoid the need for overnight shipment. The decision to ship overnight should only be made after verification of the need and only by someone qualified and authorized to make the decision. Too many decisions regarding overnight shipments are made by the shipper, a secretary, clerical worker, or warehouse employee. These are not the right people to make these decisions.

When I speak of verifying the need for overnight shipment I am talking about contacting the receiving party and finding out if they can wait another day or if they have to have it the next day. The difference between overnight shipment and 2nd day shipment can be tremendous. You must ask the questions. The questions you should ask in every area of cost control. The questions Kipling gave you.

Establish a proactive strategy for your overnight shipments. Establish a checklist that must be completed for every overnight shipment. The person requesting the overnight shipment in your company should be required to turn this completed sheet in along with the request for the overnight shipment. This checklist would require responses to questions like:

• Does it have to go overnight?

• Why must it go overnight?

• Who checked to verify it must go overnight?

• How did this get to the point where it must go overnight and how can we prevent it next time?

• Can the reason that caused this be corrected to avoid future occurrences of this type of problem?

• Can it be faxed instead with original sent by regular mail?

• Can it be sent by electronic mail instead with a hard copy sent by regular mail?

- Who is authorizing this?

- What is the material?

- Who is the customer?

- Can they be billed?

I would add a line on the form that clearly indicated that unless otherwise specified, the shipment in question will be sent for an afternoon delivery. In almost 99% of the cases when you tell someone to send something overnight they will automatically send it for AM delivery. This costs much more than overnight PM delivery and in the majority of the cases is not needed or cost justified. The costs for AM vs. PM delivery can vary by up to 40% or more.

The change in policy seems small, but in reality it is very large. You are always shipping using the higher priced method one way and with the other you are always looking to the lowest cost method first. You are also making a statement that reinforces your overall cost control and cost reduction efforts and you are removing the decision making process from someone who does not have the interest you do in saving money. Don't leave the decision in the hands of someone who simply views the process as a nuisance and ships it any way they want to simply to get the job done.

This type of checklist does a number of things. It makes the person requesting the shipment think about the real need for overnight delivery, this will cut down overnight shipments. It makes them take responsibility which will always make people think twice. It provides a written record of who sent the material, why, what it was, and if the customer can be billed.

This will allow your bookkeeping people to add applicable charges to the customer's invoice thereby recovering costs that might have otherwise slipped through. It will allow you to monitor activities for any abuses. If you have an employee who is using overnight services a great deal you can identify them and find out why. Is it legitimate or is it due to procrastination or poor organization?

Once any problem is identified you can develop the needed steps to resolve it. This is a good example of a proactive and reactive combined series of actions. It will also insure that any overnight package or letter that must go out will go out for the much lower cost afternoon delivery and not the very costly morning delivery, unless an exception is requested and cost justified.

If you use any type of overnight delivery service on a regular basis I would be shocked to find that with any effort at all you cannot at least cut the cost and usage down in this area by 25% to 50%. With phones, faxes, and E-Mail, it has never been easier to significantly reduce the need for overnight shipments. Technology and procedures are the keys.

If you needlessly send even one overnight package or letter a day at a cost of $15 per package or letter this will cost you $75 per week or $3,900 per year. You may not be impressed with saving $15, although you should be, but how about $3,900 per year? Does this interest you?

How much would you need to increase sales to make a profit equal to $3,900? Well, at a 5% pretax profit ratio you would need to increase sales $78,000 to realize a net pretax profit of $3,900. How easy is it for you to increase sales by this much? How much work is it to increase sales this much? How much does it cost you to increase sales this much?

How about if your pretax profit ratio is only 2.5%. In this case, to add the same $3,900 to your bottom line pretax profit you would have to increase sales by nearly $142,000. Now compare this to the effort required to alter your overnight shipment procedures and activities.

This $3,900 per year savings is based on eliminating only 1 needless overnight shipment a day. How about if you can eliminate 10 a day? Now you could be saving $39,000 per year. What about 100? Now you are looking at hundreds of thousands of dollars a year in savings which would be equal to the net profit on tens of millions of dollars in gross sales.

Do not ignore overnight costs, or for that matter, any shipping costs, simply because you just pass these costs onto you customers. This attitude is unacceptable. First of all, you make no profit on this added cost you bill to your customer. I would rather have my customers spending their money with me on things I make a profit on and not on items I make no profit on. If they pay less in shipping, they have more to spend on my products.

Secondly, effective customer service dictates that I do all I can to minimize secondary costs like these to my customers. You must look out for your customers and do what you can to keep their costs down. Stop wasting your customer's money. You have a responsibility.

Finally, if you are an ineffective shipper and your customer has taken the time to determine the most cost effective method of shipping or even has a good idea of what the shipping costs should be, you are going to have a problem. Not only will your customer feel you cheated them, but they may refuse to pay for your uneconomical shipping. You could lose money and perhaps a customer.

If you must use an overnight service make sure you know who the lowest cost one is based on what you are sending and know this ahead of time. See the separate strategy on selecting an overnight service. My point here is to make sure that you know ahead of time or you can be sure you will not select the lowest priced service to meet your needs.

Make sure your people understand what Federal Express, Airborne, UPS red, and other overnight services really are. I know this sounds hard to imagine that someone would not know what these services are but it is more common than you think. Even among those that know what they are many do not understand how much more expensive they are and why they should only be used as a course of last resort.

I had one customer who was sending back an order from us that was done wrong. The order was a custom order and as such had no value to us. This customer preferred to return it rather than throw it out. This was not the problem. The problem was that this customer sent it back to us via Federal Express. The cost was $311. $311 to return a product to us overnight that we were just going to throw out. This customer had no idea that Federal Express was that costly or that it always meant an overnight shipment. Don't assume understanding, make sure of it.

Control the use of all your overnight service account numbers. If someone else gets your number they can ship most anything from anywhere without your authorization. Remember the story I told you above about the $311 return of useless merchandise? Well, this material was returned on our Federal Express number.

Somehow, our salesman had obtained our account number and given it to the customer for the purpose of returning the merchandise. He had no idea either as to the cost of Federal Express and thought they also had a ground service. We paid for this ignorance. He gave out an account number he never should have had and was not authorized to give out. You must protect all your account numbers including those of your overnight services. Consider it a blank check that you are paying for. Would you leave blank checks lying around?

If you think others have this number that should not have it, call and get your current number canceled and get a new one.

If you absolutely have to ship a letter or package overnight and you can't use any of the alternative strategies I have outlined, at least find out if it can arrive in the afternoon as opposed to the morning. A number of overnight services offer both an early morning delivery which is before 10:30 normally and an afternoon delivery at 25% to 50% less. You should be thinking first must it go overnight and then if it must go overnight, can it get there in the afternoon instead of the morning?

When you ship overnight and you want p.m. delivery you must make sure that you are using a service that offers this and that you are indicating this on the overnight form.

Let me also tell you what a driver for Airborne told me. He told me that very often afternoon shipments are delivered in the morning even though they are scheduled for the afternoon. The reason for this is that they may be delivering other shipments to the same destination that are scheduled in the morning or they may already be in the area and it simply makes scheduling sense to deliver your PM package in the AM while they are in the area. The driver estimated he delivers 90% of the afternoon deliveries he gets by noon.

A driver for another overnight and 2nd day service has also told me this is very often the case for 2nd day shipments. By this I mean, 2nd day shipments very often will arrive the next day instead of the second day for the reasons I have outlined above.

Make sure your AP and AR departments are aware of all overnight shipments. You want to make sure that all applicable charges are added to your customer's invoice and you want to make sure that the invoice to you from the overnight service can be verified by cross checking. Also make sure your AR and AP people also cross check for AM or PM shipment. You do not want to overpay.

Take advantage of all money back guarantees offered by the overnight service you use. Often they will offer a money back guarantee if they do not deliver by a certain time or if they can't give you the status of your package within a specific time frame. Whatever the guarantee is, monitor the performance and file for a refund whenever they do not live up to the terms of the offer. Most people will not do this. Do not be one of them. Make them live up to the expectations they have established or make them pay as promised.

If you must ship something overnight at the request of someone else, or because of them, ship it at their cost. Ship it overnight collect or get them to have it picked up or have them give you their overnight shipment account number for whatever carrier they use. Why should you absorb this added cost if it was necessary because of someone else's action or inaction? If you do none of the above at least make sure you add the cost to their invoice if it revolves around an order or bill them separately if not.

If you must ship on a Friday to arrive Monday then use two day service not overnight. Second day service will get your package there Monday at a fraction of the cost of overnight delivery.

Always ask for lower rates. Remember, published rates are list prices, if you ship any type of volume at all you should be able to get discounted rates. If you don't ask you can be sure you won't get them. When you do ask make sure you point out that you are also asking the competition for their best rates. The knowledge of competition has always proven to be a very strong motivating factor.

How important is it to shop rates of overnight services? Perhaps a few examples will show you. As of this writing I have found that the list price to deliver an 8 ounce overnight package within the contiguous United States ranged from a low of $9.00 to a high of $15.50. This range is for AM delivery.

If you ship 20 overnight letters or packages a week that are 8 ounces or less with the service charging $15.50 you are paying $16,120 per year. This is based on list prices and does not include any volume discounts. If instead, you used the service charging $9.00 per overnight delivery you would only pay $9,360 for the exact same service. This is a savings of $6,760 per year, based only on 20 weekly overnight shipments, with no added effort and no sacrifice in the quality of service. **This is a 42% savings!**

Looking at 2 lb. packages the rates range from a low of $13.00 to a high of $24.25. If you shipped 10 packages a week at the higher rate you would be paying $12,610 per year. If you shipped these using the lower cost service you be paying only $6,760 per year. **This is a 47% savings** equal to $5,850 per year.

Who would pay these higher rates you ask? Well, somebody must because the examples I have given come from the rate charts of some of the largest companies in the overnight business. Do you know if your company is one of these customers?

Similar savings can be found in all areas of comparison among the top providers of overnight services. I have found that rates vary by up to 80%. Remember, these are list prices, since we do not pay list prices you should do even better.

You must compare and you must select the lowest cost, best value service. Do not assume that the lowest cost service for overnight delivery of an 8 ounce letter will also be the lowest cost service for a heavier package or a 2nd day delivery. In all likelihood they will not be.

Being the lowest cost in one area does not translate into the lowest cost in all related areas. In fact, my research has shown the opposite to be true. You must determine the best sources before you need to use them. You must have a reference chart of some sort so that you can quickly determine the best source for your overnight shipment based on weight, size, destination, and delivery requirements.

A simple chart that is referenced for every single overnight parcel you send out will save you thousands or, depending on your volume, even hundreds of thousands of dollars per year. This is not that complex or difficult. Update your chart at least once a year. You will find that in most cases you will be using two or three services depending on your needs. This is as it should be. As I have discussed in other strategies you should almost never use a single source.

This chart should be made after you complete your research into all your shipping options and see which are the best under the various circumstances you will encounter. This chart will allow your shipper to quickly determine, on a daily basis, the best way to ship each outgoing package based on the item, destination, and delivery requirements. If you do not have such a chart, trying to make these determinations as needed, will be too difficult and too time consuming. This means that convenience will rule. You know what it means when convenience is the criteria used to make any decision.

In Pursuit of Profits. How To At Least Double Your Profits Without Increasing Your Sales.

Don't overlook the fax. Again, I have alluded to this in a previous strategy but it bears repeating here. Whenever possible use a fax instead of an overnight delivery. This is assuming you cannot transmit electronically. The fax will cost you much less and provides a hard copy unlike the electronic transmission. If needed, the original copy can always follow by mail.

An often overlooked source for rush deliveries is the United States Post Office. As of this writing you can send a 2 lb. package to be delivered in two days almost anywhere in the country for only $2.90. This is a great price compared to other services. You can drop off or for a small fee they will pick up as many packages as you have to send.

Call them and get the details. If you ship materials that fall within these guidelines you can save significant amounts of money by using this service from the USPS. This is their priority delivery service. They also offer a competitive overnight delivery service called Express Mail.

These services deliver 365 days a year and they deliver to P.O. Boxes. No other service can offer these options. Call 1-800-222-1811 for details or to arrange a pick up or you may visit any one of the 46,000 post offices in this country.

Do you understand your options? Make sure you fully understand all the services offered by your shipping and overnight sources. Unless you know this information how will you ever be sure that you are getting the best value available?

They have express delivery, priority delivery, COD delivery, AM delivery, early AM delivery, PM delivery, 3 day delivery, 2 day delivery, hundred weight delivery, ground delivery, air delivery, domestic delivery, international delivery, and the list goes on and on. You can drop off or have picked up.

Have someone on staff who understands all your options and which is best for your company. Only by knowing your options can you effectively control your costs and reduce your expenses.

Get the free stuff. Make sure that you have any overnight service you use provide you with all your needed packaging and labeling materials. Why pay for what you can request for free? Furthermore, they look more professional and urgent. This includes tubes, packages, envelopes, labels, and flat boxes.

Over the course of a year this can save you a great deal of money. A box or tube can cost you $1 to $3 or more. Your overnight related packaging costs should be close to zero. All you need to do is request the supplies and monitor to make sure you always have an adequate supply on hand. Make sure that all mailing labels are pre-addressed with your information to save you time and money when filling them out.

Are you being penalized for being a customer? If you see a service that you are using offering special new customer rates, demand these same lower rates. You are already a customer and as such you should get rates at least equal to a new customer. If they won't give them to you cancel your account and call to open up a new customer account.

If you must ship overnight or are using any other costly method in order to comply with your customer requirements, make sure you get authorization from them in writing. If you do not, you may have a real problem when you bill them for the cost. Have them fax the authorization to you clearly indicating the method of shipment they are authorizing. You will be amazed at how often a customer has a memory lapse when they receive a very high bill for a shipment method they verbally authorized. Never incur these added costs without written authorization unless you are prepared to absorb them.

For larger overnight deliveries and 2nd day deliveries look into multiple package programs. These could save you significant amounts of money. The way they work is that for shipments of multiple packages to the same destination you can use the lower of two pricing methods. You pay based on a cost per package basis or on a cost for the total weight of the shipment as long as it exceeds a minimum weight.

You should compare both and use the lower of the two. But before you do this check with the carrier to see if they automatically give you the best price. If so, this will eliminate the need for you to determine which is best. Do not assume this is already happening. Find out and if they say you are then spot check your invoices to verify this is true.

Don't overlook UPS Hundred Weight. This is an often overlooked method of shipping larger packages or multiple packages. Let me give you an example of possible savings using UPS hundred weight. I sent a 1700 lb. shipment to New Hampshire using UPS hundred weight and it cost me $178. The same shipment sent via a trucking company would have cost me $228. This is a 22% savings. Make sure this alternative shipping source is included in your rate comparisons.

Keep up to date. Meet with the sales representatives from the major overnight services and shipping carriers at least once every six months. New programs are always being developed and you must find out about them. Never assume they will bring them to you. It is up to you to call and then determine if and how they can benefit your company.

Are you paying to ship overnight when it will get there the next day anyway? Both UPS and RPS have areas that receive shipments the next day even though they are shipped by ground and not overnight. In my area if I ship UPS ground anywhere in NE, 90% of the time it will arrive at the destination the next day.

How much can I save by knowing what areas get next day delivery on a ground shipment? Well I shipped one package to New Hampshire by UPS ground for $2.60. The UPS sales rep told me in my area 99.9% of all packages shipped to New Hampshire will arrive the next day even though I ship normal UPS ground. If I had shipped this package by UPS red, their overnight service, it would have cost me $15.75. I would have paid nearly 7 times as much for what amounted to the same service. Think about this. UPS RED is an overnight air service. Many times a plane is not even being used to transport your shipment within a certain geographical area near your location. You are paying for air when it will only go ground.

Let me give you another example to drive this point home. If I sent a 50 lb. package overnight within the geographical area near me that gets next day delivery anyway, I am going to pay $74.00. If I ship it UPS ground, it still has a 99.9% chance of getting there the next day and my cost would be $6.47. I could save $67.53 or 87%. Sending it overnight means I would pay over 11 times too much.

Find out what gets where and when.

Always look at your lowest cost options. I alluded to this in an earlier strategy but it bears a further look. A very often overlooked method to reduce the need for, and of course the cost of, overnight mail and postage is by transmitting your data and correspondence electronically via a modem from your computer to the computer at the destination.

This not only saves overnight costs and postage costs, but it also saves time, materials, and wear on equipment as you are no longer printing out information, preparing the envelope, label, or overnight package and sending it. Remember, there is always the domino effect. This will always provide you with many secondary benefits.

Sending correspondence in this manner will also be much quicker and less costly than sending the same information by fax. Lengthy documents can be sent via modem in a fraction of the time it takes to send a fax. This saves phone bills, fax machine wear, and personal time.

Finally, if you are dealing with a time sensitive issue, sending it via modem will get it in your customer's hands in seconds. Overnight mail will only get there the next day. Look at what you have accomplished. You have dropped costs from $15 to a few pennies and you get the information to it's destination in seconds instead of the next day. Better service, lower costs. This is what total cost control is all about.

Always compare the rates of trucking companies that you use with those that would like your business. Many times those companies trying to get your business will offer you significant discounts in an attempt to lure you away from your current trucker. Depending on what you ship and where, these discounts can add up to significant savings. Savings you can pass on to your customer or keep in the form of added profit. Let me give you an example.

I sent 40 boxes totaling 1,600 pounds via inside delivery. The cost with one trucking company was $313. The rate with a competing company was $494. Same contents, same destination, same number of boxes. A $181 or 37% difference. Shop around, it pays.

You must have proper controls and procedures in place to insure that you are using the most cost effective method of shipping depending on what you are shipping, when it must arrive, and where it is being sent. Using one or two carriers for all your shipments might be very convenient, but rarely will it be the most cost effective manner to run your shipping department. You have an array of choices. From UPS and RPS, to USPS and any one of the overnight services, from UPS one hundred weight to dozens of trucking companies, you must have a method to insure you are shipping with an attitude of total cost control.

Remember there is a handling cost associated with shipping. Consider adding $1 to $5, depending on the cost of the product and the base shipping costs, to the shipping costs of all orders you send out. This is a legitimate cost as long as you bill it out as shipping and handling. I would not bill it as a separate cost but instead add the handling cost to the net shipping cost and bill out as one S & H amount.

How much income could this generate for your company? If you ship out 1,000 orders per year this will generate between $1,000 and $5,000 per year. If you ship out 100,000 orders per year you are looking at an added profit of $100,000 to $500,000 per year. Think about how much you would need to increase your sales, based on your current net profit ratio, to add this amount to your bottom line!

I have done this for years and have never had one single question or complaint. Remember, you are doing all you can in other areas to minimize their shipping related costs.

If you ship products and request inside delivery I strongly suggest you verify it was actually done. My experience is that inside delivery is very often requested and not done but always charged for. I have had customers on numerous occasions call me to complain that the products we shipped them were dropped on the loading dock or outside their door when I requested inside delivery.

However, in many cases the customer will not call and complain. Instead, they will just be angry and frustrated. You can't solve the problem since you do not know one exists. In many cases you will also end up paying an invoice for a service that was never performed.

For example, I had one customer that we shipped products to and requested inside delivery. The shipping cost was $390. Of this, $90 was for inside delivery. We paid the bill and, in turn, billed our customer who paid our bill. Later in following up with this customer I discovered that the driver had never delivered the products inside.

My customer did not complain because of our long term relationship. As a result we not only forced our customer's people to undertake work they never should have had to and did not want to do, but we also overpaid the shipping bill by 30% and over billed our customer by the same amount.

In either case you have an unhappy customer.

You must verify all shipments received. Do not just accept and sign for them. Do not just accept the shipment, stick it in the warehouse and pay the bills. Once you have signed and accepted the shipment you have a problem if you find something wrong later on. What if the wrong merchandise was shipped? What if the products are damaged? What if the wrong quantity has been shipped? What if it is a duplicate shipment? What if it is something you never ordered? The packing slip may say one thing but what you may be dealing with is another thing altogether.

Your options are very limited after you have accepted shipment. By doing so you have indicated that all is in order. It will now be difficult to later on go back and claim that the goods were damaged or you received fewer than you should have.

You will also have a problem if you do not find out until days or weeks later. By now you may have paid the bill and lost any leverage you might have had. You might also need the product in question and because you are just finding out about the problem you have no time to replace the item in time to meet your requirements. This could cause a ripple effect in many areas of your business.

You also must have verification to properly compare the billing you receive so that you can conduct proper cost control procedures in your AP department. Unless you verify shipments received, any way you look at it you have a bad situation. You must find a way to verify that you have received what you are supposed to and what they claim to have shipped, and that it is not damaged.

How? Think. You know your business better than I do. Without knowing your business and the types of products in question I can't answer this for you. I will give you a few thoughts that may help you or at least get you thinking in the right direction.

If you deal in paper products that come in on a skid here are a few methods. Measure out a quantity. For example, measure 6" of products and then count it. How many are in the 6"? Once you know this you can measure the rest and divide by 6". Then multiply by the number you counted on the original 6". This should produce a count very close to what you actually received.

If you received a number of boxes of the same items, weigh one box. Then count the contents. Weigh the remaining boxes. If they are not the same weight then they do not contain the same quantity. Multiply the number of boxes that are the same weight and you should have an accurate count of what is in those boxes. Then count the contents of the boxes that do not weigh the same. Shake boxes and spot check a few to try and gauge any damage.

Worried about the truck driver waiting? Don't. Instead, worry about making sure you are not being cheated. If you don't find some way to verify what you are getting, and the condition it is in, you are giving your suppliers a license to cheat you.

If you ignore all my suggestions here do yourself a favor and at least have your receiving people sign the paperwork from the trucking company with a notation that indicates the shipment is accepted subject to your opportunity to verify contents. A stamp made up with a statement to this effect will help insure it is indicated on all unverified shipments you receive. Even in this case you must verify the contents as soon as possible.

Always ask for discounts from your shipping sources. This includes trucking companies, overnight services, and UPS. Ask for new customer discounts and volume discounts. Very often these are available but rarely will they be offered.

Low cost shipping alternatives that are often overlooked are buses and trains. Contact bus and train companies and find out about routes and rates.

They caused it, they should pay for it. Make it clear to your customer that they will be charged for any and all overnight and shipping costs that are incurred as a result of their requirements, requests, or delays .

Make sure you do not overlook the regional and local carriers in your area. Because of the higher concentration of routes they cover it is possible they could save you 20% or more when compared to the national carriers who may cover the same routes. Call them in and find out.

Do you always use first class mail? Why? Many things that you send out are not time sensitive and can be sent utilizing a much lower cost postage rate. You must have someone on staff who understands the postal rates and regulations to make sure that you are always paying the lowest rate possible depending on what you are sending and when it must arrive. The post office has a number of publications that will help you maximize your savings. Call them or visit them and educate yourself in this area. The time and effort will be well worth it.

Contact your postage meter vendor and ask them to give you prices on installing a lock on your meter. This will eliminate possible employee theft of postage and unauthorized usage of any type.

Please refer to my strategies in the equipment section for monitoring and controlling copier usage and abuse. If you recall, I have indicated that in the interest of brevity I will not list every application for every strategy. This is a good example of that. Many of the strategies I have given you to monitor and prevent abuse of your copiers apply to your postage meter as well.

This includes keeping a log of usage that records entries at the beginning of the day and the end of the day. Abuse of your postal meter can be a very costly problem. Take as many proactive steps as you can.

Ask the manufacturer of your postage meter about getting an advertising plate option for your meter imprint. This is a plate that prints the name of your company, a slogan, or advertising message at the same time as the postage imprint. Not only will this provide you with no cost advertising, it will also help to discourage employee theft of your postage for personal use.

Save all your incoming boxes to use in conjunction with your outgoing shipments. At an average cost of .50 to $1.50 per box or more, even reusing 100 boxes a week will save you $50 to $150 or more, a week. Over the course of a year this will save you $2,600 to $7,800 or more, a year. The more boxes you can reuse, the more you will save. It should be a very simple matter for a larger company to save $25,000 to $100,000 or more simply in this one area. Don't even think that you can't do this. You can and you should.

Do you want to reduce costs by 5%? Then don't tell me you can't start here by reusing 5 out of every 100 boxes. You should be able to reuse 50 out of every 100 boxes. Your goal should be to reuse 100 out of 100 boxes. This is one area that you can, with virtually no effort, reduce costs by 50%, or more.

Furthermore, you will realize a secondary savings in the area of trash disposal and labor since you are not having to spend time breaking up boxes for the trash or receiving shipments of boxes.

Of course, as always, a cost savings means increased cash flow and the opportunity to put the money you have saved to better use in other areas of your operations. Finally, recycling is something that has advantages beyond the stated economic ones. Recycling makes economic sense and environmental sense. By recycling you are being a responsible corporate citizen. You should make this known.

Don't keep this a secret. Use this to perpetuate your image. Stamp your boxes with a message indicating you are being environmentally responsible by reusing boxes and suggest your customers do the same. Put this on your packing slips when applicable as well. The goodwill you generate will be a nice bonus.

Before we move on, let me give you two tips to remove what might be two objections to recycling boxes. First, if you are worried about your customer seeing your supplier's name on a box that you might be reusing I fully understand this. A simple and inexpensive way to deal with this is to use a tan spray mask for all boxes that carry the name of some source you do not want your customer to see. This is simply a can of tan or box colored spray that masks the name and makes the area look the color of the box. This can be found in many shipping supply catalogs but in case you can't find it here are two sources.

National Box   1-800-247-6000
ULine   1-708-295-5510

The second objection that I would consider a valid reason to recycle fewer boxes is that the incoming boxes are not the right size for your outgoing shipments. This can be overcome in many cases by using a product called a box or carton sizer. This is a simple hand held tool that re-sizes oversized boxes. It will allow you to cut a box to the perfect size for your product thereby allowing you to reuse more boxes and cut down on the need for so much packing material. A better fitting package will also reduce your damage ratio on shipped products. The cost is about $18 and, again, it can be bought from many shipping and packing supply houses including ULine listed above.

Reuse all packing materials you can. Keep a large box or bin to save the various type of packing materials you receive and that are suitable for your type of outgoing packages. These would include foam peanuts, poly bags, packing paper, cardboard, etc.. This should be kept near your shipping area so the shipper can use it as needed.

Again, make sure you indicate on the box or packing slip that in an effort to help the environment you are reusing interior packaging. You are now perceived not as a cheap company, but as a very environmentally responsible company. You also will reduce your trash disposal costs.

Many of the products you receive are shipped in packaging materials that you can and should reuse. From peanuts to bubble packs, from card board to packing paper, these materials can be used by your company for a variety of outgoing shipments. You should easily be able to reduce your packing material costs by 50% or more. Depending on what you ship and receive, you may be able to eliminate these costs entirely.

This is another strategy that is both economically smart and environmentally sensitive. Take the credit as I have outlined above and get rid of these costs.

Make sure that you are using the lowest cost packaging possible while still maintaining the safety and integrity of the products you are shipping. If you follow my strategies on recycling boxes and packaging material you will greatly cut down on your costs in these areas. However, you may still have a need for other types of packaging for which your incoming boxes and material do not fulfill. If you ignore my strategies in the area of recycling, this strategy becomes even more important.

Your primary objective in shipping your products is to get them there on time and undamaged. To accomplish this you do not need custom printed fancy boxes, you do not need the most expensive packing materials you can purchase. Your customers want the product not the package it was shipped in.

If you are needlessly wasting money on unneeded and unproductive packaging you will either reduce your profits or increase your product costs. There is no in between. You either absorb these costs and, by doing so, decrease your profits, or you pass them on to your customers in the form of higher prices. Higher prices that could mean reduced sales and hinder your ability to be competitive. Higher prices could mean they have less to spend on your products. Products generate profits, packaging does not.

Make sure that at least once a year you have all your postage and shipping scales calibrated to ensure that they are weighing properly. I would prefer you have them tested every 6 months, but please do yourself a favor and have them checked at least once a year. A compromise would be to have them professionally checked once a year and to check them yourself the second time each year.

Scales get out of caliber very often. This is true of the modern electric ones as well as the older manual ones. Depending on your mail volume, if your scales are off even a few ounces you can be overspending on postage and shipping by hundreds of thousands of dollars per year. Don't expect the post office or UPS to tell you if you are overpaying. This just isn't going to happen. You have a better chance of seeing Santa.

It is equally important to verify the accuracy of any scales you are using to measure the weight of anything you use internally in the production of your products. Errors in this area can be even more costly.

Always use the postage paid envelope you have been given. If someone gives you a postage paid envelope use it. Never spend your money using or paying for something someone else has provided for you. Obvious? You would think so but my experience has proved otherwise.

What if what you want to send won't fit in the postage paid envelope they have given you? Simple, just tape the envelope to a larger one, a box or carton or anything else you are sending back. The post office will mail it and your supplier will pay for it.

Use both sides of the paper. Not only will this save you paper costs but it may save you postage. You can mail 5 sheets of most bond paper stock for the price of a first class stamp. This will weigh under the 1 ounce limit. If you have lengthy correspondence use both sides of the sheet of paper rather than exceed the 5 sheet limit.

For example, 8 sheets of paper exceeds the 1 ounce limit but printed on both sides they become 4 sheets which does not. Not only are you saving postage but you are also cutting down on your paper usage by 50%. With a savings like this you should always look to use both sides of a sheet of paper.

Chapter 28. Travel.

""Absorption of overhead" is one of the most obscene terms I have ever heard."

Peter Drucker

Tightly control all travel related expenses. Demand documentation from all your employees for all costs. No proof, no reimbursement. Establish policies that require this and that require pre-approval for travel expenses. You need the documentation not only to avoid unnecessary and perhaps bogus travel costs being submitted for reimbursement, but you must also have proof for tax purposes. By documentation I mean charge card receipts or actual receipts from the source of the expenditure. Do not accept a handwritten receipt from the employee or tear off restaurant receipts that are filled out by the employee. My experience has shown these to be greatly inflated.

Eliminate travel by using videoconferencing. If you already have this technology you know the tremendous time savings and cost savings that are possible through the utilization of videoconferencing. In many cases it can completely eliminate your need to travel. The problem is that the cost of the equipment is simply too high for many companies to justify. However, a possible option for your company may be to use videoconferencing rooms as needed. The International Teleconferencing Association and American Telephone & Telegraph Co. have joined together to publish a directory which lists all the public and private videoconferencing rooms around the world. I suggest you call 1-800-432-6600 and ask for information.

Make sure your company travel policy clearly spells out the limitations and cost control practices that you expect the traveling employee to adhere to. Unless these are clear and conveyed to the employee you will have no right to expect compliance.

Establish maximum per day expenses (if you reimburse) for all sales people, corporate entertainment, and travel. If they want to splurge beyond the per person limits let them pay for it. Remember, in business your goal should always be to obtain the desired results at the lowest cost possible. For example, if you establish a policy of allowing $25 per day for meals and $60 per day for hotels and they stay at the Ritz and dine at a 4 star restaurant, your maximum cost will only be $85 no matter what they paid.

Do not advance travel money. This is a form of prepayment which by itself will cost you money as I have outlined in other sections. But beyond this, you are encouraging a wasteful mind set. It is always easier to spend someone else's money than it is your own and money advanced will most often always be spent in total. This is exactly what you do not want.

Instead, they should use their own charge cards when traveling and they should be promptly reimbursed consistent with your written policies. By using their own charge cards they will have more than ample time to turn in receipts to you and be reimbursed before the charge card payment is due.

Let's look at air travel and how you can save here. By shopping airlines, depending on the airline, destination, travel time, and type of flight, fares can range by as much as 20% to 50%. Another way is to use discount air sellers which are sometimes referred to as consolidators. In some cases you determine arrangements. They book flights according to your instructions and usually charge a flat fee or reduced percentage. Since the normal travel agent commission on airfares is 10% the rest of the savings is rebated back to you. You are, in effect, acting as your own agent and simply paying someone a portion of your savings in exchange for doing the actual booking.

Other discount air companies have worked out large discounts with certain airlines and they will tell you if they can save money for you based on your travel plans. Since you will have already checked out the costs yourself it will be easy to see what savings, if any, you can get. Savings are claimed to be in the 5% to 16% range.

Make sure that your airline tickets are purchased so that they are refundable or can be exchanged. There may be a fee charged if you must exchange or get a refund but I can tell you first hand the cost of the fee will be well worth it. You will be protected in the event of a change in plans or if fares drop from the time you purchased the ticket to the time you fly.

I saved over $400 on four tickets last year when I was able to exchange them a few months after I purchased them and the rates had dropped almost 40% due to a rate war. The cost to save the $400 was $25 per ticket or a total of $100. I spent $100 to save $400. This is the way to make money.

On another occasion I found myself at the airport waiting for a return flight over 6 hours before it was due to depart. However, because I was able to exchange my ticket I was able to get the next flight out and for the $25 exchange cost I saved over 5 hours of waiting time. I guarantee you that if I had to wait 6 hours in that airport I would have spent a great deal more than $25 in the bar.

Whenever feasible fly round trip the same day. This will reduce your cost of food bills and eliminate hotel costs. It will cost much more if you schedule an afternoon meeting that will force you to stay over when you could have scheduled a morning meeting that enabled you to return that same day.

This may seem a bit inconvenient and you might not like missing out on staying overnight on the company's tab. Tough! The goal is total cost control not a freebie on the company. The exception to this, of course, is if your trip requires an overnight stay or a weekend stay and is cost justified and desirable.

Fly coach not first class. You are trying to control costs not boost your ego and the airline's profits.

Book with a discount air travel agency who lets you pay in 30 days. This will enable you to take advantage of the float on your money. Remember, all money has a cost. If you are earning interest on your money or avoiding borrowing for this 30 day period you have made your money make money for you. If you are paying the airline at the time you book and don't fly for a few weeks or longer you are losing money. Don't let blind loyalty or pure laziness cost you money by allowing you to simply book with a local full service full cost travel agent.

Book 7 to 14 days ahead whenever possible to allow you the lowest fares. Please understand that rules and regulations are changing rapidly in the airline industry. This may not be an issue in the near future.

You should belong to a frequent flyer plan. Compare plans among the airlines that fly where you most frequently go and when you go. Find the one offering the best frequent flyer plan. They are not all alike. There can be a 30% to 40% difference in benefits offered and miles required to earn free flights.

Look into different classes of air travel. Contrary to what most travelers think it is not just coach and first class. There are other classes and other costs. Also consider flying with a flight change if timing is not critical instead of non stop. Airfare non stop can cost twice as much or more when compared to a less direct route with a stop.

Look into different flights, routes, and times if suitable for your schedule. Depending on an airlines routes, they may be flying many more miles than another airline. Miles you are paying for. Ask what the most economical means of meeting your travel objectives are. Make sure you understand any restrictions and requirements. You must know all your options if you are to find the lowest cost way to meet your objectives.

Lest you think I am suggesting you make major changes in your travel plans to realize small savings, think again. I am not suggesting that you fly in an unmarked plane in the middle of the night surrounded by creatures with feathers. I am suggesting that it is simple to save money on most travel plans with no sacrifices and if you have a little flexibility you may even be able to save a great deal more. Hmm, maybe a camel instead of that compact.

As I was writing this section I read an article that will help drive this point home. It seems that the New York City Department of Consumer Affairs conducted a survey of over 4 dozen travel agencies in the New York area. They requested advanced ticket purchase costs to a variety of destinations. This survey of over 48 travel agencies found that fares quoted by the agencies varied by up to 50%. According to the US. Department of Transportation "Differences in air fare can be substantial. Careful comparison shopping among airlines does take time, but it can lead to real savings.". Which one would you be paying?

Use the airport shuttle service instead of a limo or taxi. They will get you there at significant savings. Call the airport for details on the many options and costs they offer to get you to the airport from points all over the state.

Frequent flyer miles. Make sure that ownership of frequent flyer miles earned for business travel is by the company. All points and bonuses should be owned by the company. This may sound foolish but believe me it is not. If the company is paying for it's people to fly frequently these can add up to tens of thousands of dollars a year.

Yes, the employee might have flown on these trips but the company paid for them and paid the employee to go on them. I strongly suggest you discuss this area with your accountant and lawyer if needed. Offsetting future costs with these earned miles can result in significant savings to the company.

Another option for these miles is to sell them to companies that buy frequent flyer miles. You can look in the back of USA Today and find companies seeking to purchase frequent flyer miles. Or you can use these miles to reinforce and motivate employees to constantly cut costs where possible. They can be given out to employees via a monthly or yearly drawing enabling them to take a trip with free airfare. Or some could be awarded to the employee that produces the best cost saving idea each year.

If you fly into a city in the early evening or late afternoon and must rent a car for the time you will be there don't rent the car until the next day. Instead, take a shuttle from the airport to your hotel. The next day you can rent the car. It makes little sense to rent a car for a full day simply to drive from the airport to the hotel.

If you or people in your company travel with any degree of regularity look into the credit cards offered by the major airlines. Compare all the rates and terms with other credit cards, but what you are also looking for is any travel related benefits that they might offer your company that other credit card companies do not. You will find that some offer the chance to earn free travel, reduced rates on everything from flights to rental cars and hotels. They may also offer frequent flyer programs with mileage earned based on card usage and discounted product and service purchases.

Don't charge calls to your hotel room unless you are clearly advised that the hotel does not charge for handling the calls. Many hotels will add a percentage of the cost of the call to your bill or a flat fee. The percentage can be as high as 30% to 40% and the flat fee can run upwards of $3.00 or more. Instead, you should charge your calls to a company or personal calling card. This will not only enable you to avoid overpaying for the call by up to 40%, but it will also provide you with a written record of the call.

While making calls away from the office access your company lines, if possible, through your phone system. This will enable you to get the largest discount for your company since you should be enjoying a discount based on volume already.

Contact AT&T and look into their AT&T TeleTravel service. If you or your people travel with any frequency you will find this service to be an excellent way to save both time and money. If you want to save time and beat the outrageous hotel service charges call 1-800-544-2222. If you travel frequently and use the phone during your travels you can easily save hundreds or even thousands of dollars a year in hotel surcharges while reducing time and frustration.

Status is not the goal. Stay at nice low budget hotels like Days Inn, Courtyard Marriott, Holiday Inn, and the like. You will save 50% or more over the cost of the 4 star Hotels. You will also save on tips, tax and food/drink. Your customers or clients should also appreciate the fact that you are not staying at the Ritz since one way or the other they will feel they are paying for it.

Ask the hotels you are considering about advance purchase rates. Many hotels offer this type of reduced rate but few, if any, will advise you of it. As I am sure many of you have experienced, hotel reservation people are often far from helpful. You must ask. For example ITT Sheraton has a plan that offers you 40% to 60% discounts off normal rates if you purchase 14 days in advance. Other hotels will have similar plans but often you must ask.

Select a hotel as close as possible to the location you are targeting during your visit. By this I mean if you are attending a convention or trade show book in advance so you can secure the best rates at the closest hotel. This can save you a great deal in cab fares, or possibly eliminate them altogether, not to mention convenience.

In Pursuit of Profits. How To At Least Double Your Profits Without Increasing Your Sales.

Always inquire about any package deals being offered by the hotel. Often these mostly unadvertised package deals will include free or discounted meals, late check out, and other free add ons. For example, I recently stayed at a hotel that was charging $115 per night. Unfortunately, this was the only hotel anywhere near the town I had to be in so I was unable to find a better price.

However, after being quoted $115 per night I inquired about package deals. They were never mentioned by the person from the hotel. Well, it turns out they had a 3 night package deal for $256 that included 2 dinners. This saved me 35% on the room and about $50 in meals. Now, granted, this did take a great deal of effort. I had to ask.

Try to get a low rate on late or last minute check-ins. The average hotel occupancy rate is about 65%. This means that on any given night 35% of the rooms for any hotel are likely to be empty. Talk about leverage. If they don't rent that room tonight they can never recover that income. This situation also exists for planes, cruises, trains, etc..

Unlike a retail store that can always sell that product tomorrow if you don't buy it today, you can't rent tonight's room tomorrow. Just by asking you should be able to get significant discounts, add ons, and room upgrades. Of course, during very busy times or in cases of special events this will not be the case. However, the smart traveler will always have made reservations already at a different hotel in the event a satisfactory discount cannot be realized. Most reservations are good up to 6 p.m. and are fully cancelable prior to that.

Look into joining one of the major hotel chain's "clubs". For instance the Holiday Inn Club or the Sheraton Club. These clubs offer built in discounts and free add ons. The cost is small and the savings can be large. But please do not always assume that the club hotel will always be the best value. Before you travel check the area you are going to for other accommodations and packages to make sure you are getting the best value for your money with the club.

If you are a Citibank credit card holder look into joining CitiTravel. The current cost of this is now $49.00 and among the benefits is a 50% off directory that will give you 50% off hotels around the country. Sears and AAA also have travel clubs. Check the costs and benefits and compare. These can be used for both business and personal travel. I can tell you one thing for sure, if you aren't looking you are not going to find anything. How could you?

Make sure that you are asking the hotel for business rates. They will often have lower rates or special packages for business travelers. When traveling on personal trips you should also ask about business rates. You might save significant money by indicating you are a business traveler who is bringing his family along on a business trip.

By staying at a less expensive hotel you will be saving money on the room and meals and you will be also be saving another 5% to 7% on every dollar you have saved due to sales and meal taxes.

Find out if the hotel you are staying at offers early bird dining. If so, you will be able to save 25% to 40% off the cost of your meals. For example, I recently ate at a restaurant that had early bird dining until 5:30. I had a meal that after 5:30 cost $14.95. I paid only $8.95 for the exact same meal. This was a savings of 41%. In case you are wondering, as I was, the meal was the same size and portions as the higher priced meal.

If you ignore my advice to stay in a nice, but inexpensive hotel and, instead, stay at a hotel with such amenities as an in-room bar, do yourself a favor and don't accept the key and make sure this is noted on your check-in slip. Why? Well, a mini bar in a room will result in charges of $2.50 or more for a can of coke and $7.00 or more for each hard drink you have. Don't despair if this seems a bit high. They do provide pretzels. At up to $8 a bag.

Think about this, according to Kiplinger's Personal Finance Magazine, rates for the same hotel room can range from $99 to $199 depending on when you book, for what dates, and from whom you book, and some in-room mini bar prices charge $2.50 for a can of soda, and $4.75 for a beer.

Do not reserve a room on the national 800#. In almost all cases when you reserve a hotel room by calling the national 800# of the chain you will be charged the highest rate per night. By calling direct to the hotel reservation department you will almost always be quoted a lower rate. They know the bookings for the dates you are seeking and they have a greater interest in getting you in their hotel. The national chain 800# does not. This is why you will often get a lower rate by calling direct.

Always ask for any supersaver packages. These will not only provide you with a lower rate but they will generally include a number of other free or discounted services and products. Even if the package is based on three nights and you are only staying two ask about it. You can always check out a day early and in almost every case your bill will reflect the lower rates as this is what is in the system.

Consider traveling by train if time is not a key factor. The savings can be significant and you will also have an opportunity to prepare for meetings and catch up on work.

Prior to renting a car discuss with your insurance agent what extra coverages can be waived. You may find that you already have coverage under your company car policy. Don't expect them to tell you this, you must ask. If you like to give your money away please feel free to send it to me. My address is at the back of the book.

Always find out if you are already covered on rental car insurance before you rent the car. Don't assume that you are, or are not, covered, find out. You may be covered under your company insurance policy or a credit card policy. By being able to refuse the rental car company insurance you will save $10 to $15 per day.

It is also a good idea to carry proof of insurance just in case the rental car company or local authorities ask for proof. I don't know if all states or all rental car companies require this but in Florida recently I had a bit of a go around with the rental car company over waiving the insurance coverage without proof of insurance. Maybe this was just the latest ploy to intimidate the consumer into taking this very lucrative coverage, I don't know but I'd rather you be safe than sorry.

If you are not covered under other policies make sure you use a credit card that allows you to waive all added insurance coverage. If you do not have a company card then use, or allow your employees to use, personal credit cards to charge the car rental. Make sure, of course, that the credit card company covers this. Most all gold cards now do. Eliminating the added rental car insurance coverage will save you 20% or more. This is where they really make their money.

In Pursuit of Profits. How To At Least Double Your Profits Without Increasing Your Sales.

Shop for a rental car just like you would for any other product or service. Look into national chains and local dealers. For 10 to 15 minutes of calling you will find rates and packages that will vary by 50% to 100%. Consider all details including mileage and other charges as you evaluate costs.

Don't assume that a 4 or 5 day rental demands that you rent the car on a per day basis. Very often rental car companies will offer weekly packages that are so low they will save you money even if you only need it for 4 or 5 days when compared to the day rate.

Always find out if your credit card company, any trade association your company belongs to, or any other organization you have a membership with, has any rental car company discounts you can use.

Always bring the rental car back with a full tank of gas. A full tank of the cheapest gas you can find. If you bring it back less than full the rental car company will charge you $2.50 to $3.00 per gallon to fill it. This means you will be paying 2 to 3 times as much for the gas.

Watch what you rent. Unless image is absolutely vital, and I doubt this very much, your people should be renting a decent sub compact car and not an executive car or even a mid-sized car. A Tempo will get you where you are going just as well as a Mercedes and it will do it for a great deal less money. Do not feed egos at the company's expense.

One side note on this strategy, very often when you reserve the lowest rate car you will find that none are available when you go to pick it up. When this happens you will get upgraded to a better car for the same cost. You can't assume this will always happen but very often it will.

Check out all options when traveling. You might find a situation where you can save the company money and enjoy the trip. For example, I recently was planning to fly down to North Carolina for a one day business meeting and fly back the same day. The cost was going to be $520 for airfare.

However, since I was planning ahead and asking questions (as you should always do), I found out that if I flew down on a Friday morning with a 7 day advance purchase and stayed over Saturday night the flight would only cost me $260. Even considering all other costs, by doing this I would still save significant money and would be able to enjoy Friday night and Saturday night virtually free.

Negotiate with hotels, travel agents, car rentals, etc.. Remember, list prices mean nothing. If the person you are talking to cannot offer you a better deal ask for the manager and explain to them that you would like to use their services but you need a better rate. You will be amazed at how often you will get a better rate, or better package at the same cost.

Always try to get volume discounts from the rental car company, hotel chain, or airline. Remember, these travel service industries are still businesses and, as with any business, the larger repeat customer deserves and usually gets the better prices / deals. If you or your company book 25 overnight stays a year you should not be paying the same rate as the traveler who books one or two rooms a year. The same applies to rental cars and flights. You may need to deal directly with the manager or corporate offices to realize the savings you want, but believe me it is done all the time.

If you are traveling to a popular destination don't ignore the typically consumer oriented travel agency. Often they will book large blocks of rooms and even charter planes to enable them to offer the best deals around. If you look around and don't mind flying with a passenger next to you in a Hawaiian shirt you might be able to save a significant amount of money. You may also be able to take advantage of low rates that exist due to empty seats on the plane or unbooked hotel rooms. This happens when the travel agent optimistically buys blocks of space and then finds out he cannot sell all spaces. Selling them outside the "package" then suddenly becomes a very attractive proposition for him.

Make sure that you check out any organization arrangements for any conventions you might attend. Depending upon the size of the organization or association, they may have very good deals on rooms and flights. Don't assume this but get information and compare to the costs of making your own arrangements.

Schedule your trips effectively. For example, if you fly to the same city each week change your schedules by setting up meetings so that you only need to travel to that city once every 2 weeks. Even if it means staying an extra day you can cut your travel costs by up to 50%.

In this day and age of faxes, overnight mail, and conference calls I would find it hard to understand the need for a weekly trip anywhere. If you must travel once a week to check on another office or store location or the progress of a project, you probably have the wrong people working for you in those areas.

Whenever possible you want to avoid the cost of renting a car or taking a cab. Most cities have excellent public transportation systems and they should be utilized instead of a cab or car whenever possible. A trip across the city by cab may cost you $25 to $50, while renting a car might cost you $50 to $75 per day but the same trip made via public transportation will only cost a few dollars.

Consider flying into alternative airports. Flying into an alternative airport can often, although not always, save you 25% to 50% or more when compared to flying into the main airport in the city you are traveling to. Alternative airports are simply smaller secondary airports that are located outside of the main metropolitan area.

They can be anywhere from 15 minutes to 90 minutes outside of the major city. Depending on where you are traveling to, the alternative airport may actually be much closer to your destination. For example, if you are flying into Washington International and your ultimate destination is Baltimore, you will not only save over 25% off the flight cost, but you will also arrive closer to your destination by flying into the alternative airport in Baltimore.

Even if a flight into an alternative airport requires that you rent a car to drive to your destination the flight savings might be so significant that even after the cost of the rental car and the 30 minute or so drive, you have still saved a great deal. If you had already planned on renting a car you would save even more.

A recent article in USA Today highlighted some of the savings you can realize by flying into an alternative airport and driving to your destination. I have listed a few below to demonstrate the potential savings. The rates indicated were in effect at the time of this writing, are round trip, did not require an advance purchase or a Saturday night stay.

In Pursuit of Profits. How To At Least Double Your Profits Without Increasing Your Sales.

Origination Point	Distance apart	Cost to fly to main airport	Cost to fly to alternative airport
Atlanta	60 miles	Cincinnati $518	Dayton $318
Orlando	60 miles	Cincinnati $558	Dayton $258
Boston	82 miles	Charlotte $598	Greensboro $298
Tampa	82 miles	Charlotte $398	Greensboro $198
Atlanta	16 miles	La Guardia $538	Newark $169
Charlotte	16 miles	La Guardia $598	Newark $398

Similar savings are available at alternative airports all over the country. If you are serious about your program of total cost control, you better get serious about checking these alternative airports out.

Travel Resources.

Inside Flyer. A newsletter of frequent flyer and travel programs. 1-800-487-8893

Frequent Flyer. A monthly magazine covering frequent flyer information. 1-800-323-3537

Consumer Reports Travel Letter. Covers hotel discounts, frequent flyer programs, car rentals, and airfare discounts. 1-800-234-1970

Best Fares. A monthly magazine dedicated to helping you find travel bargains. They also list the lowest fares for major airline routes each month. 1-800-635-3033

Call each of these and see if they offer the type of services or information you can use.

Consider flying one of the many smaller low fare airlines. These are mainly regional airlines who fly limited routes but if they go where you need to fly you will find they will offer you savings of up to 70% when compared to the larger "name" airline. Check your local phone books for these smaller airlines and call to inquire about routes, times, and costs. The service is very often excellent and the savings significant. I have listed a few of them below.

Airline	Home Base	Phone #
Carnival Airlines	Fort Lauderdale, FL	1-800-824-7368
KIWI International	Newark, NJ	1-800-538-5494
Leisure Airlines	Smyrna, GA	1-800-538-7688
National Airlines	Atlanta, GA	1-800-949-9400
Tower Air	New York, NY	1-800-348-6937
UltrAir	New York, NY	1-800-858-7247
ValuJet	Atlanta, GA	1-800-825-8538
Midway Airlines	Chicago, IL	1-800-446-4392
American Trans Air	Indianapolis, IN	1-800-225-2995
Grand Airways	Las Vegas, NV	1-800-643-6616
MarkAir	Anchorage, AK	1-800-627-5247
Reno Air	Reno, NV	1-800-736-6247

Closing thoughts.

"The seeds of dissatisfaction will produce a harvest of change."

Derrick W. Welch

You can't be satisfied with your current profitability or you would never have purchased this book. The fact that you did means you are ready to start making changes in the way you run your business, to not only increase profitability, but I hope also to improve every area within your organization. This is what a program of total cost control is all about.

Total cost control is not about merely increasing profitability. Without question, a program of total cost control will have stunning results on your bottom line, but more importantly it is about improving every area of your business. It is about establishing a common unified goal for all within your company to work towards. It is about providing the best product or service you can, selling at the highest feasible price, while producing at the lowest possible cost.

I hope I have shown you that total cost control is really a program of total improvement for your company which leads to a much more efficient and **profitable** organization. The key to success in any type of improvement plan, be it one of cost control and expense reduction, or one of quality control, is a change in attitude. The attitude of acceptance for the old way of doing things must be replaced by an attitude of doing things a new way.

The key to changing an attitude is to change perception. By changing the perception of how important something is you can change the attitude about how it is looked at. Changing the perception of your employees is the challenge you face.

"Example is contagious behavior."

Charles Reade

It begins with you. Before you can change their perception you must change yours. Before you can change their actions you must change yours. Controlling and reducing expenses must be a priority with you. Improving the way you operate starts with you. Improving the way you produce, sell, and deliver starts with you. Commitment starts with you. **It is not someone else's job. It is everyone's job, including yours.** The opportunity for improvement in your company is endless. The quest for improvement must be never-ending.

Improvement begins with you and ends in increased profitability. Don't think "How can I stop costs from going up?". Think "How can I reduce costs?". Don't think about ways to justify that cost, think about how you can eliminate that cost or how not to incur that cost. There is a significant difference in mind set between these two ways of thinking. One assumes a defensive posture while the other assumes an offensive posture.

"Knowing is not enough, we must apply. Willing is not enough, we must do."

Goethe

Your cost control and cost reduction efforts will pay you handsome dividends, year after year, for as long as you are in business. I have given you many tools to use in your total cost control efforts. It is up to you to use them.

Just as the quest for improvement must be never-ending, so too should your quest for increased profits. Your program of total cost control is not a one time program. It must be an ongoing, never completed, process. The tools and ideas I have given you are merely a beginning. A starting point.

"Choose to be uncommon. Think of the alternative."

Derrick W. Welch

A starting point in a quest that has no ending. You and your people must always be reaching for ways to improve. You must always be striving to provide a better product or service for a lower cost and to sell it for a higher price. The process is evolutionary.

Increasing profits is not brain surgery. All it takes to increase profits is simple common sense applied with an unwavering commitment that is demonstrated day in and day out. As I stated at the beginning of this book there is no magic involved.

Sometimes we lose sight of the real reason we are in business. The day to day business of running a company, division, or department, seems so all consuming that we have trouble keeping things in perspective. Let me just close this book by reminding you of why you are in business, of why you have a job and of what your real responsibility is.

The bottom line responsibility of any business person, employee, manager, or owner is simple. It is to produce profits. The goal of your business must be to produce an acceptable level of profit. Products and services are merely the vehicles used to accomplish the goal. Don't ever lose sight of this. Don't ever let your people lose sight of this.

If you would like help in reaching your goals I would welcome the opportunity to help you.

My best,

Derrick W. Welch

About the author.

Derrick Welch is currently Chief Operating Officer and Vice President of a multi-million dollar Massachusetts based company that manufactures and distributes products for sale nationwide. <u>The strategies and philosophy represented in this book were used to increase the profits of this company over 450% in the first two years after Derrick took over operations.</u>   Prior to that he served as Vice President of Client Services for a major Boston based advertising agency for 6 years. Mr. Welch has degrees in business administration, marketing, and management.

Derrick has a simple goal. It is to help you succeed. It is to help you reach your business goals. It is to help your company become more profitable. He hopes this book is a strong start in that direction.

Derrick has two other books currently nearing completion. These books, titled "A Businessman's Book of Wisdom" and "In Pursuit of Excellence", will both be available in the early part of 1995. Both of these books will have the same goal. To help you become more successful and your company become more profitable.

If you would like to contact Derrick for more direct assistance he can be reached through our offices at:

LeeMar Publishing
Suite 178
319 Centre Ave.
Route 123
Rockland, MA 02370

Phone 1-617-499-1970
Fax   1-617-871-6025

Your comments and suggestions regarding this book are both welcome and appreciated!

Additional copies of this book can be ordered directly from the publisher by phone, fax, or mail.

Quantity	Cost per book
1-25	$34.95
26-50	$32.95
51-75	$30.95
76-100	$28.95
101-150	$26.95
150+	$24.95

To insure prompt and safe delivery all orders are shipped via UPS unless otherwise requested.

Individual orders must be prepaid and must include $5 shipping and handling for the first book and $1.00 for each additional book. Individual orders from residents of MA must include 5% sales tax.

Corporate orders from publicly held companies need only indicate a purchase order number. Shipping, FOB Rockland, MA will be added to your invoice. MA orders will also incur a 5% added sales tax.

Number of books ordered _____

Payment enclosed for individual purchase _____   **Purchase order number** _____

(Including applicable S&H / MA sales tax)   (Applicable S&H / MA sales tax will be added)

Name _____

Title _____

Company name _____

Ship to _____

_____

_____

Telephone _____

Signature _____

Please photocopy, fill out, and mail or fax to: **LeeMar Publishing**
Suite 178
319 Centre Ave.
Route 123
Rockland, MA 02370

Phone 1-617-499-1970◆Fax 1-617-871-6025

Thank you for your order!